AMERICAN EDUCATION

Purpose and Promise

AMERICAN EDUCATION

Purpose and Promise

Peter Hlebowitsh

University of Iowa

Kip Téllez

University of Houston

West / Wadsworth
I⊤P® **an International Thomson Publishing Company**

Belmont, CA • Albany, NY • Bonn • Boston • Cincinnati • Detroit • Johannesburg
London • Los Angeles • Madrid • Melbourne • Mexico City • Minneapolis/St. Paul
New York • Paris • San Francisco • Singapore • Tokyo • Toronto • Washington

Production Credits
Education Editor: Joan Gill
Production Editor: Brenda Owens
Designer: Roslyn Stendahl, Dapper Design
Copy Editor: Allen Gooch
Illustrator: Julie Horan, Radiant Illustration and Design
Cover: Cynthia Mailman, *Homeroom,* Art and the Law 1986. Photo courtesy of West Publishing Company, Eagan, MN.
Compositor: Carlisle Communications, Ltd.
Printer: West Publishing Company

COPYRIGHT © 1997 by Wadsworth Publishing Company
A Division of International Thomson Publishing Inc.

I(T)P The ITP logo is a registered trademark under license.

Printed in the United States of America
1 2 3 4 5 6 7 8 9 10

For more information, contact Wadsworth Publishing Company, 10 Davis Drive, Belmont, CA 94002, or electronically at http://www.thomson.com/wadsworth.html

International Thomson Publishing Europe
Berkshire House 168-173
High Holborn
London, WC1V7AA, England

International Thomson Editores
Campos Eliseos 385, Piso 7
Col. Polanco
11560 México D.F. México

Thomas Nelson Australia
102 Dodds Street
South Melbourne 3205
Victoria, Australia

International Thomson Publishing Asia
221 Henderson Road
#05-10 Henderson Building
Singapore 0315

Nelson Canada
1120 Birchmount Road
Scarborough, Ontario
Canada M1K 5G4

International Thomson Publishing Japan
Hirakawacho Kyowa Building, 3F
2-2-1 Hirakawacho
Chiyoda-ku, Tokyo 102, Japan

International Thomson Publishing GmbH
Königswinterer Strasse 418
53227 Bonn, Germany

International Thomson Publishing
Southern Africa
Building 18, Constantia Park
240 Old Pretoria Road
Halfway House, 1685 South Africa

Library of Congress Cataloging-in-Publication Data

Hlebowitsh, Peter S.
American education, purpose and promise / by Peter S. Hlebowitsh and Kip Téllez.
p. cm.
Includes bibliographical references and index.
ISBN 0-314-20220-X (alk. paper)
1. Education—United States—Philosophy—History. 2. Education--Social aspects—United States. 3. Education—Aims and objectives--United States. I. Téllez, Kip. II. Title.
LA205.H544 1997
370'.973—dc21   96-45058

This book is printed on acid-free recycled paper.

To Our Families

Erica, Margaret, Paul, Nadia, and Nikolai Hlebowitsh

and

Sarah, Carmen, and Catrina Téllez

PHOTO CREDITS

02 Robin Sachs, 04 Corbis-Bettmann, 10 Corbis-Bettmann, 25 Liaison International, 26 Brenda Owens, 26 Brenda Owens, 36 Robin Sachs, 46 Corbis-Bettmann, 50 Corbis-Bettmann, 51 Bettmann, 53 Corbis-Bettmann, 53 Elizabeth Crews, 64 Robin Sachs, 66 Bettmann, 73 AP/Wide World Photos, 78 Corbis-Bettmann, 80 Bettmann, 92 Robin Sachs, 100 Corbis-Bettmann, 104 Tony Freeman/PhotoEdit, 118 D. Young-Wolff/PhotoEdit, 126 Robin Sachs, 128 Mary Kate Denny/PhotoEdit, 130 Elizabeth Crews, 140 Brian Smith/ Liaison International, 142 Corbis-Bettmann, 145 UPI/Bettmann, 147 Ulrike Welsch/PhotoEdit, 151 Courtesy of Harvard Graduate School of Education, 162 Robin Sachs, 173 AP/Wide World Photos, 188 Richard Hutchings/ PhotoEdit, 213 Mary Kate Denny/PhotoEdit, 218 Douglass Borrows/Gamma Liaison Network, 226 AP/Wide World Photos, 224 Elizabeth Crews, 229 Robin Sachs, 230 Reuters/Bettmann, 236 Jeremy Bigwood/Gamma Liaison Network, 242 Bettmann, 246 Corbis-Bettmann, 252 Robin Sachs, 255 AP/Wide World Photos, 256 AP/Wide World Photos, 275 Robin Sachs, 284 Robin Sachs, 289 Elizabeth Crews, 295 Robert Brenner/PhotoEdit, 297 Jerry Bauer, 305 Elizabeth Crews, 308 Michael Newman/PhotoEdit, 318 Robin Sachs, 333 Merritt Vincent/PhotoEdit, 338 D. Young-Wolff/PhotoEdit, 345 AP/Wide World Photos, 356 Robin Sachs, 361 Robin Sachs, 366 AP/Wide World Photos, 369 Kathy Ferguson/PhotoEdit, 377 Elizabeth Crews

CONTENTS

**Visit our Education web site at
http://www.wadsworth.com/education.html**

PREFACE

This book begins with a historical survey of how the public school came into existence in America, explaining the uniquenesses of the American school system while also underscoring the importance of the most progressive dimensions in the public school's development. Although much of the narrative speaks to the particular traditions of governance and legislation that helped to fashion the school, we also wanted to write a historical story that reflected on what was occurring in the practice of the school and in the argumentation and debate that shaped the school curriculum. Thus you will find that the historical section of the book deals with events and persons that influenced curriculum formulations, with the focus fixed on questions about what we should teach, how we should teach, and why we should teach. In this manner, we integrated philosophical dimensions in the historical story, rather than isolating them in a separate chapter. All along we were driven by Dewey's thoughtful reminder that the history of the past is always the history of the present, that what we derive from the past only makes sense and has relevance as it touches upon current conditions and problems.

We also wanted to show the relation of the school to society and decided to situate our treatment in thematic issues that highlighted the problems of equity and the problems of school achievement. We chose vital themes that continue to daunt even the most well-intentioned policy making—desegregation, funding inequities, curriculum tracking, and gender and race inequities. We balanced this examination with a more positive appraisal of school achievement, especially as it related to democratic causes such as the role that the school plays in advancing social mobility and in closing of certain achievement gaps in gender, class, and race. There is quite a bit of good news to report about the American schools that we tried to cover fairly. The nature of school reform since midcentury was also discussed. We showed, for instance, the vulnerability of the school to sociopolitical forces, and we provided an in-depth analysis of the main rationales for and against arguably the most important educational policy issue of our time—school choice. The idea of school choice, especially if it includes private school options, represents a turn away from the historic traditions and purposes of the public school.

Lastly, we discussed the actual practice of the American school, focusing on specific design issues and actual classroom-based problems. Here we spoke most directly to the prospective schoolteacher, suggesting ideas in areas of classroom discipline and curriculum development. In advancing this advice, we tried to make a renewed case for the concept of comprehensive schooling, which is a progressive vision of school that aims at the widest marks of enlightenment. Under such a design, the focus of teaching shifts away from an attitude of strict academics to a comprehensive method that stresses the value of academic, vocational, personal, and sociocivic growth in learning.

This book was written for prospective teachers. It was designed to be the first word, not the last, on issues that we believe are fundamental to the growth of people who plan to work with children in schools. We want it to fund the knowledgeability of the teacher, to start conversations, and perhaps even to provoke debates. Thus, the success of this book will very much be measured by the conversations that it might engender and by the social circulation of ideas that will follow these conversations. As Dewey observed, democracy begins with conversation. Schools, as embryonic democracies, start the same way.

ACKNOWLEDGMENTS

Because the manuscript for this textbook has gone through so many iterations and so many different review stages, we cannot possibly thank all those who have been kind enough to give us criticism and helpful suggestions. The many blind reviews commissioned by our editor helped to transform our work into a document that better reflects school policy conditions and practical classroom considerations.

Our thanks to the following list of reviewers:

Dr. Fred Baker
1829 Shenandoah
Claremont, CA 91711
(909) 869-2308

Phil Bassett
Box 601 251 N. Main St.
Cedarville College
Cedarville, OH 45314

Richard R. Farmer
Southeast Missouri St. Univ.
MS 5550
Cape Girardeau, MO 63701
(314) 651-2427

Gordon G. Barkell
Michigan Tech. Univ.
1400 Townsend Dr.
Houghton, MI 49931-1295
(906) 487-2171

Dr. John Petry
Leadership Dept.
Univ. of Memphis
111A Patterson
Memphis, TN 38152
(901) 678-3407

Dr. Fritz Mengert
Curry Bldg. Rm. 246
Univ. of North Carolina-Greensboro
1000 Spring Garden
Greensboro, NC 27412
(910) 334-5100

Doris McGrady
Minot State Univ.
Main 206G-MSU
Minot, ND 58701
(701) 857-3016

Paul C. Deacon
Lynchburg College
1501 Lakeside Dr.
Lynchburg, VA 24501
(804) 522-8480

Beth Laforce
George Fox College
414 N. Meridian Box 6062
Newberg, OR 97132
(503) 538-8383

James Maryott
NWOSU Box 191
Alua, OK 73717
(405) 327-1700

James Alarid
New Mexico Highlands Univ.
Education Dept.
Las Vegas, NM 87701
(505) 454-3535

David Noonan
University of Nevada-Reno
Educational Leadership
Reno, NV 89557
(702) 784-4084

Doris Gardner
3224 Happy Valley Drive
Little Rock, AR 72212
(501) 543-8058

Dr. Donna Keenan
COEHS Dept.
University of North Florida
4567 St. Johns Bluff Rd.
Jacksonville, FL 32216
(904) 646-2578

Rhonda Baynes Jeffries
Education Dept.
University of Wisconsin-Milwaukee
Franklin, WI 53132
(414) 229-4150

Edwina Pendarvis
College of Education
Jenkins Hall 110
Marshall University
Huntington, WV 25705
(304) 696-2855

Doug MacIsaac
College of Education
McKee Room 213
University of Northern Colorado
Greeley, CO 80639
(970) 351-2610

Johanna Nel
Division of Leadership and Human Dev.
College of Education Box 3374
University of Wyoming
Laramie, WY 82071-3374
(307) 766-5327

Steve Pawluk
Walla Walla College
204 S. College Ave.
College Place, WA 99324
(509) 527-2272

Kenneth D. McCracken
Educational Studies
U of TN at Martin
205 Gooch Hall UTM
Martin, TN 38232
(901) 587-7201

Dr. Vilma Seeburg-King
Kent State Univ.
405 White Hall
Kent, OH 44242-0001
(216) 672-2294

Dr. Claudette Morton
Western Montana College
710 South Atlantic
Dillon, MT 59725
(406) 683-7121

Tim Heaton
Cedarville College
Box 601
Cedarville, OH 45314
(513) 766-7782

Prof. Baust
Murray State Univ.
University Station
Murray, KY 42071
(502) 762-3011

We are also very grateful to the feedback provided by our many friends and colleagues. We know that over the years we have tried their patience by often forcing ideas taken from our book into our conversations or correspondence. This too is a long list, but several people deserve to be mentioned, including William Wraga, University of Georgia; Daniel Tanner, Rutgers University; Richard Gibboney, University of Pennsylvania; and Gregory Hamot of the University of Iowa. Our students, of course, have also given us useful advice. Several semesters of feedback to the manuscript from our undergraduates have helped us immensely. And no one worked more closely with the narrative, looking for ways to improve the experience with the book, than Lucy Payne and Liz Ann Miller, both Ph.D. students at the University of Iowa.

All along we have been very lucky to have worked with a very fine team of editors who put great care and thoughtfulness into the development of the book. Joan Gill, Becky Stovall, and Brenda Owens represented a powerful combination of wisdom and understanding. Their encouragement and enthusiasm helped us to write a sincere book.

It goes without saying, however, that our true source of inspiration and strength has come from our families. This book is dedicated to them.

PSH
KT

PART I

TOWARD A HISTORY AND PHILOSOPHY OF AMERICAN EDUCATION

Knowledge of the past is the key to understanding the present. History deals with the past, but this past is the history of the present. John Dewey

1 **EARLY IDEAS IN THE DEVELOPMENT
OF THE AMERICAN SCHOOL**

Janice Herbranson's school in McLeod, North Dakota, is one of the few remaining images of America's rural public school past. Like many teachers in early rural schools, Herbranson serves as teacher, principal, cook, and janitor. As the very beginnings of public schooling in the United States are explored, think of the challenges Herbranson faces. How are her challenges different from those of teachers in urban and suburban schools? Think, too, about the general challenge of providing free public education to an entire nation. Although the nation's schools did not begin in rural settings like the one in which Herbranson teaches, the one-room schoolhouse is what many Americans equate with early schools.

The history of public schooling in the United States began in the colonies of the Northeast. As the Puritans began to mark a new life in America, they initiated a system of schooling tied to religious teachings. However, as the nation diversified, these provincial ideas had to give way to a more comprehensive education. It is important to remember that no other nation has made such a commitment to comprehensive education.

Public education in America arose out of an early union between the church and the state. Puritans living in the Massachusetts Bay Colony during the 17th century were the first to support state-sponsored education. Their interest was driven by a commitment to inject religion into the life of the state. Publicly funded schools, in effect, became the main messengers of the Word.

The religious homogeneity of the New England colonies made such an arrangement between church and state interests not only possible but also compulsory. What was good for the Puritan faith was also good for government; there could be no real separation. Colonial New England, after all, was a settlement that, in the words of Lawrence Cremin (1977), was founded in the unsettlement of Europe, in a movement to find new expression for religious conviction, and in the general mood of adventure believed to be guided by God's grand design.

But in the more diverse regions of the colonies, the idea of commingling state and church concerns was problematic, and the idea of using public monies for public schools was difficult to understand. The hurdles were obvious. Questions would be raised about which church, which doctrine, and which ecclesiastical slant on learning could be viewed as best for all children. Given the difficulties of such questions, much of the education of children outside New England occurred in nonpublic places, including the church and the household. As all the colonies became more diverse, the Puritan belief in using the public school for denominational purposes would clearly become increasingly unmanageable.

It was not until the postrevolutionary period, however, that a new school agenda began to take shape. A new regard for sociocivic obligations was slowly succeeding the traditional regard for religious doctrine that dominated the school for so many years. Such a shift was influenced by the writing and the ratification of the U.S. Constitution and by the growing belief that the new American nation had to find itself in a practical commitment to social democratic causes. No longer able to support sectarian views, the publicly funded school had to aim at a wider mark, at a mandate that stressed the inclusivity of a wider range of youth. This meant that the public school had to examine its place as an agency that ensured national unity, strengthened opportunities for economic and social mobility, and ultimately socialized a new generation of youth into the skills and dispositions needed to conduct an intelligent life in a democracy.

The Emerging Public School in Colonial America

The history of American education dates from the early 17th-century settlements in New England. The center of the action was in colonial Massachusetts, where the Puritans took an active hand in promoting publicly funded education at virtually every level of school organization. The Puritans were well known for their efforts in providing a beginning education, up to age 7, to all the children in their communities, and in providing continued education, up to age 15, for a select group of boys.

They also founded many colonial colleges, the first and most famous being Harvard College, which was chartered in 1636. They had, in the end, built an educational structure that set the basis for a town-controlled system

The early Puritans based their brand of schooling on the teachings in the Bible.

PART ONE: TOWARD A HISTORY AND PHILOSOPHY OF AMERICAN EDUCATION

of compulsory education and that, by the close of the 17th century, could boast of having produced higher literacy rates than those in England (Cohen, 1974).

The Puritans' attraction to public education was not at all moved by democratic or egalitarian principles but by a desire to use the school as an agency for church doctrine. Despite escaping religious harassment in Europe, the Puritans had no intention of establishing a New World community open to all religious creeds. To the Puritans, such an arrangement could only lead to anarchy and to a serious falling away from God (Cohen, 1974). They were strong headed about these matters, denying suffrage to nonchurch members and tolerating no dissent against the church. The Puritan embrace of the state in establishing schools was moved by an effort to create a government in the image of their church, making the state's purpose allegiant to sectarian priorities.

Because the Puritans believed that they needed mass education to bring the gospel of Christian faith to all their children, they committed themselves, with the urging of the church, to publicly funded schools that openly aimed to socialize youth in doctrinal faith. To the Puritans, the road to personal salvation was always traveled through the Bible, and unlike other colonial Americans, they were willing to use the school as one of the main vehicles for this most important journey. As shall be explained, the Puritan idea of using the state to enforce and otherwise support a tax-based public education for all youth set an early pattern of organization and governance for American public education that was sustained long after the state and church went their separate ways (Cubberley, 1947).

As in most colonial settlements, the Puritan home or family unit was considered the wellspring for moralistic and religious education. A family, in fact, was not considered very civilized if it did not properly attend to the religious education of its children (Rippa, 1984). But under the hardships of conducting a life in the New World, many parents were neglectful of their duty, so much so that the Puritans enacted legislative statutes compelling families, under the threat of financial penalties or the potential removal of custodial rights, to teach reading and religion to their children. The result was the **Massachusetts Law of 1642,** which was passed at the behest of the church and which made education compulsory for all youth in the Massachusetts Bay Colony. The law empowered town officials, also known as selectmen, with the responsibility of ensuring that children in the community received an education that, among other things, taught them to read and to understand the principles of religion. The officials periodically paid visits to homes, where they would expect parents or masters (hired teachers) to account for the education of the children. Thus, the nature of the 1642 law made education compulsory, but it did not necessarily establish schools. The form of education was still essentially as it was before the law; it was largely a family matter and was conducted in the home.

Within five years, however, the Puritans took an even larger step toward establishing a public system of schooling by passing a law, known as the **Massachusetts Law of 1647,** that specifically required all townships to maintain schools and hire teachers (see Figure 1.1). The actual maintenance of some type of school represented a much stronger commitment to education because it required public monies and public accountability. Again the driving force behind the legislation was the church. As far as the church was concerned, children could not be expected to understand the Bible unless

FIGURE 1.1

MASSACHUSETTS LAW OF 1647

It being one chiefe project of that ould deluder, Satan, to keepe men from the knowledge of the Scriptures, as in former times by keeping them in an unknowne tongue, so in these latter times by perswading from the used of tongues, that so at least the true sence and meaning of the originall might be clouded by false glosses of saint seeming deceivers, that learning may not be buried in the grave of our fathers in the church and commonwealth, the Lord assisting our endeavors,—

It is therefore ordered, that every towneship in this jurisdiction, after the Lord hath increased them to the number of 50 housholders, shall then forthwith appoint one within their towne to teach all such children as shall resort to him to write and reade, whose wages shall be paid either by the parents or masters of such children, or by the inhabitants in generall, by way of supply, as the major part of those that order the prudentials of the towne shall appoint; provided, those that send their children be not oppressed by paying much more than they can have them taught for in other townes; and it is further ordered, that where any towne shall increase to the number of 100 families or househoulders, they shall set up a grammer schoole, the master thereof being able to instruct youth so farr as they may be fited for the university, provided, that if any towne neglect the performance hereof above one yeare, that every such towne shall pay £5 to the next schoole till they shall performe this order.

Source: Shurtleff, N. B. (Ed.). (1853–1854). *Records of the governor and company of Massachusetts Bay in New England.* In S. Cohen. *Education in the United States:* A documentary history (Vol. 1). New York: Random House. p. 394.

they possessed the basic rudiments of reading. The thinking in the church was that the old deluder, Satan, was always among the people, looking for opportunities to exploit them, and that direct measures had to be taken to protect the community, especially its children. The best protection was to be charged with the Word of the Lord, and at least to the Puritans, the best way to secure this effect was to erect a school system that imbued all youth with the spirit of the Bible and the skills needed to read the Bible. In the words of the law, schools had to be maintained to thwart the "chief project of the old deluder Satan to keep men from the knowledge of the scriptures" (Meriwether, 1907).

Thus the Massachusetts Law of 1647, also known as the Old Deluder Act, authorized, depending on the size of the town, the provision of schools and the employment of teachers. For towns having 50 households, a teacher of reading and writing had to be employed at a wage determined by the town; for towns with at least 100 households, the same requirements applied, but a Latin grammar school (a secondary school) had to also be provided (Colony of Massachusetts, 1853). The Massachusetts law was copied in Connecticut in 1650, although compliance to the law became increasingly problematic as populations spread along the frontier (Noble, 1959).

School Life

Among the Puritans there were essentially two types of schools: **dame schools** and **Latin grammar schools.** Dame schools were elementary or primary schools typically conducted in the home of a widowed or otherwise

This early American painting depicts a dame school setting

unmarried woman in town. Early in their development, they were either private neighborhood schools that survived off small weekly fees paid by parents or semipublic schools that received marginal assistance from the town treasury (Small, 1969). Without the compulsion of law, dame schools emerged idiosyncratically. As a mother taught her own children the rudiments of reading, other neighborhood children might be included for a small fee of perhaps a few pence per week (Small, 1969). But as the dame schools began to receive some public support, they started to take on a more deliberate focus. With the passage of legislation compelling the establishment of schools, the dame schools eventually garnered more substantive support from town sources and in time evolved into town elementary schools.

The town schools, in effect, became the elementary schools of New England, providing an essential education in the ABCs and in elementary reading up to the age of about 7 or 8. The age limit slowly extended upward over time. Such schools were moved out of the households and into their own facilities. These town schools ultimately set the early tradition of instruction in the three Rs in elementary education and compelled the increasing use of local taxes to support public education. Later in their development the dame schools existed coterminously with the town schools, offering their graduates at about age 7 to the local town schools for further education, especially in writing and counting.

As reported by Rippa (1984), a harsh and dogmatic atmosphere characterized the dame schools and town schools. The teaching revolved around the alphabet and the scriptures in the Bible. Usually, the formal education of children in the dame schools was concluded by age 7, and for the overwhelming majority of the population, there was no other opportunity for further public education. Household duties awaited the girls and various apprenticeships or work on the farm awaited the boys (French, 1964). And for both boys and girls, it was the household that continued to be the strongest source of education (Cremin, 1977).

For a small group of boys, however, formal schooling continued in an institution known as the Latin grammar school, which was a school design imported from England. The sole purpose of the Latin grammar school was to educate an elite group of boys for college study. Latin was at the center of instruction because it was the sacred language of religion, which presumably made it good for the mind and for the soul. Education in the Latin grammar school ran until approximately age 15. Upon graduation, the boys were expected to enroll at Harvard College.

Girls, as a rule of thumb, were excluded from the grammar schools and from higher education. Many males believed that higher education would come at the cost of a female's health, reveal their innate mental inferiority, deprive them of their most delicate and effeminate qualities, and generally lead to the neglect of children (Douglas & Greider, 1948). As Figure 1.2 shows, among those who shared this view was John Winthrop, the first governor of Massachusetts Bay Colony. Few male colonists saw the contradiction between their religious views and the manner in which they disregarded the education of girls beyond the most rudimentary levels (Harris, 1899). French (1964) cites work that claims very high illiteracy rates for women in the colonies, especially in relation to the rates for men. Women would only begin to benefit from opportunities for a higher education during the early 19th century.

As with the dame schools, religious exercises and a rote/recitation style of learning also governed the Latin grammar school. Great faith was placed on the act of memorization, which was encouraged through skill-drill exercises and repeated recitations. Memorizing grammatical rules and a multitude of Latin equivalents for English words and translating Latin passages to English and back again to Latin constituted a good share of the pedagogy (Cohen, 1974). Students also read notable classical authors, such as Cicero, Horace, and Virgil, and were subjected to rigorous religious training that entailed the daily recitation of prayers, catechisms, and translations of the Latin New Testament (Cohen, 1974). Writing and the fundamentals of arithmetic were optional, but were frequently ignored (French, 1967). Class discussions were abhorred, and a climate of control and order, with all of its attendant punishments and regulations, pervaded the school.

FIGURE 1.2

JOHN WINTHROP OF MASSACHUSETTS ON THE EDUCATION OF WOMEN (1645)

Mr. Hopkins, the governour of Hartford upon Connecticut, came to Boston, and brought his wife with him, (a godly young woman, and of special parts,) who was fallen into a sad infirmity, the loss of her understanding and reason, which had been growing upon her divers years, by occasion of her giving herself wholly to reading and writing, and had written many books. Her husband, being very loving and tender of her, was loath to grieve her; but he saw his errour, when it was too late. For if she had attended her household affairs, and such things as belong to women, and not gone out of her way and calling to meddle in such things as are proper for men, whose minds are stronger &c. she had kept her wits, and might have improved them usefully and honourably in the place God had set her. He brought her to Boston, and left her with her brother, one Mr. Yale, a merchant, to try what means might be had here for her. But no help could be had.

Source: Winthrop, J. (1826). *The history of New England from 1630–1649.* In S. Cohen *Education in the United States: A documentary history* (Vol. 1) New York: Random House p. 383.

PART ONE: TOWARD A HISTORY AND PHILOSOPHY OF AMERICAN EDUCATION

Graduates of the Latin school were essentially innumerate and unable to write with much fluency, but they were usually quite literate in Latin (Cubberley, 1934). No allowance was made in such schools for technical, business, or commercial education, or for what were viewed then as "polite accomplishments," such as music or dancing (Cohen, 1973). Ultimately, the failure of the Latin grammar school to be in touch with the matters and demands of colonial life led to its demise (Tanner & Tanner, 1987).

The teachers in these schools were poorly trained and the conditions for teaching did not encourage very thoughtful experiences in the classroom. Everyone followed the same instructional pattern, as all the children memorized and recited their ways through their lessons. Except for some reading materials, there was no classroom equipment to facilitate instruction. Paper and individual desks were rare; slates would not arrive in school until the early 1800s.

The school buildings were undersized and were often in a state of physical calamity (Cohen, 1974). For instance, the most common building design was a simple carpenter box, usually 25 feet by 25 feet, 6 to 9 feet high, and presumably big enough for 60 pupils (Small, 1969). These schools, more often than not, were built cheaply and hastily and were known for falling into quick and dramatic disrepair. A Roxbury citizen in 1681 recorded one complaint:

> The inconveniences I shall instance no other than that of the schoolhouse, the confused and shattered and nasty picture that it is in, not fitting for to reside in; the glass broken and thereupon very raw and cold; the floor very much broken and torn up to kindle fires; the hearth spoiled; the seats, some burnt and others out of kilter, so that one had as well nigh as good keep school in a hog-sty as in it (Small, 1969, p. 258).

The furnishings in the school buildings were threadbare, consisting of planks on barrels or stakes for desks, and benches for seats (Small, 1969). In the winters, many schools went unheated and those that were heated relied on poorly ventilated fireplaces or stoves. Complaints were sometimes noted about how the air became burned up by the fireplaces to such an extent that it actually became difficult to breathe (Small, 1969). The heating of the school building also consumed much wood, which was the only heating fuel available, and frequently led to a wood-tax levy on families with children attending school (Small, 1969).

Some schoolrooms were equipped with whipping posts, which were used on unruly students (Cubberley, 1934). Even the use of the whipping posts had an ecclesiastical rationale. Children were believed to be born sinful and often had to have "old Adam beaten out of them" (Knight, 1951, p. 127). Because children were believed to be better off whipped than eternally damned, teachers could easily justify their punitive measures. The reasons that they gave for punishment were often arbitrary. In an example taken from Small (1969), a boy who made a bad recitation caused his teacher to flog "another boy for not exercising a better influence over the delinquent" (p. 386). Other teachers were more creative in their offerings of punishment. One teacher after securing several offenders, asked one to get on all fours, the other to mount his back and the third to whip the other two around the room. They then changed positions until each boy had his turn at whipping once and being whipped twice (Small, 1969). Milder forms of punishment included demanding that pupils "sit on air" or stand in the corner with their face to the wall, taps on the head with a steel-thimbled finger, and slaps with a rawhide ruler (Small, 1969).

Throughout colonial America, the curriculum materials were wedded to the notion of building knowledge in reading as a way to build knowledge in religion. To this end, the **hornbook** was among the earliest pedagogical devices used. Brought from England, the hornbook, which was used in virtually every colonial school, was not really a book in the sense that we might know it today. It was made out of a thin piece of wood with a handle, looked much like a paddle, and was, by some accounts, periodically used for hitting children (Meriwether, 1907). On the top of the wood was a paper that usually contained the alphabet, various letter combinations, and the Lord's Prayer. The paper was covered with a thin, translucent sheet of cow's horn that protected the print and made the book durable.

The hornbook kept instruction fixed on phonemic representations of letters (*B* as in bear, *H* as in horse) and on nonsense jingles that represented the sounds that the letters make (Art we add, Ben is bad, Cat she can, Dad or Dan, Ear and eye). Some hornbooks also carried the emblem of Christ's cross at the very top of their front side. Once the children finished all of their lessons on the hornbook, they were ready for catechisms, which entailed the memorization and recitation of various religious texts. At the level of catechisms, the children were subjected to texts like the *Westminster Catechism* and the Reverend John Cotton's *Spiritual Milk for American Babes Drawn Out of the Breasts of Both Testaments for Their Souls' Nourishment* (Callahan, 1963).

Girls in dame and town schools also were often required to practice their embroidering and knitting skills by sewing what were known as samplers. Girls took quite a bit of care in stitching the alphabet, a verse from the Bible, the Lord's Prayer, and an ornamental border of flowers and sometimes animals on a piece canvas or linen. The samplers, in effect, served the same purpose as the hornbooks and over time, largely because of their beauty, became family heirlooms handed down through generations (Johnson, 1917).

The most influential text used in the education of young colonists, which eventually replaced the hornbook as introductory reading material, was the ***New England Primer,*** a document that embodied the Puritan outlook of moral depravity in humankind (Ford, 1899). The *Primer,* which first appeared in 1690, was saturated with religiosity—moral maxims, hymns, and prayers. It had the tone and the language of the Bible—the Ten Commandments, the Lord's Prayer, various samples from the Old Testament, and unique verses that taught literacy within the story of Christianity. The *Primer,* for instance, contained rhymes and poems to help children learn the phonetic sounds represented in various letters and letter combinations. These rhymes were also used to teach children something about their own innate proclivity toward sin (see the Objects of Teaching feature in this section for examples from the *Primer*). The book, for instance, covered the alphabet in the following manner: *A*—"In Adam's Fall, We sinned all," *B*—"Thy Life to mend, This Book attend" (a pictured Bible), and so on (Rippa, 1984). One particularly popular poem, reproduced in Alexander Rippa's (1984, p. 39) history of the schools, captures the miserable moralistic tone of the text. The poem reminds children of their sinful nature and of their destiny with the fires of hell. Children often memorized and performed the poem in school.

Samplers like the one pictured here were part of the curriculum in America's earliest schools

The New England Primer

In Adam's Fall
We finned all.

Thy Life to mend,
This Book attend.

The Cat doth play,
And after flay.

A Dog will bite
A Thief at Night.

An Eagle' flight
Is out of fight.

The idle Fool
Is whipt at SchooL

Praife to GOD for learning to Read.

THE Praifes of my Tongue
I offer to the LORD,
That I was taught and learnt fo young
To read his holy Word.

2 That I was brought to know
The Danger I was in,
By Nature and by Practice too
A wretched flave to Sin:

3 That I was led to fee
I can do nothing well ;
And whether fhall a Sinner flee
To fave himfelf from Hell.

Cubberley, E. B. (1934). *Public Education in the United States.* Boston: Houghton-Mifflin Company. p. 45.

What conclusions about teaching and learning might be drawn from this sample of the *New England Primer?*

You sinners are, and such a share
    as sinners many expect
Such you shall have, for I do save
    none but mine own elect.
Yet to compare your sin with their
    who liv'd a longer time,
I do confess yours is much less,
    though ev'ry sin's a crime:
A crime it is; therefore in bliss
    you may not hope to dwell;
But unto you I shall allow
    the easiest room in hell.

The merging of reading instruction with the moralistic preachments of the Puritan faith was the rule of thumb in the *New England Primer.* Proper child-rearing values at the time promoted the need to instill children with fear, obedience, and discipline (Karier, 1967). However, with changing social conditions, later editions of the *Primer* deemphasized stories about sin and eternal punishment and instead stressed patriotic themes and the practical values of learning to read (Butts, 1955). The *Primer* was used in school for well over a century. An estimated 3 million copies were sold during its use. It was said to have "taught millions to read, and not one to sin" (Callahan, 1963, p. 116).

Regional Differences

Not all the colonies were as strongly committed to establishing a public school as were the Puritans. In Anglican Virginia, for instance, religion was simply not as strong a factor in dictating a public school response. The character of life in Virginia, with its dispersed plantations as opposed to towns, and its general lack of good transportation made "public" schooling much more difficult to achieve (Cubberley, 1934). Moreover, the South was much slower at establishing local colleges and at setting up printing presses that might have provided materials to the populace (Cremin, 1977). Wealthy parents in the South relied on tutors and private schools for the education of their children, while the children of the poor were left to the largess of charity, which often led to church-sponsored **pauper schools.**

The societal fabric of the South was also quite different from the more homogeneous North. Black slaves and White indentured servants working on the plantations were considered too lowly for even the most basic education. Such a population was not likely to win public support for the schooling of its children, thus providing little motivation for free and common public schools. The idea that one school could be fashioned to serve these antagonistic social classes was simply unthinkable. As a result, education in the colonial South resided neither with the state nor with the church, but with private tutors and private schools. Education in the South was a sport for the rich, and those without means simply could not play.

The education of girls was probably even more restricted in the South than in the North because the Anglicans did not share the Puritan zeal for bringing the creed to both sexes (Cohen, 1974). But like the North, the Southern attitude toward women and education rarely went beyond expectations of knowledge in cooking, sewing, and the basic rudiments of reading, writing, and arithmetic. Depending on the region, girls could gain an education through charity schools, dame schools, private schools, and for the most wealthy, boarding or finishing schools, but these were relatively rare. Most girls were taught at home to do those things that contributed most directly to their roles as wives and housekeepers (Cohen, 1974). This generally meant that the training of women paid closest attention to the attitudes of modesty, gentleness, and piety and to the skills of the household.

The education of slave children had, by and large, no legislative support in the South during the 17th century and beyond. The institution of slavery required submission, obedience, and the essential evisceration of individualistic thought. To most slave owners, education provided a potential tool of empowerment that opened disturbing possibilities for insurrection (Cohen, 1974). Some colonial masters wanted to educate their slaves to save their souls and some saw an economic benefit in slave education, but such thinking was uncommon. Most of the slave owners understood that education was a liberating force and thus a menace to their system of enslavement. The ability to read might give slaves "dangerous" ideas about their own abilities and might ultimately allow them to see new life possibilities (Beale, 1975). Many Southerners also held to the idea that Black slaves were uneducable and acted on this conviction by forbidding the teaching of Blacks. Slaves, especially on the larger plantations, relied on their own wit and will to educate themselves. This was done through family or community storytelling and through various clandestine meetings, which tended to focus on Black folklore, on know-how with some agricultural and artisan skills, and on Christian precepts (Cremin, 1977).

Blacks in the South also had found some educational opportunities in the evangelical activities of the **Society for the Propagation of the Gospel in Foreign Parts** (SPG). The organization, which was chartered in England, was dedicated to conducting missionary work in English colonies. The missionaries targeted the Southern colonies of America, seeking converts, distributing Bibles, and founding churches in the hope and the intention of bringing Blacks, Indians, and some Whites into the Episcopal faith (Cohen, 1974). Like the Puritans, the SPG believed in the importance of education in bringing the Word of God to the people. Thus the SPG established a network of charity schools, taught by missionaries, that emphasized Episcopal religious tenets and basic instruction in literacy and numeracy. The SPG's efforts reached out to Black children, Indian children, and poor White children, and in the end the SPG had succeeded in providing some semblance of a centrally administered system of schooling for Black children in the South (Cohen, 1973). As a result, the organization was not always popular. The conversion of Southern Blacks to Christianity obviously raised the question of whether they inherited their freedom with their newly professed Christianity.

The issue of slavery clearly compromised the emerging democratic spirit of the nation. Even later statesmen, like Thomas Jefferson, were vulnerable on the issue of slavery and education. Although Jefferson drafted some early legislation to abolish slavery and favored the antislavery provisions of the Northwest Ordinance, he never freed his own slaves and he did not play much of an activist role in fighting for the causes of the slaves during his lifetime (Butts, 1978). As we shall find, even Jefferson's modest proposal for free schools was overwhelmingly rejected by Virginia legislators, and any hope for winning more radical changes that altered the educational conditions of slaves in the South was slight indeed (see Figure 1.3). Still, Jefferson's lack of action was symbolic of the slaves' situation in America. Even arguably the greatest American voice for liberty and equity of the 18th century could not fathom the reality of including Blacks as free people who could be peacefully and fruitfully integrated into what was clearly developing into a pluralist constitutional democracy. This became a battle, quite literally, for another time.

The middle colonies, which comprised different groups of Protestants, Catholics, and Jews, also made no strong claim for the role of public

AN ACT PROHIBITING TEACHING SLAVES TO WRITE IN SOUTH CAROLINA (1740)	**FIGURE 1.3**

And *whereas,* the having of slaves taught to write, or suffering them to be employed in writing, may be attended with great inconveniences; *Be it therefore enacted* by the authority aforesaid, That all and every person or persons whatsoever, who shall hereafter teach, or cause any slave or slaves to be taught, to write, or shall use or employ any slave as a scribe in any manner of writing whatsoever, hereafter taught to write, every such person and persons, shall, for every such offence, forfeit the sum of one hundred pounds current money.

Source: Cooper, T., & McCord, D. (Eds). (1836–1841). *The statutes at large of South Carolina.* In S. Cohen *Education in the United States: A documentary history* (Vol. 1) New York: Random House p. 574.

education. As in the Southern colonies, there was no uniform ethnic or religious monopoly to make such a claim. Thus the state played a marginal role in the education of youth, and no one church dominated the political landscape. (Cubberley, 1947). Although the belief in educating youth for personal salvation existed among the middle colonists, these obligations were handed to the church and to private schools. The result was that families had to depend on the church or private advantage for even a rudimentary education. The state was, for all intents and purposes, out of the picture. The laissez-faire attitude toward public education in the middle colonies continued into the 19th century and was not surmounted until the migration of New Englanders created a critical mass that helped to agitate for free-school legislation (French, 1964).

All in all, three movements marked the colonial educational scene (Cubberley, 1947). In New England, particularly in Massachusetts, efforts were directed at establishing state-sponsored common schools that carried a clear religious mandate. The preponderance of towns and the lack of religious diversity made it easy for the citizens of Massachusetts to conduct such schools. As a nation, the United States inherited its present system of governance, with some obvious changes, from the Puritan New England model. In the middle colonies, which were populated mostly by Protestants and Catholics, the church stood alone as the main player in the education of youth. Education proceeded along denominational lines, and the role of the state in such affairs was viewed as repugnant by the people. In the South, the attitude toward education favored private tutoring or private schooling and church-sponsored pauper schools for the poor.

Of course, the New England tradition eventually prevailed in the country. Had the middle colonists had their way, the structure of schooling in America might have evolved into a partnership between private and public schools; had the Southern colonists' views become popular, the nation's schools might have developed into an openly private and parochial system (French, 1964). Clearly, the events of the colonial period were central to the development of how we see the public school today.

 ## The Movement Toward a Sociocivic Mandate

As an American-born generation of colonists began to move inland to expand its settlements, new attitudes began to prevail toward schooling and religion. Having never carried the yoke of religious oppression in Europe, the American-born colonists were less absorbed with religious zeal and much more civic-minded in their approach to government and business. The increasing circulation of denominational faiths in the colonies made the relation between church and state much more complicated, and the hard work of frontier settlement life pointed to a more practical outlook toward life overall and toward schooling in particular.

The colonies were also beginning to move toward a sense of national identification, a position eventually strengthened by a revolutionary tempest. One major consequence of the American Revolution was that school education had to take on a clearer role in civic affairs and economic needs. Knowledge of Latin and Greek was simply not going to take the new generation of youth far enough in dealing with the nation's growing economic, political, and social demands. A new method of schooling was on the horizon.

Bringing the School to the People

By 1750, an entirely new vision for a secondary institution, known as the **Academy school,** was beginning to take shape. First advanced by Benjamin Franklin, the American Academy was designed to make the curriculum more utilitarian than the Latin grammar school and more responsive to emergent economic and social needs. The Academy did not abandon the traditional courses in Latin and Greek, but it gave such courses a less exalted status in the curriculum. Franklin believed that the Academy's teaching had to encourage scientific observation and that the course work had to be broadened to include practical insight on learning to write, on agriculture and gardening, and on commercial skills in navigation and surveying. Even physical education had some currency in the curriculum. Of course, the curriculum also possessed all the traditional academic disciplines. As a deist, Franklin also wanted to avoid religious or sectarian instruction in the Academy, except as it might be related to other academic studies. In essence, his idea for schooling in the Academy marked an early movement toward a new and comprehensive form of education.

Not only was the curriculum different, but those admitted into the school were different as well. For the first time, girls were being freely admitted into postelementary education. The Academies, however, were still not truly public institutions. They were open to the public but they were not free of cost. In practice, the Academy did not go as Franklin had hoped or expected. The classic tradition provided too strong an undertow for the utilitarian brand of education promoted in Franklin's Academy, and some Academies actually became breeding grounds for the college bound (Butts, 1955), very much to Franklin's dismay.

Still, the Academy was a significant step in the development of a new kind of school that argued that education should be more useful and more attentive to real life issues and experiences (Butts & Cremin, 1953). The actual range of offerings in the Academy's curriculum is highlighted in Figure 1.4, which was taken from Will French's (1967) work on secondary education. The list itemizes the subjects taught during different years in various New York Academies from 1787 to 1881. It does not, however, show which subjects were more popular. Collectively the offerings represent a much more free-wheeling and practical-minded perspective on learning than what was typically provided in the Latin grammar school. By the end of the 18th century, the Latin grammar school had expired or transformed itself into an institute looking more like an Academy. A new curriculum prototype was born in the Academy design, one that underscored the significance of comprehensiveness in schooling.

Changes were also occurring at the level of school governance. During the early phases of the colonial settlement, the New England town was marked by central locations for public meetings and public schooling. The requirements for universal church attendance and the fear of Indian attacks kept most settlements within one-half mile of most towns (Cremin, 1951). In time, more inland settlements arose at the extreme peripheries of the central town. For those living in the removed areas, the centralizing functions of the town (the church and school) became difficult to reach and were less widely used. Because they supported the town school with their taxes, those living in the outlying sections asked central town officials to find a way to share school facilities with them. The original solution was something known as a moving

FIGURE 1.4

SUBJECTS TAUGHT IN THE NEW YORK ACADEMIES (1787–1881)

The Academies

Subject	Year	Subject	Year	Subject	Year
Acoustics	1850	French	1787	Music	1827
Algebra	1825	Geography	1787	Music, vocal	1832
Archaeology	1844	Geography, ancient and Biblical	1826	Mythology	1829
Architecture	1830	Geography, physical	1828	Natural history	1830
Anatomy	1837	Geography, political	1830	Natural and moral chemistry	1829
Arithmetic	1787	Geology	1830	Natural theology	1828
Arts and sciences	1797	Geometry, analytical	1828	Nautical astronomy	1831
Athletic exercise	1828	Geometry, descriptive	1828	Navigation	1826
Astronomy	1797	Geometry, plane	1825	Needle-work	1828
Belles lettres	1817	Geometry, solid	1885	Optics	1831
Biblical antiquities	1832	German	1825	Orthography (spelling)	1796
Biography	1831	Globes	1827	Ornamental needle-work	1828
Blair's lectures	1827	Grecian antiquities	1828	Ornithology	1847
Bookkeeping (accountantship)	1787	Greek	1787	Painting	1826
Botany	1827	Gymnastics	1849	Penmanship (writing)	1787
Calculus	1830	Hebrew	1829	Perspective	1828
Calisthenics	1841	Higher mathematics	1825	Philosophy	1825
Carpentry	1844	History of England	1841	Philosophy, intellectual (mental)	1826
Chaldee	1838	History of France	1841	Philosophy of language	1827
Chemistry	1825	History, general	1787	Philosophy, moral	1804
Chemistry, agricultural	1841	History of Greece	1881	Philosophy, natural	1787
Chronology	1826	History of literature	1867	Philosophy, natural and chemical	1828
Classical biography	1832	History of N.Y.	1831	Philosophy, vegetable	1831
Commerce	1873	History of Rome	1881	Phonography	1846
Composition	1804	History, Tytler's	1829	Phreno-mnemotechny	1844
Conchology	1840	History of U.S.	1827	Physics	1879
Conic Sections	1827	Hydraulics	1850	Physiology	1835
Constitution, New York	1841	Hydrostatics	1832	Political economy	1832
Constitution, U.S.	1841	Hydrostatics and pneumatics	1844	Pronunciation	1834
Criticism, elements of	1826	Hygiene	1849	Psychology	1847
Dancing	1837	Intellectual arithmetic	1831	Reading	1787
Declamation (elocution)	1787	Isoperimetry	1841	Rhetoric	1799
Dialing	1830	Italian	1828	Roman antiquities	1827
Domestic economy	1850	Jewish antiquities	1828	Spanish	1825
Drawing	1826	Latin	1787	Statics and Dynamics	1852
Draughting	1851	Law (civics)	1826	Stenography	1831
Ecclesiastical history	1830	Laws of interpretation	1833	Stewart on the mind	1825
Electricity	1843	Lectures on English language	1833	Statistics	1831
Elements of taste	1832	Leveling	1834	Surveying	1801
Embroidery	1836	Logarithms	1825	Teaching, principles of	1831
Engineering	1828	logic	1787	Technology	1830
Engineering, civil	1835	Mapping	1839	Technology, mathematical	1831
English, elements of grammar	1787	Mathematics	1787	Theology	1830
English literature	1804	Mechanics	1830	Topography	1830
Ethics	1827	Mensuration	1827	Trigonometry	1825
Evidences of Christianity	1827	Mental arithmetic	1826	Trigonometry, plane	1831
Evidences, Parley's	1827	Metaphysics	1827	Trigonometry, spherical	1831
Evidences of religion	1832	Meteorology	1838	Warts on the mind	1827
Extemporaneous speaking	1834	Military education	1827	Waxwork	1841
Fencing and military tactics	1828	Military tactics	1826	Zoology	1828
Fine needle-work	1827	Mineralogy	1828		
Fluxions	1825	Mnemonics	1832		

Source: French, W.M. (1967). *American Secondary Education*. New York: Odyssey Press, pp. 74–75.

school. The town sent an itinerant teacher to each of the more rural communities for a designated period of time to teach the children. This meant that a teacher might arrive in a particular precinct for an agreed period and then leave for another part of town for an agreed period, and continue with such a schedule until completing a rotation that covered all the town's territory.

This solution, however, eventually gave way to the proportional sharing of property taxes so that each subdivision could independently govern its own schools. Soon the districts, also known as parishes, obtained their own common schools and private tuition schools, and the education of children began to be deliberated as a district concern as opposed to a town concern. With such a measure, the districts, in essence, rediscovered the dimension of local school governance that was once fundamental to the central town. Such an arrangement, however, did not have legal sanction until the passage of the **Massachusetts Law of 1789.** This law established the district as the basic unit of organization for the public school and reconfirmed the essential logic of the Massachusetts Law of 1647, which assigned the function of the school to local governance (Cremin, 1951). Each town or district was now quite free to go along its own individual lines. Like the Law of 1647, the new legislation also encouraged the local inspection of schools by town or district officials, stressing the responsibility that ministers had in supervising the curriculum and in encouraging attendance among the youth (Cremin, 1951).

One should observe, however, that the functional governance of the school was entrusted to civil authorities, not religious ones. Town funds, not church funds, were used to finance the schools. To the Puritans, the idea of moving the school into the province of the civil government was never a problem and was accomplished without much friction (Cubberley, 1947). The objectives of the church were still superordinate to the objectives of the

A village in early colonial times

school district. In assigning the governance of the school to the civil government, the Puritans were confident that religious instruction had a sound advocate. In this way, the American idea of local initiative was born out of a religious agenda.

Although great strides were taken to provide a basic and religious education to youth in New England and in some middle colonies, it should be remembered that, with the possible exception of Massachusetts, there was very little success at universalizing even an elementary education for children. The state laws were permissive, and the local districts were not equally committed to the provision of common schools. Those who had means could find schools for their children, but for most of the population, life was still marked by illiteracy. Whatever strides, however, that might have been taken in the 17th century toward the provision of a public education in the colonies were essentially reversed with the start of the revolutionary conflict. Many colony schools closed under British occupancy, and in the midst of military engagement, many others fell into disarray and disrepair. Educational options decreased and illiteracy increased.

Education in the New Nation

After the colonists defeated England, their new nation was impoverished and was faced with establishing an independent government amid a society growing in cultural and religious diversity. The U.S. Constitution provided the first signs of how the public school might evolve in the new nation. As indicated, in England the tradition had been to leave the state out of the affairs of education. The writers of the U.S. Constitution, virtually all privileged men of the old aristocracy, left out any reference to education in the document. This has led to speculation about how the original framers saw the role of the school in the society (Butts, 1978), with some scholars arguing that its absence in the Constitution meant that the framers wanted to leave it to private efforts. The fact that no direct reference to education can be found in the nation's most important legal document is not exactly an endorsement of the centrality of public education to the workings of the new democracy (Power, 1991).

But the founders' views on education were couched in other positions, the most prominent being the separation of church and state. When the attenders of the Constitutional Convention contemplated the growing pains of the new nation, they were quickly drawn to the question of how the state and church might be able to reconcile their agendas. Among the problems facing the new nation was a growing religious diversity. The writers of the Constitution posed a solution by supporting the free exercise of religious faith for all and by banning the state sponsorship of any particular religious view. The state and the church could no longer be brothers under the same skin, as they once were in some of the more homogeneous colonies. Moreover, when the ratification of the **10th Amendment to the Constitution** in 1791 declared that any power not specifically delegated to the Constitution become the property of the states, public education secured a place as a state function as opposed to a federal one. To this day, the public schools in the United States are marked by a state-specific strategy of governance that allows for the exercise of local district views—a decentralized system of schooling without precedent in the world.

PART ONE: TOWARD A HISTORY AND PHILOSOPHY OF AMERICAN EDUCATION

Taking religion out of the governance of the state set the course for a common, nonsectarian, state-funded public school. Public monies could no longer be used to support a religious education, though it would take some time to realize this prohibition, and with the apparatus for publicly funded schools already in place in Massachusetts, the common public school had just begun to start its transformation from an institution dominated by religiosity to one that carried the obligations of enlightening a diverse citizenry for sociocivic intelligence. The development of a new democracy was now dependent on a public school system that had to move its interests into the civic arenas of building common political communities (Butts, 1978). The very system that had its beginnings in religion was now poised to be used as a protection against it. The new charge for the school was civic in character and was generally associated with the need to socialize good citizens.

Many early advocates of a public system of schooling referred to the need for education to become a source of general enlightenment for the people of a new democracy. These were essentially the sentiments expressed by early statesmen such as Thomas Jefferson, Thomas Paine, John Adams, John Jay, James Madison, and George Washington. The dominant themes of religious fervor were now replaced with more secular discussions that dealt with issues of equity, liberty, individualism, and reason. Jefferson, more than anyone in his time, made a direct appeal to the logic of allying democracy with public education. In a famous statement, he declared that "if a nation expects to be ignorant and free in a state of civilization it expects what never was and never will be. . . ." (Quoted in Callahan, 1963, p. 125). Jefferson took these ideas to heart and proposed in 1779 a plan for public education in Virginia that mandated public schooling for all free children, at public expense, for three years. Then the best and brightest would be chosen for secondary education at state expense, with the aim of eventually entering the College of William and Mary, again at public expense (Callahan, 1963).

But state-supported education in the South was resented, and even a political statesman with the credentials of Jefferson could not convince the legislature to accept his proposal. Jefferson's proposal was rejected, and his hope of realizing a state-funded system of schooling that provided a primary education for a wider group and a more advanced education for the meritorious, including what he hoped would be the first state university, was lost and not regained until after his death.

The universalization of the basic elementary schooling was still many decades into the future, but Jefferson and others planted the idea for it. By the end of the 18th century, state governments throughout America, with some regional variations, were beginning to confront the reality of funding public education. Governments in the New England colonies, for instance, were responsive to the causes of public education. As early as 1776, many of these governments reflected a commitment to a publicly funded general education in their state constitutions (Butts, 1978). By the late 1780s, states such as Vermont, Massachusetts, and New Hampshire had instituted general state school laws, mandating compulsory public education (Cubberley, 1947). Not only were elementary and Latin grammar schools supported in New England, but new colleges were also being founded, including Yale College and Dartmouth College. Thus, in New England and in the westward expansion from New England into New York and Ohio, the belief in state-sponsored schooling continued, even after the religious justification for it had deteriorated (Cubberley, 1947).

In the middle colonies, however, the situation was much less attuned to the objectives of general education in the population. Some legislative support was garnered for the public financing of pauper schools, but the tradition of privately funded education continued to prevail. In a similar fashion, the colonies in the South, as well as Rhode Island (which was the first state to support legislatively the freedom to exercise any religion) essentially held their ground with a position that maintained that the state had no business in the affairs of educating children.

Consciousness for public education was not strictly a state matter. Various states incorporated a commitment to public schooling in their constitutions and laws, but the national government was also underscoring the importance of education through its regulation of the westward settlements (Cubberley, 1947). As settlers purchased land in Ohio and territory north of Ohio, Congress demanded that land surveys be conducted and that one section of the land surveyed (640 acres) in every township be reserved as a place for the maintenance of schools (Butts, 1978). Known as the **Land Ordinance of 1785,** the land grants enticed a settlement population from the New England colonies and helped to create a conducive condition for the rise of publicly funded schooling among the more northern inland settlements. Because the people of New England migrated at a very strong rate to the west, the development of schools in the Northwest territories (northern Ohio, northern Indiana, northern Illinois, Michigan) often followed that same pattern set by the early Puritans. Wherever the people of New England prevailed in the population, particularly Ohio, Wisconsin, and Michigan, state-funded public schooling was on firm ground; wherever the population was dominated by settlers whose origins were in the middle or Southern colonies, such as Kentucky, Tennessee, and the southern portions of Ohio, Illinois, and Indiana, no such conviction existed (Cubberley, 1947). Still, by 1876, nearly 20 million acres—a territory the size of Great Britain—were allocated by the federal government for educational purposes (Harris, 1899).

Despite the efforts to support education through land grants, state laws, and state constitutional protections, the free public school in America was still largely an abstraction. The country was still quite poor and the citizenry had not worked out how it could fund the high-minded idea of public education. Moreover, the agrarian lifestyle, the relative isolation of villages, and the fact that education was not yet central to the political or business practice of the time (even **universal manhood suffrage** was not yet achieved) gave education a low priority.

The Struggle for the American Public School

As the nation entered the 19th century, a philanthropic movement to offer free education to children of the poor was thriving in the cities of the North. The thinking behind these actions was imported from Europe, where public education was considered an act of alms for the poor (Power, 1991). To wealthy Europeans who could afford to educate their own children, public schools were utterly unacceptable because of the stigmatization of pauperism that they carried. The idea of publicly supported schools in Europe was anathema. Despite the considerable legislative support given to the public school in America, to many wealthy citizens the tradition of education as alms took root in some parts of the country. At the turn of the 19th century, for instance, public schools were funded by various agencies and philanthropists, including some free schools for Black children, which existed in New York City as early as 1787. Many of these charity schools were later absorbed by the public school system itself and got their charter from the state (Cubberley, 1947). Ironically, philanthropically funded public schools, as shall be explained, would ultimately give quite a boost to the idea of publicly funded schools.

During the early 1800s, among the more significant events emanating from the philanthropic school movement was a pedagogical innovation known as the **Lancaster method,** which originated in England and was popular in many of its pauper schools. The major appeal to the method was that is was a cheap and efficient way to educate many children in an equal and common manner (see The Historical Context feature in this section). The idea was rather simple: the school congregated a large class of children in a room, anywhere from 200 to potentially 1,000 students, and then sorted them into even rows. One pupil was then chosen as the monitor of the row or part of it and, with the other chosen monitors, was instructed by the teacher in the lessons for the day. The monitor's responsibility was to return to his group or row and instruct it in the very lesson that he had just completed with the teacher. This system was used for teaching reading, catechism, simple computations, writing, and spelling.

The beauty of the idea was that one teacher could presumably educate hundreds of youth in one room, with results that were no worse than those achieved in the Latin grammar schools or dame schools. With the Lancaster method, students no longer had to wait their turn at their teachers' desk to read or recite their lessons. Moreover, the method protected against student idleness and offered a climate of order and control. Used on a wholesale basis, the Lancaster method greatly cheapened the potential costs of providing a public education (Cubberley, 1947). With classroom sizes literally in the hundreds, per-pupil expenditures could be kept low. This served the causes of publicly funded education because it kept the price of conducting a school very low. In the words of one admirer,

> When I behold the wonderful celerity in instruction and economy of expense and when I perceive one great assembly of a thousand children, under the eye of a single teacher, marching, with unexampled rapidity and with perfect discipline to the goal of knowledge, I confess that I recognize in Lancaster the benefactor of the human race (Clinton, 1809, p. 121).

Another idea inspired by a philanthropist and brought to the colonies from England began to take hold at the level of primary education. In 19th-century England, it was usual for children as young as 5 to be employed in factories, working up to 12 hours a day. One manufacturer, Robert Owen, attempted to remedy this situation by offering an education to children from ages 3 to 5, partly to provide them with some early enjoyment and play before entering factory life and partly to offer them moral and intellectual training. These schools were known as **infant schools.** In the cities on the northeastern shores of the United States, where similar conditions existed for poor children, infant schools were supported by various philanthropists for the same purposes. The infant schools were used rather widely in Boston, New York, and Philadelphia.

The Lancaster Method

Monitor inspecting written exercises at signal "Show slates."

The above pictures demonstrate how the Lancaster method was used. Its virtues were believed to be tied to its efficiency and economy. Assume that you had the responsibility of teaching 365 elementary-aged students in one setting. What strategies might you apply? Would you use the Lancaster method? What alterations might you make to it? What general effects would such a situation have on your teaching and on the student's learning?

Source: Cubberley, E. B. (1934) *Public Education in the United States.* Boston: Houghton-Mifflin. p. 130,131,133.

They signified an early organizational distinction between primary and elementary education. Unlike the Lancaster schools, the infant schools actually tried to advance a new theory of teaching driven by a psychological view of children (Cubberley, 1947). The introduction of the infant school to America represented the simultaneous introduction of the learner (his or her needs and interests) into the teaching/learning equation. This was fundamentally different from the Lancaster effort, which was influenced entirely by business values and efficiency concerns.

As the country grew and stabilized during the early 19th century, and as it slowly moved into the early stages of industrial development and the building of its infrastructure, a new regard was struck for the ideals of equality among the settlers. The country now had to conceive of itself as a national entity, with national needs and goals, as opposed to the distinct state identities that existed among the settlers of the colonial period. The national hopes for the fledgling democracy naturally found its way into the schools. It was during this period that the school became conceived, particularly among various social reformers interested in bringing better equity to the social landscape of America, as a great leveler of economic differences and as an agency that could provide social and economic opportunities to all.

One of the first steps taken in the direction of developing a national consciousness was tied to the goal of using the school to build a common language and a common history. Noah Webster helped the school to serve this end by publishing his *Grammatical Institute of the English Language,* which was a three-part book containing sections on spelling, grammar, and readings. The spelling section, which was published separately as the **American Spelling Book,** eventually superseded the *New England Primer* as the most widely used text in the schools in the late 1700s (see Figure 1.5). It was said to have gone west with the settlers, often being the first book printed by the local presses in the small frontier towns (Pangle & Pangle, 1993).

Webster, of course, later wrote and published the *American Dictionary of the English Language.* But it was his speller that gave impetus to a common language without accents and that contributed to the ideal of a common classless society. All along, Webster's work stressed the Puritan values of thrift, diligence, and work, but Webster broke ranks with the rather stern style used in the *New England Primer* and used images of animals and other childhood pleasantries to convey his messages to children, although moralistic proclamations were in constant use in the text (Pangle & Pangle, 1993).

The rise of the industrial age also influenced the renewed call for public education. Industrial development brought factory work into the life of the new America, and many of these factories led to the rapid growth of cities, particularly in the northeastern and north central regions of the country. In the North, as the general concentration of manufacturing facilities developed within cities, a concentration of investment and labor followed. Where the colonial village was once homogeneous and tied to work on the land, the new cities brought together a wide mix of people whose life work was associated with the factory (Cubberley, 1947).

It became clear that as the United States continued to attract diverse populations, some type of amalgamating institution was going to be needed to build common communities. The common public school was one answer to this question of advancing a common national experience. By the 1850s, the annual immigration rate was exceeding 500,000 and was representing a wider range of national origins. From 1840 to 1870, the population of the country doubled, and then doubled again from 1870 to 1900. At the dawn of the new century, virtually one out of every seven Americans was foreign-born (Butts, 1955). No other nation had faced the challenge of socializing a largely uneducated pluralist population into a new whole. Moreover, the argument that children needed basic reading skills for manufacturing work and general levels of enlightenment to stay away from crime and other socially undesirable behavior entered the discussions. Thus, the school was taking on the role

FIGURE 1.5

Of the Boy *that stole* Apples.

An old Man found a rude Boy upon one of his trees stealing Apples, and desired him to come down; but the young Sauce-box told him plainly he would not. Won't you? said the old Man, then I will fetch you down; so he pulled up some tufts of Grass and threw at him; but this only made the Youngster laugh, to think the old Man should pretend to beat him down from the tree with grass only.

FABLE I.—*Of the* **Boy** *that ſtole* **APPLES.**

From a Webster's speller dated 1789.

Well, well, said the old Man, if neither words nor grass will do, I must try what virtue there is in Stones: so the old Man pelted him heartily with stones, which soon made the young Chap hasten down from the tree and beg the old Man's pardon.

MORAL

If good words and gentle means will not reclaim the wicked, they must be dealt with in a more severe manner.

Source: Johnson, C. (1917). *Old-time Schools and School Books.* New York: Macmillan, p. 179.

as a leveler of economic differences, as an assimilator of ethnic differences, and as a nest for learning what it meant to be an American.

Simultaneous with the growth of the industrial base of the country and the increasingly overt signs of class differences was the desire to secure universal suffrage for White men. Until the early 1800s, the right to vote was severely restricted to men with property qualifications; that is, landowners who could pay for the education of their own children. Therefore, the argument that Jefferson made about the need for the citizenry to be educated did not apply because a good share of the people simply did not have the full rights of citizenship—women did not, Blacks did not, and White men without means did not. But with the extension of voting rights to all White men, irrespective of class, occurring on a state-by-state basis during the early 1800s, the arguments for a free general education for all youth, though obviously

The statue of Liberty remains a powerful symbol of immigration into the United States. America's new citizens dramatically changed the public schools.

qualified, nevertheless became more compelling. In terms of suffrage, the basic hurdle of class as it related to White men was cleared. The hurdles of gender and race were still insurmountable.

The idea of a publicly funded school system for all youth had its share of detractors. Opponents essentially believed that state-supported education was a luxury that the nation could not afford and that such a system would cause the industrious people to support the education of the stupid and the lazy. Critics also used the old English argument that maintained that the state had no business in education, that such an institution was best left to the church and the family. There was even an aristocratic view that maintained that the poor did not need education because they had no time to use it (Callahan, 1963).

Given these views, there were some battles yet to fight in gaining widespread public support for a school tax. The argument for school taxation was laid on a principle that equated taxation with the price that must be paid for social order (for courts, jails, roads, police, and so on). By this rationale, free public schooling was an investment in the stability and progress of society, in making life more civilized and more likely marked by enlightened behaviors. Many states experimented with a wide range of tools to garner monies for schools. Lotteries, occupational taxes, bank taxes, and money taken from license fees were popular. Some states also used rate bills, another practice inherited from England, which were charges levied on parents whose children were in school.

But as the population and its problems grew, these sources proved to be much too scanty, and other avenues were explored and exploited, which led to the idea of school support through local property taxes. In Massachusetts, the legislature passed the Law of 1789, which gave local districts full power to tax and control their own schools. Such a system was well aligned with the structure of school organization established in early New England and was popular in several Northern states. "For the purpose of public instruction," declared Daniel Webster, "we have held, and do hold, every man subject to taxation in proportion to his property; and we look not to the question whether he himself have or have not children, to be benefitted by the education for which he pays" (Quoted in Harris, 1899, p. 44). The idea of the local tax was grudgingly accepted (Power, 1991). But permissive state laws gave local schools all kinds of leeway, and rate bills continued to be used. Still, a corner was turned for public education in America in that the European school tradition of pauperism was rejected.

Under the new scheme of tax funding, it became incumbent on the community to control and regulate the quality of schooling offered to its youth. But there were dangers. Public apathy, local infighting, rampant poverty, and the rise of individualism led to a decline in community interest in schooling (Cremin, 1951). Moreover, districts not disposed to funding public schools were really under no compulsions to do so. Early state laws were highly permissive, and there was little organized authority at the state level in public education. Under these conditions, local decision making thrived, but not always in ways that were in the interests of the public school. Clearly, the universalization of the public school could not be accomplished under circumstances that allowed local initiatives to prevail without necessarily accounting for state needs. Local concerns were obviously important, but the state would clearly need to take an active hand in developing, facilitating, and supervising public education.

The naming of schools is a way to bestow honor upon those who worked in the interest of public education. On the left, is the Horace Mann school in St. Paul, Minnesota, and on the right, the Christa McAuliffe school in Hastings, Minnesota. Mann and McAuliffe, each in their own way, dedicated their lives to improving public schooling.

Eventually, the state moved in on the public school by establishing forms of state aid, which led to setting criteria for the securing of these monies and later to supervising roles in accounting for these monies. States often forced local taxes on schools by making state monetary commitments to local districts contingent on in-kind or matching monetary commitments at the local level. In other words, no state monies were forwarded unless the local district made an equal-share investment in the school. To accomplish all its new functions, the state had to create an administrative structure, led by a state school officer, that would be responsible for the leadership and supervision of the public schools. In the 1830s, a legislator by the name of James Carter argued long and hard for a more direct state role in the conduct of public schooling in Massachusetts. He wanted a state board to be established so that efforts to create public high schools and normal schools (training institutes for teachers) could find some central authority and advocacy. In 1837, Carter succeeded in winning approval for a state board and proceeded to help appoint Horace Mann as the first state secretary of education in Massachusetts in 1837. This appointment would eventually take on historic significance.

The Rise of State Authority

Probably more than anyone who lived in the 19th century, Horace Mann used his new office to reawaken the Jeffersonian concept of mass education for sociocivic gain. In his leadership role in Massachusetts, Mann worked to widen schooling opportunities for all children in the state, to elevate the base of tax support for schools, to upgrade the hygienic standards of schoolhouses, to support the training of teaching in normal schools, to bring more women into the profession, to increase the number of school libraries, and generally to improve upon the pedagogical practices of teachers. During his tenure, teachers' salaries increased substantially, the school year was lengthened, and the general appropriations to schools increased (Rippa, 1984).

Mann studied the emerging educational theories of his time and attempted to apply the best of these ideas in Massachusetts. For instance, he was among the first to try to improve on reading instruction by considering what was then known as the whole-word method of teaching reading, which essentially rejected the phonetic alphabetic treatments of words in favor of whole-word recognitions (Tanner & Tanner, 1987).

Although he understood there was a clear limit to what he could accomplish in the school politically, Mann was quite an activist. He was very unhappy with the district system used in Massachusetts that allowed local schools to regulate themselves and not be accountable to concerns that transcended local matters. To Mann, the district school needed to be given a center of gravity that brought things together under a common civic mission, as opposed to a local or sectarian one, and that provided an overseeing agency devoted to maintaining certain standards of quality in education. Mann saw little more than anarchy in the idea of local school control (Power, 1991).

Much to the chagrin of many citizens, Mann also wanted to keep the function of the state-funded school separate from sectarian religious instruction. He wanted to use the school to promote a civic community that would subject children to a political education and that would offer a common discourse for mutual understanding and tolerance. Although Mann was severely critical of the way schooling was conducted in Massachusetts, he understood its promise and was ever faithful and optimistic about the powers of free common schools, thinking that the public school would help eliminate poverty and class distinction and become "the great equalizer of the conditions of men."

Mann also had a keen political sense and generally avoided matters on the curriculum that might divide the population (Butts, 1978). Therefore, not only was religion generally avoided in the school, though Mann advised that the Bible be read without commentary, but potentially fractious political issues were also avoided. Mann understood that the common public school was a fragile institution, and he did not want to imperil its future by generating controversies in the curriculum that might spill into the community. Thus he generally held the line on controversies in the curriculum and focused more on literacy instruction, moral training, and knowledge of government (Butts, 1978). As Karier (1967) explains, Mann also viewed the American public school as a form of protection against social revolution and as an important contrast to the European model of schooling that accepted the inevitability of class differences.

Because of his many progressive ideas, Mann was not the most popular man in Massachusetts. The early history of Massachusetts upheld the right of the church to dictate school practice, and Mann was breaking with tradition by trying to erect a wall of separation between the two. Thus it was not long before Mann was faced with an onslaught of criticism that contended that he (and the State Board of Education that he led) were trying to take God out of the public schools, to make them Godless, which in the eyes of many citizens made them worthless. Mann was subjected to vicious attacks from the pulpit and through the press. In his third year in office, Mann had to face the indignity of two legislative attempts, led by religious forces, to abolish the State Board of Education (Rippa, 1984). The attempts failed, and Mann kept his position as secretary of education for 12 years.

Mann also made quite a few enemies among teachers, mostly because he was so unabashedly critical of their work. A skilled writer, Mann used the annual reports on education in Massachusetts to provide commentary on many educational problems of the day. In the Seventh Annual Report of his term, Mann took direct aim at the poor teaching in the schools and spoke admiringly about how education in Prussia, which he visited for a period, might provide some thoughtful lessons for educators in Massachusetts. In the Prussian schools, Mann (1844) observed, "I never saw a blow struck, I never heard a sharp rebuke given, I never saw a child in tears. . . . I heard no child ridiculed, sneered at, or scolded, for making a mistake" (p. 187). Could a visitor, Mann added rhetorically, spend six weeks in schools in Massachusetts and walk away with the same impressions?

Mann also accounted for the style of instruction in Prussia, noting the scholarly insight of the teachers, whose books (to paraphrase Mann) were in their heads, not in their hands. He recounted classroom observations that allowed for student questions, classroom discussions, and more humane and empathic treatments of youth. Not surprisingly, his report spawned a harsh response from the Principal's Association in Boston and set off a yearlong written debate between Mann and the principals. Each of the 12 annual reports written by Mann is full of commentary on various school-related issues, many of which are still relevant today (Rippa, 1984).

The genius of Horace Mann had to do with the way in which he understood the changing social landscape of Massachusetts and America. Although he was a deeply religious man, he knew that battles over which religious creeds to read and study in the school would eventually destroy the chances of establishing a universally accessible common public school. Instead, Mann worked out of a sociocivic tradition that stressed democratizing themes in the schools and that opted for the professionalization of teaching. It was largely through his work that a strong model for free common schooling existed during the 1840s in Massachusetts, a model that not only influenced other states but also other countries. Mann and his ideas traveled widely. He advised other state authorities on matters of school administration and counseled the development of public schools in such distant places as Chile and Argentina (Noble, 1959).

The Upward and Outward Extension of Schooling

Massachusetts was also the place where the American high school was preliminarily formed. As indicated earlier, by the mid-1700s, the Latin grammar school was waning as an option for secondary school instruction and the Academy was on the rise. By the mid-1800s, the Latin grammar school had essentially disappeared, becoming an anachronism of an earlier time and place, and the tuition-based Academy had taken its place. In Massachusetts, where free public schooling at the elementary school level was becoming more of a reality, free schooling was making an upward extension into the secondary school years. The Academies were still tuition based, but Massachusetts was ahead of its time by enacting legislation in 1827 that required the establishment of tax-supported high schools in towns with 500 or more households. Over the next two decades, at least 100 public high schools were maintained in Massachusetts.

The first public high school opened in Boston in 1821. It was designed more in the image of the Academy than the Latin grammar school. Latin and Greek were not part of the school's curricular offerings. Instead, the center of the curriculum consisted of English, mathematics, science, logic, and history (Boston Records, 1820, p. 134). In 1826, a separate high school for girls opened in Boston, which became so oversubscribed that the mayor closed it down after two years, fearing that the city might bankrupt itself (Rippa, 1984).

The idea for public high schools spread to other states, most particularly to those in the North. But the development of the public high school in other states was still being held back by a district system that allowed local districts to decide whether they would erect such schools. Most of the state laws requiring free public education were lenient and did not compel compliance to the state's wishes. Districts sometimes abused their power, which led to uneven tax support for the schools and uneven access to quality schooling. But by 1860, a free common public schooling system more or less existed at the elementary level in Massachusetts, while free public high schools were becoming more popular, even in more rural areas.

It was only a matter of time before the constitutionality of tax-supported high school education was tested. The most prominent court case that spoke to this issue was in Kalamazoo, Michigan, where a citizen, in 1872, tested the school board's right to levy taxes in support of high schools (Tanner, 1972).

The complainant argued that high schools were not institutions designed to educate all the children, as evidenced by their relatively low attendance, and were, therefore, not under the purview of public taxes. The State Supreme Court, however, ruled that tax monies could be used to support high school education because they aimed to provide an advanced education to rich and poor alike (Butts, 1955). The schools, in other words, were not widely attended, but they were presumably accessible to all. The ruling in the Kalamazoo court case was significant because it gave the high school a secure place in the common, publicly supported school system.

As the concept of the public school began to take hold in cities and towns across the nation, fundamental changes were occurring in school organization. The evolving common elementary school, which had long practiced nongraded instruction, was undergoing divisional changes that separated primary education from intermediate education (Douglas & Grieder, 1948). Soon, actual grade divisions followed. This change was facilitated by the construction of new school buildings that tried to accommodate smaller groups and by the provision of smaller classes, which were reduced to between 50 and 75 students per class (Cubberley, 1947).

Thus, with the high school in place and the elementary school carved into three parts (primary, intermediate, and grammar), the American ladder system of education was born. The virtue of the ladder (grade one through college) was that it represented one unified pathway for schooling that all students could theoretically access, as opposed to the dual ladders that existed in Europe (one for the college bound and one for the vocational bound). Even higher education had received a boost with the congressional passage of the Morrill Act of 1862, which authorized federal subsidies and land grants for the endowment of state universities given the mission of educating all the classes in a liberal and practical education (see the Web Points feature in this section). Many of these early land grant universities featured education in agriculture and mechanics and have since grown to be among the largest and most comprehensive universities in the world. The land grant act also represented a new pedagogical priority in the education of young adults because practical studies, as opposed to classical studies, now had a justifiable place in the postsecondary curriculum.

As the 20th century loomed, religious concerns no longer dominated the character of instruction in the common schools, though the Bible still often made its way into the curriculum. The new priority was knowledge accumulation, which typically meant knowing the rules of arithmetic and grammar, the conventions of spelling and reading, and various geographic information. The Americans might have rejected various European school traditions, but they were receptive to new theoretical ideas on education being forwarded by more progressive European educators and thinkers. The work of Pestalozzi and Herbart, and the development of new teacher training institutes, known as normal schools, generated new outlooks on the classroom and the curriculum in America.

Moreover, with the passage of the 13th Amendment in 1865, slavery was abolished in the country, and with the passage of the 14th and 15th Amendments, Black Americans now had equal protection under the law and open access to voting. In the South, of course, these initiatives were undermined by Jim Crow laws and by other efforts to deprive the rights of citizenship to Blacks. Still, in the decades to come, the public school would emerge at the

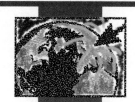

Land Grant Legislation

The Morrill Act of 1862 represented a massive federal investment in the construction and development of state colleges. To learn more about different land grant efforts and about the history of land grant legislation, visit the following web site: http://www.ifas.ufl.edu/WWW/LS_GRANT/INDEX.HTM.

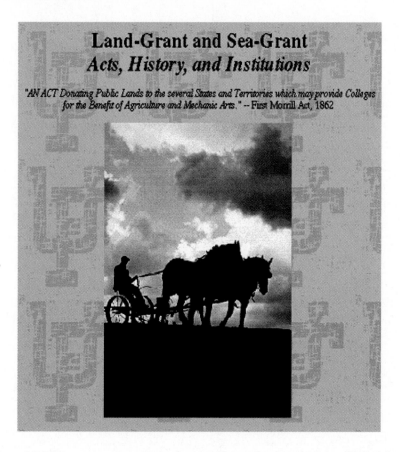

Land-Grant and Sea-Grant
Acts, History, and Institutions

"AN ACT Donating Public Lands to the several States and Territories which may provide Colleges for the Benefit of Agriculture and Mechanic Arts." -- First Morrill Act, 1862

Education - UF/IFAS can trace its roots to the Morrill Act of 1862 which established the Land Grant university system. On July 2, 1862, President Abraham Lincoln signed into law what is generally referred to as the Land Grant Act. The new piece of legislation introduced by U.S. Representative Justin Smith Morrill of Vermont granted to each state 30,000 acres of public land for each Senator and Representative under apportionment based on the 1860 census. Proceeds from the sale of these lands were to be invested in a perpetual endowment fund which would provide support for colleges of agriculture and mechanical arts in each of the states. The establishment of Florida Agricultural College at Lake City in 1884 under the Morrill Act marked the beginning of what became the College of Agriculture of the University of Florida in 1906.

FIGURE 1.6

TIME LINE OF EVENTS IN THE DEVELOPMENT OF PUBLIC SCHOOLS

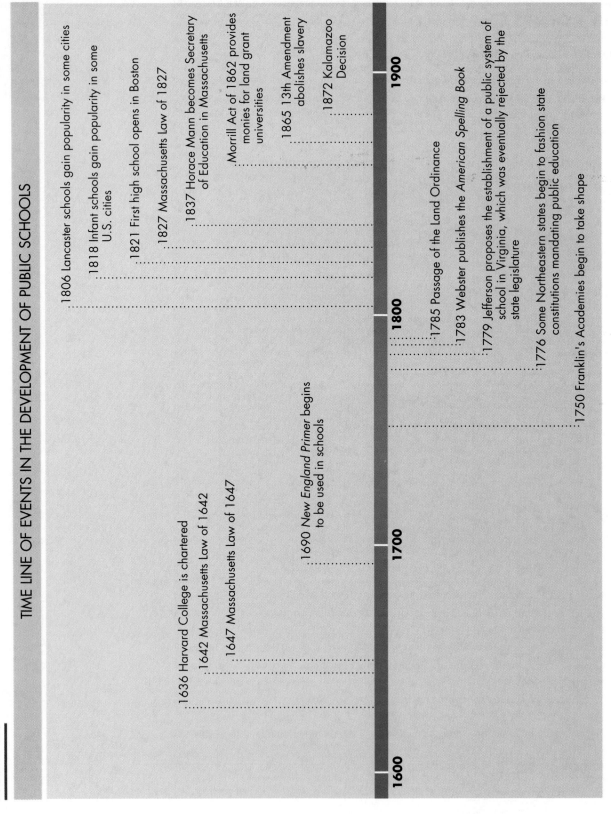

1600

1700

1800

1900

1636 Harvard College is chartered

1642 Massachusetts Law of 1642

1647 Massachusetts Law of 1647

1690 *New England Primer* begins to be used in schools

1750 Franklin's Academies begin to take shape

1776 Some Northeastern states begin to fashion state constitutions mandating public education

1779 Jefferson proposes the establishment of a public system of school in Virginia, which was eventually rejected by the state legislature

1783 Webster publishes the *American Spelling Book*

1785 Passage of the Land Ordinance

1806 Lancaster schools gain popularity in some cities

1818 Infant schools gain popularity in some U.S. cities

1821 First high school opens in Boston

1827 Massachusetts Law of 1827

1837 Horace Mann becomes Secretary of Education in Massachusetts

Morrill Act of 1862 provides monies for land grant universities

1865 13th Amendment abolishes slavery

1872 Kalamazoo Decision

very forefront of a civil rights struggle, continuing to try to find its way as an agency of and for the people.

There is little question that the development of the school in New England had indeed swayed the course for public education in America. (See Figure 1.6 for a time line of events that were important in the development of public education.) On principle, the foundation for tax-supported public education was secure at the turn of the century. Opportunities for an education were no longer dependent on the philanthropy of industrialists and other elites, or on the church. A new democratic vista was now before the nation—public schools, free and open to all, supported by the public, regulated by the state, free from sectarian control, and still responsive to local conditions and priorities.

KEY TERMS

Academy school
American ladder system of
  education
American Spelling Book
Dame schools
Hornbook
Infant schools
Kalamazoo court case

Lancaster method
Land Ordinance of 1785
Latin grammar schools
Massachusetts Law of 1789
Massachusetts Law of 1647
Massachusetts Law of 1642
Morrill Act of 1862

New England Primer
Pauper schools
Society for the Propagation of the
  Gospel in Foreign Parts
10th Amendment to the
  Constitution
Universal manhood suffrage

KEY QUESTIONS

1. Why did regional differences exist in the colonies toward the provision of public education?

2. How did the Lancaster method of teaching contribute to the argument for publicly funded education?

3. How does one account for the slight attention given to the education of women and girls in the colonies?

4. Explain the decline of religious bodies in the control of education.

5. Characterize the overall nature of teaching in a New England dame school or Latin grammar school.

6. Explain the shift from religious instruction to sociocivic objectives in the historical development of the public school.

7. Why was the Massachusetts Law of 1647 also known as the Old Deluder Act?

8. Explain the stages of development in the growth of the Massachusetts school district system.

9. Explain how the constitutional recognition of religious freedom contributed to the growth of the public school.

10. How did the extension of universal manhood suffrage serve the causes of public education?

11. Explain the methods of, and the justification for, discipline in the schools of the Puritans.

12. In what way was the American public school born out of a religious mandate?

13. Why did the Puritans want to hand over control of education to civic government?

14. In what way was the Law of 1647 a greater stride toward the development of the public school than the Law of 1642?

15. What was meant by the observation that the *New England Primer* "taught millions to read and not one to sin"?

16. In what ways was Benjamin Franklin's Academy a reaction against the Latin grammar school?

17. Why were not many slave owners interested in educating their slaves?

18. How did the national government support the development of the public school through its regulation of westward settlements?

19. As the nation grew in number and diversity, what were the more important mandates facing the schools?

20. How did the growth of cities support the public schools?

21. What were some of the early arguments made against publicly funded education?

22. In what way was the virtue of the district system also its fundamental weakness?

23. What was Horace Mann's main argument for more active state control over public schools?

24. Why did not Mann support the introduction of controversial topics in the school curriculum?

25. Why was Mann not always the most popular public official in Massachusetts?

26. What made the American ladder system of education unique for its time?

27. Explain the work of the Society for the Propagation of the Gospel in Foreign Parts.

REFERENCES

Beale, H. K. (1975). The education of negroes before the Civil War. In J. Barnard & D. Burner (Eds.), *The American experience in education*. New York: New Viewpoints.

Boston Records. (1820). Proceedings of town meeting, XXVII. In D. Calhoun, *Educating of Americans: A documentary history* (pp. 168–171). Boston: Houghton-Mifflin Company.

Butts, R. F. (1978). *Public education in the United States*. New York: Holt, Rinehart and Winston.

Butts, R. F. (1955). *A cultural history of Western education: Its social and intellectual foundations*. New York: McGraw-Hill.

Butts, R. F., & Cremin, L. A. (1953). *A history of education in American culture*. New York: Holt, Rinehart and Winston.

Callahan, R. (1963). *An introduction to education in American society*. New York: Alfred A. Knopf.

Clinton, D. W. (1809). Address on the opening of a new school building. In D. Calhoun, *Educating of Americans: A documentary history*. Boston: Houghton-Mifflin Company.

Cohen, S. S. (1974). *A history of colonial education, 1607–1776*. New York: John Wiley and Sons.

Cohen, S. (1973). *Education in the United States: A documentary history* (Vol. 1). New York: Random House.

Colony of Massachusetts. (1853). *Records of the governor and company of the Massachusetts Bay in New England*. Boston: William White.

Cremin, L. A. (1951). *The American common school: A historic conception*. New York: Teachers College, Columbia University.

Cremin, L. A. (1977). *Traditions of American education*. New York: Basic Books.

Cubberley, E. B. (1934). *Public education in the United States*. Boston: Houghton-Mifflin Company.

Douglas, H. R., & Greider, C. (1948). *American public education*. New York: The Ronald Press Company.

French, W. M. (1964). *America's educational tradition*. Boston: D C Heath and Co.

French, W. M. (1967). *American secondary education*. New York: The Odyssey Press.

Ford, P. L. (1899). *The New England Primer*. New York: Dodd, Mead.

Harris, W. T. (1899). *Education in the United States*. New York: D. Appleton and Co.

Johnson , C. (1917). *Old-time schools and school books*. New York: Macmillan.

Karier, C. J. (1967). *Man, society and education*. New York: Scott Foresman and Co.

Knight, E. W. (1951). *Education in the United States*. Boston: Ginn and Company.

Mann, H. (1844). Seventh annual report of the Board of Education, In D. Calhoun, *Educating of Americans: A documentary history*. Boston: Houghton-Mifflin Company.

Meriwether, C. (1907). *Colonial curriculum 1607–1776*. Washington, DC: Capital Publishing Co.

Noble, S. G. (1959). *A history of American education*. New York: Rinehart and Company, Inc.

Pangle, L. S., & Pangle, T. L. (1993). *The learning of liberty*. Lawrence, KS: University Press of Kansas.

Power, E. J. (1991). *A legacy of learning*. Albany, NY: SUNY Press.

Rippa, S. A. (1984). *Education in a free society: An American history*. New York: David McKay Company, Inc.

Small, W. H. (1969). *Early New England schools*. New York: Arno Press and the *New York Times*.

Tanner, D. (1972). *Secondary education*. New York: Macmillan.

Tanner, D., & Tanner, L. N. (1987). *History of the school Curriculum*. New York: Macmillan.

2

DEFINING THE SCHOOL CURRICULUM AT THE TURN OF THE 20TH CENTURY

With the beginning of the 20th century, the public school system took hold and attention turned from the objective of simply providing school to the question of what would be taught inside the school. In this photograph, Mary Laycock of the American School in Lahore, Pakistan, compels a student to solve a problem using the base cubes. Such a strategy is designed to help students understand the concepts of math, not just to remember the steps in solving math problems. As questions about the subject matter in school gained prominence, educators moved toward a wider vision of schooling. This raised the idea that schools did not necessarily have to reflect society but that they could be used to "make" a different kind of society.

John Dewey, perhaps the greatest American philosopher, argued that public schooling had the potential to change society. Through activities designed to provoke a sense of community in students, he and other progressive educators were convinced that public schooling had great potential to change the character of American life. This chapter examines the earliest attempts at curriculum design formulations.

A new day was dawning for the public school at the turn of the 20th century. The school gates were just beginning to swing open, and the very idea of pedagogy was taking on new scientific and philosophical slants. A new progressive force was gathering strength in American education, setting a counterbalance to traditionalist thinking. With the idea of a public school now in place, a struggle over the character of the school curriculum was taking shape between conservative and progressive thinkers, as new questions were being raised about the content, the instructional practice, and the evaluation of the school curriculum.

Policy issues were also being raised, particularly in relation to perennial issues of equity and opportunity to learn. The early tradition of the American school was about to get an injection of new ideas that challenged the old and that set the course for an entirely new way of looking at teaching and learning. At the same time, traditionalist measures of teaching were themselves getting a boost from advocates in the liberal arts, who were arguing for a highly academic subject-centered curriculum. The conditions were set for a debate over the practice of the American school, a clash of ideas that featured an early child-centered form of progressivism against the subject-centered thinking of traditionalism (Dewey, 1902; Bode, 1938).

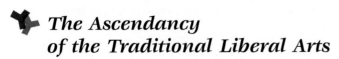 The Ascendancy of the Traditional Liberal Arts

The progressive reaction in the schools at the turn of the century was due in part to the ascendancy of traditionalism in the schools during the late decades of the 19th century. During this period, traditional approaches to teaching youth, which stressed the Old World methods of rote and recitation, were still quite popular. In fact, new advocates for such instruction were emerging from the ranks of the liberal arts, equipped with a new psychology and an associated doctrine of learning that gave justification to the old pedagogy. Many of these thinkers were what one might tentatively classify as adherents of **traditional humanism** (Kliebard, 1986). These scholars generally believed that a good education entailed an immersion in the disciplines and the great works of the liberal arts. During the early development of the American high school, which spanned the middle and late decades of the 19th century, such thinkers dominated the educational scene.

The Doctrine of Mental Discipline

The character of education supported by the traditional humanists is probably best broached by starting with an explanation of the learning doctrine that drove their thinking about the curriculum. Virtually everything done in the school by the traditionalists was rationalized through a learning doctrine known as **mental discipline.** The central principle was derived from a theory of learning, known as **faculty psychology,** that held that the mind was made up of separate faculties that collectively comprised the human mind. According to faculty psychology, responses related to emotions, affections, the will, and the intellect all had their "place" in the mind. While more progressive thinkers, such as Pestalozzi, used faculty psychology to argue for a more holistic approach to education that encompassed all the so-called faculties (mental, physical, moral, emotional), advocates of the doctrine of mental discipline used it to justify a preoccupation with the intellect, with the task of finding a way to train the intellectual faculties. Thus, through mental discipline, it was thought that intellectual faculties could only be developed and improved through certain mental exercises. Proponents believed that such exercises could so strengthen the mind that the benefits to learners would be transferable to most life situations, making them better able to handle their lives with intelligence.

The key to the teaching/learning process under these assumptions was ensuring that students were exposed to subject areas believed to be intrinsically empowered with the capacity to cultivate the mind's intellectual faculties. This meant that students needed to be trained in the study of certain subjects. Skills of memory, judgment, imagination, and other mental processes could only be sharpened if students were regularly immersed in the proper academic subjects. The "mind as muscle" metaphor became associated with the doctrine of mental discipline because it captured the idea that the mind, like a muscle, had to be exercised through a rigorous mental workout. Such a workout, however, could only be accomplished with the heavy mental equipment that the traditional academic disciplines provided. Latin, Greek, mathematics, rhetoric, grammar, and the Great Books were, more or less, believed to be at the core of a good mental routine, while anything that dealt with vocational, interdisciplinary, or more experiential studies was clearly not up to the task of bulking the mind's muscle. The idea was to inherit the intellectual force of the subject matter, a priority that led to intensive drill and practice in the school, as well as to much student memorization (Rippa, 1984).

Mental discipline was clearly an early expression of a classical dualism in education that placed the power of the mind over the power of the body. It led to an early bias favoring "mindful" intellectual activity, as it might be construed in its most puristic academic sense, over vocational and experiential activity, which was perceived to be anti-intellectual and not worthy of much attention in the school.

But the doctrine of mental discipline was able to answer two essential curriculum questions, which helped to give it staying power. It had a ready answer to the question of what should be taught in the school curriculum and an equally clear, though less obvious, answer to the question of how one should teach. What one taught in school from the standpoint of mental discipline was a traditional body of academic knowledge built largely on the liberal arts. But since the subject matter did the "teaching" through its inherent intellective capacities, mental disciplinarians did not believe that they needed any particular instructional methodology to actualize the connection between the subject matter and the mind. Teachers, of course, had to be well schooled in the subject matter, but their role in the classroom was to be the purveyors and guardians of the liberal arts tradition. Thus, the teacher, who was frequently without much professional training, was not expected to do much more than establish order in the classroom, fulfill the primary needs for basic skills instruction, which was typically approached through skill-drill strategies, and ensure an exposure to the proper academic traditions. The high regard placed on basic skills, especially in the elementary school, had to do with the fact that such skills were seen as preparatory for later academic study. In other words, mental disciplinarians held few worries about instructional methods. They opted to put their faith in the power of the subject matter.

Because of its fixation on mental manipulations, the school (especially the high school) was characterized by a uniformity of instructional routines that did little to attract the learner's interests and needs. As long as mental discipline prevailed as a learning doctrine, this was the way that it was likely to stay because any studies that could not find a rationale through mental discipline were seen as potential distractors from the central function of cultivating the mind.

The adherents of mental discipline were convinced that they had identified a central core of studies needed to develop the human mind. But they also hit on an even more important revelation. They maintained that their core of mental studies was appropriate for the education of all youth, not simply those aiming to go to college. The mental training not only represented the best preparation for college but also the best preparation for ordinary citizens. This egalitarian principle in the traditional humanist position turned out to be crucial to its influence in the curriculum. It gave the traditional humanists a platform upon which the education of all youth could be maintained (see the Scholarly Voices feature in this section). At the level of the high school, this position was made quite clear in a curriculum document sponsored by the National Education Association (NEA) and published in 1893 by a committee of traditional humanists known as the **Committee of Ten.**

The Committee Reports and the Identification of the Curriculum

The Committee of Ten report (1893/1969) was written under the chairmanship of Charles Eliot, who was then president of Harvard University. Funded

THE SCHOOL EXPERIENCE IN LITERATURE

Mr. Gradgrind

Charles Dickens's memorable *Hard Times* describes many harsh episodes of teaching. Here is a famous one taken from the beginning of the book. The teacher, Mr. Gradgrind, and a government officer engage in a pedagogy that reflected early conceptions of learning.

'Girl number twenty,' said Mr. Gradgrind, squarely pointing with his square forefinger, 'I don't know that girl. Who is that girl?'

'Sissy Jupe, sir,' explained number twenty, blushing, standing up, and curtseying.

'Sissy is not a name,' said Mr. Gradgrind. 'Don't call yourself Sissy. Call yourself Cecilia.'

'It's father as calls me Sissy, sir,' returned the young girl in a trembling voice, and with another curtsey.

'Then he has no business to do it,' said Mr. Gradgrind. 'Tell him he mustn't. Cecilia Jupe. Let me see. What is your father?'

'He belongs to the horse-riding, if you please, sir.'

Mr. Gradgrind frowned, and waved off the objectionable calling with his hand.

'We don't want to know anything about that, here. You mustn't tell us about that, here. Your father breaks horses, don't he?'

'If you please, sir, when they can get any to break, they do break horses in the ring, sir.'

'You mustn't tell us about the ring, here. Very well, then. Describe your father as a horsebreaker. He doctors sick horses, I dare say?'

'Oh yes, sir.'

'Very well, then. He is a veterinary surgeon, a farrier, and horsebreaker. Give me your definition of a horse.'

(Sissy Jupe thrown into the greatest alarm by this demand.)

'Girl number twenty unable to define a horse!' said Mr. Gradgrind, for the general behoof of all the little pitchers. 'Girl number twenty possessed of no facts, in reference to one of the commonest animals! Some boy's definition of a horse. Bitzer, yours.'

'Bitzer,' said Thomas Gradgrind. 'Your definition of a horse.'

'Quadruped. Graminivorous. Forty teeth, namely twenty-four grinder, four eye-teeth, and twelve incisive. Sheds coat in the spring; in marshy countries, sheds hoofs, too. Hoofs hard, but requiring to be shod with iron. Age known by marks in mouth.' Thus (and much more) Bitzer.

'Now girl number twenty,' said Mr. Gradgrind. 'You know what a horse is.'

She curtseyed again, and would have blushed deeper, if she could have blushed deeper than she had blushed all this time. Bitzer, after rapidly blinking at Thomas Gradgrind with both eyes at once, and so catching the light upon his quivering ends of lashes that they looked the antennae of busy insects, put his knuckles to his freckled forehead, and sat down again.

The third gentleman now stepped forth. A mighty man at cutting and drying, he was; a government officer;

'Very well,' said this gentleman, briskly smiling, and folding his arms. 'That's a horse. Now, let me ask you girls and boys, Would you paper a room with representations of horses?'

—*Continued*

Mr. Gradgrind

—Continued

After a pause, one half of the children cried in chorus, 'Yes, sir!' Upon which the other half, seeing in the gentleman's face that Yes was wrong, cried out in chorus, 'No, sir!'—as the custom is, in these examinations.

'Of course, No. Why wouldn't you?'

A pause. One corpulent slow boy, with a wheezy manner of breathing, ventured the answer, Because he wouldn't paper a room at all, but would paint it.

'You *must* paper it,' said the gentleman, rather warmly.

'You must paper it,' said Thomas Gradgrind, 'whether you like it or not. Don't tell *us* you wouldn't paper it. What do you mean, boy?'

'I'll explain to you, then,' said the gentleman, after another and a dismal pause, 'Why you wouldn't paper a room with representations of horses. Do you ever see horses walking up and down the sides of rooms in reality—in fact? Do you?'

'Yes, sir!' from one half. 'No, sir!' from the other.

'Of course no,' said the gentleman, with an indignant look at the wrong half. 'Why, then, you are not to see anywhere, what you don't see in fact; you are not to have anywhere, what you don't have in fact. What is called Taste, is only another name for Fact.'

Thomas Gradgrind nodded his approbation.

'This is a new principle, a discovery, a great discovery,' said the gentleman. 'Now, I'll try you again. Suppose you were going to carpet a room. Would you use a carpet having a representation of flowers upon it!'

There being a general conviction by this time that 'No, sir!' was always the right answer to this gentleman, the chorus of No was very strong. Only a few feeble stragglers said Yes; among them Sissy Jupe.

'Girl number twenty,' said the gentleman, smiling in the calm strength of knowledge.

Sissy blushed, and stood up.

'So you would carpet your room—or your husband's room, if you were a grown woman, and had a husband—with representations of flowers, would you?' said the gentleman. 'Why would you?'

'If you please, sir, I am very fond of flowers,' returned the girl.

'And is that why you would put tables and chairs upon them, and have people walking over them with heavy boots?'

'It wouldn't hurt them, sir. They wouldn't crush and wither, if you please, sir. They would be the pictures of what was very pretty and pleasant, and I would fancy—'

'Ay, ay, ay! But you mustn't fancy,' cried the gentleman, quite elated by coming so happily to his point. 'That's it! You are never to fancy.'

'You are not, Cecilia Jupe,' Thomas Gradgrind solemnly repeated, 'to do anything of that kind.'

'Fact, fact, fact!' said the gentleman. And 'Fact, fact, fact!' repeated Thomas Gradgrind.

'You are to be in all things regulated and governed,' said the gentleman, 'by fact. We hope to have, before long, a board of fact, composed of commissioners of fact, who will

—Continued

THE SCHOOL EXPERIENCE IN LITERATURE

Mr. Gradgrind

—Continued

force the people to be a people of fact, and nothing but fact. You must discard the word Fancy altogether. You have nothing to do with it. You are not to have, in any object of use or ornament, what would be a contradiction in fact. You don't walk upon flowers in fact; you cannot be allowed to walk upon flowers in carpets. You don't find that foreign birds and butterflies come to perch upon your crockery; you cannot be permitted to paint foreign birds and butterflies upon your crockery. You never meet with quadrupeds going up and down walls; you must not have quadrupeds represented upon walls. You must use,' said the gentleman, 'for all these purposes, combinations and modifications (in primary colours) of mathematical figures which are susceptible of proof and demonstration. This is the new discovery. This is fact. This is taste.'

Source: Dickens, Charles. (1868). *Hard Times* NY: President Publishing Company, originally published in 1854, pp. 3–6.

by the NEA for the purpose of providing some curriculum direction to the American high school, the Committee of Ten fashioned a clear statement about what should be taught. The hope was that the committee's report might set a standard for American high schools to follow. Many secondary schools, which served less than 5 percent of the student population in the 1890s, were facing a dizzying set of requirements from different universities and colleges and were quite confused over which way to proceed to ensure the postsecondary admission and success of their graduates. Moreover, participation in public secondary education was on the rise, forcing many to think about high school as not only a preparation for college but also as a preparation for life itself. The committee (1893/1969), in fact, took this trend quite seriously, stating that

> A secondary school programme tended for national use must be made for those children whose education is not to be pursued beyond the secondary school. The preparation of a few pupils for college . . . should in the ordinary secondary school be the incidental, and not the principal object. (p. 481)

The Committee of Ten was dominated by strong believers in the doctrine of mental discipline. It included 10 men: 5 college presidents, 1 professor, 2 private school masters, a principal of a public school, and the sitting U.S. Commissioner of Education (Rippa, 1971). The actual report provided a single curriculum prescription for the high school, advancing what was, in effect, a highly traditional set of studies, rooted in the liberal arts, believed to be valuable to the goal of disciplining the mind. The committee supported nine broad subjects: Latin, Greek, English, modern languages, physics, astronomy and chemistry, natural history, history, and geography (see Figure 2.1). The inclusion of science courses was unconventional for its time and was likely the result of Charles Eliot's influence, who, as a former professor of chemistry, believed that there were mind-training possibilities in studies not traditionally conceived in the liberal arts.

But the report made no provision for physical education, the fine arts, or for any vocational subject. Such matters in the curriculum were thought to

Hutchins on the Virtues of Developing the Mind

The following statement was made by Robert Hutchins, a scholar whose philosophical leanings favored traditional humanism. Do you agree with his statement?

> The ideal education is not an ad hoc education, not an education directed to immediate needs; it is not a specialized education, or a preprofessional education; it is not a utilitarian education. It is an education calculated to develop the mind.
>
> I have old-fashioned prejudices in favor of the three R's and the liberal arts, in favor of trying to understand the greatest works that the human race has produced. I believe that these are the permanent necessities, the intellectual tolls that are needed to understand the ideas and ideals of our world.

Source: Hutchins, R. M. (1936). *The Higher Learning in America.* New Haven: Yale University Press, p. 66.

have no relevance to the strengthening of the mind. Thus, by virtue of what it included and excluded, the Committee of Ten helped to erect a high school curriculum on nine subjects conceived as equally able to train the mind. As indicated, these subjects were upheld as appropriate for the education of all youth, including those whose plans did not lead to college. In this manner, the committee had set a new curriculum pattern for the American high school that was disciplinary and subject focused. What was best for the preparation of the college scholar was best for the preparation of all youth.

Interestingly, Eliot did not give full support to the committee's work. He had already been on record for his support of free electives in the curriculum, a cause that he championed at Harvard University during his tenure as president (Rippa, 1971). Eliot, who accepted the value of mental training, simply did not think that only certain subject areas had a monopoly on mind development. Eliot thought, in fact, that nearly all subjects had value in this regard as long as they were taught in a manner that attempted to cultivate reason and morality. At Harvard, Eliot had managed to reduce the number of classical courses in the interests of expanding the curriculum offering, providing more space for the technical and scientific areas (Tanner & Tanner, 1990). Thus, when the Committee of Ten limited its recommendations to nine essential subjects, Eliot had to face an inevitable compromise. But the committee had a little bit of compromising to do as well because without Eliot it would not have likely supported even as many as nine core areas of study. Eliot's lobbying helped to secure a place for courses in the modern sciences in the curriculum, which was a breakthrough for the time.

Still, Eliot's friction with his own committee underscored a fundamental question in the development of the school. Eliot had raised some interesting and important questions: Should the school stand by a uniform academic curriculum that treats every student more or less the same, or should it aim to widen its offering beyond the scope of core academic subjects? Should the school experience be tethered to the acquisition of a formalized body of knowledge, or should it look more comprehensively at student and societal needs? At the secondary school, the Committee of Ten had opted for uniformity and for focused instruction in nine academic areas.

FIGURE 2.1

COURSE OFFERINGS PROPOSED BY THE COMMITTEE OF TEN

1st Secondary School Year

Latin		5 p.
English Literature,	2 p.	4 p.
English Composition,	2 p.	
German [or French]		5 p.
Algebra		4 p.
History of Italy, Spain, and France		
Applied Geography		3 p.
(European political—continental and oceanic flora and fauna)		4 p.
		25 p.

2nd Secondary School Year

Latin		4 p.
Greek		5 p.
English Literature,	2 p.	4 p.
English Composition,	2 p.	
German, continued		4 p.
French, begun		5 p.
Algebra,*	2 p.	4 p.
Geometry,	2 p.	
Botany or Zoology		4 p.
English History to 1688		3 p.
		33 p.

*Option of book-keeping and commercial arithmetic.

3rd Secondary School Year

Latin		4 p.
Greek		4 p.
English Literature,	2 p.	4 p.
English Composition,	1 p.	
Rhetoric,	1 p.	
German		4 p.
French		4 p.
Algebra,*	2 p.	4 p.
Geometry,	2 p.	
Physics		4 p.
History, English and American		3 p.
Astronomy, 3 p. 1st 1/2 yr.		3 p.
Meteorology, 3 p. 2nd 1.2 yr.		
		34 p.

4th Secondary School year

Latin		4 p.
Greek		4 p.
English Literature,	2 p.	4 p.
English Composition,	1 p.	
English Grammar,	1 p.	
German		4 p.
French		4 p.
Trigonometry,		2 p.
Higher algebra		
Chemistry		4 p.
History (intensive) and Civil Government		3 p.
Geology or Physiography, 4 p. 1st 1;2 yr.		4 p.
Anatomy, Physiology, and Hygiene, 4 p. 2nd 1.2 yr.		
		33 p.

Committee of Ten (1893). Report on the Committee of Ten on Secondary School Studies. Washington, D.C.: National Education Association.

Before the dust settled from the Committee of Ten report, another NEA-sponsored committee, known as the **Committee of Fifteen,** engaged in a reconsideration of elementary education in America. Eliot was in the thick of the debate relating to this report also. Although not a member of the Committee of Fifteen, Eliot (1893) used various forums to argue that the elementary school curriculum had to be broadened and enriched with a new diversity of offerings. This was a matter of considerable significance to Eliot. He believed that too much time and energy were being spent on a narrow range of subjects, including holdover subjects from the Latin grammar school, such as Latin and grammar. He also thought that conceiving of elementary education as a single program of studies for all students was essentially wrong and that efforts had to be undertaken to recognize the value of some individualization in the curriculum. Eliot wanted to integrate a new science course in the elementary school and generally to pull back on the time devoted to traditional courses.

When the Committee of Fifteen submitted its recommendations in 1895, however, it was clear that it had only partially accepted Eliot's views. The report of the committee (1895/1969) supported the inclusion of some new courses, including one dedicated to "Natural Science and Hygiene," but overall the report sanctioned the status quo and helped to solidify the traditionalist grasp on the curriculum (Tanner & Tanner, 1990). Even where new courses were added, the time devoted to such courses, relative to the traditional subject-centered courses, was slight. The central subjects that the committee advanced for the elementary school were those that the traditionalists viewed as most worthy—grammar, literature, arithmetic, geography, and history.

The central figure in the Committee of Fifteen's work was William Torrey Harris, then U.S. commissioner of education. Harris, who had a respected background in philosophy and once held the job of superintendent of schools in Saint Louis, was the chair of the committee and the main author of the report. At the turn of the century he was emerging as one of the more outspoken and intelligent proponents for a conservative liberal arts education. Harris, in fact, had cultivated a new rationale for the subject-centered thinking that dominated the curriculum for years to come. He believed that public education had everything to do with transmitting the race or cultural experience of the nation and he was convinced that this could best be accomplished by elevating the importance of five central academic areas (grammar, literature and art, mathematics, geography, and history) in the curriculum, which he likened to the five windows of the soul.

To Harris's (1888) thinking, the schools could best serve the nation by actively transmitting the clear concept of culture embodied in "the five windows." The "windows" were believed to open up to the world of nature and humanity, providing a view to the learner of all that was worthy in the culture (Cremin, 1988). Hence, it was through "the windows" that the society became civilized and enlightened; life was in the subject matter.

Due, in part, to his high standing as commissioner, Harris was able to carry quite a bit of weight in the deliberations of both the Committee of Ten and the Committee of Fifteen. By virtue of his high regard for subject-centered study, Harris became an active critic of anyone who argued for the inclusion of course work in the natural sciences, the vocational arts, interdisciplinary studies, and any other "nonacademic" pursuits.

 ## The Child-Centered Counterreaction

As mentioned, part of the reaction against traditionalist thinking in the schools had to do with a desire to bring the consideration of children to the heart of teaching and learning formulations. Many of the early impulses on this front were developed in Europe. The philosophical discourses of Rousseau, the practical work supported by Robert Owen in the infant schools, and the new pedagogical theorizing offered by Pestalozzi and others all delivered messages about the importance of recognizing the life of children in schools.

The American scene capitalized on these influences and gave birth to a movement dedicated to giving learners their due in the school. This commitment, however, ultimately glorified learners and their innate capacities to decide what was best for their own education.

The Doctrine of Original Goodness

The major philosophical voice helping to clear the way for more expressly child-centered views in education was Jean Jacques Rousseau. The starting point in his thinking was to undermine the doctrine of original sin that the Calvinists and others promulgated. Children were not born sinful, proclaimed Rousseau. Quite the opposite; they were born good and innocent, and were made sinful and depraved at the hands of adults and the social institutions to which adults subjected children. Rousseau was, in effect, proclaiming a doctrine of original goodness.

Rousseau's thinking on these matters was likely influenced by the manner in which children were exploited in 18th-century France and by the vicious upbringing that he received at the hands of a cruel master (Rippa, 1971). It is not so much that Rousseau had trouble envisioning healthy and active interactions between children and adults, but rather that he thought nature was right in its original construction of children and that adults had to follow its lead (Thayer, 1960). Thus, spontaneity and natural interests were very important to any education justified by Rousseau.

Throughout his works, Rousseau glorified the early or primitive savagery of humanity as a natural and good period, as a time when humankind was in a state of equilibrium with nature. "Civilized" humans, according to Rousseau, severed this connection and corrupted themselves through social inventions of greed and power. Because children were born as one with nature, without the contamination provided by society, Rousseau celebrated their innocence and their beauty. His message was that children as raw products of nature,

Raphael's Renaissance painting "The Sistine Madonna" anticipated Romantic ideas about the goodness of children.

PART ONE: TOWARD A HISTORY AND PHILOSOPHY OF AMERICAN EDUCATION

were born good, but that society corrupted them and eventually made them evil. This was a recurring theme in his work. In *Emile,* originally published in 1762, he stated:

> Everything is good as it leaves the hands of the Author of things; everything degenerates in the hands of man. . . . He turns everything upside down; he disfigures everything; he loves deformity, monsters. He wants nothing as nature made it, not even man. (Rousseau, 1762/1979, p. 37)

According to Rousseau, the pedagogical antidote to the depravity of "civilized" humanity was for adults to take a more limited and distant role in the education of children, to regulate, if the need arose, the education of children from afar, but to always allow children to unfold and develop under their own initiative, will, and interest. It was the child, not the church and not the state, who was at the center of Rousseau's universe.

Rousseau's theorizing had a dramatic influence on the thinking and actions of a small group of school reformers in Europe whose ideas would eventually enter America during the mid-1800s. This group, comprised, most prominently, of Johann Pestalozzi, Johann Herbart, Friedrich Froebel, and Maria Montessori, helped to set an early condition for the rise of an important branch of the American progressive movement.

European Influences

In elementary education, the colonial style of rote and recitation was challenged directly by a view of teaching developed in the late 17th century by European reformer Johann Pestalozzi. Inspired by the child-centered thinking of Rousseau, Pestalozzi (1894) experimented with new forms of teaching that were expressly built on what he believed to be the natural inclinations of children. Pestalozzi viewed learning from the standpoint of faculty psychology, as an experience that nurtured all the mind's separate faculties (emotional, intellectual, physical, and moral). He vested discipline in the activity of learning, rather than in external prodding and compulsion, and he saw motivation as emerging out of the inner instincts and desires of children. Pestalozzi did not abide by the Calvinist view of **child depravity** and argued instead that all children should be treated with gentle discipline. These were the Pestalozzian principles that so impressed Horace Mann during his visit to the Prussian schools in the 1840s.

According to Pestalozzi, teaching had to move away from the act of memorizing and reciting, which he likened to "empty chattering," and toward the acts of sensing, interpreting, observing, and questioning. Teaching had to engage students in language and thinking; it had to proceed along the lines of a child's organic development and be planned and organized ahead of time. In this manner, Pestalozzi emancipated teachers, not only by liberating them from the dreary recitation style of instruction that bound them and their students to the text, but also by giving them initiative and purpose to consider their own ideas in the light of the learner's needs. As Power observed (1991), the implications of Pestalozzi's work meant that "teachers could no longer be regarded as mere hearers of lessons" (p. 203). This amounted to a virtual sea change in the school curriculum. Observations, investigations, discussions, individual expressions, and activity, all ignored in the early American schools, now had an arguable place in the classroom.

Pestalozzi also stressed the role of objects in teaching. He wanted children to study real objects found in nature for the purposes of cultivating their sense of observation and their overall understanding of objects in the world. Relying on his observations of children, Pestalozzi believed that sense perception was the most important path to good learning for children. This perspective, of course, was diametrically opposed to the memoriter exercises of the colonial schools and the instructional reliance that such schools put on reading and reciting books. Pestalozzi wanted to connect the sights, sounds, and touch of learning into the development of language and thought.

This perspective on learning had specific implications in the teaching of science because it led to a higher regard for nature study, observational insight, outdoor learning, and less "bookish" or abstract attempts to understand the world (Cubberley, 1947). It also influenced the placement of drawing, modeling, music, and general sense or physical activity in the school. With Pestalozzi, the schools now had a way to justify a break with the instructional tradition of memorization exercises and a way to offer activities that encouraged expression and sense perception. Ironically, as the years went by, the object lesson became a kind of tradition in early childhood education that often lost its sensory and observational slant and became yet another way to teach facts (Meyer, 1975; Cubberly, 1947). As stated by Thayer (1960), Pestalozzi's **object teaching** did indeed "open the door of the classroom to the outside world of objects and events, but, in the course of time, it also degenerated into a barren verbalism" (p. 230). Today we can still find the legacy of object teaching in classroom demonstrations and in the continuing custom of "show and tell" in early education.

Although Pestalozzi's work clearly advanced teacher professionalism and brought the interests of the learner into pedagogical consideration, Pestalozzi did not promote a social theory to accompany his thinking about schooling. This gave his work some currency among economic elites who saw no real social threat in the kind of education that Pestalozzi was proposing (Karier, 1967). The Prussians apparently were attracted to Pestalozzi's methods and to the broader implications that his work had for the training of teachers precisely because his ideas were so socially neutral.

As reported by Karier (1967), the rise of the normal school (teacher training institutes) in Prussia was partly a function of the fact that such places taught teachers *how* to teach, not *what* to teach, leaving the graduates of such places without the kinds of content skills or knowledge that might sow the seeds of revolution or might otherwise threaten the stability of the society. In America, the development of the normal schools followed the same emphasis and today many teacher training programs continue to stress the value of methods over content.

Another European thinker who gained some ascendancy in the American schools during the 19th century was a German professor of philosophy named Johann Herbart. Herbart was very much sympathetic to the work of Pestalozzi, fundamentally agreeing with his open rejection of the rote and recitation approach to instruction, with his regard for the use of real objects in teaching, and with his belief that education was a process of social and moral development. Herbart, however, asked new and different questions and approached the problem of developing an educational theory and method with novel insight.

First, Herbart shed the Pestalozzian concern for the faculties of the mind. It was not the mind that needed to be developed in individuals but rather the social character and morality of individuals, of which the mind was but a part. Thus, the purpose of the school was not about cultivating the different faculties of the mind but rather cultivating the social powers of the individual. This meant that schooling had to be more expressly social and less tied down by the content of the academic traditions. Herbart maintained that school experiences had to be framed around the problems and concerns of the social environment, and he contended that the study of history and literature, which were not popular in school curricula at the time, were absolutely vital to the fulfillment of such a purpose.

As a result, Herbart (1901) wanted to use history and literature to synthesize the subject matter in school so that it could be better associated with the social environment. This was another way of saying that the convention of organizing knowledge along strict disciplines was illogical and not attendant to the living conditions of individuals. No one subject area had a monopoly on the interests and needs of a child, and thus no one subject could be promulgated as most appropriate for all children. Focal points of concentration that took on a historical focus and that conveyed a literary tradition had to be found.

These units of subject matter were known as correlations or concentrations. Supporters of Herbart, for instance, frequently used *Robinson Crusoe* as a way to unify all inquiry in the third-grade classroom, a fact the traditionalists derided as bad pedagogy. But to a Herbartian, such an activity had all the essential ingredients of a good curriculum. *Robinson Crusoe,* after all, was a literary work that followed the historical development of a family that had to solve the basic problems of survival; it correlated history with literature. One American proponent of Herbart reported an example of a way that an elementary school might use basic historical topics as correlations in the curriculum. In the fifth grade, for instance, the synthesizing theme for the curriculum was the story of John Smith. For planning purposes, the correlation could be seen as carrying a geography component that might highlight the study of Chesapeake Bay (its climate, its main crops, and natural resources), a science component that might focus on the flora and fauna of Virginia, a mathematics ingredient that might offer mathematical queries into the production, marketing, and consumption of vital crops in Virginia, and a language component that might focus on the adventure of Smith's life (McMurray, 1946). Butts (1955) believes that the Herbartian effort to bring a sense of convergence to literature, history, and the social environment helped to develop the role of social studies in the school curriculum.

In a way, then, Herbart was the first to argue for a more integrated and interdisciplinary curriculum. Such a belief was anathema at the time, given the high regard placed on the knowledge power of the separate disciplines. In fact, when Herbart's ideas began to establish a following in the United States, they were attacked vigorously by William Torrey Harris, who, as the defender of the liberal arts tradition in the schools, felt that the more integrated schemes contemplated by the Herbartians could not effectively transmit American culture. The correlations advanced by the Herbartians eviscerated Harris's five windows of the soul. Obviously, this was no small problem to Harris, who thought that Herbart's views threatened the school's capacity to bestow children with the cultural treasures of the past, with the very tools that Harris believed children needed to understand themselves and their society.

THE

LIFE

AND

STRANGE SURPRIZING

ADVENTURES

OF

ROBINSON CRUSOE,

Of *YORK*, MARINER:

Who lived Eight and Twenty Years,
all alone in an un-inhabited Iſland on the
Coaſt of AMERICA, near the Mouth of
the Great River of OROONOQUE;

Having been caſt on Shore by Shipwreck, where-
in all the Men periſhed but himſelf.

WITH

An Account how he was at laſt as ſtrangely deliver'd by PYRATES.

Written by Himſelf.

LONDON;
Printed for W. TAYLOR at the *Ship* in *Pater-Noſter-
Row*. MDCCXIX.

The title page and illustration taken from an early edition of Robinson Crusoe

The most visible battle between Harris and the American Herbartians occurred over the release of the Committee of Fifteen report. The report raised the ire of the Herbartians because they hoped that the report would sanction the place of correlations in the curriculum. Although the committee dealt with the idea of correlations, its curriculum recommendations suggested, at least to the Herbartians, a complete repudiation of the idea of correlation (McMurray, 1946). Harris, who was the author of the Committee of Fifteen report, was not shy about expressing his disdain for Herbartian thinking, referring at one point to the integrated use of *Robinson Crusoe* in the curriculum as "shallow and uninteresting" (Krug, 1964, p. 103).

Out of Herbart's work also arose an unusual theory of teaching that equated the maturational development of the individual with the evolutionary

PART ONE: TOWARD A HISTORY AND PHILOSOPHY OF AMERICAN EDUCATION stages of the species. Known as the **cultural-epochs theory,** this idea implied that the proper instruction of a child had to be connected with the period of human development that likely corresponded with the child's age. Hence, the youngest schoolchildren might be given activities dealing with primitive life and the hunting and gathering period of human history, while older children (grades two and three) might be subjected to activities based on early agricultural life and early civilization. Similarly, children in the later elementary grades might engage in activities rooted in the medieval period, the early explorers and settlers, and so on, until they reached the industrial age.

Followers of Herbart saw a wonderful sense of unity between the individual and the race experience in cultural-epochs theory. Such a theory contained the vast character-building potential of historical study, and the actual cultural epochs provided focal points for a more unified arrangement of the subject matter in the curriculum. For instance, at Dewey's laboratory school, where cultural-epochs ideas were tested, children studied the race experience by focusing on the occupations of humankind in the preindustrial period. In the course of their studies, the children made cloth from fleeces (weaving, spinning, and dying), lead castings, Indian baskets, candles, soap, and so forth (McMurray, 1946).

Herbart also spoke directly to the issue of teaching methodology. Like Pestalozzi, he did not want to resort to external devices to inspire motivation; he wanted it to emerge out of the conditions of learning. Using principles taken from Pestalozzi, Herbart developed a method of instruction based on the notion that all learning is a process of assimilating knowledge with what one already knows. The idea was to connect new knowledge to existing conditions and existing understandings. According to Herbart, if such a connection was properly made, the learner was in an ideal learning situation; her interests would be aroused, and her mind would be prepared to absorb the new material.

Herbart tried to formalize this process into five steps (Butts, 1955).

- First, the teacher had to make formal preparations by recalling or otherwise stimulating prior ideas and experiences in the child (to which the new material can be related).
- Following the step of preparation, the teacher presented all the new material to the student.
- This was then followed by an effort to build associations (through comparisons and contrasts) between the old and the new.
- The fourth step called for the teacher to draw generalizations from the individual cases discussed in class.
- The fifth step was to find examples and practical situations highlighting the generalizations.

This method lent some sense of standardization to instruction and very much dominated the training given in the normal schools in the 1890s. To this day, there is much in Herbart's "five steps" that is still basic to good teaching, including the effort to find application contexts and to engage students in inductive reasoning.

Whereas Pestalozzi influenced instruction at the elementary school level and Herbart at the secondary school level, two more important European figures emerged to influence instruction at the primary school level: Friedrich Froebel and Maria Montessori.

Jean Piaget was also influenced by the cultural-epoch theory. He began studying children because he believed they provided a window into early human thought.

Froebel's interest in education was also sparked by the work of Pestalozzi. He visited his schools in Switzerland and was impressed with the value Pestalozzi placed on play and "nonacademic" pursuits such as art and music. Froebel, however, formulated his own views on education by merging the sense perceptions that were fundamental to Pestalozzi with a philosophy of romantic idealism.

Through idealism, Froebel (1826/1887) saw his work in kinship with the absolute spirit of God, as drawing out the innate gifts given to children by God—gifts that allowed children to appreciate a closer identification with the divine spirit. Froebel, in this manner, felt that his instructional efforts awakened the inner strengths of children, which in turn, allowed them to find an essence of unity under the service of the divine. To free children, to liberate their "gifts," and to encourage their spontaneous and natural curiosity were the ways that one started down the path toward perfect unity (Butts, 1955). This was Froebel's method of facilitating the work of God. "Education," he observed, "consists in leading man, as a thinking, intelligent being, growing into self-consciousness, to a pure and unsullied, conscious and free representation of the inner law of Divine Unity and in teaching him ways and means thereto" (1826/1887, p. 2).

Froebel opened his own school for very young children in 1837, in which singing, drawing, painting, coloring, dancing, dramatics, and self-selected activity were encouraged. He called the school kindergarten, a garden where children grew. Froebel advanced beyond Pestalozzi in several ways. To Pestalozzi, learning still tended, despite his efforts to bring sense perceptions to learning, to be passive and mental. Froebel, however, awakened the spirit of "learning by doing," the physical/motor side of learning, and the ideal of directing the desires of children in socially satisfying ways. He was not preoccupied with the faculties of the mind, nor with the Herbartian idea of finding unity between the child and cultural history. What he wanted most was for children to find themselves through play, and he envisaged growth as a social concept, as part of the quest to find the whole. He provided children with balls, blocks, and paper and encouraged them to use them at their will. In this way, Froebel gave new respect and authority to children, to their individuality, and to the dynamic qualities of their personalities.

The child to Froebel, after all, was anointed with the inner spirit of God, and play, liberated from the exigencies of survival, represented a high spiritual form. This, in the end, was the moving idea that Froebel brought to educational thought—the notion that the actions of play brought one closer to finding a unity with the highest orders of life. Education, then, could not revert to prescriptive or coercive measures; it had to engage the student in a facilitative role that enlivened the inner spirits of play and self-activity. Moreover, the child himself, a kind of replica of God, was to be revered and his inner spirit cherished as the main pathway toward growth and understanding.

In the course of time, the metaphysical justifications that Froebel used to sanction his kindergarten had to give way to different criteria. The consideration of the child in the curriculum could not settle for a mystical explanation about how the child's consciousness was part and parcel of the divine spirit, and in this way, Froebel could only advance the curriculum so far. The legacy of Froebel, however, can still be appreciated in the design and function of the kindergarten today, where children, by and large, are still allowed to play, where social activities are viewed as educative, and where the embrace of the child, especially relative to the upper grades, continues to be warm and protective.

Maria Montessori worked along the same lines as Froebel, but she brought a different level of analysis to the problem of teaching children. Trained in engineering, medicine, anthropology, and experimental psychology, Montessori had a comprehensive lens with which to view the problem of educating children. She started her work in education in 1898 by focusing on the education of "idiot children" housed in the insane asylums of Italy. She spent two years preparing methods of instruction for these children, discovering that many of their problems were educational in nature, not biological. The children, in other words, were usually victimized by poor environmental experiences; they were deprived of the early stimuli needed to develop into intellectually and emotionally healthy people. Montessori validated her thesis by teaching these "deficient" children to read and write and to compete successfully with so-called normal children. Montessori's success with these children, which was seen by outside observers as bordering on the miraculous, inspired her to move forward with formulations on early education for all children (Rippa, 1984).

After years of advanced study in experimental psychology, Montessori opened a preschool in 1907 for the education of children living in the tenements of San Lorenzo, a poverty-stricken section of Rome. She noted how these poor children, like the "feebleminded" children in the asylums, were at a considerable disadvantage because they were not benefiting from any of the basic early childhood experiences that were preparatory to later success and health.

In her school, which was called "Casa dei Bambini" (The Children's House), Montessori set out to help correct the early education problems of the poor. She formulated a pedagogical model that worked off Pestalozzi's idea of sense impression, which aimed to foster the growth of intelligence through

Maria Montessori's pedagogical theories have had great influence on early education in the United States.

With the help of a teacher, children use materials based on Montessori's theories.

a. Colored Numerical Rods

c. Contemporary Individual
Sandpaper Letters

b. Sound Cylinders

Here are some samples of the didactic materials that Montessori developed. How do such materials logically follow from Montessori's views on learning?

Montessori, M. (1965) Dr. Montessori's Own Handbook. N.Y.: Schocker Books. Originally published in 1914, pp. 67, 111, 149, 167.

the senses. She developed quite a few original games and tasks that highlighted the sense experience. These activities came with certain "didactic apparatus"—blocks, cylinders, and other manipulatives that children could select at their discretion. The didactic materials represented a form of sensory gymnastics to Montessori (see the Objects of Teaching feature in this section). Children could engage in their use freely, which meant that individual youngsters could occupy themselves by selecting into and out of various tasks associated with the materials. Thus, a new level of individualization was recognized in the Montessorian classroom. Montessori also designed and developed children's furniture for the classroom to encourage real social interactions among the children, which included social events such as preparing lunch and cleaning up afterward. She asked teachers to be cognizant of the particularities of each child and to encourage free choice among the children. The success of her school took on international proportions; the children had learned basic elements of cleanliness and manners and were equipped with the basic skills of reading and writing (Rippa, 1984).

Montessori's work made it clear that early education was fundamental to the sound development of humans. She countered the argument for biological determinism by showing what a good early educational environment can do. Historically, her work has been criticized for being too programmatic and for relying too much on the didactic apparatus, which tended to reduce learning to the completion of predesigned tasks as opposed to creative and experimental problem solving. She was also criticized for not understanding the importance of reflecting social needs and collective group actions in her teaching (Kilpatrick, 1971). The individual was always the central variable to Montessori; she did not stress the importance of the group project and social intercourse. Montessori's ideas are still vital in early education programs throughout the nation. The idea of providing youth with early sensory experiences as an investment in later development has stayed vital, long after Montessori's death.

American Child-Centeredness

A burgeoning **child-study movement** in America also furthered the emerging recognition of the child in school deliberations. This movement had begun to take on some real force during the 1890s and the first decade of the 20th century, particularly as it was steered by the able hand of G. Stanley Hall, an American psychologist who brought credibility to the task of child study by making it accountable to modern scientific methods.

The idea behind the child-study movement was to examine the nature of the child in ways that might inform the practical judgments of the schoolteacher. Hall, for instance, conducted studies on the muscle use of children in school and concluded that very young children needed to have opportunities for large muscle development, a finding that had clear and practical use in the school (Tanner & Tanner, 1987). He even went as far as developing a systematic survey of what primary schoolchildren knew about common animals, insects, plants, and other phenomena, which he wrote up in an essay titled "The Contents of Children's Minds" (Hall, 1883/1969). This was the style of the child-study movement—to find insight about children that might lead to better teaching. Even teachers got into the act by beginning to study children for the purpose of improving their practice, by questioning them, keeping observational notes on them, and checking their vision and hearing.

Hall's influence in education, however, transcended his work in the child-study movement. As Harvard's first doctoral graduate in psychology and as a German-schooled scientist, Hall had the credentials and the intellectual prowess to speak directly to a newly developing pedagogy, one that accounted for the natural development of the child. At the turn of the 20th century, he was indeed emerging as one of the new titans in education, as one who spoke for the causes of children in education from the stage of science (Cremin, 1961). In this way, Hall represented a position that was diametrically opposed to the work of William Torrey Harris, the great defender of the centrality of the liberal arts in the curriculum.

Hall, in fact, made quite a spirited criticism of the Committee of Ten report, through which he helped to frame an important counterposition to the traditional liberal arts argument (Kliebard, 1986). The report, he stated, was faulty in very fundamental ways. First, Hall observed that the report failed to understand the importance of individual differences among students by trying to adjust them uniformly to preexisting subject categories. Second, he simply did not see or appreciate the so-called transferable life skills that were supposedly being effected in the kind of studies supported in the report. Hall was no mental disciplinarian, and he did not accept the view that certain subjects had mind-training powers that were transferable as life skills. Clearly, Hall wanted to scuttle the traditionalist version of learning that treated children as passive receptors in need of having their heads filled with disciplinary knowledge. In its place he wanted to see a curriculum that showed some responsiveness to the individual, a desire that inevitably led to the idea of differentiation or individualization in the school experience. Hall (1901/1969) argued that the curriculum had to be differentiated so that each individual is given the chance to grow and unfold according to her own potential. Interestingly, one might have expected, given Hall's concern for child study, that he would be a strong believer in the powers of the environment. But Hall's commitment to individualizing the curriculum was justified paradoxically by **social Darwinism,** where heredity, not the environment, was the ruling law.

To Hall, the school curriculum had to be determined by student needs, but since these needs were native, the school had to encourage, through curriculum differentiation, the development of the most gifted students ("the best blood"). This also meant that all "nongifted" could be treated in a more simple manner, all in the name of the learner. To know children, then, was to appreciate their native endowments, something that Hall believed would become obvious to teachers as they allowed their students to develop freely. In this way, Hall helped to toe the Rousseauian line about the virtues of a laissez-faire education, as he encouraged teachers and parents to stay out of nature's way and to act only as guardians of the child's health and natural endowments (Cremin, 1988). Ironically, such an attitude contradicted the very role and purpose of child development, which would presumably encourage teachers not to leave students alone but to take an interventionist role attuned to the developmental nature of the learner. This, however, was no contradiction from Hall's standpoint. Because child study pointed to certain development patterns in all learners, Hall argued that such patterns might help teachers foster certain learnings for children, but that, in the end, the child's endowments would determine his progress. Teachers could facilitate the growth of the child, but without native endowments, they could not realize certain potentials in children. Growth was largely preordained.

Through examining the character of development among children, Hall also became a proponent of the cultural-epochs theory that was gaining ground with the American Herbartians. The theory, to recall, was tied to the notion that the development of the individual recapitulates the course of human history (from presavagery to civilization). The more sophisticated way of putting this is to say that ontogeny (the development of the individual) recapitulates phylogeny (the evolution of the species). To Hall, the natural development of children went through the various stages of the experience of the human race. Making the connection between the two was essential to good pedagogy. Such ties helped the student along an already predetermined path. With young children, these ties also helped to justify the indulgent treatment that they received at the hands of teachers working with Hall's ideas. As young children recapitulated the experiences of the species, they could not be asked, in any way, to meet adult standards of punishment and adult prohibitions; they had to be treated at their level of development (Cremin, 1988).

Although the cultural-epochs theory had its share of problems, it still represented a breakthrough in the curriculum that favored the child. The content of the curriculum could now be argued to be with and in the child (part of her natural development), not in the liberal arts. Furthermore, the right of education, which was long seen as a luxury or privilege, was now naturally embedded in the child (Cremin, 1961).

All in all, the child-centered focus had done a fairly successful job of securing the place of the child in the curriculum equation. The problem was that the thinking started and stopped with the child. In the course of time, a good share of the school community embraced child-centered reasoning, so much so that many of the private and university lab schools of the 1920s highlighted a curriculum that encouraged children to follow their momentary interests and wishes. Many of these schools concentrated on the education of young children. But there were also elements of the progressive community that were distressed to see the level of individualism being advanced in many of these so-called progressive schools. In 1928, Rugg and Schumaker published a book that appraised the first quarter century of child-centered education in these mostly private schools, showing how a desire to reflect children's interests in the school frequently supplanted wider pedagogical initiatives. Others critics, including John Dewey, eventually offered more strident criticism of the child-centered perspective.

The child-centered schools represented a classic counteraction to the traditionalism that had dominated the schools. The traditional school, long a bastion of order and control, had deliberately squelched student expression and initiative and showed little regard for the interests and welfare of the learner. **Child-centeredness** found its way as a palliating force against traditional extremes. But by casting its floodlights on the child, the child-centered school created its own counterextreme. Thus, much of the early debate in the 20th century over the definition of the school curriculum was waged between subject-centered (traditionalist) views and child-centered views. This was an inadequate framing of the curriculum problem because it posed the curriculum in dual terms—either subjected-centered or child-centered. As we will learn, another progressive group will demand that both factors (the learner and the subject matter) be integrated with yet another important factor (the society). But during the 1920s and 1930s, child-centered thinking was basking in the newly found respect for the child and in the recognition that activity was central to learning. The height of its rise in school practice was witnessed in the development of a new pedagogical concept known as the Project Method.

In 1918, William Kilpatrick published a paper, called the "Project Method," that underscored the "purposeful act" as the key focal point for subject organization in the curriculum. Kilpatrick wanted to bring activity into the curriculum; he wanted to break the mold of passive rote/recitation, and like some other progressives, he wanted the subject matter or content of the curriculum to be remade according to emergent sociopersonal problems. (In the traditionalist schemes of things, it is important to remember that the subject matter is predetermined; the curriculum is of the subject matter). Kilpatrick believed that the curriculum should take on the organizational form of projects (problem-focused, group-oriented inquiries) rather than formal school subjects. The so-called academic subjects would not be forgotten but would be used as needed during the course of investigation in the projects. The subject matter became a means of education as opposed to an end of instruction. When one used the method, education was not about knowledge accumulation but about thinking and testing ideas against experience.

At higher levels of school organization, the Project Method helped school practitioners to see the value of laboratories in teaching science. It was also used in the teaching of agriculture in high schools, particularly in schools that did not have experimental farm fields. Students engaged in "home projects" that involved the testing of ideas relevant to the care of poultry, cattle, pigs, sheep, and horses, the rotation of crops, the use of fertilizers, and the functions of the household (including canning, cooking, and making clothes). Under such conditions, the Project Method upheld the value of problem-focused inquiry that was directly tied in to the improvement of present conditions on the farm (Childs, 1956).

In the elementary school, the Project Method led to the development of "teacher units" that favored thematic treatments of the subject matter. Kliebard (1986) describes one project developed in 1927 for a second-grade classroom in the Lincoln School, the experimental laboratory school of Teachers College, Columbia University.

> In a "Study of City Life," . . . children began with the study of the city's transportation, one boy making a model of Grand Central Station while others made trains, trucks, buses, taxis, and boats. Next they constructed buildings—a wholesale market, a bakery, a post office, a fire station, a bank and so on. . . . Eventually the project led to a six-week study of foods, where various food stuffs were prepared and sold at various market prices. (p. 168)

Another unit study, again taken from the Lincoln School, epitomized the nature of the subject matter used in the Project Method. A synopsis of the unit is reproduced in Special Insert 2.3. As one can see, the subject matter follows the course of questions to be explored, emerges out of inquiry, is not prefashioned in any way, and is interdisciplinary in its character.

Naturally, there were problems with the Project Method idea. One problem was that Kilpatrick did not set strong delimiting factors on the use of the Project Method. He had essentially equated its social dimension with child interest. Thus, when pressed to define what was a worthwhile project, Kilpatrick noted that it had to be marked by purposeful activity as defined by the child's interest. This was a virtual admission that the Project Method was any activity that a child was committed to do. If a child had a reason to pursue a form of activity (any activity), it could be rationalized as a manifestation of the Project Method. Not surprisingly, the Project Method began to be used as a way to justify child-centered actions in the school. It should be said, however, that Kilpatrick did send clear signals about the dangers of making the curriculum subordinate to the whims of children in his original essay on the Project Method (Kilpatrick, 1918) and in a later textbook (Kilpatrick, 1925), where he openly advised teachers to avoid projects that did not encourage growth.

In a way, Kilpatrick had become an unwitting accomplice in the child-centered movement. But the Project Method was still vulnerable to the accusation of child-centeredness, despite Kilpatrick's admonishments to the

A UNIT OF STUDY RELATED TO
BOATS
THIRD GRADE

PROBLEMS-QUESTIONS

To construct boats that will look like a certain kind and with which children can play.

How do boats "go"?

Who first thought of making a sailboat?

How did people get the idea for different shapes for boats?

To know more about the people who traveled on the seas in early times.

To find out about the making of boats.

How many different kinds of boats do we have today and how is each kind used?

How did early people use their ships?

To find out about the different parts of a boat.

How do people know how much to put into a boat before it will sink?

SUBJECT MATTER CONTENT

INDUSTRIAL ARTS
Construction of boats: Making pattern, shaping hull, making sail, making keel, casting weight for keel, making rack for boat, and testing boat.
How boats developed from early times to the present day.
The difficulty involved in building a toy boat so it will balance in water.
Different kinds of sail boats.
The need for a keel on a boat.
Different methods of propelling a boat.
Modern inventions in connection with the propulsion of boats.
What makes boats float.
Different uses of boats today.

HISTORY
The Half-Moon directed interest to Hendrick Hudson and his ship.
Historic ships: Santa Maria, Mayflower.
Reference work, reading and discussions about:
Vikings: What color and kinds of clothing did they wear? What did they eat? What kind of houses did they have? What were their boats like? Did Vikings have stores? How did Viking writing look? Story of Lief Erickson. The gods of the Vikings. Their beliefs.
Phoenicians: Scenery, boats, people, trade, beliefs, clothing, cities, industries, etc.
Egyptians: Scenery, country, boats, beliefs, tools, writing, etc. Story of the building of Solomon's Temple.
Early Mediterranean peoples.

GEOGRAPHY
Pictures of boat from newspaper which interested children in world geography.
Geography related to countries studied.
Norway: Country, climate, people and occupations.
Phoenicia: Country, climate, people, trading routes, daily life of early people compared with that of today.
Egypt: Country, climate, trading, etc.
Map interest: Norway, showing ancient home of the Vikings.
The Mediterranean countries, showing cities of Phoenicia and routes on which the King of Tyre sent materials for Solomon's Temple.
Plasticene map of Mediterranean Sea and surrounding countries on which children sailed card-board models of early boats.
Globe in frequent use to locate places mentioned.
Outline world map, locating countries.
Interest in determining distances (reading scales on map).
How far is it from Norway to Phoenicia?
How far is it from Norway to America?
Building Lower Manhattan on floor with blocks to exhibit boats.
Map was drawn on floor; buildings in New York City that helped most with sea travel.

ARITHMETIC
Measuring for best patterns and measurements in boat making.
Figuring the number of board feet used by class in building boat racks.
Arithmetic problems in connection with science experiment of water displacement and floating objects.
What is a gram?
What is a cubit?
Dimensions of Solomon's Temple compared with dimensions of the Lincoln School.
Children saw a cubit measure at the Museum.

FINE ARTS
Sketching and painting pictures of Half-Moon.
Sketching and painting boat models.
Drawing blackboard frieze showing history of boats.
Ten easel pictures showing story of Lief Erickson.
Cut paper pictures of boats.
Painting Egyptian boats seen at Museum.
Painting Viking pictures showing clothing.
Painting modern boats.
Making clay tablet.

COMPOSITION--LITERATURE
Stories written about the trip to see Half-Moon.
Stories of other trips by individual children.
Original poems about boats and the sea.
Labels and invitations for best exhibit.
Written and oral reports about boats, Vikings, Phoenicia and Egypt.
Stories for bulletin, room paper, council news, or absent class members, telling of class interest and study.

READING
Reference material pertaining to topics under discussion, found in school library or at home.
Children's reading material: Lief and Thorkle, Viking Stories. Early sea people. Boat Book prepared by other Third Grade, material prepared by student teachers.

SCIENCE
How can we tell if our boats will float and balance? Try out in delta table.
Three experiments: Why do some objects float and why do some sink?
How do people know how much to put into boat before it will sink?

DRAMATIZATION
Play-Story of Lief Erickson, spontaneously prepared by class.

MUSIC
Old Gaelic Lullaby. Volga Boat Song. Sail Bonnie Boat.

PROBABLE OUTCOMES

DESIRABLE HABITS AND SKILLS

Better skill in sketching.
Better skill in handling brush and paints.
A beginning of the development of how to sew.
Developing the habit of making a pattern before con structing an article.
Developing skill in shaping wood by means of plane and spokeshave.
Developing skill in using gouge and mallet.
Developing skill in reading distances on map.
Rapid growth in map drawing.
Developing habit of reading the newspaper.
Better skill in measuring.
Ability to gather information on a certain subject and reporting to class.
Increased ability in writing.

ATTITUDES AND APPRECIATIONS

Economic:
An appreciation of the use of weights and measures.
What it means to construct a real boat that will float and balance properly.
Appreciation of the change in the lives of the people caused by the discovery of iron and the use of sails.
Appreciation of paper as a writing material.
Appreciation of the modern inventions in connection with the propulsion of ships.

Social:
What the early people contributed to the world.
The number of people and industry it takes to supply materials for the construction of one building.
Comparison of the ideas of fairness of the early people with the present day.

Recreational:
Developing a joy in painting, sketching and drawing.
Growing interest in reading books about historical peoples, inventions or boats.
Playing with boats made.
Interest in the construction of a toy-boat.
Interest in the construction of a real boat.
The pleasure in making maps.
The pleasure of playing with maps.

Aesthetic:
Appreciation of the beauty in line and construction of boats.
The adventure of the ship.

INFORMATION

Knowledge of the development of the boat from raft to steamship.
Who Hendrick Hudson was.
General idea of historic ships.
An interesting acquaintance with Vikings, Phoenicians and Egyptians.
General geographical knowledge of the world.
What a cubit measure is.
Knowledge of how to draw maps.
Some idea of what makes objects float.
Some idea of how to make boats balance in water.
Some idea of how to construct a toy-boat.
How the early people made their clay tablets.
How to make a clay tablet.
The need for molds in casting metals.
Some idea of how iron is made into different shapes.

Cremin, L. (1961) *The Transformation of the School*, N.Y.: Alfred A. Knopf, pp. 284–285.

Adapted from a graphic in Otis W. Caldwell, "The Lincoln Experimental School," in *Curriculum-Making: Past and Present*, Twenty-Sixth yearbook of the National Society for the Study of Education, Part 1, edited by Guy M. Whipple (Bloomington, IL: Public School Publishing Company, 1926). pp. 221–289. Adapted with permission of the society.

contrary. It was clear that the method, which was designed as a group initiative, had, in its application, lost sight of common social problems and concerns, and was, instead, preoccupied with individual issues. Some scholars even charged that it had ignored the act of thinking, the idea of keeping the learning process focused on problems that required thoughtful adjudication (Bode, 1927). To many progressives who saw the role of the school from its democratizing functions, the Project Method was theoretically flawed because it abided by no social theory and no sense of what knowledge was most worthwhile (Bode, 1927).

The Progressive Criticism of Child-Centeredness

In general, the notion of **child-centeredness** was sullied in both the traditional and progressive quarters. John Dewey, for instance, could not fathom how any form of education could deny children the wisdom and maturity of experience offered to them by adults, especially ones professionally trained to deal with children. He was usually a gentle critic, but here Dewey (1929) was strong worded in condemning **child-centeredness.**

> There is a present tendency in so called advanced schools of educational thought to say, in effect, let us surround pupils with certain materials, tools, appliances, etc. and let pupils respond to these things according to their own desires. Above all let us not suggest any end or plan to students; let us not suggest to them what they shall do, for that is an unwarranted trespass upon their sacred individuality since the essence of such individuality is to set up ends and aims. Now such a method is really stupid. For it attempts the impossible, which is always stupid; and it misconceived the conditions of independent thinking. (p. 153)

Dewey believed in the need to reflect the nature of the learner in school decisions, but he also believed that the learner, as an immature organism, could not be effectively socialized into the canons and the learnings of the social group (the culture) without the active intervention of adults. Boyd Bode, who was among the most penetrating progressive critics of his time, sided with Dewey in assailing the thinking of those who opted for **child-centeredness** and in worrying about the negative effects that such a view might have on the progressive movement.

> The failure to emancipate ourselves completely from Rousseauism . . . is responsible for most, if not all, of the weaknesses of the progressive movement in education. . . . The insistence that we must stick uncompromisingly at all times to the "needs" of childhood has bred a spirit of antiintellectualism, which is reflected in the reliance on improvising instead of long-range organization, in the overemphasis of the here and now, in the indiscriminate tirades against "subjects" [and] in the absurdities of pupil planning. (Bode, 1938, p. 70)

Dewey and Bode were at the forefront of a very different version of progressivism, one that honored the child but that also brought other fundamental variables to the act of teaching and learning. In the eyes of Dewey and other like-minded progressives, child development could not be contemplated without thinking about the child in the context of the society. It was ridiculous, they believed, to think about the child in terms that were independent of the society or of the skills, attitudes, and knowledge the child needed to be successful in society. This new attitude pervaded the progressivism explained in the next chapter.

KEY TERMS

Child depravity	Committee of Ten	Object teaching
Child-centeredness	Cultural-epochs theory	Social Darwinism
Child-study movement	Faculty psychology	Subject-centeredness
Committee of Fifteen	Mental discipline	Traditional humanism

KEY QUESTIONS

1. What was the doctrine of mental discipline, and how did it help to give rise to a subject-centered view of learning?

2. What was the central recommendation of the Committee of Ten report, and how did such a recommendation influence the character of high school education?

3. In what ways did Charles Eliot, the chairman of the Committee of Ten report, differ with the committee's recommendations?

4. Describe the fundamental differences between the way that William Harris and Charles Eliot conceived of the school curriculum.

5. Both Pestalozzi and mental disciplinarians used faculty psychology to justify their school actions. Explain how this could be so.

6. What was the central message that Pestalozzi wanted to send to the school?

7. Why were supporters of Herbart turning toward thematic treatments in the curriculum, using, as described, the novel *Robinson Crusoe* as a way to unify all studies in the third-grade classroom?

8. Describe how the Herbartian idea of correlations might be used in an elementary school.

9. Why was William Harris utterly distressed at what the Herbartians were advocating in the curriculum?

10. Describe cultural-epochs theory, and explain why many Herbartians were attracted to the idea.

11. Explain how Froebel believed that he was facilitating the work of God through the way that he was educating small children.

12. How did Maria Montessori's work with "feebleminded" children lead her toward early childhood instruction?

13. In what ways was Maria Montessori's work in early childhood education criticized?

14. How did the philosophical work of Jean Jacques Rousseau contribute to the child-centered movement in education?

15. Explain the significance of G. Stanley Hall in the development of the child-centered movement in education.

16. In what ways did social Darwinism contradict Hall's work in the area of child development?

17. What was the essential argument that Dewey and some other progressives made against child-centered thinking?

18. In what ways was the child-centered movement a counterreaction to the traditionalist curriculum?

19. Describe the Project Method and explain how it, in the end, became a child-centered phenomenon.

20. How did the work of Pestalozzi lend itself to the development of teacher professionalism and the growth of normal schools?

REFERENCES

Bode, B. H. (1927). *Modern educational theories.* New York: Macmillan.

Bode, B. H. (1938). *Progressive education at the crossroads.* New York: Newson and Co.

Butts, R. F. (1955). *A cultural history of Western education: Its social and intellectual foundations.* New York: McGraw-Hill Book Co.

Childs, J. (1956). *American pragmatism and education.* New York: Henry Holt and Co.

Committee of Fifteen. (1969). *Report of the Committee of Fifteen.* New York: Arno Press. (Original work published in 1895)

Committee of Ten. (1969). Report of the Committee of Ten on secondary school studies. In D. H. Calhoun, (Ed.) *Educating of Americans: A documentary history.* Boston: Houghton-Mifflin Co. (Original work published in 1893)

Cremin, L. A. (1961). *The transformation of the school.* New York: Alfred A. Knopf.

Cremin, L. A. (1988). *American education: The metropolitan experience.* New York: Harper and Row.

Cubberley, E. (1947). *Public education in the United States.* New York: Houghton-Mifflin Co.

Dewey, J. (1902). *The child and the curriculum.* Chicago: University of Chicago Press.

Dewey, J. (1929). Individuality and experience. In J. Dewey, *Art and education.* Merion, PA: The Barnes Foundation Press.

Eliot, C. (1893). Can school programs be shortened and enriched? *National Education Association Proceedings.* Washington, DC: The Association.

Froebel, F. (1887). *The education of man* (Translated from German). New York: Appleton. (Original work published in 1826)

Hall, G. S. (1969). The contents of children's minds. In D. H. Calhoun, (Ed.) *Educating of Americans: A documentary history.* Boston: Houghton-Mifflin Co. (Original work published in 1883)

Hall, G. S. (1969). The ideal school as based on child study. In D. H. Calhoun, (Ed.) *Educating of Americans: A documentary history.* Boston: Houghton-Mifflin Co. (Original work published in 1901)

Harris, W. T. (1888). What shall the public schools teach? *The Forum, 4,* 573–81.

Herbart, J. F. (1901). *Outlines of educational doctrine.* New York: Macmillan.

Karier, C. J. (1967). *Man, society and education.* New York: Scott Foresman.

Kilpatrick, W. H. (1971). *The Montessori system examined.* New York: Arno Press and the *New York Times.* (Original work published in 1914)

Kilpatrick, W. H. (1925) *Foundations of method* (N.Y.: Macmillan Co.)

Kilpatrick, W. (1918). The Project Method. *Teachers College Record, 19*(4), 319–335.

Kliebard, H. M. (1986). *The struggle for the American curriculum.* New York: Routledge Kegan.

Krug, E. A. (1964). *The shaping of the American high school.* New York: Harper and Row.

McMurray, D. (1946). *Herbartian contributions to history: Instruction in American elementary schools.* New York: Bureau of Publications, Teachers College, Columbia University.

Meyer, A. E. (1975). *Grandmasters of educational thought.* New York: McGraw-Hill.

Pestalozzi, J. H. (1894). *How Gertrude teaches her children.* Syracuse N.Y.: C. W. Bardeen.

Power, E. J. (1991). *A legacy of learning.* Albany, NY: SUNY Press.

Rippa, A. (1984). *Education in a free society: An American history.* New York: David McKay Co.

Rousseau, J. J. (1979). *Emile* (A. Bloom, Trans.). New York: Basic Books. (Original work published in 1762)

Rugg, H., & Schumaker, A. (1969). *The child-centered school.* New York: Arno Press and the *New York Times.* (Original work published in 1928)

Tanner, D., & Tanner, L. N. (1990). *The history of the school curriculum.* New York: Macmillan.

Thayer, V. T. (1960). *The role of the school in American society.* New York: Dodd, Mead and Co.

3

**DEFINING THE SCHOOL
CURRICULUM INTO
THE 20TH CENTURY**

C harline Rice, a third-grade teacher in Fort Worth, Texas, is pictured here with some of her students. The diversity represented by her students is emblematic of the wide net public schooling has cast in the US.

This chapter continues to explore the contributions of John Dewey. As a progressive, Dewey was particularly concerned about the experiences of immigrant children in the schools. Other progressives, such as Jane Addams, committed their lives to the education and betterment of immigrant families. In addition, the progressives made forceful arguments about the need for democratic activities in schools. Such efforts, however, were not always welcomed, especially as the model of the "efficient" factory was applied to schooling. The tension between the child's needs and the society's needs was a center of debate in the early 20th century.

W hile the early debate between progressives and traditionalists was mired in a debate between child-centered versus subject-centered views, other progressive thinkers began to look directly at the school in the light of its ameliorative purpose in society. As a result, the dominant curriculum question was no longer whether the child was being served in the school or whether the omnipotent subject matter was being transmitted to the masses. Instead, the focus shifted toward the question of how to use the school to build a democratic society. During the early decades of the 20th century, the struggle for the school curriculum was actually a struggle over how the school would factor into the causes of social reform. Varieties of progressives had different answers to these questions.

Progressivism and the Cause of Social Reform

Led by the work of John Dewey, one progressive rank emerged in the early decades of the 20th century wanting to reawaken a social democratic view of public schooling. Among Dewey and others, the conception of the child in the development of the curriculum had to be tempered with a vision of society, with a belief in using the school as an agency for the improvement of social conditions, for the advancement of democratic principles, and for the formation of common democratic communities. Whereas the child-centered movement focused on the individual and promoted a pedagogical agenda that valued individualistic pursuits of self-expression, self-meaning, and self-development, the progressivism of Dewey emphasized the importance of developing social insight and community consciousness. Dewey conceived of schooling as operating within a miniature unit of democracy that was deliberately and consciously conceived to produce a comprehensive and enlarging social experience, where children learned about their differences and their commonalities, where vocational pursuits coexisted with academic ones, and where the needs for dissent and critical mindedness met the ideals of tolerance and social mutuality.

John Dewey and the Democratic Community

John Dewey was born in 1859. He was a child of preindustrial New England, born and raised in Burlington, Vermont, where his father was a storekeeper and where Dewey himself would grow to maturity and eventually attend the University of Vermont at age 16 (Wirth, 1989). Graduating in 1879, Dewey became a high school teacher. Within three years, however, he entered a doctoral program at Johns Hopkins University, where he was tutored by some of the greatest academic stars of his time, including G. Stanley Hall, with whom Dewey studied psychology (Cremin, 1961). Dewey took only two years to complete his doctoral studies, which prepared him for work in psychology and philosophy.

His first academic appointment was as an instructor at the University of Michigan. In 1894, however, he moved to the University of Chicago, where he put a great deal of energy into the development of a laboratory school that allowed him to test his school-related ideas against the experience of teaching children (Dewey, 1902). By working in an experimental school, Dewey had placed his ideas in the living context of children and teachers, a tradition already established by the likes of Parker, Pestalozzi, and Froebel. But in 1905, in a squabble over the leadership of the laboratory school, Dewey left Chicago for Columbia University. He remained at Columbia until his retirement and died in New York City at age 92.

During his long life, Dewey engaged in a philosophy that not only addressed traditional philosophic pursuits in logic, ethics, political science, religion, psychology, and aesthetics, but that also spoke to issues in the public arena. Dewey, for instance, had substantive things to say about issues related to the suffragette movement, labor unions, birth control, world peace, social class tensions, and societal transformations in Mexico, China, and Russia (Dworkin, 1954). A corpus of Dewey's work has been captured in a 37-volume edition edited by Jo Ann Boydston (1979).

Although Dewey started his career in the field of psychology, he soon came to know and appreciate the philosophical work of the American pragmatists. The philosophy of pragmatism gained a foothold in the consciousness of Dewey largely because it stressed a social psychology that examined human behaviors and that resonated well with democratic values and traditions. In American pragmatism, thought and knowledge were only relevant as action, as working power in the conduct of the individual and the society. Truth itself was a tentative condition, always under inspection and always being tested by the consequences that it produced under real life conditions (Childs, 1956).

Similarly, society was viewed as an ever changing organism that required a vigilant treatment of its problems and a method of adjudicating its problems. The very sustenance and health of the society, according to pragmatism, was dependent on a commitment to understanding the prob-

This portrait of Dewey is how many of his followers remember him.

lems of present living conditions, and this, in turn, meant that some method of intelligence or inquiry, qualified by democratic values, had to be found as a way to regulate, understand, and ultimately ameliorate present conditions. The present, in the custom of the early pragmatists, was (to borrow Whitehead's metaphor) "holy ground" that gave the past relevance and that provided the working conditions for a better future.

Pragmatism came as a serious turn in direction for Dewey, who took his first academic appointment as a professed idealist, where reality was bound to a working spiritual connection with an absolute and everlasting truth. Under idealism, humankind could only begin to find and understand the truth and unity of the external world by committing itself to the study of intellectual traditions. Learning, in other words, had to be immersed in the wisdom accumulated by humanity as it was embodied in intellectual knowledge. Dewey's ultimate rejection of idealism could not have been more complete, in the sense that he embraced a pragmatist's perspective that looked to the here and now and that saw the living problems of humankind as the driving forces for education.

Dewey, of course, eventually made his own contributions to American pragmatism by stressing the role that the scientific method could play in improving the human condition and by openly committing his philosophy to the values and aims of democracy. To Dewey, democracy was less of a political concept than a moral one. When married to a method of inquiry (essentially found in science), democracy represented a moral method of understanding. Dewey, in this sense, became the chief axiologist for American pragmatism, a role that likely led George Herbert Mead to observe that "in the profoundest sense John Dewey is the philosopher of America" (quoted in Morris, 1970, p. 8).

In 1902 Dewey made it quite clear that the educative process was composed of three fundamental factors: the nature of the learner, the values and aims of the society, and the wider world of knowledge represented in the subject matter. This was his way of saying that all good learning had to be attuned to the character of the learner (his interests, problems, developmental nature, and so on), to the highest values of the society (democratic principles of cooperation, tolerance, critical mindedness, political awareness), and to the reflective representation of the subject matter (the knowledge in the disciplines that helps the teacher to provide learnings that are in alignment with the learner and the society). Moreover, these factors had to be conceived as interrelated elements. Thus, the learner had to be seen in the context of the society, forcing a consideration of the needs and interests not just of the learner, but also of the learner living in a democracy. Similarly, the choice of subject matter in the curriculum had to be made on the grounds of what was most worth knowing for a learner living in a democracy.

Dewey's ideas about the school curriculum can be cautiously classified as experimentalist-progressive (Tanner & Tanner, 1990). The reference to **experimentalism** had to do with Dewey's advocacy of the scientific method in the conduct of teaching and learning. According to Dewey, science had given humanity a method of intelligence that can transform problems into progress. Being ever aware of the need to develop autonomously thinking, socially responsible citizens through the school, he embraced the scientific method as a mainstay in the teaching of children. However, he merged his embrace of science with the ethics of democracy and thus hoped to instill schoolchildren with a scientific attitude toward truth and

SCHOLARLY VOICES

The Progressive Views of John Dewey

Familiarity breeds contempt, but it also breeds some thing like affection. We get used to the chains we wear, and we miss them when removed. 'Tis an old story that through custom we finally embrace what at first wore a hideous mien. Unpleasant, because meaningless, activities may get agreeable if long enough persisted in. *It is possible for the mind to develop interest in a routine or mechanical procedure if conditions are continually supplied which demand that mode of operation and preclude any other sort.* I frequently hear dulling devices and empty exercises defended and extolled because "the children take such an 'interest' in them." Yes, that is the worst of it; the mind, shut out from worthy employ and missing the taste of adequate performance, comes down to the level of that which is left to it to know and do, and perforce takes an interest in a cabined and cramped experience.

Source: Dewey, J. (1902). *The Child and the Curriculum.* Chicago: University of Chicago Press, pp. 27–28.

Put in your own words what Dewey was trying to say in this excerpt. What are the fundamental progressive principles that Dewey is elucidating?

understanding that was informed by and associated with democratic ideals and principles.

Dewey (1916), who wrote extensively about the act of thinking, structured the act of learning along lines that resembled the scientific method. Good learning, he believed, was based on a method of inquiry. It originated in the difficulties and problems of experience and was then focused and intellectualized into a problem that could be investigated. This led invariably to the careful consideration of the problem itself and to the positing of tentative resolutions. Such resolutions were then further refined into hypotheses and developed in a way that anticipated their overall effect in experience. Finally, the hypotheses were brought to bear on the problem in experience and were tested for the purpose of yielding new insight on the original problem. Dewey wanted the spirit of such inquiry to be marked by social problems rooted in the soil of democratic communities. He wanted schooling to ingrain youth with an experimental habit of mind and with an ethical disposition toward the aims of democracy. Under the conditions just described, learning is anchored in the real problems of experience. It is problem focused and democratic in its purpose and intent, and built on the principle that truth is never absolute.

This latter point was particularly relevant to Dewey. In fact, he often discussed the need for education to proceed as an act of reconstruction. By this, he meant that the school had to look continually at society's problems as opportunities for improvement and growth. When one subjected social problems to a method of intelligence, found in the admixture of science and democracy, one allowed for experience to be reconstructed and renewed with new insight and value. More than anything, Dewey's commitment to the **reconstruction of experience** made him a progressive in the true sense of the word—one who looks for progress and change (see the Scholarly Voices feature in this section).

Dewey, however, balanced this regard for reconstruction through inquiry with an argument that spoke to the value of common communities, particularly to their value as unifying and conserving forces. One could not have a community, he argued, unless the people shared elements of commonality (common problems, common ideals, common language, and a common history). Given the pluralistic character of the population in America, Dewey thought that using the school to build common bases of understanding was imperative. The school, in other words, had to transmit a heritage of ideals to schoolchildren and had to provide a common ground for discourse that would bond the nation in some basis of commonality (Dewey, 1916). He did not want the school to transmit culture through the liberal arts, as Harris and others did. He wanted this basis of commonality to be built on conversation and to be devoted to problems and principles rather than preexisting subject matter.

Dewey's entrance into the school reform fray at the turn of the century was to become legendary. After spending 10 years as a professor of psychology and philosophy at the University of Michigan, he moved more directly into educational circles after accepting a position at the University of Chicago, which entailed, among other duties, the directorship of a university laboratory school.

Dewey, like many of other progressives of his time, started to test his ideas in an actual school. In developing his school, he was naturally drawn to questions of what knowledge was most worthwhile, and what instructional procedures could be employed in the development of an experiential and democratic education. Dewey, of course, wanted to integrate the problems and disturbances of experience in the education of the children, but he also wanted to be sure that such an objective did not collapse into child-centeredness. Dewey's curriculum, it should be remembered, had to be attuned not only to the learner, but to the society and to a sense of subject matter as well. Dewey understood that if children were going to learn to control their own destinies, they obviously had to learn basic literacy skills and basic knowledge embodied in organized subject matter.

As a result, he decided to build the lab school curriculum around what he called **social occupations**— cooking, carpentry, and sewing (Dewey, 1902a; Wirth, 1989). Out of these occupations children could learn arithmetic, reading and writing, and the sciences. The subject matter came to the occupations, as it were, which meant that the curriculum was interdisciplinary in its organization. The occupations themselves were worthwhile only to the extent to which they informed problems and needs in experience. For instance, the 12-year-olds in the laboratory school had at one time made it clear to their teachers that they needed their own place in school where they could hold meetings without interruption and where materials could be kept for their ongoing projects. Out of this need, the children developed a plan to build a clubhouse. In consultation with adults,

> committees on architecture, building, sanitation, ways and means, and interior decoration were formed, each with a head chosen because of experience in directing affairs. The site for the building was chosen under the guidance of the teachers in the different departments; plans were made and the cost estimated. A scheme for decoration was worked out, designs for furniture made. The choice of a location was prefaced by a study of the formation of soil, the conditions of drainage, climate, exposure to light or wind, which must be taken into account in building a house. (Mayhew & Edwards, 1936, p. 229)

All this activity led to the actual building of the clubhouse and to the extended study of the physical geography of Chicago in relation to its building sites. It was out of such problem-driven projects that Dewey taught children to think, act, and express themselves in intelligent ways while simultaneously developing basic skills and basic knowledge.

Dewey's desire to integrate skills and knowledge into the experience also led to a very different attitude toward interest and motivation (Tanner & Tanner, 1990). Whereas the idea of motivating children had long been seen as something marked by threat or coercion, Dewey argued that interest and motivation had to be vested in the actual conduct of the learning experience. If one had to resort to pleadings, threats, punishments, or some kind of trickery to get children to do their schoolwork, it probably meant that the schoolwork was not very worthwhile and not likely connected to ideas and experiences. In a manner of speaking, the development of student interest and motivation was always an act of curriculum development. It had everything to do with the construction of attractive and engaging learning experiences (see The School Experience in Literature feature in this section).

Lester Ward and the Founding Principles of a New Progressivism

Dewey was not alone in his effort to create a new form of education that was openly devoted to the idea of using the school for social democratic purposes. The very same idea was emerging from other scholars, the most notable being Lester Ward, who in 1883 produced a two-volume work, titled *Dynamic Sociology*, that helped him earn the title as the "father of American sociology."

Ward was trained as a geologist, but he used his analytical talents to test the prevailing social doctrines of the day. His book took direct aim at the assumptions of social Darwinism, which presumed that a "survival of the fittest" attitude was the best policy toward the school and the society. One should recall that even G. Stanley Hall, the champion of the child-study movement, had bowed to social Darwinism, believing that children were genetically wired for success. Ward, however, had come to quite a different conclusion. He believed that environmental factors were at the very forefront of an individual's chance to succeed in life, and he thought that the uneven distribution of wealth and all its concomitant inequalities (access to knowledge, to nutrition, to the fulfillment of material needs) ensured the continued poverty of underclass citizens. Intelligence to Ward was evenly distributed across social, economic, and gender lines. The trick was to develop a system of education that distributed equal qualities of experience. There was no lack of intelligence among poor people or among women; there was only the lack of opportunity (Tanner & Tanner, 1990).

Ward, not surprisingly, put his faith in the public school, believing that it was the most important function of government—the main engine for social correction and social improvement. Through the school, he wanted to lay to rest the idea of biological inheritance in intelligence and proceed with operationalizing the idea that healthy environmental interventions were the key to improving the lives of people. He was also not shy about encouraging government intervention in ways that helped to close the chasm of inequity in people's lives, a view that has led some to describe him as "the prophet of the welfare state" (Kliebard, 1986).

THE SCHOOL EXPERIENCE IN LITERATURE

Miss Weber's One-Room School

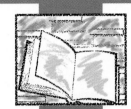

In the mid-1940s, Julia Weber Gordon was invited to prepare for publication the diary of a remarkable teacher. Miss Weber, as she was known to her students, taught in a small one-room schoolhouse in Minnesota during the 1930s. Miss Weber's teaching methods represented a radical departure from the normal recitation instruction. Instead of memorizing, she invited students to explore the issues that surrounded them in their rural community. The children, ranging in age from 5 to 16, studied the government's role in milk production, including the price supports so central to life in a dairy community. Most importantly, instead of ruling from a position of authority, Miss Weber created an atmosphere of shared decision-making and collegial debate in which her students had a significant voice in the activities of the classroom. Not surprisingly, she faced many of the same problems any teacher today would encounter in trying to wean children from the traditional role of teacher as authoritarian. In the following passage, we hear that frustration:

****

TUESDAY, SEPTEMBER 14. Last night I thought my problem through carefully. The children are having their difficulties, it's true, but so am I. I want so much to meet genuinely the needs of these boys and girls, but I'm having such a struggle. I've done more things wrong than I have done right since school began, it seems. This work taxes my ingenuity and patience heavily. How easy it would be to settle the problem by going back to an autocratically managed school. But I am not willing to give up the purposes of a democratic one, and these purposes cannot be accomplished by force.

I must give the children more challenging work to do. If I can keep them busy and interested perhaps I can guide their energies into more worth-while channels. . .

Using the social studies period to make improvements in the appearance and efficiency of our room has been good. In addition to this, I decided to capitalize on the interest of the children in my trip to Michigan to give them something more definite to do. This morning I listed on the board the interesting things I saw in Michigan: many fossils, windmills, barns with round roofs and lightning rods, fields of wheat and corn, square farms and straight roads, sheep and hogs, oil fields, much flat country, few trees, and many lakes. We talked about the meaning of these. We found a map in our geographies and traced the route I took. Ruth read that I went through part of the corn belt. She explained that more corn was raised here than in any other part of the United States.

What features of progressivism are evident in Miss Weber's teaching strategies?

Gordon, J. W. (1946). *My country school diary.* New York: Dell.

While Ward underscored the sociological need for schools to lend themselves to social progress and social change, Dewey, as it were, put the flesh on the bones, by discerning just how schools should conduct themselves under Ward's sociology. In the end, Ward helped to cripple the inherent laissez-faire attitude of social Darwinism and provided the main rationale and conceptual foundation for a method of schooling that looked to prepare a rising generation for social insight and social gain.

Ward's ideas got an early test at the hands of educational progressives, but there were other social reformers who were working from an agenda even wider than schooling.

Driven by the need to take direct action against the poverty and squalor of city life for factory workers, social activists, such as Jane Addams and Lillian Wald, opened **settlement houses** for the indigent. Located in the poorest neighborhoods of the cities, settlement houses were community centers that provided local residents, including children, with educational experiences that helped them to deal with the emergent needs of their difficult and often painful lives. The key to their function was to deal with neighborhood needs. Cremin (1961) describes the kinds of questions that moved the spirit of the settlement house:

> Were the streets dirty and the tenements infested with vermin? Settlements founded antifilth societies to induce people to rid their rooms of bedbugs, lice, cockroaches, and rats. Were gangs of street urchins a menace to life and property? Settlements established boys' and girls' clubs to channel the ebullient energy of adolescence into athletics, arts, and crafts, and constructive recreation. Were death and disease rates in the slum pitifully high? Settlements became first-aid centers, clinics, headquarters for visiting nurses, and schools of preventive medicine. Were young men unable to obtain jobs? Settlements experimented not only with trade education but with devices for fitting individuals to the trades for which they were best suited. Were mothers required to work? Settlements introduced kindergartens and day nurseries. Were workingmen illiterate? Settlements taught them to read. Was summer oppressive in the city? Settlements established playgrounds and vacation centers. (pp. 60–61)

Jane Addams was among the most prominent directors of a settlement house in America. She established her house in a Chicago neighborhood populated by immigrants living under the most horrific conditions of poverty. At her settlement, which was called the **Hull House,** Addams placed education at the center of all the action. There was a kindergarten for toddlers and clubs for boys and girls. For adults there were classes in English, cooking, nutrition, dressmaking, child care, the trades, and the like (Cremin, 1961). For the children, Addams also tried to provide a comprehensive education that went beyond the three Rs offered in the schools; she stressed art, literature, and history in ways that related to industrial life. Moreover, Addams agitated for reform in factory legislation and for improved city services for the poor. She worked directly out of the tradition of Lester Ward in committing herself to providing environmental stimuli for those who had little means and even less hope. Addams wanted to take some of the pain out of the lives of the poor but she also wanted to help them develop the life skills needed to combat the oppressive focus of poverty with their own initiative and power.

Here was an example of progressive ideas in their full bloom of practice. Addams worked directly with people needing help, using the very problems of their lives as targets for instruction and improvement. She was driven by the ideal of developing and liberating community insight, of directing the community to work in the interest of political reform and social reconstruction. Whereas Dewey turned to the school to fulfill his hopes for social reform, Addams remained anchored in the community, living amid the very

The Hull House, located in a poor neighborhood in Chicago, is where Jane Addams and other progressives developed their zeal for community action through education.

problems and perturbations that took place in the community of poor people. John Dewey was a frequent visitor to the Hull House even before he opened the doors to his own school. He became a great admirer of the Hull House and of Jane Addams. He and Addams, in fact, became close friends, so much so that Jane Addams became the namesake for John and Alice Dewey's child Jane Dewey. It has been observed that Dewey himself acknowledged a deeper faith in the guiding forces of democracy by witnessing Addam's work at the Hull House (Cremin, 1988). Jane Addams eventually achieved world-wide recognition for her work, winning the Nobel Peace Prize in 1931 for the humanitarian causes that she championed in the Hull House (Lagemann, 1985).

There were, of course, other notable progressives who tested their ideas in the application of a school. Francis Parker, whom Dewey called the "father of progressive education," was advancing progressive ideas in the school several years before Dewey even got started in education. Unlike Dewey, who operated out of a private lab school, Parker's ideas found a home in the public schools that he commanded as superintendent of schools in Quincy, Massachusetts, from 1875 to 1880.

Influenced by progressive Europeans, such as Pestalozzi and Froebel, Parker settled into his appointment as superintendent with a comprehensive reform mandate. Before hiring Parker, the Quincy schools conducted examinations of their students to discern their levels of skill and knowledge. The findings were discouraging, to say the least. Children knew the rules of grammar but not how to write; they could read from their texts, but not from any other materials (Cremin, 1961). They had essentially been trained for the examination but had no generalizable skills. As one school committee member put it, the school "had turned his scholars into parrots and made a meaningless farce of education" (Adams, 1881, p. 318). Change was definitely in the air at Quincy, making Parker the right person for the job. Parker's innovations were known as the **Quincy Methods.**

Among Parker's first actions was to try to integrate more natural methods of learning in the school, methods built around child play and activity. Here his bias for Pestalozzi was most clear. More natural methods included the whole-word reading strategy, the use of classroom field trips, the embrace of conversations in the classroom, and the willingness to bring motor activities into teaching (Cremin, 1961). Object lessons were used in the teaching of geography, and teachers were encouraged to look at ways to individualize instruction. The whipping or flogging of children was not tolerated because the doctrine of child depravity was openly rejected.

Parker was on the side of the child in the curriculum, but he was also energized by the social reform spirit of education, referring to the school as an upbuilder of democracy, as an embryonic democracy, descriptors that Dewey himself would later use in his own work. Parker understood the sociocivic purposes of education and thoroughly supported the idea of using the school to build communities and to teach tolerance and understanding. The means that he used in achieving such effects, however, were child-centered; they were primarily Froebelian, meaning that through individualization better forms of social unity and cohesion could be formed.

Thus, while Parker's rhetoric supported the expression of schooling as a democratizing institution, his heart was always with the child. The child was the center, and it was through the child that all else proceeded, including the growth and profit of a democratic society. As a result, Parker put forward a child-centered strategy as a means for obtaining sociocivic objectives. The school would have to wait for Dewey and others to supply social democratic means for the achievement of social democratic objectives.

Although Parker was one of the earliest progressives to try his ideas in the public schools, his school, as indicated, was more Froebelian than Deweyan. However, over time, there were other school-reform efforts that were more closely aligned with the emerging experimentalist thinking of the early decades. Many of these are described in the *Twenty-sixth Yearbook of the National Society for the Study of Education,* edited by Harold Rugg (1927), and in a small book that John Dewey coauthored with his daughter Evelyn Dewey called *Schools of Tomorrow* (1915).

Among the interesting schools working out of the more experimentalist tradition of Dewey were the Denver public schools, which undertook a complete curriculum revision project during the 1920s under the superintendency of Jesse Newlon. Like Parker before him, Newlon saw the management of a public school system as a curricular problem. Newlon started the reform effort at Denver by involving teachers in the act of curriculum revision and curriculum experimentation. He appointed committees composed almost entirely of teachers and asked them to read and study the school literature with a view toward reworking the course work in the Denver schools. He imposed no administrative edict on the selection of content and organization of the courses of study, and he provided the time and the resources that were needed for teachers to make these decisions themselves (Newlon, 1927).

Most of the committees opted to build the curriculum on the basis of **life situations.** What this meant was that the curriculum would be based on situations of daily living, involving work, leisure, the family, and the social community. Commercial courses for junior high school students, for instance, were built around an investigation of commercial practices in the Denver business community; the social studies dealt with civic and social problems; in the mathematics, students were expected to understand modern business practices, the expenditure of public money, and the world's commerce system (Cremin, 1961). In general, ideas in the disciplines had to find a specific ground of application in life situations.

The implications of these initiatives were quintessentially progressive. First, the subject matter of the course work in the Denver schools was drawn out of life conditions and was not predetermined (as in the traditional-humanist sense). Second, the focus on life situations and problems underscored the need for continual curriculum revision. Because life itself was dynamic, curriculum development had to be dynamic—new courses would evolve and old courses would be continually revised. Third, the curriculum itself was framed as a hypothesis, as something to be tested and evaluated. Fourth, the character of the learning was openly experiential, having to do with the problems and conditions of life. Lastly, the idea that teacher intelligence and creativity were central to good schools was promoted.

A Tidal Change in Secondary Education

The Denver reforms, however, were simply the manifestation of a broader curriculum movement that was based on a famous report sponsored by the National Education Association (NEA). Much of the curriculum experimentation occurring in the schools, including what was described in Denver, would not likely have taken form without the influence of the **Cardinal Principles Report of 1918.** It, more than any document of its time, led to a national call to broaden the fundamental scope of the schools' offerings. As mentioned, the Committee of Ten and Fifteen reports had kept the schools centered largely on an academic plane, within the limits of a very few subject areas. The Cardinal Principles report changed this completely.

In 1913, the National Education Association appointed another committee, aptly named the Commission on the Reorganization of Secondary Education, to reconsider the pattern of course work in the high school. After five years of deliberation, the committee offered its recommendations in a report known as the Cardinal Principles Report of 1918. Whereas the Committee of Ten report itemized subject areas to be taught, the Cardinal Principles report itemized practical objectives to be met. These objectives included the command of the fundamental processes (basic skills), worthy home membership, health, vocation, citizenship, worthy use of leisure time, and ethical character. These were, in fact, the seven cardinal principles of the report.

The listing of seven principles or objectives foretold a new sense of a school. If the report was to be taken seriously, the character of secondary education now had to shift from its solid academic emphasis in the traditional liberal arts to a more comprehensive emphasis that included academic concerns but that placed equal value on vocation development, citizenship education, and personal needs. It was precisely in the context of these recommendations that the blueprint for the comprehensive high school was fashioned. The American comprehensive high school acknowledged two main functions: the provision of specialized studies for the purpose of dealing with issues related to individual interests and talents in areas of college and vocational preparation and personal development; and the provision of unifying studies for the purpose of dealing with the vital problems of social life in a democracy as they related to citizenship, ethical character, and worthy home membership.

The notion of providing new breadth in the course work of the curriculum had very direct effects in the way that the school had to be organized. Differentiation in the curricular program was going to be needed to allow students to pursue their own plans, interests, and needs. The curriculum could no longer be seen as one monolithic block of courses, a problem that hounded the Committee of Ten report from its inception. As a result, specialized courses designed to meet vocational, college preparatory, and special interest needs were all supported in the Cardinal Principles document. At the same time, course work in general education was going to be needed. Such courses had to be expressly designed to provide a common social discourse for students. They represented a place where sociocivic issues could be broached and where the society could be funded with common ideals and common understanding. In the Cardinal Principles report, the unifying studies of general education represented the curriculum ground for democracy. Through common experiences, the pluralistic dimensions of the population could find a common ground—the nation's diversity could be made whole.

The Cardinal Principles report has often been cited as a turning point in American education, primarily because it offered a comprehensive school model as an alternative to the strictly academic curriculum of traditional education. Partly as a result of the report, the idea of mental discipline was rejected and the search for life activities responsive to individual and social needs was enacted. As Butts (1978) put it, "What the seven cardinal principles did was shift the emphasis in schooling away from the preoccupation with the academic and intellectual disciplines and to broaden the social role of education almost beyond recognition" (p. 194).

The report can be viewed as a uniquely American effort to educate youth in a unified setting in ways that allowed for sociocivic education (general education) and specialized education. Such a system diverged markedly from the separatist, dual system that existed in Europe. Instead of going to separate trade schools, American students interested in vocation education found a hospitable climate in the unified cosmopolitan school. Vocational education was, after all, one of the cardinal principles. But no matter what their specialization might be, students were always required to participate in heterogeneously grouped common learning, which aimed to build common communities along common knowledge and common values. William Wraga (1994) captures the history of the comprehensive high school in his recent work, showing its development from the Cardinal Principles report.

A More Radical Progressivism

Also arising out of the new regard for the school's role in the areas of social progress and social consciousness was a more radical group of thinkers that wanted the school to take a direct interventionist role in making America into a classless workers' society built largely on socialist principles.

Much of this thinking started with the social class analysis of George Counts, who, in the 1920s, took on the cause of empirically showing how the goals of democracy and equal opportunity were unfulfilled in the public school. Counts had a keen eye for demonstrating how the school not only failed to ameliorate economic disparities but also how it actually had a hand in their perpetuation. "In a very large measure," wrote Counts in 1922, "participation in the privilege of secondary education is contingent on social economic status" (p. 149). Counts showed how socioeconomic factors affected various levels of school operation. He observed, for instance, that the membership of school boards was drawn from favored socioeconomic classes that had little interest in drafting educational policy that altered the status quo (Counts, 1927). Elsewhere, he bemoaned the disproportionately large numbers of dropouts who came from poor backgrounds, noting that high school education "was a privilege being extended at public expense to those very classes that already occupy the privileged positions in modern societies" (Counts, 1922, p. 152).

To Counts, the problems with schooling had less to do with the institution itself than with the socioeconomic conditions in which the institution found itself operating. Counts likened the socioeconomic situation in America to an economic aristocracy where the masses barely got by while a small culture of elites flourished. The implication was that the solution in reforming the society was rooted in changing the economic order; otherwise, the school would always be a handmaiden to economic interest. On this point, Counts was forthright in stating that the maintenance of existing patterns of economic inequities would always lead to differential forms of education constructed along class lines. To avoid this condition, Counts reasoned that the schools needed to resist the dominance of the economic aristocracy by championing collectivist democratic causes and principles in the school. Because the controlling hand of economic oppression infused the school with the philosophy of economic individualism, which fostered egoistic and competitive values in education, the schools themselves, particularly the teachers, needed to defuse this power by committing themselves to the reordering of the economic order in the direction of a collectivist or workers' society. This attitude removed Counts from the progressive-experimentalist of Dewey and placed him more directly in what could be called a perspective of **social reconstructionism** concerning education.

Counts articulated his socialist themes most powerfully in a speech that he gave at a meeting of the National Education Association. Written in 1932, Counts's voice reflected the temperament of the Great Depression and the overwhelming concerns that he had for social and economic inequalities:

> Here is a society that manifests the most extraordinary of contradictions: a mastery over the forces of nature, surpassing the wildest dreams of antiquity, is accompanied by extreme material insecurity; dire poverty walks hand and in hand with the most extravagant living the world has ever seen; an abundance of goods of all kinds is coupled with privation, misery, and even starvation; . . . breakfastless children march to school past bankrupt shops laden with rich foods gathered from the ends of the world; strong men by the million walk the streets in a futile search for employment and with the exhaustion of hope enter the ranks of the damned; great captains of industry close factories without warning and dismiss the workman by whose labor they have amassed huge fortunes over the years; . . . racketeers and gangsters with the connivance of public officials fasten themselves on the channels of trade and exact toll at the end of the machine gun; . . . the wages paid to the workers are too meager to enable them to buy back the goods they produce; . . . the

science of psychology is employed to fan the flames of desire so that men may be enslaved by their wants and bound to the wheel of production; . . . federal aid to the unemployed is opposed on the ground that it would pauperize the masses when the favored members of the society have already lived on the dole. . . . (1932, pp. 33–35)

Counts used attention-commanding language to make a case for the primacy of economic factors in the rehabilitation of the U.S. democracy. He wanted the schools to be open about indoctrinating youth according to certain "democratic" tenets, which to Counts translated into an embrace of a more socialist societal arrangement that teachers would lead. Impatient with the child-centered nature of the new progressivism, which dodged the issues of inequity and injustice (all in the name of the goodness of the learner), Counts embraced an educational program that carried a powerful theory of social welfare and that provided a quick fix to the problems that he described so vividly in his NEA speech.

Bode and Dewey criticized Counts and other social reconstructionists for misconceiving the functioning of a democracy. Using a strategy that resonates with current discussions about politically correct thinking, Bode (1938) observed that what the social reconstructionists were proposing was not education at all, but training toward a particular programmatic position that equated democracy with a specific scheme of ownership and distribution. "Education becomes propaganda when we set out deliberately to make converts," observed Bode (quoted in Childs, 1956, p. 291), even if the instruction dealt with obvious democratic principles. Clearly, the problems that concerned Counts also concerned Dewey and Bode, but to them the judgments of a democracy had to be conducted democratically. Such problems were opportunities for reconstruction, a process, as discussed, that was scientific and moral in its orientation and that harbored no prior commitment to a socialist collectivism. Counts wanted revolutionary change. Dewey wanted evolutionary change. Counts, in fact, discussed the prospect of

The abject social conditions of the depression were partly responsible for the progressives' interest in the development of a new society.

PART ONE: TOWARD A HISTORY AND PHILOSOPHY OF AMERICAN EDUCATION

enacting the most revolutionary concept of all—institutionalizing revolutionary change in a democracy without resort to violence or war (Childs, 1956, p. 285).

Thus, where Dewey and like-minded progressives were interested in dealing with socioeconomic issues in the school for the purpose of developing a critical consciousness about the society, the social reconstructionists aimed to deal with the same issues for the purpose of installing a workers' society. The difference here is crucial. To Dewey, ideas proceed from inquiry and cannot be known preliminary to democratic and scientific procedures. To Counts, the primacy of economic problems in the society made him unapologetic about predetermining the kind of social and economic arrangement that was best for America. To experimentalists, learning could not be democratic and intelligent if it was encumbered with a mission of imposing and inculcating particular ideological viewpoints. This did not mean that schooling had to be neutral, but it did mean that the methods used in dealing with socioeconomic factors in the school had to be those of investigation and cooperative discussion. The work of Counts and other social reconstructionists helped to inform and develop a neoradical group of educators in educational studies that became vital in later decades and that focused most of its attention on issues of race, class, and gender. We will discuss these more contemporary movements later.

 ## Education and the Rise of Social Efficiency

There was yet another group of thinkers that was quite intent on bringing life activity to the curriculum. It differed substantively from most progressive groups because it supported the application of business values and principles to the condition of education. Advocates of such a view wanted the curriculum to be used to strike the chord of order, control, and social harmony; they wanted to use the curriculum as a mechanism to sort and slot the population in ways that adjusted everyone to a place in society. Thus, out of this group of thinkers arose a new conception of curriculum that was management oriented, efficiency driven, and highly prescriptive in its details. It was out of this early tradition, which is known in the literature as the tradition of **social efficiency,** that later formulations revolving around competency-based instruction were made. It was also out of this tradition that the primacy of measurement began to take hold in the school.

Several forces shaped the movement toward social efficiency concerns in the curriculum. First, there was a recognition that the modern methods of science might be able to bring the school under the umbrella of standardization and control. Given the general disillusionment with the traditional school, some scholars were demanding standardization as the only way to ensure quality of results. Rather than seeking to release the intelligence of teachers, the belief was that teachers should be programmed or scripted. Second, the rise of industrialization and the embrace of business values in the American ethic gave way to a new set of principles in education that stressed waste elimination, procedural compulsion, cost savings, and efficiency. This historical phenomenon was captured in Raymond Callahan's book, *Education and the Cult of Efficiency.*

Frederick Taylor and the Ideal of Efficiency

The commitment to social efficiency in the curriculum was naturally preceded by a commitment to social efficiency in the society. During the early 1900s, the business community led the way with a new efficiency strategy known as **scientific management.** Developed by an engineer named Frederick Taylor (1911), scientific management promised to provide a method for businesses, particularly factories, that would increase production while also lowering costs.

The key to the idea had to do with identifying and then standardizing the action of the most productive workers. The premise was that there was one best way to do any job, and that such a way could be discerned through careful study. To Taylor, if the most productive worker had an output of x, then there was no reason all workers could not meet the same output figure. By using various incentives, Taylor identified the best workers, meaning those who produced the most in the least amount of time. Taylor then analyzed their actions and tried to note, in behavioral terms, what made them so productive. After having secured a sense of what factors were central to the most productive workers, Taylor itemized and then standardized the practice so that other workers could be taught to produce at the same level.

It is instructive to explain how Taylor's management system worked in an actual case study taken from his writing (Callahan, 1962). The setting was the Bethlehem Steel Company at the turn of the century. After building up a huge surplus of pig iron during the 1890s, Bethlehem Steel had entered into healthier economic times. A new market was found for the pig iron, and vigorous sales were cutting into the accumulated surpluses. Bethlehem Steel hired Taylor to examine how these surpluses could be moved out for sale as quickly and efficiently as possible. The pig-iron, which weighed 92 pounds, had to be carried approximately 40 feet to a railway car, where it would be shipped out for sale.

When Taylor arrived at the work scene, each worker was lifting about 300 pigs during his 10-hour shift. Armed with the tools of scientific management, Taylor set out to improve this figure. First, he conducted time-and-motion studies that itemized exactly what was involved in moving the pig iron. The time per foot of travel and the time taken to pick up, throw down, and lay the pig in a layer were recorded. Allowing for various fatigue factors, Taylor's time-and-motion studies indicated that each man was capable of carrying 1,100 pigs per day, a more than threefold increase that translated into a daily rate of more than 50 tons of iron per man. According to Taylor, the men were simply not accomplishing what science indicated a healthy man could accomplish. Perhaps they were dawdling or simply lazy, but the crucial point was that the men were simply not working efficiently.

Having determined his target, Taylor tried to find the men he thought were best able to meet his goal and make his productivity objective a reality. He finally settled on one, a small but sturdy Pennsylvanian Dutchman who was witnessed trotting to and from work each day at a distance of about a mile and who was building a house for himself before and after work (see The Historical Context feature in this section). Taylor gave this worker a monetary incentive to increase his productivity up to the new target. The man was given a 60% increase in pay (from $1.15 per hour to $1.85) and was followed during the ensuing work days by an efficiency expert who told him exactly when to pick up the pig and when to rest. The results spoke for

The application of Frederick Taylor's scientific management practices to education spurred a new science of school measurement.

Taylor's Conversation With Schmidt

The following was taken from Taylor's own account of his interaction with Schmidt, the Pennsylvania Dutchman targeted to be the ideal worker in Taylor's scientific management strategy.

He was a little Pennsylvania Dutchman who had been observed to trot back home for a mile or so after his work in the evening about as fresh as he was when he came trotting down to work in the morning. We found that upon wages of $1.15 a day he had succeeded in buying a small plot of ground, and that he was engaged in putting up the walls of a little house for himself in the morning before starting to work and at night after leaving. He also had the reputation of being exceedingly "close," that is, of placing a very high value on a dollar. As one man whom we talked to about him said, "A penny looks about the size of a cart wheel to him." This man we will call Schmidt.

The task before us, then, narrowed itself down to getting Schmidt to handle 47 tons of pig-iron per day and making him glad to do it. This was done as follows. Schmidt was called out from among the gang of pig-iron handlers and talked to somewhat in this way:

"Schmidt, are you a high-priced man?

Vell, I don't know vat you mean?

Oh yes, you do. What I want to know is whether you are a high-priced man or not.

Vell, I don't know vat you mean?

Oh, come now, you answer my questions. What I want to find out is whether you are a high-priced man or one of these cheap fellows here. What I want to find out is whether you want to earn $1.85 a day or whether you are satisfied with $1.15, just the same as all those cheap fellows are getting.

Did I vant $1.85 a day? Vas dot a high-priced man? Well, yes, I vas a high-priced man.

Oh, you're aggravating me. Of course you want $1.85 a day—everyone wants it! You know perfectly well that that has very little to do with your being a high-priced man. For goodness sake answer my questions, and don't waste any more of my time. Now come over here. You see that pile of pig-iron?

Yes.

You see that car?

Yes.

Well, if you are a high-priced man, you will load that pig-iron on that car tomorrow for $1.85. Now so wake up and answer my question. Tell me whether you are a high-priced man or not.

Vell—did I got $1.85 for loading dot pig-iron on dot car tomorrow?

Yes, of course you do, and you get $1.85 for loading a pile like that every day right through the year. That is what a high-priced man does, and you know it just as well as I do.

Vell, dot's all right. I could load dot pig-iron on the car tomorrow for $1.85, and I get it every day, don't I?

Certainly you do—certainly you do.

Vell, den, I vas a high-priced man.

Now, hold on, hold on. You know just as well as I do that a high-priced man has to do exactly as he's told from morning till night. You have seen this man here before, haven't you?

—Continued

Taylor's Conversation With Schmidt

—Continued

Well, if you are a high-priced man, you will do exactly as this man tells you tomorrow, from morning till night. When he tells you to pick up a pig and walk, you pick it up and walk, and when he tells you to sit down and rest, you sit down. You do that right straight through the day. And what's more, no back talk. Now a high-priced man does just what he's told to do, and no back talk. Do you understand that? When this man tells you to walk, you walk; when he tells you to sit down, you sit down, and you don't talk back at him. Now you come on to work here tomorrow morning and I'll know before night whether you are really a high-priced man or not. . . ."

Schmidt started to work, and all day long, and at regular intervals, told by the man who stood over him with a watch, "Now pick up a pig and walk. Now sit down and rest. Now walk—now rest," etc. He worked when he was told to work, and rested when he was told to rest, and at half past five in the afternoon had his 47 ½ tons loaded on the car. And he practically never failed to work at this pace and do the task that was set him during the years that the writer was at Bethlehem. And, throughout this time he averaged a little more than $1.85 per day, whereas before he had never received over $1.15 per day, which was the ruling rate of wages at that time in Bethlehem. That is, he received 60 per cent higher wages than were paid to other men who were not working on task work. One man after another was picked and trained to handle pig-iron at the rate of 47 ½ tons per day until all of the pig-iron was handled at this rate, and the men were receiving 60 percent more wages than other workmen around them.[57]

Source: Taylor F. (1911). *The Principles of Scientific Management.* New York: Harper and Brothers, as quoted in Callahan, R.E. (1962). *Education and the cult of efficiency.* Chicago: University of Chicago Press, pp. 36–38.

What is your reaction to this conversation? What are the basic principles that Taylor sees as central to increasing efficiency?

themselves: the man received a 60% increase in pay but he met Taylor's objective and more than tripled his productivity. The effect was that the company was getting more for less, a threefold increase in output vis-à-vis a 60% increase in input (wages). Stories of Taylor's successes sparkled like shining stars in the business community. In time, all the roads to success in business were paved with the insights of scientific management.

The lesson that Taylor provided to businesses soon reached the schools. Applied to the curriculum, scientific management was deceptively simple: find the best practices, standardize them, and make them part of the school routine. The "best" practices under Taylor's conditions, however, were always those that managed to secure the highest productivity with the least amount of effort. Applied to education, there were going to be complications. It was one thing to note the productivity of an assembly line worker or a man lifting pig iron, but it was quite another to make similar judgments with something as complex and dynamic as the education of children. To make it work, substantive changes had to be made in the way that the curriculum was to be conceived. Generally speaking, a factory model had to be embraced for the curriculum. The idea of productivity in the school meant that actual learning outcomes needed to be identified and that measurements needed to be taken to determine whether they had been reached. The Taylorian regard for efficiency had in fact set the wheels in motion for a new science of school measurement, a numerical way of demonstrating achievement and mastery.

Curriculum Design and Social Efficiency

The implications of Taylor's work were also very clear in the early curriculum construction designs that were being promoted by like-minded thinkers in the burgeoning field of curriculum studies, the most prominent being University of Chicago Professor John Franklin Bobbitt. For the curriculum to be manageable and operative, Bobbitt believed that learning had to take on a character of specificity that had never before been seen. Many social progressives, like those that supporting the Cardinal Principles report, had built the school experience on the ground of generalizability, talking of the need for broadly framed objectives that were more statements of principle than specific actions to be undertaken. Bobbitt thought such thinking was unrealistic and irresponsible and he wanted to change it:

> Objectives that are only vague, high-sounding hopes and aspirations are to be avoided. Examples are: "character building," "the harmonious development of the individual," "social efficiency," "general discipline," "self-realization," "culture," and the like. All of these are valid enough; but too cloud-like for guiding practical procedure. They belong to the visionary adolescence of our profession—not to its sober and somewhat disillusioned maturity. (Bobbitt, 1924, p. 32)

Out of this demand for a new level of specificity arose a method of curriculum development known as activity or **job analysis.** An admitted admirer of Taylor's work, Bobbitt believed that the school curriculum was best served by preparing the learner for specific activities in adult life. He wanted the school to survey all the relevant activities in the lives of adults (as they related to occupations, family, society, and so on) and then, like Taylor's standardized production model, to teach directly to each activity. Bobbitt (1918) expressed his theory in clear terms:

> The central theory is simple. Human life, however varied, consists in the performance of specific objectives. However numerous and diverse they may be for any social class, they can be discovered. This requires only that one go out into the world of affairs and discover the particulars of which these affairs consist. These will show the abilities, attitudes, habits, appreciations and forms of knowledge that men need. These will be the objectives of the curriculum. They will be numerous, definite and particularized. The curriculum will be that series of experiences which children and youth must have by way of attaining those objectives. (p. 42)

The intent was to be as specific as possible in framing activities because the job of the curriculum was to prepare the learner for specific tasks through a process of habit formation. As a result, Bobbitt's curriculum was filled with thousands of skills and behaviors that were, by virtue of their specificity, fixed at rather low, mechanistic levels. This made the method of job analysis amenable to the behavioristic psychology emerging at the time, the stimulus-response connectionism of behavioristic theory. It is important to note that

Bobbitt provided no way to screen curriculum objectives and activities. He did not ask if certain objectives were important to the learner or to the society. He simply observed the adult environment and chose objectives that emerged out the common judgments of teachers and other curriculum participants. This was curriculum making for the status quo, a decidedly antiprogressive outcome.

Bobbitt believed that the curriculum could be reduced to a conveyorlike process preoccupied with the finished product. Bobbitt (1913) was not subtle about such matters. "Education," he declared, "is a shaping process as much as the manufacturing of steel rails" (p. 11). The factory metaphor captured the essence of education that Bobbitt promoted. Students were the raw products. The school was the assembly line and the society the consumer. The world of philosophy and concerns for social reform and sociopersonal growth were simply not important considerations. The charge of the school was to fit the individual into life, into a slot that ensured the stability of order in an industrial society.

To its advocates, the method of job analysis carried certain positive results. By virtue of the method, for instance, the school curriculum was apparently more closely connected to life; it was based on activity. Moreover, job analysis was said to have been better suited for teachers because it offered prefashioned and ready-made activities that did not require the teachers to think independently. "The burden of finding the best methods," stated Bobbitt, "is too large and too complicated to be laid on the shoulders of the teachers" (1913, pp. 51–52). One could see how different this idea was from those being proposed in the Denver schools and in the work of the experimentalists. Job analysis also pointed to new promises in the area of waste elimination and institutional order by making it clear that scales of measurement were needed for assessment or valuative purposes. Lastly, the method, by aiming to teach children according to their needs and abilities, provided differential experiences that led to different social and vocational destinies. This willingness to differentiate in the school curriculum helped it to secure a world where everyone could find her place, where the individual was adjusted to a social order that stabilized society.

Job analysis had its share of critics. No one offered critical remarks, however, that were more penetrating and thoughtful than Boyd Bode's. Bode attacked Bobbitt for the manner in which Bobbitt discerned his objectives, noting how Bobbitt drew entirely from adult activities. Bode (1927) contended that by disregarding the lives of children, Bobbitt had set into motion a condition for education that simply served the status quo (things as they already exist). To Bode, job analysis was clearly little more than training for adjustment to existing social conditions. In a democracy, Bode continued, the society would be better served if education proceeded from the level of general training, with abilities that cut across particular conditions and particular problems. The individual and the collective society could only grow and develop if they had the skills needed to deal with emergent problems and issues, as opposed to being adjusted to and knowledgeable of particular existing conditions. Specific activities change over time. The activities of being a citizen or a farmer are different now from what they were decades ago. Thus, to look at specificity as the answer to the curriculum was to promote outdated training that would not likely have much currency beyond the present. Bobbitt was no progressive in Bode's estimation.

Opting for Specificity in the Curriculum

Despite the criticisms, job analysis received a boost of support from the landmark experimental work that Edward Thorndike had done in the area of mental training. Thorndike had conducted experiments to test the validity of the doctrine of mental discipline, which was, to recall, the belief that certain subjects had greater disciplinary value in developing intelligence than others. Thorndike's (1924) experiment was elegantly simple. After correcting for initial ability and special training, Thorndike tested the disciplinary value of Latin by comparing the gains in intelligence scores of students who studied a series of subjects plus Latin against those who studied an identical series of subjects plus shop work. This same experimental procedure was used to test each of the subject areas. The results were clear. No one subject had a grasp on the intelligence; there was no hierarchy of studies. In Thorndike's (1924) words, "We found notable differences in gain in ability to think as measured by these tests, but they do not seem to be due to what one studies" (p. 94).

This finding was a boon for Bobbitt and other curricularists smitten with the notion of job analysis. If Thorndike was right, then clearly the academic subjects did not possess the transferable effects of intelligence as was originally believed. Because a subject could no longer be claimed as an instrument of intelligence, Bobbitt and others could say with more confidence that education had to proceed by direct route, by an effort to teach each activity and conditions in life, a position that eliminated discussions of transfer since each particular situation was dealt with directly.

Bobbitt's penchant for specificity was also drawing support from other sources, including the earlier work of a prominent journalistic critic of education named Joseph Rice. During the late 19th and early 20th centuries, Rice had written several important magazine pieces about the state of education in America. Rice, who wrote in the style of the muckraking journalism that was popular at the turn of the century, was a tough critic with a searing commentary. Having surveyed American elementary school education through a 36-city tour, Rice wrote several articles that told the story to the American public about what was actually happening in the schools. In city after city, he outlined the character of incompetence, corruption, and apathy that was, in his view, conspiring to ruin the hearts and minds of schoolchildren. Although he did report on some positive developments in the schools, particularly in the Indianapolis schools where the Herbartians influenced the curriculum, Rice clearly believed that schools were in a calamitous state. In his writing he frequently targeted the mindlessness of the pedagogical exercises used in school and the petty triviality that marked much of the teacher's actions. In an elementary school in Saint Louis, for instance, Rice observed the following scene:

> During several daily recitation periods, each of which is from twenty to twenty-five minutes in duration, the children are obliged to stand on the line, perfectly motionless, their bodies erect, their knees and feet together, the tips of their shoes touching the edge of the board in the floor. The slightest movement on the part of a child attracts the attention of the teacher. The recitation is repeatedly interrupted with cries of "Stand straight," "Don't bend the knees," "Don't lean against the wall," and so on. I heard one teacher ask a little boy: "'How can you learn anything with your knees and toes out of

order?. . . The teacher never forgets the toes; every few moments she casts her eyes "toeward." (Rice, 1893/1969, p. 98)

Rice, discouraged by what he saw in the schools, could conceive of only one solution. Believing that teachers were the main perpetrators of stupidity in the school, Rice recommended that the curriculum be built around specific objectives and skills so that teachers knew exactly what they were to do. Rather than attempt to cultivate the teacher's intelligence and creativity, Rice wanted to find a way to protect children from the teacher's incompetence. In this manner, he opted for a Bobbitt-like design that featured specificity. What was forgotten was the possibility that learning could proceed from the basis of high generalizability for transfer to a wide range of situations, not unlike the training that Bode discussed when he criticized Bobbitt.

This inclination to teach by direct route and to provide a differentiated curriculum that had different social and vocational destinies was also bolstered by a new faith in the measurement of intelligence. To have confidence in the intelligence quotient (IQ) of students was also to be confident of its capacity to place students in a differentiated curriculum. With a quantifiable number, curriculum developers could be sure that they had identified the proper intellectual rank of the individual, which then paved the way for the creation of curriculum tracks that provided an appropriate education for each rank of intelligence. Ross Finney, a professor of sociology, expressed this attitude with stunning openness. Armed with IQ data, Finney envisaged a curriculum for dullards and a curriculum for leadership, both of which would make their contribution to the order and maintenance of society. "Instead of trying to teach the dullards to think for themselves," Finney (1928) observed, "the intellectual leaders must think for them, and drill the results, memoriter, into their synapses" (p. 395). Similarly, other sociologists argued that separate schools, divided along vocation and academic lines, were needed to teach to the different intelligence levels (Snedden, 1914).

The growth of the intelligence quotient test in America started late in the first decade of the 20th century, at the hands of Alfred Binet and Theodore Simon, two French psychologists (Cremin, 1961). Over a decade or so, discussions related to IQ testing stayed in the province of professional circles. But during the earlier stages of World War I, the IQ test attracted the attention of the United States Army, which was looking for a way to "quantify" the intelligence of its recruits, particularly those soldiers who fell on either extreme end of the IQ scale. Although the developers of the IQ test admitted that the test was irrelevant to character concerns, they did assert that the test had the capacity to assign mental ages to all test participants. Using norms taken from children, which turned out to be quite a mistake, the Army tests found that the average "mental age" of the American soldier was 14. This was a dangerous turn for American education because now various commentators could claim that schooling beyond a certain age was essentially worthless. A student with an IQ that corresponded with a mental age of, say, 13 presumably did not need to go to school beyond that age. His inherent skills could only take him so far. Clearly, Lester Ward's hope to enliven the social environment and to expand the educational opportunities for all youth was imperiled by the prospect of educational retrenchment based on IQ points.

John Dewey on Mental Measurement

The following story about John Dewey was once told by one of his students:

> I remember once when he [Dewey] was presiding at an educational evening in Teachers College, there was a series of papers on mental testing. And it was all on norms and so on. And at the end of the meeting—I have to tell this story just for the record—at the end of the evening he said, "Listening to these papers I was reminded of the way we used to weigh hogs on the farm. We would put a plank in between the rails of the fence, put the hog on one end of the plank and then pile the other end of the plank with rocks until the rocks balanced the hog. Then we took the hog off; and then we guessed the weight of the rocks!" [*Laughter.*]

Source: Lamont, C. (Ed.) (1959). *Dialogue on John Dewey,* N.Y.: Horizon Press, pp. 113–114.

What is the essential point of Dewey's criticism here?

In time, the faith taken in IQ scores was fought with full force by progressives and traditionalists alike, who tried to show how hazardous the IQ was as a measurement and who also argued that even accurate IQs were not fixed and changeless but were very much influenced by educational opportunity. Bagley, for instance, conducted studies showing a high correlation between IQ points and educational opportunity (Cremin, 1961). Bagley (1925), made it clear that the results of IQ tests spoke not for educational restriction, but for educational opportunity (see the Scholarly Voices feature that recounts Dewey's perspective on measurement).

Dewey offered similar argumentation to the problem of the IQ test. Dewey feared that the teacher might see IQ measures as complete and final statements of a student's ability to learn. He saw children as always in the state of becoming, of growing and developing. This was his faith as an educator, to be more concerned about what might be than what is. "At all events," observed Dewey (1928), "quality of activity and of consequence is more important for the teacher than any quantitative element" (p. 174).

In the end, those who supported efficiency strategies in the curriculum helped to bring several new elements to bear on the school. A new trend toward specificity was initiated as was an accompanying trend for measurement and objective-driven action in the school. In these developments lay the foundation for later competency-based or mastery-learning designs in the curriculum.

FIGURE 3.1

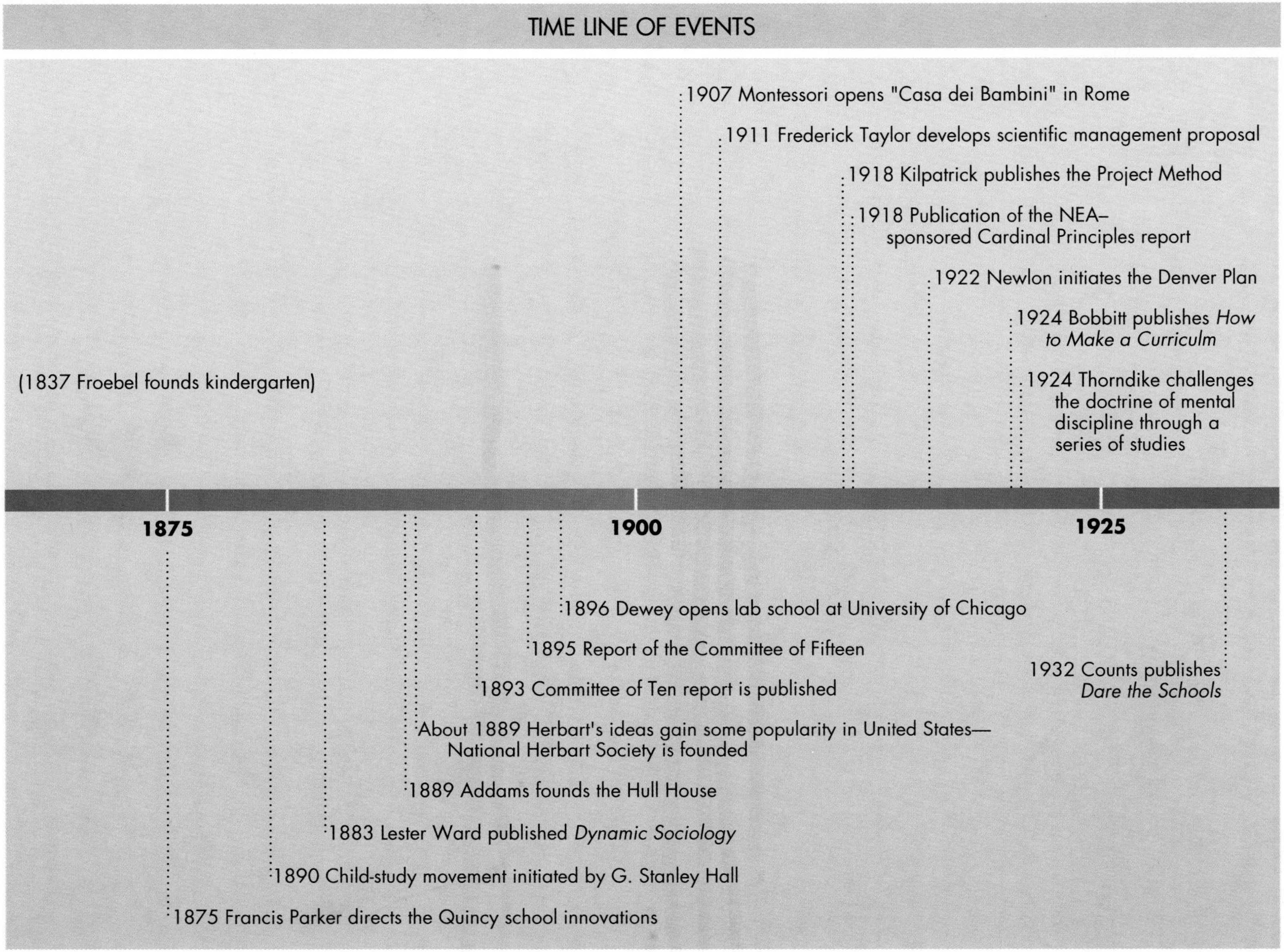

TIME LINE OF EVENTS

(1837 Froebel founds kindergarten)

1875 Francis Parker directs the Quincy school innovations

1875

1890 Child-study movement initiated by G. Stanley Hall

1883 Lester Ward published *Dynamic Sociology*

1889 Addams founds the Hull House

About 1889 Herbart's ideas gain some popularity in United States—National Herbart Society is founded

1893 Committee of Ten report is published

1895 Report of the Committee of Fifteen

1896 Dewey opens lab school at University of Chicago

1900

1907 Montessori opens "Casa dei Bambini" in Rome

1911 Frederick Taylor develops scientific management proposal

1918 Kilpatrick publishes the Project Method

1918 Publication of the NEA–sponsored Cardinal Principles report

1922 Newlon initiates the Denver Plan

1924 Bobbitt publishes *How to Make a Curriculum*

1924 Thorndike challenges the doctrine of mental discipline through a series of studies

1925

1932 Counts publishes *Dare the Schools*

KEY TERMS

Cardinal Principles Report of 1918

Experimentalism

Hull House

Job analysis

Life situations

Quincy Methods

Reconstruction of experience

Scientific management

Settlement houses

Social efficiency

Social occupations

Social reconstructionism

KEY QUESTIONS

1. Describe in general terms what Dewey supported as the main factors in the educative process.

2. How did the scientific method relate to Dewey's ideas about learning?

3. Dewey balanced his regard for change with an equal regard for conservation through a sense of commonality. Explain this position.

4. Explain Dewey's curriculum experiment with social occupations. Why was he attracted to using social occupations as focal points in the curriculum?

5. What were some of the main principles of American pragmatism and how did they inform Dewey's thinking?

6. What was Lester Ward's main contribution to the progressive movement?

7. What were settlement houses and how did they fit into Lester Ward's thinking about school and society?

8. Why do you think Dewey called Francis Parker the "father of progressive education?"

9. What was the essential difference between the way that Parker and the way that Dewey saw the agency of public education?

10. Explain the curriculum revision work done in the Denver schools under the leadership of Jesse Newlon.

11. Why did the Cardinal Principles Report of 1918 represent a proverbial tidal change in the way that high school education was conceived?

12. Explain the social reconstructionism of George Counts and describe how Dewey and others criticized it.

13. What was scientific management and how did it relate to the development of the school curriculum?

14. What was the main rationale behind the use of job analysis in the curriculum?

15. How did Thorndike help to erase the dominance of mental discipline as a learning doctrine, and in what way was such a development helpful to Franklin Bobbitt and the method of job analysis?

16. What were Boyd Bode's main complaints about the work of Bobbitt?

17. Who was Joseph Rice, and how did his work contribute to the rise of scientific management procedures in the school?

18. How did the priorities of social efficiency set a favorable condition for the rise of educational measurement in schools?

19. Explain how the development of IQ testing led to curriculum differentiation and educational restrictionism.

20. What were some of Dewey's fears about the use of IQ scores in public education?

REFERENCES

Adams, C. F. (1969). The Development of the Superintendency. In D. H. Calhoun, *Educating of Americans: A documentary history.* Boston: Houghton-Mifflin Co. (Original work published in 1881).

Bagley, W. (1925). *Determinism in education.* Baltimore: Warwick and York.

Bobbitt, J. F. (1913). The supervision of city schools: Some general principles of management applied to the problems of city-school systems. *Twelfth yearbook of the National Society for the Study of Education* (Part I). Bloomington, IL: Public School Publishing Co.

Bobbitt, J. F. (1918). *The curriculum.* Boston: Houghton-Mifflin Co.

Bobbitt, J. F. (1924). *How to make a curriculum.* Boston: Houghton-Mifflin Co.

Bode, B. H. (1927). *Modern educational theories.* New York: Macmillan.

Bode, B. H. (1938). *Progressive education at the crossroads.* New York: Newson and Co.

Boydston, J. A. (Ed.). (1979). *The complete works of John Dewey.* Carbondale: Southern Illinois University Press.

Butts, R. F. (1978) Public education in the United States. N.Y.: Holt, Rinehart and Winston.

Butts, R. F. (1955). *A cultural history of Western education*. New York: McGraw-Hill Book Co.

Callahan, R. E. (1962). *Education and the cult of efficiency*. Chicago: Phoenix Books, the University of Chicago Press.

Childs, J. (1956). *American pragmatism and education*. New York: Henry Holt and Co.

Commission on the Reorganization of Secondary Education. (1918). *The Cardinal Principles of secondary education*. Washington, DC: U.S. Government Printing Office.

Counts, G. S. (1922). *The selective character of American secondary education*. Chicago: University of Chicago Press.

Counts, G. S. (1927). *The social composition of boards of education*. Chicago: University of Chicago Press.

Counts, G. S. (1932). *Dare the schools build a new social order?* New York: The John Day Co.

Cremin, L. A. (1988). *American Education: The metropolitan experience 1876–1980*. New York: Harper and Row.

Cremin, L. A. (1961). *The transformation of the school*. New York: Alfred A. Knopf.

Dewey, J. (1902). *The child and the curriculum*. Chicago: University of Chicago Press.

Dewey, J. (1902a). *The school and society*. Chicago: University of Chicago Press.

Dewey, J. (1916). *Democracy and education*. New York: Macmillan.

Dewey, J. (1928). Progressive education and the science of education. In R. D. Archambault (Ed), *John Dewey on education*. New York: The Modern Library.

Dewey, J., & Dewey, E. (1915). *Schools of tomorrow*. New York: Dutton.

Dworkin, Martin. (1954). *Dewey on education*. New York: Teachers College Press.

Finney, R. L. (1928). *A sociological philosophy of education*. New York: Macmillan.

Kliebard, H. M. (1986). *The struggle for the American curriculum*. New York: Routledge and Kegan.

Lagemann, E. (1985). *Jane Addams on education*. New York: Teachers College Press.

Mayhew, K. C., & Edwards, A. C. (1936). *The Dewey school*. New York: Atherton Press.

Morris, C. (1970). *The pragmatic movement in American philosophy*. New York: George Braziller Inc.

Newlon, J. (1927). Curriculum development in the Denver schools. In H. O. Rugg (Ed.), *Twenty-sixth yearbook of the National Society for the Study of Education* (Part I: Curriculum making: Past and present). Bloomington, IL: Public School Publishing Co.

Rice, J. M. (1969). *The public school system of the United States*. New York: Arno Press. (Original work published in 1893).

Rugg, H. O. (Ed.). (1927). *Twenty-sixth yearbook of the National Society for the Study of Education* (Part I: Curriculum making: Past and present). Bloomington, IL: Public School Publishing Co.

Snedden, D. (1914, May). Vocational education. *The New Republic, 3,* 40–42.

Tanner, D., & Tanner, L. N. (1990). *The history of the school curriculum*. New York: Macmillan.

Taylor, F. W. (1911). *The principles of scientific management*. New York: Harper and Brothers.

Thorndike, E. L. (1924). Mental discipline in high school studies. *Journal of Educational Psychology 15,* 1–22, 82–98.

Ward, L. (1883). *Dynamic sociology*. New York: D. Appleton.

Wirth, A. (1989). *John Dewey as educator*. Landam, MD: University Press of America.

Wraga, W. G. (1994). *Democracy's high school*. Landam, MD: University Press of America.

PART TWO

THE SCHOOL AND SOCIETY

The conception of education as a social process and function has no definite meaning until we define the kind of society we have in mind. John Dewey

4

THE STRUCTURE OF
AMERICAN EDUCATION

Jenlane Gee of Modesto, California, stands in front of a door. For a good part of her day, she is the teacher in the classroom behind that door. The ease with which she stands, her dress, and her soft smile indicate to us that she is a teacher.

As this chapter explores the structure of American schools, it is interesting to note how much of schooling is taken for granted. Schools, of course, did not simply appear. It took time for schools to take their present shape. For example, the general movement from elementary school to high school and on to college or university is taken for granted. But how did such a system begin?

The structure of schools is related to the way they are funded. This chapter examines the important but often misunderstood issue of school funding. Finally, the issue of religion in a diverse and often contentious society is raised. The division between church and state is clearly stated in the U.S. Constitution, but the specific meaning of this division is still unclear and must often be addressed in the highest courts.

The organization of the American school has historically been built on a relationship between state and local jurisdictions. Early state laws gave school districts the liberty to conduct themselves as they wished. But as the nation developed and as the teaching profession began to inherit a theoretical foundation, states became more adamant about the establishment of public schools in district areas and more focused about how such schools should go about educating youth. As discussed, Horace Mann set the historical model for the state supervision of local schooling during his tenure as the first secretary of education in Massachusetts. But the very notion of giving the steerage of the school to the state is rooted in the Massachusetts laws of 1642 and 1647. The legislators of the Massachusetts Bay Colony were the first to mandate public education, the first to require the maintenance of town schools, and the first to use public taxes for public school appropriations.

The early pattern for the place of the federal government in the governance of the school was decided in the 1791 ratification of the 10th Amendment to the Constitution, which essentially gave states full powers in the operation of the public schools. Although the Constitution delegated no duties to the federal government in the arena of public education, the federal government still had a role to play through legislation. In fact, the nature of federal intervention in schooling was given an early precedent when Congress drafted the Land Ordinance of 1785, which demanded that federal grants of land be contingent on the parceling of land for local public schools. Here the federal government was enacting the legislation drafted by Congress and was promoting the general welfare of the nation by encouraging public schools without stipulating what such schools should be like (Cremin, 1951).

CHAPTER OUTLINE

Grade and School Level Orientations

The American system of education, which is structurally organized as one path (or one ladder) from kindergarten to college, did not come into existence overnight. In the 18th century, there were no graded public schools in America. Dame schools and common elementary town schools were largely ungraded and made no effort to articulate with more advanced schools, such as the Latin grammar schools or the Academies (Douglas & Greider, 1948). In other words, the elementary school simply did not flow curricularly into the secondary school; they were not component parts of one larger unit. But as the nation took on a national identity, so did the school, and the establishment of the graded educational ladder gave the whole system a unified focus (see Figure 4.1).

Most American public schools use grade levels to organize instruction, but the grade pattern that comprises each school district varies (Jones, Salisbury, & Spencer, 1969). Many school districts use a 6/3/3 configuration, which includes 7 years of elementary school (counting kindergarten), 3 years of **junior high school,** and 3 years of high school. Increasingly, however, school districts are recognizing the value of a **middle school,** as opposed to a junior high school, for the education of preadolescents. School districts so inclined lean toward the adoption of a 4/4/4 or 5/3/4 pattern, which often results in the placement of the ninth grade in high school and the sixth grade in middle school.

Middle schools were developed in response to the accusation that junior high schools were little more than imitations of senior high schools (Tanner, 1972). Middle schools reawakened the spirit of the preadolescent in the curriculum by promising to provide learning experiences less wrapped up with college bound concerns and more directly committed to exploratory, enrichment, and general education opportunities. The junior high school, which was originally rationalized as a transition or intermediate institution between the **self-contained classroom** setting of elementary school and the departmentalized setting of the senior high school, had failed to become a distinctive institution for preadolescents. Moving the course work for the ninth grade out of the intermediate grades was significant because ninth-grade course work counted toward admission to college and provided a departmentalizing pressure on the curriculum. Similarly, moving the sixth grade into the middle school setting better captured the developmental period of preadolescence. This way the middle school could explore curriculum options attuned to the early adolescent. It could stress interdisciplinary themes, exploratory learnings, and more multiage grouping strategies (Wiles & Bondi, 1993).

For every rule in American education, there are always notable exceptions. Because the American schools are designed for **decentralized governance** (without a single federal or national authority), it is difficult to draw a generalization about American schooling. The structural configurations discussed here are by no means universal. Small rural districts might organize their schools with a 6/6 configuration, and where the population is especially small, the district might adopt one unified K-12 setting. Moreover, the manner in which a school district structures its grade levels may have nothing to do with pedagogical principles, but rather with the size of its facilities and its enrollment distributions across age levels.

There are, however, some common threads. For instance, with few exceptions, school districts recognize the divisions of elementary, middle or

FIGURE 4.1

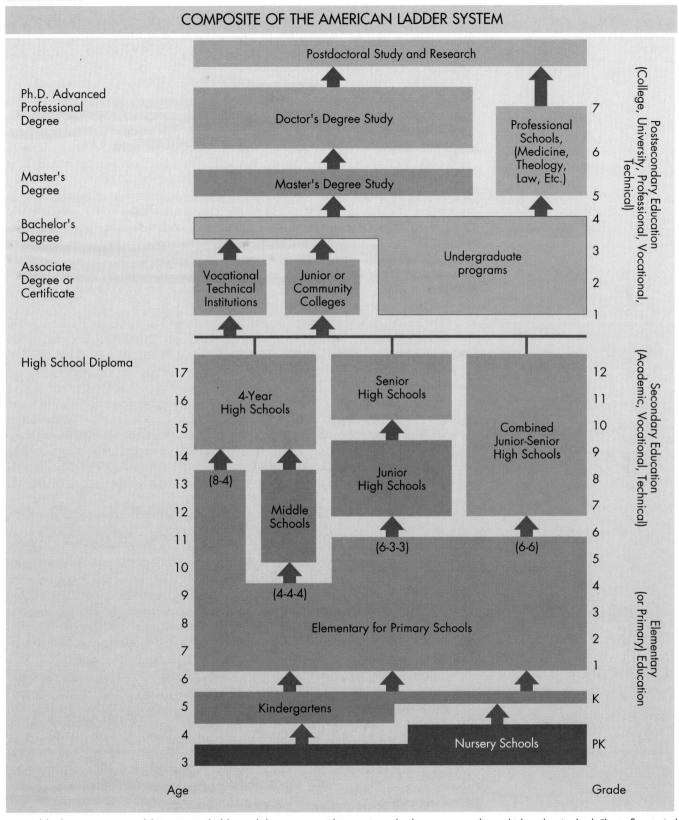

COMPOSITE OF THE AMERICAN LADDER SYSTEM

Note: Adult education programs, while not separately delineated above, may provide instruction at the elementary, secondary, or higher education level. Chart reflects typical patterns of progression rather than all possible variations.

Source: National Center for Education Statistics. (1995). *Digest of education statistics* (p. 7). Washington, DC: U.S. Department of Education.

intermediate, and secondary schools. In recognizing these distinctions, they also recognize the pedagogical orientation of each division. Thus, while the secondary school and the junior high schools have, historically speaking, been openly departmentalized in the manner that they have structured teaching, elementary schools and the new middle schools have been less inclined toward departmentalization.

Much teaching at the elementary school continues to be treated through rather traditional subject lines (math, science, language arts, and so on), but the actual makeup of an elementary school classroom is often self-contained, meaning that one educator is responsible for teaching all the standard academic areas in one heterogeneously grouped classroom. Because elementary education does not need to be too concerned with college preparation, it can be more attendant to interdisciplinary studies. Moreover, the child development strategy in elementary education sees the classroom as a miniature society, where young people learn about each other, about basic principles of cooperation, and about other standards of group living. Elementary schools are designed to be responsive to the developmental tasks of early, middle, and late childhood. They center on social adjustment, physical development, an awareness of self, academic readiness, and sensory development (Wiles & Bondi, 1993). Subject-centered learning should not be a major consideration.

The self-contained classroom design used in elementary schools is ideal for group-centered learning that promotes interdisciplinary learnings, but it has always been criticized for its failure to deal properly with individual variations. Critics have argued that by putting a heterogeneous group of youth together in one room, the self-contained classroom has no good way of dealing with individual talents and skills. The classroom is said to follow the pace of the slowest learner, thereby compromising the education of the more academically inclined students. Because of this concern, grouping procedures have become quite popular in self-contained settings, especially in the elementary subjects of reading and mathematics. Grouping, of course, has its advantages and disadvantages, but it should be made clear that intraclass grouping is a practice different from ability-based interclass grouping, something also known as curriculum tracking, an issue discussed in the next chapter.

In some school districts, the self-contained system in the elementary schools has been abandoned in favor of departmentalization. Today, some elementary schools are teaching children within an organizational scheme that is not unlike what one might expect at a high school level. Specialized teachers are teaching specialized subjects, sometimes in ability-grouped settings. In elementary schools employing specialized teachers, sometimes there is an effort to temper the arrangement by using heterogeneous groups taught by a team of teachers, sometimes known as a house or unit. This team-teaching arrangement allows for collaborative curriculum planning and some articulation across the subjects and grades.

Middle schools have, by and large, featured curriculum designs that are more like the self-contained elementary schools than the high schools in that they aim at connections between subject areas for the purpose of providing integrated and sociocentered learning opportunities. Like the elementary school, the middle school is not under direct college preparatory pressures. Under ideal circumstances, the curriculum in the middle school should take good account of the psychosocial development of the early adolescent and deal with items related to health, social responsibility, basic communication, and human relation skills. The development of more complex thinking skills should be center stage because, developmentally speaking, many preadolescents are just entering the Piagetian stage of formal operations, which stresses hypothetical thinking. The academic subject areas of the curriculum should not be disciplinary but should aim at sociopersonal issues that speak to life interests, peer relations, questions of social identity, and the like. Exploratory learning should be valued as a way to open the world up to the preadolescent and to develop early interests in various new ideas and subjects.

At the secondary school level, public education follows two different styles. Many high schools are known as comprehensive institutions, meaning that they provide educational programs for both college- and noncollege-bound students in a unified setting. The purpose of the **comprehensive high school** is to provide comprehensive learning experiences for all youth. College preparatory programs are offered to college-preparatory youth and vocational programs are offered to students destined for work. All youth, however, are given opportunities in exploratory, enrichment, and general education programs, with the latter representing sociocivic learnings in common heterogeneous settings (see chapter 9). The other secondary school form is the **specialized high school,** which, depending on the school, offers specialized training in a particular academic or vocational area. Specialized vocational schools, in fact, are popular in some states. Specialized magnet schools, which can offer unique academic or trade programs for students, are growing in stature and popularity in school districts, especially in large urban districts.

School Governance

Today, three interrelated sources govern the ladder system of American education: the federal government, the state government, and the local school board. The legal governance of the school falls entirely into the hands of the state. Each state conducts its schools as it sees fit, as long as it abides by the laws of the nation. Thus, in effect, 50 states translate into 50 systems of education. Although each state is, of course, influenced by nationalizing factors reaching down from the federal government and the national media, there is no centralized national control of education. The public school system in the United States is among the few in the world to be governed by an open decentralized system. Other advanced nations, such as Japan and most of the European nations, have central ministries of education that dictate national policy and practice for schooling.

Ultimately, state legislatures are responsible for the public schools. They authorize funding and contemplate legislative support for the schools. But most of the actual day-to-day supervision of the state system is done by a state-level board of education. All the states in America, except one, have **state boards of education.** Their services extend into the areas of policy development, school personnel, budget appropriations, curriculum, and the law. Among other duties, state boards of education appoint and supervise the chief state officer, or **state superintendent,** of education, manage budgetary appropriations for school spending, fashion licensure regulations for the preparation of teachers, establish standards for accrediting schools, enforce

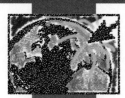

School Districts on the Internet

As more school districts establish a presence on the Internet, anyone interested will be able to find out about a particular school district's location, student population, and even ongoing special projects. At this time, however, only a handful of school districts have developed an extensive web site. We have chosen to highlight the Spring Branch Independent School District, a mid-urban district in Houston, Texas. Spring Branch's web site is home to several links that represent the common structure of many U.S. schools. For instance, the superintendent has a home page welcoming the browser to the district's web site and other background information. Other links lead to the district's mission statement and the strategic plan. Yet another link takes the browser to a page listing the school board members.

The browser may also choose to visit the home pages of specific schools, where some of the principals of those schools have their own home pages. Several schools have enhanced their web site, describing special projects at the school. And at some schools, individual students have developed their own web site.

As you examine Spring Branch's web site and others on our home page, is the common hierarchy of the school represented? Is the division between the school administration and the schools themselves made clear?

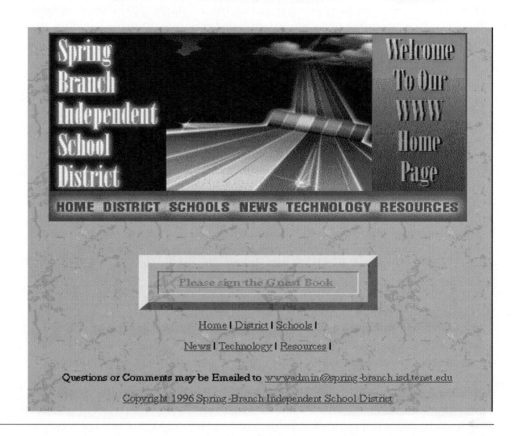

compliance to state school laws, provide an annual report on educational progress, and distribute funds from state and federal coffers to various local districts. In some states, the state board of education might be more interventionist than in others. In Texas, for instance, the state board is involved in appointing a committee to screen school textbooks for the purpose of identifying an adoption list from which schools can make selections; it also tries to supervise the instruction offered by schoolteachers in each local school district with a statewide model of pedagogy, and, at one time, required a basic literacy examination be taken by all the state's professional educators.

In most states, the governor appoints the members of the state board, but in 15 states, membership is by popular vote, and in five states, the legislature appoints the school board. The board commonly consists of lay people. Membership rarely requires being a professional educator.

The chief officer of the state, who can also be either appointed or elected (depending on the state), takes much of his or her charge from the state board of education, especially if he or she is an appointed official. Frequently the chief officer is also the executive chairperson of the state board. The chief officer, often known as the state superintendent, makes the decisions on appointments in the state department, offers budgetary and legislative recommendations to the state board, and is responsible for determining the status and the needs for public education, particularly as they relate to improving the conditions of schooling. The state superintendent is also responsible for the function of the state department of education, which often operationalizes the work of the state board by helping to regulate teacher certification, school accreditation, attendance, and finance. The state department is often active in compiling statistical data on the schools. It is the main administrative agency for education in the state.

The chief school officer is an elected position in 18 states and an appointed position in the remaining states. The appointment can come from the state board of education or from the governor, which represents two sides of the same coin because the governor also appoints boards of education in such states.

Often overlooked is the power that the state governor has in this arrangement of authority. Usually, the governor appoints the state superintendent of education and the state board of education. The governor also approves the state school budget, proposes bills to the legislature, vetoes bills brought forward by the legislature, and uses the office as a platform for the promotion of reform. During the 1980s, governors became active in the school reform movement. Because the Reagan administration abhorred the idea of federal intervention in schooling and tried to reduce the federal presence in education, the state governors took up the torch for reform and responded with a consolidated effort that led to widespread institutional changes in the practice of the school (U.S. Department of Education, 1984). With federal programs being slashed, more monetary and program responsibilities were being placed on the shoulders of state governors. The governors targeted everything from the length of the school day to the nature of teacher certification.

Every public school is, of course, part of a local school district arrangement, and in this sense, local communities still have an important voice in their schools. In fact, one can consider the local district the basic administrative unit for the implementation of state policy. But the local district is an agent of the state, essentially sanctioned by the state to carry out its functions. The state can intervene virtually as it wishes in the action of the local school. It can change its boundaries, authorize an evaluation of its curriculum, or if warranted, entirely usurp its governing powers.

There were in 1930 well over 120,000 school districts in America. By 1950, the number dropped to about 80,000 districts, and today the number stands at about 15,000. The dramatic reduction in the number of districts has been the result of consolidation. Various legislative and monetary inducements have been used to influence districts to accept consolidation as a means of providing a more resourceful and comprehensive education.

Each local district also has its own **local school board,** which again, depending on the district, might be appointed or elected, although the overwhelming majority are elected. Given the history of the relation between the state and local district, local school decision making is frequently given wide latitude. Local school boards need to be compliant to state requirements, especially, for instance, in areas of institutional regulation. State laws and regulations might specify the length of the school year, the standards of preparation required of teachers, minimal teacher salaries, required subject areas to be taught, the forms of tax that can be used, and other essential aspects of the school's operation. But within this framework of regulations, the local school district usually has ample opportunity to influence practice in ways that are honest to its own prerogatives. Local school boards, after all, authorize the monies to be raised through local taxes. They hire the district superintendent of schools, and they make all the decisions related to personnel and property. Within certain boundaries, local school boards are

As governor of Arkansas, Bill Clinton was a powerful voice for Goals 2000, the governors' education initiative. In this 1989 photograph, Former President George Bush, Iowa Governor Branstad and Clinton share a moment of bipartisan unite.

expected to plan local school policy and ultimately to appraise the work of their personnel, especially the superintendent. They approve budgets, determine schools and attendance boundaries within the district, enter into labor negotiations, and make numerous decisions about the curriculum. Their work, however, is not administrative. They are charged with the formation of policy, not the implementation of policy.

The actual implementation of the local board's policy wishes is typically delegated to the superintendent of schools. But, as a professional educator, the superintendent also acts in an advisory capacity to local districts in the area of policy (Tanner, 1972). As the chief officer of the school district, the school superintendent makes recommendations to the board on various fronts, including appointment of personnel, drafting of labor policies, curriculum reform actions, physical plant issues, and public relations concerns. The local school superintendent is also responsible for submitting a budget to the board for its analysis and eventual approval.

The idea of the local school district is distinctively American; it is a function of the unique history of the United States. Advocates of localism have hailed the idea of keeping the school close to the people. Local school control, however, also carries its share of problems. As we will find, the district system tends to lead to funding inequities between schools, a problem that has stymied many states. And too often local school boards overstep their responsibilities and attempt to micromanage their schools, which sometimes results in the promotion of narrow political or even religious agendas in the school. The state, of course, oversees these actions and can apply remedies. Nevertheless, these problems still find their way into the courts and often prove costly to schoolchildren.

The federal government also has a place in the governance of the school. Historically, the character of its intervention has been to carry out any federal legislation related to the functioning of the school, which has frequently meant providing monies to schools through federal programs sanctioned by Congress. The federal government also has the duty of evaluating the status of American education at the national level. The federal role, however, has little jurisdiction in the area of policy or practice.

Most of the action of the federal government has been operationalized through the **Department of Education** and a cabinet-level **secretary of education** (see the Web Points feature on the department in this section). The secretary can influence the course of education by speaking from the bully pulpit, which can influence the course of debate and discussion in educational circles as well as the course of media coverage related to education. The Department of Education and its secretary also oversee the Office of Educational Research and Improvement, which assumes all of the main responsibilities for the analysis and reported progress of achievement among American schoolchildren. This office conducts the National Assessment of Educational Progress (NAEP), which provides a national glimpse at the level of understanding and competence achieved by students in various subject areas, including math, science, reading, and writing.

Historically, the federal government has had a very visible position in the development of the public school. Among its more prominent initiatives has been the Morrill Act of 1862, which was largely responsible for the development of the nation's state universities, and the Smith-Hughes Act of 1917, which provided massive funding for the support of vocational education in secondary education. More recently, the federal government has sponsored

Eliminating the Department of Education

Here is a campaign statement popularized by Lamar Alexander during the 1996 primary presidential elections. Alexander wanted to eliminate the Department of Education "in order to liberate parents and schools." What are some of the ways that the Department of Education might get in the way of schools and parents? Do you agree that the Department of Education is an unnecessary agency?

Abolish the Department of Education in order to liberate parents and schools. On January 26, I testified before the U.S. Congress and argued that it should take each activity currently housed in the Department of Education and do one of three things with it: (a) send it home to states and communities; (b) entrust it to another federal agency; or (c) terminate it and return the money to the taxpayers. I've been looking at this issue for more than 15 years and I am convinced that the people in a position to know what is best for education are those closest to the child. Education policy should be geared toward giving parents and teachers more control over what goes on in the classroom.

the GI Bills, which have supported the cost of postsecondary education for military veterans; the National Science Foundation, which has historically shown a presence in the area of math and science education; the National Defense Education Act of 1958, which funneled federal monies for the improvement of instruction in math, science, and foreign language instruction and for the development of early instructional technologies; the Elementary and Secondary Act of 1965, which targeted the education of children in low-income brackets; the National Merit Scholarship program, which recognized and supported the most academically talented students in the country; and a host of initiatives dealing with special education, bilingual education, vocational education, and compensatory education. Various areas of the federal government, including the Departments of Defense, Justice, the Interior, and Labor, have also, at one time or another, provided federal education programs for youth at some level of the educational ladder. Lamar Alexander, former secretary of education and a candidate for U.S. president in 1996, argued for the elimination of the Department of Education. See The Contemporary Debate feature in this section for his comments.

Funding Public Education

The way that the educational system is funded is of obvious importance. Money is not everything, but without adequate levels of support, most schools cannot offer resourceful experiences to children.

The education of the American schoolchild is supported by taxes paid for by the adult citizens of the nation. Such taxes, in most cases, are drawn from some combination of local, state, and federal sources. In general, the average breakdown is about evenly split between local and state revenues. The local district and the state each take on between 40% and 50% of the funding

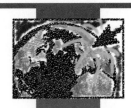

The Department of Education

An excellent web site for educators is the U.S. Department of Education's main page. The top page address is:

http://www.ed.gov/

This web site features the National Center for Education Statistics (NCES) data page, which maintains data on several major school achievement projects. In addition, the site reprints some of their more popular reports. Relevant to the work of this chapter is the document, "Educational Progress of Women," which suggests that the large gaps in educational attainment between men and women have essentially disappeared. However, despite their gains in educational attainment, female college graduates earn, on average, 20 percent less than their male counterparts.

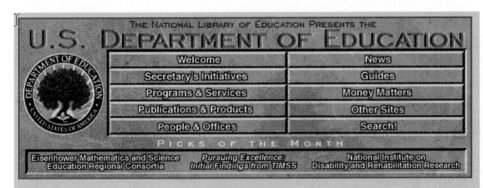

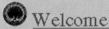

obligation, although in some states, such as Hawaii, there is full state funding and in others, such as New Hampshire, there is heavy reliance on locally raised revenues. Across the nation, the federal government averages less than 10% of the full funding composite.

The typical pattern for financial support in the schools follows the governance structure discussed earlier. The state creates the local school districts and authorizes levy taxes to raise funds for the support of public schools. The local district raises these funds through property taxes. Obviously, the value of real estate properties will affect how successful a district might be in finding the proper level of financial support. The basic capacity of a local school district to raise monies for the school is always a function of the property wealth of the district combined with the tax burden or tax effort that the community is willing to accept. There are often remarkable disparities in spending between different local districts that the state is responsible for closing.

Differences in funding at the local level usually result from differences in the amount and the value of local commercial and residential property. A district wealthy in property value can raise more revenue for its students, and often at a lower tax rate, than a property-poor district. When local districts have no state restrictions over their school budgets, the differences in spending between high- and low-spending districts can reach mind-boggling proportions, as in some states where the highest spending districts had a per pupil expenditure rate eight times greater than the lowest spending district.

Although the local district has to rely almost exclusively on property taxes, states can turn to other sources for revenue. Each state is different, but typically state revenue systems are a combination of general sales taxes, personal income taxes, and corporate taxes. Recently, state lotteries have also become popular fund-raising mechanisms. Once the state collects its money for public education, it has to have a way of deciding how each district will get its share of the revenues. Because one of the functions of the state is to help equalize differences in per pupil expenditures across school districts, districts that are less wealthy and less able to invest large sums of money in education are supposed to find relief from the state. Many states tackle this problem with a **minimal provision philosophy** toward finance that maintains a required minimal baseline investment in a school district. The baseline represents a commitment of money that supposedly ensures an adequate education for youth in the state (Guthrie, Garms, & Pierce, 1988).

For several decades now, several lawsuits have been filed against state systems of funding. In 1973, the U.S. Supreme Court heard the case of

State sponsored lotteries have become part of the national character. The money they earn for states, however, rarely amounts to much of the public school budget.

PART TWO: THE SCHOOL AND SOCIETY

Rodriguez v. the San Antonio Independent School District, in which the plaintiffs charged that the inequities in the funding of the local schools violated their children's equal protection guarantees under the 14th Amendment to the Constitution. The plaintiffs argued that the funding extremes were illegal because they failed to secure equal educational opportunities. The Supreme Court, however, did not accept the plaintiffs' argument and upheld the Texas system of funding, observing that absolute equity between the districts was not required, and that, while children in poorer districts were likely getting an inferior education to children in wealthy districts, they were still getting an adequate education. The effect of this ruling placed the question of funding in the states' courts, and it was not long before a major court challenge arose, this time in California, in a 1974 case known as *Serrano v. Priest.* This time, however, the California State Supreme Court pronounced the system of financing its schools to be in violation of the state's constitution. This ruling precipitated a national round of lawsuits against various states, resulting in widespread state legislative measures to ensure more equitable forms of spending across districts (Munley, 1993).

Historically, when states began to give money to districts, their thinking was that each district, irrespective of its local investment, should be given a flat rate grant of money that would provide enough of a monetary base for a minimal education (Swanson & King, 1991). These grants were known as **flat grant programs.** Schools spending in excess of the flat rate were believed to be indulging in a luxury that was their right. But the minimal guarantees of an adequate education were thought to be supported under this scheme; basic equalization, in this sense, was upheld. The problem, of course, was that minimal support was an arbitrary amount, especially since the conditions of learning across city and rural landscapes vary so widely. Some schools, moreover, were already vested with local monies at a rate well above the flat grant line drawn by the state. Because the flat grant provided a level bed of money on which each district could depend, it had little impact on the variance in spending seen across districts. Flat grant programs were eventually abandoned by the states in favor of what is known as **foundation programs.**

The foundation program is also driven by a minimal provision philosophy, but it is a wiser way of setting an adequate minimal level of funding for each school district (see Figure 4.2). As with the flat grant program, the foundation program sets a minimal funding level that represents what each district will need in order to provide an adequate education. At the same time, it requires each district to levy a property tax at a fixed rate. If a property-rich local district meets the baseline or foundational figure with its local monies, it receives nothing from the state, but if a less wealthy district falls short of this figure, the state provides the difference. The architects of this program also designed a recapture clause that required any districts spending above the foundational level to return those monies to the state for redistribution (Guthrie, Garms, & Pierce, 1988). Few states, however, have been willing to add this clause, arguing that a property-rich district cannot be so compelled. Under the foundation program, the state does not provide money to districts spending above the minimal line, and it can set a minimal investment level at a considerably higher rate than what was possible with flat grants.

The problem, however, is that the local funding disparities are so wide that many states cannot afford to bring the lower districts up to a competitive level. Furthermore, the state responsibility in closing the funding gap is

FIGURE 4.2

FLAT GRANT AND FOUNDATION FUNDING STRUCTURES

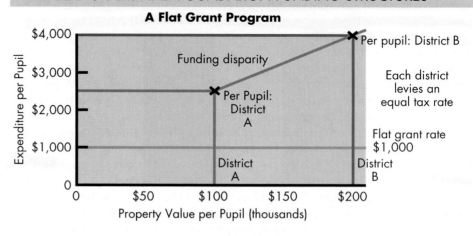

A Flat Grant Program

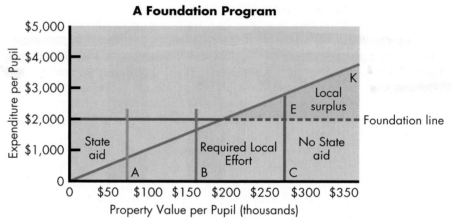

A Foundation Program

Source: Guthrie, J. W., Garms, W. I., & Pierce, L.C. (1988). *School finance and education policy* (pp. 134, 136). Englewood Cliffs, NJ: Prentice-Hall.

typically to ensure that students in lower spending districts receive a fair and basic education, which means that they aim at a minimal compensation figure rather than at a full and comprehensive one. In Montana, litigation was filed against the state for operating a foundation program that equalized at a level below the average spending of districts. But even if average levels were met, the poorest districts would still be at a disadvantage because in most cases their needs and problems are not average. In many cases, the problems emanating from poverty make education in such places more costly, often requiring an above-average investment. Moreover, each school district, irrespective of its wealth, will usually receive some funds from the federal government, often because of categorical aid programs that designate monies for special purposes (like the education of the handicapped or the education of students from low-income backgrounds). These also have a disequalizing effect (Guthrie, Garms, & Pierce, 1988).

The state usually handles somewhere between 40% to 50% of the total budgetary commitment to public schooling. These monies are typically drawn from sales and income taxes, but many states are also engaging in special programs, such as state lotteries, to earmark funding for education.

Although there is quite a bit of variance, on the average 33% of state tax revenue for public schools is from sales or gross receipt tax, 30% from personal income tax, 8% from corporate tax, and the remainder from excise and business taxes. Most states are, as indicated, under increasing pressures to find a way to distribute monies to school districts to equalize the conditions of schooling.

Many states have long looked at equalization as simply a matter of meeting a base or minimal level of funding. But these minimal or foundational provisions are usually not high enough to compete with the dramatic per pupil expenditures that are occurring in property-rich districts. As a result, many states are exploring funding structures that pay school districts monies according to their rank on a scale of wealth, on weighted formula scales that account for the special needs of children in the school districts, and on formulas that provide state aid inversely proportional to the local property wealth (Munley, 1993). Increasingly, there is also talk of full state funding, which means that each state would assume the costs of running each of its school districts. Local revenues, in such a case, would likely become state property and be redistributed on an equitable level. Of course, such a scenario might also result in the forfeiture of local decision making and local preferences and priorities.

Over the past decade, the states have taken a more active hand in the financing of schools (see Figure 4.3). This presence will likely increase since a reliance on state taxes will probably be the only way to equalize the resources of the schools. This fact has been made quite clear in the recent voters' decision in Michigan to opt for what amounts to full state funding of

FIGURE 4.3

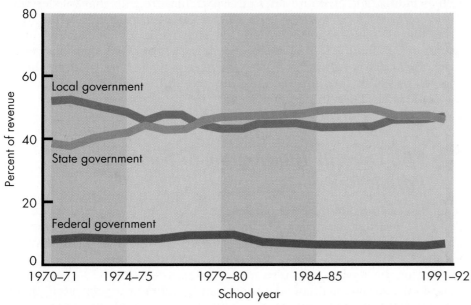

PROPORTIONS OF LOCAL, STATE, AND FEDERAL SCHOOL SPENDING (1970–1990)

Source: National Center for Education Statistics. (1994). *Digest of education statistics* (p. 49). Washington, DC: U.S. Department of Education.

the public schools. The schools in Michigan are no longer dependent on property tax for funding because of the voters' decision to increase the sales tax in the state from 4% to 6% and to triple the tax on cigarettes in exchange for dramatic reductions in the property tax. Under the new funding conditions, all the schools in the state will draw their monies from state coffers and will be guaranteed a minimum investment of $4,200 per student, giving most poor districts in the state about $1,000 more per student than they have been spending.

Michigan, relative to other states, did not have a serious spending gap between the richest and poorest school districts (the range of spending was from about $3,200 to $10,000 per pupil), but the wealthier school districts in the state will now be operating under a state funding cap of about $4,200. This has generated criticism from several school leaders who claim that assistance for the lowest-spending schools should not have to come at the expense of the highest-spending schools. The Michigan plan has also been criticized by the state's teachers union, which believes that a reliance on the sales tax for school funding is dangerously unstable. Because sales revenues fluctuate, there will be years, it claims, when the state's sales revenues will not be able to fund the schools properly. The union petitioned for an increase in the state income tax, instead of the sales tax, arguing that it was more trustworthy. Others have argued that the sales tax is a regressive tax that asks citizens with lesser means to take a disproportionately large share of the burden in funding the schools. What occurred in Michigan may be a sign of the times. As of 1994, 28 states were involved in lawsuits that relate to financing inequities resulting from a reliance on property tax funding (Celis, 1994).

Despite the changes occurring at the state level in school funding, the limited role of the federal government in the economic arrangement of schooling will likely remain in tact. The federal role in school financing is essentially limited to aid enacted by congressional legislation. This includes direct grant programs and compensatory aid for children of poor families, as well as indirect aid given to states or geographical regions that trickles down to school districts. Historically, the federal government has invested in the expansion of educational opportunities, showing a lot of visibility in the education of handicapped children and in the areas of bilingual instruction and compensatory education. It has also been active where there has been a compelling national defense interest and where the economic livelihood of the country has been in question.

 ## The Overall Investment in American Education

Much has been made in the popular media regarding the overall investment that the United States makes in public education. Most of the coverage has promoted the belief that the United States outspends all other advanced nations.

During the Reagan administration, spokespersons in the Department of Education tried to show how the American investment in education, though high, had little to show for it, especially in terms of achievement. Chester Finn (1991), for instance, observed that "solid analysis has shown that there is no reliable relationship between school spending and pupil achievement"

(p. 77). Although Finn is not necessarily saying that money does not matter, he believes that spending has diminishing results at current levels of investment, that much money is being funneled to noninstructional sources, and that we should start to look for ways to make better use of existing monies. One of the problems in Finn's argument, however, is the manner in which he conceives achievement. He equates it with higher norm-referenced test scores, which conceivably can be raised without much investment, through teaching to the test strategies and other test-driven tactics. He also fails to acknowledge the uneven spread of monies across school districts and the strong association that obviously exists between high-spending districts and high-achieving districts. As Kozol (1991) and others indicated, those who claim that more money is marginal to the achievement of schools still send their children to wealthy private schools or public schools with high per pupil expenditures. The uproar over inequities in the funding across school districts itself speaks to the relevance and importance of spending. It is clear, however, that some reform can be conducted in the schools without a huge investment, as we will discuss later (see also The School Experience in Literature feature on Kozol's visit to a Chicago classroom). But a wealthy education is also a resourceful one, and such a thing is difficult to accomplish without a substantive investment.

Of course, if measured with absolute dollars, the United States does spend more on public education than most other nations. Part of this figure is inflated by the extensive commitment that the United States makes to higher education, which, in many others countries, is still a relatively closed institution. But when one examines the financial commitment to public schooling as a percentage of gross domestic product (GDP) from public sources, the United States does not rank high but is in a crowded middle range. The largest shares of GDP (from public sources) dedicated to education are in Hungary and the Nordic nations. The United States, however, stands tall when the GDP also accounts for private sources, though the comparison between nations is not complete because of unreported data on private expenditures in other nations (Center for Educational Research and Innovation, 1993). See Figure 4.4.

Since 1950, the average per pupil expenditure for elementary and secondary education has increased, as indicated in Figure 4.5. As of 1991, the United States led the world in per pupil expenditures levels (only Switzerland spent more). However, when the public funding allocations are analyzed, one finds that the bulk of the funding has been earmarked for special education programs, not regular education programs. Thus, one can argue that the increase in public funding did not have a direct line into the mainstream or regular classroom. It was largely driven by growth in the costs associated with special education and the increasing percentage of students enrolled in special education programs (see Figure 4.6). The investment in regular education, in fact, remained rather flat.

The issue of how school money is being put to use has become an increasingly interesting and controversial one. In New York City, where per pupil expenditure rates level out to about $7,500 a year, the actual allocation to the classroom for instructional purposes comes out to about $2,500, roughly one third of the total expenditure. The remaining amount (about $5,000) goes to building maintenance, security, overhead, counseling, bus contracts, fringe benefits, administration, and the like (Barbanel, 1994). The costs of court-mandated special education programs and special education

Mrs. Hawkins

Mrs. Hawkins is an educator working in the Chicago Public Schools. In *Savage Inequalities,* Jonathan Kozol describes an interaction he had with her that demonstrates how good teachers can indeed elevate the education of children in schools where the resources are greatly limited.

The room looks like a cheerful circus tent. In the center of it all, within the rocking chair, and cradling a newborn in her arms, is Mrs. Hawkins.

The 30 children in the class are seated in groups of six at five of what she calls "departments." Each department is composed of six desks pushed together to create a table. One of the groups is doing math, another something that they call "math strategy." A third is doing reading. Of the other two groups, one is doing something they describe as "mathematics art"—painting composites of geometric shapes—and the other is studying "careers," which on this morning is a writing exercise about successful business leaders who began their lives in poverty. Near the science learning board a young-looking woman is preparing a new lesson that involves a lot of gadgets she has taken from a closet.

"This woman," Mrs. Hawkins tells me, "is a parent. She wanted to help me. So I told her, 'If you don't have somebody to keep your baby, bring the baby here. I'll be the mother. I can do it.' "

As we talk, a boy who wears big glasses brings his book to her and asks her what the word *salvation* means. She shows him how to sound it out, then tells him, "Use your dictionary if you don't know what it means." When a boy at the reading table argues with the boy beside him, she yells out, "You ought to be ashamed. You woke my baby."

After 15 minutes she calls out that it is time to change their tables. The children get up and move to new departments. As each group gets up to move to the next table, one child stays behind to introduce the next group to the lesson.

"This is the point of it," she says. "I'm teaching them three things. Number one: self-motivation. Number two: self-esteem. Number three: you help your sister and your brother. I tell them they're responsible for one another. I give no grades in the first marking period because I do not want them to be too competitive. Second marking period, you get your grade on what you've taught your neighbors at your table. Third marking period, I team them two-and two. You get the same grade as your partner. Fourth marking period, I tell them, 'Every fish swims on its own.' But I wait awhile for that. The most important thing for me is that they teach each other. . . .

"All this stuff"—she gestures at the clutter in the room—"I bought myself because it never works to order things through the school system. I bought the VCR. I bought the rocking chair at a flea market. I got these books here for ten cents apiece at a flea market. I bought that encyclopedia—she points at the row of World Books—"so that they can do their research right here in this room."

I ask her if the class reads well enough to handle these materials. "Most of them can read some of these books. What they cannot read, another child can read to them," she says.

"I tell the parents, 'Any time your child says, "I don't have no homework," call me up. Call me at home.' Because I give them homework every night and weekends too. Holidays I give them extra. Every child in this classroom has my phone."

Cradling the infant in her lap, she says, "I got to buy a playpen."

Source: Kozol, J. (1991) *Savage Inequalities.* New York: Crown Publishing Inc. pp. 48–49.

FIGURE 4.4

EXPENDITURES FOR EDUCATION AS A PERCENTAGE OF GDP (1991)

Chart 1: Primary and secondary education

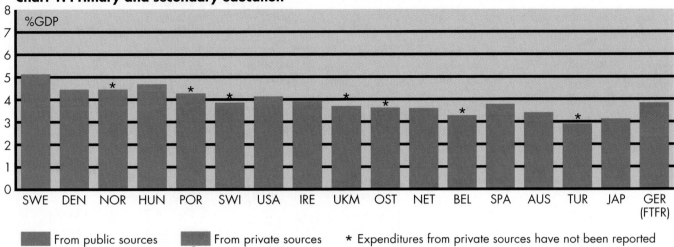

From public sources   From private sources   * Expenditures from private sources have not been reported

Source: Center for Educational Research and Innovation. (1993). *Education at a glance* (p.67). Paris: Organization for Economic Cooperation and Development.

AVERAGE PER PUPIL EXPENDITURE FOR THE UNITED STATES SINCE 1980

FIGURE 4.5

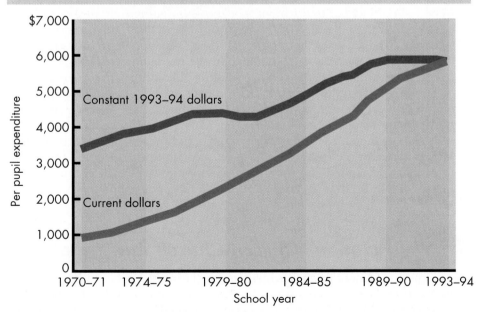

Source: National Center for Education Statistics. (1994). *Digest of education statistics* (p. 49). Washington, DC: U.S. Department of Education.

FIGURE 4.6

TOTAL PUBLIC SCHOOL EXPENDITURES, REGULAR VERSUS SPECIAL EDUCATION STUDENTS

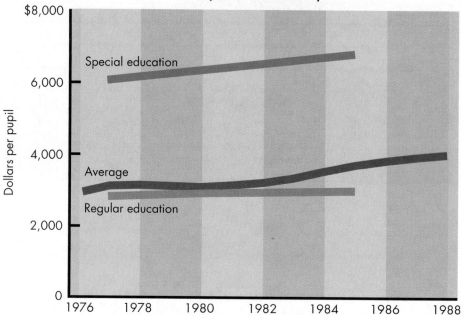

K–12 Current Public Expenditures per Pupil (1987–88 Dollars)

Source: Carson, C. C., Huelskamp, R. M., & Woodall, T. D. (1992). *Perspectives on education in America.* Albuquerque, NM: Prepared by Sandia National Laboratories.

standards of service often take a large bite out of these monies also. The national average for classroom expense is closer to 60% of the school budget ("To Aid U.S. Schools," 1993).

The issue of school investment is a zero-sum game that always calls for difficult decisions in the area of resource allocation. If the building is old and dilapidated, what share of the money should be directed to its improvement? If school security is an issue, should expensive metal detectors be purchased and security guards hired? If the school library's holdings are too low, should more books be bought, or if technological needs are believed to be important, should more computers be purchased? Is a particular inservice program needed for the teachers? And what happens when all the issues implied in these questions need to be dealt with at once and there is not nearly enough to cover the cost of the solutions? Per pupil expenditures never tell the whole story because one needs to know how the monies are being spent and the extent to which the monies are reaching the classroom and child.

 The Relation Between Church and State

One of the fundamental legal principles regulating the relation between the church and the state derives from the First Amendment to the Constitution: "Congress shall make no law respecting an establishment of religion, or prohibiting the exercise thereof. . . ." The purpose of the principle ensures religious freedom for all by protecting against the governmental establishment of any one sectarian view and by protecting against government impairment of any individual's religious expression. The 14th Amendment to the Constitution extended this restriction to state and local governments, including public school districts.

Many scholars have characterized the relation between the church and state as marked by a wall of separation, a metaphor taken from an early Supreme Court decision. As shall be explained, there are indeed important prohibitions against certain religious activity in the school, but the image of a wall of separation between church and state is not completely accurate. Religion has a role in the school curriculum if it maintains an overarching secular purpose, and the free expression right of students in school has to make allowances for religious conviction. Students, for instance, have every right to be excused from school to attend to religious obligations or desires, and with certain qualifications, to be excused from classroom activity if it is viewed by students or parents as offensive to their religion. The school, in a sense, cooperates with the church in the interests of the student's free expression rights (Power, 1991).

Contrary to popular opinion, schools are *not* designed to be religion-free. Although there have been episodes in public schools, especially in the development of curriculum materials, where religion has been systematically and unreasonably culled out of the learning experience (Vitz, 1986; Nord, 1995), many schools have been accommodating to religion. Students, for instance, have the right to pray individually or in groups when attending public school, as long as they do not improperly compel others to do the same and as long as they do not undermine the educative nature of the school experience. Student prayer groups, in fact, enjoy some popularity in the public schools. According to some estimates, 12,000 Bible clubs are operating in American public high schools ("Prayer in Public Schools?" 1994). Students may also carry and read religious material in school and, within certain boundaries, even distribute religious material in school. Some school coaches still like to ask for a pregame or postgame prayer, and many school graduation ceremonies continue to be prayful occasions. Nevertheless, there is quite a bit of confusion regarding the relation between religion and the school. In 1995, President Clinton asked the Department of Education to draw up guidelines that might help local school districts to understand what is generally permissible school behavior in relation to religion ("Clinton Defines Religious Role in U.S. Schools," 1995). The guidelines, of course, do not carry the force of law, but they make it clear that the school need not be dismissive of religion.

In adjudicating cases that test the interference of government in the religious lives of citizens, two main questions have to be considered: 1) whether or not an individual's religious faith is being handicapped by government, which is known as the **free exercise clause;** and 2) whether or not there is excessive government involvement in supporting a particular religion, which is something known as the **establishment clause.** To deal with the latter, the Supreme Court advanced a three-part framework. It asked whether or not government action fulfilled a clear secular purpose, whether or not it advanced or inhibited religion as its primary effect, and whether or not it avoided excessive entanglement with religion (*Lemon v. Kurtzman,* 1971). To this day, these three conditions are usually at the center of a Court's judgment in cases related to the entanglement of government in religion. To deal with the free exercise clause, the Court has to weigh the interests of the government against the interests of the individual. All persons are free to think and believe according to their will, but because of the establishment clause, there are qualified protections for the freedom to engage in public religious activities (Sendor, 1988).

Among the more interesting and ongoing court battles testing the legal boundaries of church and state relates to the issue of school prayer (see the From the Editorial Page feature in this section). Historically, of course, biblical texts were used with frequency in schools, and school personnel often invoked Christian prayers. Over the years, however, school prayer has been litigated as a First Amendment violation, and the courts have, by and large, judged that the conditions of the establishment clause ("shall make no law respecting an establishment of religion") could not be met when one considered the place of prayer in the school (Sendor, 1988). Generally speaking, the courts found that by allowing audible prayer and Bible reading, the school district (the government) was no longer acting toward a clear secular purpose and was advancing religion as a primary effect.

However, because there is protection for the freedom to hold religious beliefs, private prayers, if voluntary and nonofficial, are clearly supportable in a school. The school cannot tell students that they may not pray, but it also cannot condone public prayer. As a result, so-called moments of silence have been treated more leniently by the courts because they are less vulnerable to the conditions of the establishment clause. If the school designates a moment of silence or silent meditation without formally sanctioning prayer or any other denominational method of reflection, it will likely be on more constitutional ground than if it refers to a period of voluntary prayer (*Wallace v. Jaffree,* 1985). A period of meditation seems to be clearly secular in purpose and has no real connection with advancing or inhibiting a religion, since youth can meditate about anything they choose. All this assumes that there is no compulsion in the school to embrace a particular form of reflection or meditation. This means that teachers have to be scrupulous about their own behaviors during official moments of silence. Some school districts have told their teachers not to bow their heads, fold their hands, close their eyes, or provide any hint that they may be actually praying ("When Quiet Is Pervasive in Schools," 1994). The concern here is over the issue of perceived teacher entanglement with a religious or prayful view.

Laws mandating a moment of silence at the beginning of the school day exist in Alabama, Georgia, South Carolina, and Tennessee ("Prayer in Public Schools?" 1994). Several other states allow for a moment of silence but do not require it. Recently a public school teacher in Georgia refused to obey a state law requiring a moment of silence at the start of the school day. He personally believed such a law to be little more than state-ordered prayer. The teacher was dismissed and the law remained in tact largely because it required students to pause for a moment of reflection, not prayer ("Teacher Ignores Georgia Law," 1994).

A variation of this problem is the issue of prayer held at special school ceremonies. Although most courts have acknowledged prayers at graduation ceremonies as advancing religion, they have been lenient toward them because they are not officially part of the school curriculum program and can be viewed as ceremonial rather than educational in purpose. Moreover, because attendance at such events is typically voluntary and because there is usually a strong gathering of parents and other mature adults at such events, there is not as much of a concern over potential proselytism (*Grossberg v. Deusebio,* 1974). If a school, however, made a habit of having prayers at public meetings without the buffeting presence of parents (pep rallies, assemblies, and other special school events), made such meetings mandatory, and used school personnel to lead the prayers, the courts would likely see violations to the establishment clause: excessive entanglement of school personnel with religion being the most obvious.

Another area of legal debate concerns the role of religious clubs on school grounds, especially secondary schools. The place of an extracurricular religion club in a school has historically not been supported in the courts on the grounds that it advances a religious belief in school and produces an excessive entanglement of school officials in religion (*Brandon v. Board of Education of Guilderland,* 1980/1981; *Johnson v. Huntington Beach Union High School District,* 1977). In most schools, to qualify as an extracurricular group, a student club requires school supervision. If such a club has a religious mandate, school supervision represents an excessive entanglement. But the courts have not been all of one mind. The thinking on the role of the religious clubs has also maintained that such clubs have a clear secular purpose because they are part of an extracurricular policy that is open to student interests, that secondary school students are mature enough to understand that the functioning of such a club is not a school endorsement of its doctrine, especially if there are many different clubs with competing mandates, and that teacher supervision is strictly administrative and entails no sympathetic or visceral involvement of school personnel (*Widmar v. Vincent,* 1981).

In 1984, Congress passed a law, known as the Equal Access Act (EAA), that confused matters even more. The EAA stated that any school receiving federal monies that allows a political, religious, or philosophical group (which is not directly related to the school curriculum) to meet on school grounds must then grant equal access to all groups. In other words, once a political group, such as the Young Republicans, is granted use of the school grounds, all other groups, mainstream and fringe alike, must be granted access (Sendor, 1988). This is usually not a problem with the courts when such groups meet during nonschool hours, carry no official school sanction, entangle no school officials, and generally can be seen as helping to maintain the secular purpose of using the school facility for community activities.

The EAA legislation was originally sponsored by a conservative senator from Utah who wanted to find a way to allow Bible clubs to meet in schools. However, in an interesting twist of events, the EAA legislation unwittingly paved the way for a Salt Lake City high school student to form an extracurricular club dedicated to gay lifestyle issues. Because the federal law said that local schools cannot discriminate among school clubs, Salt Lake City's board of education had three choices: 1) allow the gay club to operate unimpeded in the school, 2) ban all clubs from the city high schools, or 3) violate the law by not allowing the gay club to exist and risk the loss of approximately $100 million of federal aid. It opted to ban all student clubs ("To Be Young, Gay and Going to High School in Utah," 1996).

The observation of holidays that have clear religious overtones is also an area that has required the clarification of the court. Christmas, Easter, Saint Patrick's Day and others are each religious holidays with some basis in secularity. One could argue that Christmas has actually become a kind of capitalist or commercial holiday celebrated by Christians and non-Christians alike. By applying the three conditions of the establishment clause, a school cannot observe such holidays if such observations advance a religious belief or fail to reflect a clear secular purpose. Thus, holidays such as Christmas can be observed in the school as long as the instruction is clearly secular in its orientation (*Florey v. Sioux Falls School District,* 1980). Teachers can discuss the commercial aspects of the holiday, the cultural folklore surrounding the holiday, and the festival traditions of the holiday, but if they raise ideas related to the birth of Jesus, they will likely to be on less steady establishment clause grounds.

Music teachers who direct school choir and band performances at various holiday seasons have sometimes fallen into controversy in this area. Can "Silent Night," for instance, be sung without violating the establishment clause? The answer is argumentative and contextual. The teacher has to demonstrate that the choice of songs advances a secular learning purpose, which in the case of "Silent Night" might include an appreciation for different festival songs and the performance of artistically meritorious works. But to advance such secular instructional goals, the teacher would have to be sure to include other festival songs on the program, including perhaps Hanukkah and Kwanza songs. Thus, the performance of "Silent Night" might not be viewed as an establishment issue if the teacher can show that it was one of several important festival songs that were sung by the choir in the interests of fostering a secular learning objective.

This same principle applies to the general treatment of religion in the curriculum. One cannot effectively study early America, for instance, without understanding how religious faith drove much of the actions and thinking of the people. Similarly, one could not effectively understand the civil rights movement in America without knowing that much of the prominent leadership came out of the Southern Christian Leadership Conference and that Christian doctrine partly justified the idea of nonviolent civil disobedience. In such cases, religion is honestly integrated with a secular instructional purpose and will not be likely seen as a trespass on someone's religious sensibilities.

Similar issues are raised when a teacher openly wears religious apparel to school. But in such a scenario, the issue not only becomes whether such apparel comprises the establishment of religion but also whether restrictions on apparel might violate the teacher's rights under the free exercise clause, which, to recall, prevents the government from impairing the free exercise of religious faith. As with most issues, there is no consensus on this issue. Some courts have reasoned that attire itself is not objectionable because it represents an affiliation with a faith but not the open promotion of a faith. As long as the attire is not part of an open plan to inject personal religious views by the teacher, it is not a problem. Other courts have maintained that the wearing of religious attire, if occurring on a daily basis, represents a subtle signal about religious faith and leads to clear associations between the supervisory authority (the teacher) and a particular religious faith, which itself would be indicative of an excessive entanglement of school personnel with a religion (Sendor, 1988).

Students, of course, generally have no regulations on their religious apparel, unless their clothes are found to disrupt the learning climate of the school. This was precisely the problem that surfaced in an interesting case that occurred in California. Three elementary school students of the Hindu Sikh faith were banned by their school principal from carrying their sacred knives, known as kirpans, to school. The students, who are mandated by their faith to carry their kirpans as a sign of their devotion to God, violated the school's weapons policy and created, at least in the mind of the principal, an unsafe condition for learning. The knives were 4-inch blades that could do appreciable harm in the event of an accident or deliberate mischief. The question was whether the safety and security of the learning environment was compromised by the Sikh students' kirpans and whether the Sikh students were being subjected to an unreasonable burden on their freedom of religion. The courts ruled in favor of the Sikhs and stated that every reasonable accommodation had to be taken to allow the Sikh youngsters to wear their knives. In this case, the court was convinced that the religious expression needs of the students could be secured without harming the educative environment of the school. The court, in fact, suggested that certain safeguards, such as blunting the blades of the knives and sewing the knives into cloth sheaths ("School Told to Allow Sikhs to Have Knives," 1994), could be reasonably imposed.

In recent years, objections have been raised over the manner that science educators have privileged the theory of evolution over biblical accounts of the origin of human life. Those offended by this imbalance have argued that **creationism** (the biblical interpretation of the beginning of humankind) must be given equal treatment in the curriculum. At face value, given the clear linkage that creationism has in the Bible, one could argue that the public school would violate the establishment clause by giving creationism an airing in the classroom. Creationism is, after all, an unambiguous Christian version of truth that the school is being asked to perpetuate.

What made the argument particularly provocative, however, was that creationists argued that those teaching evolution were already violating the establishment clause—that evolutionary theory was part and parcel of an atheistic civil religion called **secular humanism.** Their thinking was that if evolution can be proved to be religious, the establishment clause could be used against teaching it (*Wright v. Houston Independent School District,* 1972). The courts, however, rejected this line of thought, arguing that evolution was a scientific theory sanctioned by a method of science, not by a preexisting religious faith. The courts did not find that evolution advanced a religion or that it failed to promote a secular end, but they did suggest that excusal policies be used in cases where students might find the teaching of evolution offensive to their religious views. In other cases, the courts later found that creationism could not be supported as a scientific theory; it failed to abide by the most elemental principles of evidence in establishing a theory (*McLean v. Arkansas Board of Education,* 1982; *Edwards v. Aguillard,* 1987). It could not be justified as promoting a secular end and was therefore purely religious doctrine.

Despite this ruling, the creationism versus evolution debate has remained vital. In several school districts, especially in the South, creationism continues to be endorsed. Some high school teachers report that the atmosphere surrounding the teaching of evolution has become so wrapped up in controversy and confrontation that they often skip the subject rather than teach it and tempt political trouble ("70 Years After Scopes Trial, Creation Debate Lives," 1996). The courts have been definitive in this area but the struggle to balance the secular priorities of the school with appropriate religious ones continues even in the face of the court's will.

The court decision on the place of secular humanism in the school experience is also interesting. Secular humanism is a deeply disturbing idea to some Christians. As mentioned earlier, some fundamentalist Christians believe that the school is peddling a humanistic "religious" doctrine that destroys family values, advances moral relativism, promotes world government, and essentially sets the conditions for the reign of the Antichrist. Through secular humanism, for instance, boys and girls allegedly learn nontraditional sex roles that could imperil the nuclear family. It also teaches children to think independently and critically, to look at some problems as not having right or wrong answers and to engage in imaginative ponder. All this, it is claimed, leave youngsters with the view that values and truths are relative and that humans, not God, are the main determinants in influencing the direction of humanity. In 1984, a court in Alabama was convinced that such secular views were indeed extant in the curriculum materials of the school and ordered the immediate removal of 455 history, social studies, and home economics books. In the view of the judge, the books supported the religion of secular humanism and thus violated the prohibition against state establishment of religion (*Smith v. Board of School Commissioners of Mobile County*). This was the first time that a federal court recognized humanism as an equivalent to a religion.

The ruling, however, was eventually overturned. Rather than seeing the values of secular humanism being promoted in the texts, the court overturning the Alabama case perceived the basic principles of secular humanism (independent thought, tolerance for diversity, self-respect, self-reliance, and rational decision making) to be nonreligious virtues that transcended religious lines. In other words, the "religious" virtues of secular humanism were often found in the context of the secular and the nonreligious and were taken to be less strictly religious than civic. Correspondence between the nonreligious and religious did not mean that the nonreligious was automatically converted into the religious. The theory of evolution is supported in secular

Religious and ethnic diversity in American public schools requires a deep commitment to the separation of church and state.

humanism, but many persons agree with the theory without subscribing to secular humanism. The law against murder is found in the Ten Commandments of the Bible, but to subscribe to such a law does not convert such a conviction into a religious belief (Sendor, 1988). The public school carries a public mandate that includes characteristics and competencies that serve a wide public interest. These might include competencies such as independent thought, self-reliance, social tolerance, and the like. The public school has a public job that is strictly civic, not religious, in nature.

In cases where the school is accused of damaging the free exercise of religious thought, an excusal or alternative assignment policy might be weighed. If a book is objectionable, for instance, another book might be assigned. But the school may not always be able to pose alternatives, due to any number of factors including financial duress, and it may not believe that an excusal policy is appropriate, especially if it sees the material in question as central to the curriculum (Sendor, 1988).

Among the more interesting cases testing a school district's resolve to not provide an alternative or excusal policy was litigated in Hawkins County, Tennessee, in *Mozert v. Hawkins County Public Schools* (1986/1987/1988). It started when fundamentalist Christians objected to the required reading materials used in the elementary school, materials that they claimed were in violation of the free exercise clause of the Constitution. Their children, they asserted, were being forced to read materials that were wholly objectionable to their religious faith. They further claimed that the reading series used in the school promoted a secular religion that supported world government, nontraditional gender roles, moral relativism, nonreligious views of death, critical views of the founders of the country, socialism, universal communication, magic, environmentalism, kindness to animals, vegetarianism, negative views of war and hunting, disarmament, gun control, and several other "unacceptable" perspectives (Delfattore, 1992).

The parents offered many examples. They objected, for instance, to the reading and teaching of Jack London's story "To Build a Fire." To recall, the main character in London's story is a Yukon traveler who accidently got his feet and legs wet. In the Yukon, such a condition is life threatening. The traveler had to build a fire to thaw out his feet and legs. Without it, he would surely die. He succeeded in building a fire but made the fatal mistake of setting the fire under a tree branch that was heavy with snow. The snow eventually fell on the fire and put it out. The man was doomed. The complaint lodged by the parents was that the man in the story failed to understand that God is responsible for the physical survival of individuals. The children who read the story would not learn that it was God, not the failed decisions of the man, that dictated the man's destiny. Because the man eventually dies in the story, the complainants also objected to the fact that his death made no reference to an afterlife. This lack of reference presumably taught children to accept the humanistic view that there is no God and no hereafter (Delfattore, 1992). Similar complaints were lodged against the reading of the *Wizard of Oz,* in which the characters again failed to pray for wisdom and salvation and in which the satanic practice of witchcraft was condoned. The same logic applied to the complaint against the reading of "Cinderella" (Delfattore, 1992). The plaintiffs simply did not want their children exposed to cosmopolitan ideas that went against their particular world view. They admitted, for instance, that if given a choice, they would not expose their children to any knowledge of other races, religion, or ethnic groups, expect perhaps to know that such groups were wrong and inferior. (Delfattore, 1992). Did the school have to accommodate such views because they were based on religion?

The school's response to these criticisms was that it was conducting reading instruction well within its public school mandate and that it would not excuse any students from reading instruction. Because of the number of students involved and because of the integrative nature of reading in the subject matter of the curriculum, the school claimed that any accommodation would be disruptive to the whole learning process and would result in considerable financial and administrative distress.

After a volatile period of debate, the parents filed suit against the school, claiming a burden to their freedom of religious expression. The state court eventually agreed that the books did indeed pose a clear trespass on the religious sensibilities of the children. Observing that a uniform series of books was not a necessary condition for teaching children to read, the court looked for a solution that might accommodate the freedom of religious expression rights of the children in question. But the court also noted that asking the school to provide an alternative arrangement would be an unreasonable impingement on the school and might potentially be in violation of the establishment clause since reading instruction had to be customized for a group with one religious belief. So, instead, the court ordered the school to provide an option out of the reading instruction for the children and suggested that reading be taught to them privately. For the complainants' children, reading instruction would now be done at the home or in some other private setting, apparently in accordance with their religious faith. This would, in effect, become state-sponsored home education for reading.

This ruling, however, was eventually overturned by an appeals court panel. The judges on the panel argued that the mere exposure to beliefs in books did not constitute an active advocacy for or against a particular religion. It also stated that since reading was integrated into other aspects of the curriculum, the removal of students from reading class would have ripple effects throughout the curriculum and would essentially undermine the entire educative process. The ruling went even further and observed that if a burden was imposed on the religious views of the plaintiffs' children, it was done with a compelling state interest in mind. Teaching students to draw conclusions, express opinions, and deal with the controversies and diversities of public life were appropriate school objectives for public education. The school, in the interest of securing the widest educative effect, could continue to forbid alternative reading instruction.

In the end, the plaintiffs lost the case, but there were lessons learned for public school authorities. The *Mozert* case made it clear that school districts should honor excusal requests from parents as long as such requests do not produce unreasonable financial, pedagogical, and administrative hardships. The school, however, could now be more confident that if such burdens do exist, alternative teaching need not be provided. In other words, the school district's interest in providing a public education to all students seems to outweigh the free exercise rights of the parents (Sendor, 1988).

In the *Mozert* case, the school faced freedom of religion pressures because of what it compelled students to read and do, but in another interesting case the school faced similar pressures over what it would *not* allow a student to do in school. In 1991, a student in a Tennessee public school was given a grade of zero for a research paper that she submitted to her teacher. The paper topic was not approved by the teacher because the student wanted to write a report about Jesus. The teacher would not allow the assignment because, in her view, the student's strong Christian faith made it impossible for the student to approach the topic with any objectivity or scholarly distance. In other words, the paper was not viewed as an educative experience for the child. The family of the student objected on the grounds of free speech and religious expression. Did the teacher's action fall within the leeway given to educators as they fashion their assignments and grading procedures, or was the teacher engaging in viewpoint discrimination and violating freedom of expression protections? The court ruled in favor of the teacher, arguing that, in such a case, "learning is more vital than free speech" ("Justices Won't Hear Student Who Sought to Write About Jesus," 1995). Again where the educative interest of the child is demonstrably at stake or in question, the court seems to favor the professional judgment of the teacher and the societal agenda of the school.

The United States Supreme Court in 1994 adjudicated another case that tested the extent to which the state can accommodate religious needs in a public school. In the town of Monroe, New York, a group of Satmar Hasidim incorporated an independent village, known as **Kiryas Joel.** The Hasidim are a deeply religious people, derived from European Jewry, who speak Yiddish as their primary language, renounce many modern conveniences of life (including television and radio), and generally resist assimilation with other groups. They have a distinctive style of dress and head cover, and eschew public schooling for their children.

With the assistance of some state legislation, the group formed its own village and set up its own public school district. The purpose behind the district, however, was not to educate the majority of the school-aged children in the district, who attended private religious schools, but to serve a small group of handicapped children in the village whose education could not be met adequately in the private religious schools. The handicapped children in Kiryas Joel were, of course, entitled to receive their education in the local public school district, but their parents found such an option to be highly unsatisfactory. The Hasidim children who attended public school in the past were said to have suffered from panic and trauma induced by leaving their village and by being educated among strangers whose ways were so different from theirs and whose attitudes were often ridiculing toward the distinctive nature of dress and custom among their children. The Hasidim wanted to care for their own handicapped children in their own public schools.

A single school was eventually established, with about 40 children attending. It maintained a secular curriculum and was taught by non-Hasidic teachers. The problem, however, was that the creation of such a district (and school) looked very much like the government had yielded to the separatist nature of the Hasidim. In the eyes of some critics, the government's action in allowing for the creation of such a school was tantamount to using the government for the purposes of establishing a religion. The school district was created solely for the purpose of keeping the Hasidim children among their own kind. The United States Supreme Court, in a 6–3 decision, eventually agreed with this line of thinking and outlawed the school district. The majority opinion stated that the establishment of the district was an absolute bow to religion, resulting in the segregation of people on the basis of religion. Justice Anthony Kennedy wrote, "Just as the government may not segregate people on account of their race, so too it may not segregate on the basis of religion. The danger of stigma and stirred animosities is no less acute

Personal Prayer Is Not Illegal

The following is an editorial written in the *New York Times* in response to the allegation, often made by various politicians, that personal prayer is not being allowed in public schools. What are your views on this matter? Do you know of anyone whose freedom of religious expression rights were violated by the public school?

When Representative Newt Gingrich complains that it is 'illegal to pray' to oneself in public school, he misstates the law and the Constitution. The Constitution forbids organized school prayer because that is government action for the advancement of religion, a violation of the First Amendment's ban on religious establishment. Individual students remain free to bow their heads and pray or meditate in their own unobtrusive way.

Mr. Gingrich misrepresents the law to promote his agenda—a prayer amendment to the Constitution. He cites the dubious case of Raymond Raines, a pupil in St. Louis allegedly disciplined for praying over his cafeteria lunch. School officials say the episode never happened and imply that he might have been disciplined for other, unspecified conduct. But even if the accusation were true, it would not prove the need to alter the Bill of Rights.

Raymond and his mother, Ellen Raines, are suing the St. Louis school system, charging that he was punished last year for piety that bothered none of his fourth-grade classmates but allegedly upset school authorities. The suit contends that the school's action drove Raymond out of a public school into a private one where he is now free to exercise his Christian faith.

A trial is a long way off, but some things are clear now. First, if the punishment occurred as the lawsuit charges, it should not have. If a school principal or teacher punishes a child for praying silently, that official misapplies the Constitution and violates the child's right to the free exercise of religion, a breach of the First Amendment. Second, if the punishment did occur, it would prove at most that school officials misunderstand the law. Such misunderstanding is fed in part by cries like Mr. Gingrich's that the Supreme Court has driven God out of the schools and that quiet reverence at mealtime amounts to 'illegal' prayer.

In some school districts, principals and teachers need more education on the proper boundaries between personal, private prayer and improper state promotion of religion. Just as many districts countenance organized prayer that unconstitutionally coerces some youngsters into group prayer, others may wrongly deny students the chance to pray quietly and unobtrusively.

Schools must also make those boundaries clear. St. Louis did not, when asked by Mrs. Raines's lawyers for clarification of school policy. A fair answer, authorized by the Supreme Court, would have been that any child can pray or pause reverently over a school meal just as Raymond says he did. That answer would demonstrate how wrong Mr. Gingrich is to say that the Supreme Court has outlawed all prayer in the schools.

Source: *New York Times.* (1994, December 10). Sec. 1, p. 22. Copyright 1994 by The New York Times Company.

for religious line drawing than for racial . . ." ("The Supreme Court," 1994). The Court believed that the needs of the handicapped children could be met in the wider school district in ways that showed sensitivity to the village children and that the establishment of the Kiryas Joel school district was based entirely on a religious criterion.

Edwards v. Aguillard

Edwards v. Aguillard was an important Supreme Court case that provided some direction on the question of creationism in the science education curriculum. Visit the web site to read more detailed text on the case: http://earth.ics.uci.edu:8080/faqs/edwards-v-aguillard.html.

Edwards v. Aguillard:
U.S. Supreme Court Decision
Transcribed by Clark Dorman
[Last Update: Febrary 8, 1996]

(This was put into html form by Clark Dorman <dorman@cns.bu.edu>. All errors without a sic after them are probably mine.)

The Supreme Court affirmed the judgment of the court of appeals, which in turn had affirmed the District Court's decision finding the Louisiana act unconstitutional.

The decision had Brennan, Marshall, Blackmun, Powell, Stevens, O'Connor, and White on the majority, with Scalia and Rehnquist dissenting.

Held Opinion
Majority Opinion by Brennan I, II, III (A) (B), IV, V
Concurring Opinion by Powell I (A), (B), II, III
Concurring Opinion by White
Dissenting Opinion by Scalia I, II, (A) (B), III

KEY TERMS

Comprehensive high school
Creationism
Decentralized governance
Department of Education
Establishment clause
Flat grant programs
Foundation programs
Free exercise clause
Junior high school

Kiryas Joel
Local school board
Middle school
Minimal provision philosophy
Mozert v. Hawkins County Public Schools
Rodriguez v. the San Antonio Independent School District
Secretary of Education

Secular humanism
Self-contained classroom
Specialized high school
State boards of education
State superintendent

KEY QUESTIONS

1. Why is the ninth grade typically excluded from the middle school arrangement?

2. Why is the self-contained classroom more popular in elementary schools than in secondary schools?

3. What is the fundamental difference between a comprehensive high school and a specialized secondary school?

4. What makes a governor of a state especially influential in public education?

5. Explain the relation between local and state school authorities.

6. What were some of the more significant initiatives sponsored by the federal government over the years?

7. What was at issue in the case of *Rodriguez v. the San Antonio Independent School District*? What was the Supreme Court's ruling and reasoning?

8. What is the main difference between flat grant and foundation financial programs?

9. Why do foundation programs often fail to have much impact on local funding differences?

10. Explain the new funding structure in Michigan and why it might promise to be helpful in other states. What is the main argument against the funding arrangement in Michigan?

11. Is there validity to the view that funding is incidental or not always meaningful to good public education?

12. Why is the per pupil expenditure rate not always a telling index of quality in schooling?

13. Explain how public investment in schooling has increased while the investment in regular classroom instruction has remained flat.

14. Explain the establishment and free exercise clauses as they relate to the relation between church and state.

15. How have the courts dealt with the role of creationism in science education?

16. How have the courts dealt with the issue of silent school prayer? How does voluntary prayer in school differ from a moment of silence?

17. Explain the Equal Access Act of 1984.

18. How have the courts dealt with the contention that public schools uphold the religion of secular humanism?

19. Can religion be properly and honestly integrated in the school curriculum? If so, how?

20. Explain the ruling in Kiryas Joel. Do you agree with the position taken by the Supreme Court?

REFERENCES

Barbanel, J. (1994, January 23). $7,512 per pupil: Where does it go? *New York Times*, Sec. 13, p. 1.

Celis, W. (1994, March 17). Michigan votes for revolution in financing its public schools. *New York Times*, Sec. A, p. 1.

Center for Educational Research and Innovation. (1993). *Education at a glance*. Paris: Organization for Economic Cooperation and Development.

Clinton defines religion's role in U.S. schools. (1995, August 26). *New York Times*, Sec. 1, p. 1.

Cremin, L. A. (1951). *The American common school: A historic conception*. New York: Teachers College, Columbia University.

Delfattore, J. (1992). *What Johnny shouldn't read*. New Haven: Yale University Press.

Douglas, H. R., & Greider, C. (1948). *American public education*. New York: The Ronald Press Company.

Finn, C. E. (1991). *We must take charge*. New York: The Free Press.

Guthrie, J. W., Garms, W. I., & Pierce, L. C. (1988). *School finance and education policy*. Englewood Cliffs, NJ: Prentice-Hall.

Jones, J. J., Salisbury, G. J., & Spencer, R. L. (1969). *Secondary school administration*. New York: McGraw-Hill.

Justices won't hear student who sought to write on Jesus. (1995, November 28). *New York Times*, Sec. B, p. 9.

Kozol, J. (1991). *Savage inequalities*. New York: Crown Publishers.

Munley, V. (1993). The structure of K-12 school finance in the United States. In R. J. Thorton & A. P. O'Brien (Eds.), *The economic consequences of American education*. Greenwich, CT: JAI Press.

Nord, W. (1995). *Religion and American education*. Chapel Hill: University of North Carolina Press.

Power, E. J. (1991). *A legacy of learning*. Albany, NY: SUNY Press.

Prayer in public schools? It's nothing new for many. (1994, November 22). *New York Times*, Sec. A, p. 1.

School told to allow Sikhs to have knives. (1994, September 4). Sec. 1, p. 24.

Sendor, B. B. (1988). *A legal guide to religion and public education*. Topeka: National Organization on Legal Problems of Education.

70 Years after Scopes Trial, creation debate lives. (1996, March 10). *New York Times*, Sec. 1, p. 1.

The Supreme Court; Excerpts from opinions and dissent on religion. (1994, June 28). *New York Times*, Sec. D, p. 20.

Swanson, A. D., & King, R. A. (1991). *School finance*. New York: Longman.

Tanner, D. (1972). *Secondary education*. New York: Macmillan.

Teacher ignores Georgia law on moment of quiet. (1994, August 24). *New York Times*, Sec. B, p. 8.

To aid U.S. schools, a simple spending model. (1993, March 22). *New York Times*, Sec. 1, p. 19.

To be young, gay and going to high school in Utah. (1996, February 28). *New York Times*, Sec. B, p. 8.

U.S. Department of Education. (1984). *A nation responds*. Washington, DC: U.S. Department of Education.

Vitz, P. (1986). *Censorship: Evidence of bias in our children's textbooks*. Ann Arbor: Servant Books.

When quiet is pervasive in school. (1994, September 4). *New York Times*, Sec. 1, p. 25.

Wiles, J., & Bondi, J. (1993). *The essential middle school*. New York: Macmillan.

LEGAL CASES

Brandon v. Board of Educ. of Guilderland, 635 F.2d 971 (2d Cir. 1980), *cert. denied,* 454 U.S. 1123 (1981).

Florey v. Sioux Falls School Dist. 49–5, 619 2d 1311 (8th Cir.), *cert. denied,* 449 U.S. 987 (1980).

Grossberg v. Deusebio, 380 F. Supp. 285 (E. D. Va. 1974).

Johnson v. Huntington Beach Union High School Dist., 68 Cal. App. 3d 1, 137 Cal. Reptr. 43, *cert. denied,* 434 U.S. 877 (1977).

Lemon v. Kurtzman, 403 U.S. 602 (1971).

McLean v. Arkansas Board of Educ., 579 F. Supp. 1255 (E. D. Ark. 1982).

Mozert v. Hawkins County Public Schools, 647 F. Supp. 1194 (E. D. Tenn. 1986), *rev'd.* 82 F.2d. 1058 (6th Cir. 1987), *cert. denied,* 108 S. Ct. 1029 (1988).

Smith v. Board of School Commissioners of Mobile County, 655 F. Supp. 834 (S. D. Ala.), *rev'd,* 827 F.2d 684 (11th Cir. 1987).

Wallace v. Jaffree, 105 S. Ct. 2479 (1985).

Widmar v. Vincent, 454 U.S. 263 (1981).

Wright v. Houston Indep. School Dist., 366 F. Supp. 1208 (S. D. Tex. 1972).

All legal cases were originally cited in: Sendor, B. B. (1988). *A legal guide to religion and public education.* Topeka: National Organization on Legal Problems of Education.

5

THE QUESTION OF SCHOOL EQUITY

Karen Hudson Ashbrook, who has been a special education teacher for more than 20 years, reads to one of her students. It should come as no surprise that in earlier times, Ashbrook would not have been given the opportunity to teach such exceptional youth. The school doors were open to only the most able. Now, of course, legislation mandates that all children receive a free public education.

This chapter discusses the question of school equity. Although it is easy to be convinced of the equity of public schooling, the equality of public schooling is another matter. For instance, all students cannot be treated equally, but all should be treated fairly. Students with special needs, such as Ashbrook's student pictured here, obviously require an education that is different from many other students. This point is obvious. However, there are subtle ways that schools can treat students unfairly. For instance, the idea of grouping students by ability may seem to be a logical teaching design, but such a strategy can also be unfair, especially to those who are believed to have low ability. Segregated schools were once thought to be equitable—a point struck down by the nation's courts. A current debate over whether schools are fair to girls represents still another issue to discuss.

The role and the function of the school can only be understood in the context of the values and aims of society. As a public institution, the school is obligated to reflect the highest ideals of society and to provide an experience that is rich in what it means to be "a good person leading a good life in a good society." As Plato explained, to understand the good life, one is inevitably drawn to the question of the good society, which itself leads one to contemplate how such a society will be brought into existence and sustained, a concern that, at least to Plato, had everything to do with the development of educational policy and practice (Cremin, 1965).

A more simple way of thinking about this is to realize that the means of a school should always be contiguous with the aims of its society—that a democratic society demands a democratic school system, one that strives to create an intelligent, socially responsible, and autonomously thinking individual. In the context of the United States, this means that the public school should embody, among others, the ideals of tolerance, equity, justice, dissent, and liberty. Public education should also provide youth with various skills of individual control, socializing them in the ability to make decisions according to a method of intelligence and a democratic standard of ethics.

The United States has long been recognized as a nation that has put its faith in its public school system. Over the years, public schools have been described as central to the functioning of virtually every aspect of life—from building a strong economy to building good character, from being seen as a

OUTLINE

127

place that builds a common identity to being seen as a place that builds individual identity. The schools have been described as the great equalizers in the society and have long been perceived as the fundamental variable to economic and social mobility.

Not surprisingly, the very notion of universalizing secondary education and opening the gates of college and university education to the masses has had its roots in America. To this day, many other advanced countries offer secondary and postsecondary education to a comparatively small percentage of the student-age population. The United States, however, has retention rates in high school that are among the highest in the world (despite the dropout problem) and has a large group of universities, both public and private, to which a high school graduate can usually find admission. The United States still leads the world in the percentage of 22-year-olds obtaining bachelor's degrees and, as discussed in another chapter, continues to lead the world in the percentage of degrees obtained by women and minorities in both technical and nontechnical fields (Carson, Huelskamp, & Woodall, 1993). On the whole, America's educational system offers the greatest educational opportunity to the greatest number of students (Husen, 1983). On an international scale, U.S. schools, relative to the schools of other advanced nations, have historically been documented as having a low socioeconomic bias (Tyler, 1981; Husen, 1983; Tanner & Tanner, 1995).

There is, however, another side to American education, one that runs counter to its egalitarian and democratic ideals. Education continues to suffer from clear inequities both across and within public schools. Many of these inequities affect children from poor families, the very children who stand to gain the most from equal educational opportunities. Many schools are inequitably funded, racially stratified, and curricularly sorted in a way that works against those who have the least.

Many urban schools, lacking the funds for regular maintenance, present a dismal face to inner-city learners.

PART TWO: THE SCHOOL AND SOCIETY

Inequities in Society and School

Alex Kotlowitz describes the frustrations of a teacher in inner-city Chicago. The description documents the difficulty of trying to conduct public education in an environment that is obviously not conducive to learning.

> Ms. Barone tired of the large classes, which at one point swelled to as many as thirty-four students—they now numbered around twenty-five—and of the funding cutbacks. And she worried so much about her children, many of whom came in tired or sad or distracted, that she eventually developed an ulcerated colon.
>
> The relentless violence of the neighborhood also wore her down. The parking lot behind the school had been the site of numerous gang battles. When the powerful sounds of .357 Magnums and sawed-off shotguns echoed off the school walls, the streetwise students slid off their chairs and huddled under their desks. The children had had no "duck and cover" drills, as in the early 1960s, when the prospect of a nuclear war with Cuba and the Soviet Union threatened the nation. This was merely their sensible reaction to the possibility of bullets flying through the window. Ms. Barone, along with other teachers, placed the back of her chair against a pillar so that there would be a solid object between herself and the window.
>
> She dreaded the walk each morning and afternoon from and to her car. She no longer wore jewelry or carried her leather purse. Instead, she used a cheap plastic handbag. She regularly slipped her paycheck into her bra before making the short trek to her car.

Source: Kotlowitz, A. (1991) *There are no children here.* New York: Anchor Books, pp. 66–67.

The Curriculum Tracking Problem

Curriculum tracking is a phase of the school that aims to provide differential instruction for students with differential ability levels. Tracking is usually done by categorizing students into instructional groups based on judgments of individual intelligence and skill, often for the purpose of providing a more homogeneous instructional target for the teacher. In essence, tracking represents an encompassing use of grouping designed to structure an entire class according to an ability level.

There is, however, a difference between tracking and ability grouping. The use of reading groups based on ability within a self-contained heterogeneous classroom, for instance, is technically not tracking because such a classroom will presumably offer other experiences inclusive of the whole heterogeneous group. However, if reading instruction is sorted by ability and taught in separate classrooms, and if this or a similar sorting system is also used to teach science, math, and language arts in separate ability-based classrooms, then it would be fair to say that the school is tracked. Similarly, the availability of accelerated or advanced placement courses for a small percentage of high-aptitude students in various areas of study is not tracking if these students spend most of their time in a heterogeneously grouped class and if access to such placements is demonstrably fair and based on educational principles.

There are many schools that engage in ability grouping without resorting to tracking. Pervasive ability grouping (or tracking) across several subjects, for instance, is not at all popular in elementary schools. Ability grouping, of course, is used with some frequency by elementary school teachers, but it is usually narrowly scoped, meaning that it is used only in a few areas of instruction, and it is often contained within a mixed-ability classroom setting. Among the more popular approaches to grouping in elementary schools is something known as the Joplin Plan, which uses cross-grade grouping for instruction in only one or two areas, usually reading and math. The idea is to keep the inclusive nature of the self-contained classroom in tact, while still targeting instruction according to ability in one or two areas. The Joplin Plan is not considered tracking precisely because it allows for heterogeneously grouped experiences. Most elementary school teachers use within-class grouping for limited instructional purposes, a practice that, at least in terms of achievement effects, seems to work well when compared with nongrouped instruction (Slavin, 1987).

Tracking, however, starts to become a real force in the curriculum in the middle school and junior high school. Although middle schools are ideally designed to keep the learner away from tracked experiences and more substantively involved in exploratory and general education, national survey data suggest the persistent presence of tracking in schools serving preadolescents. According to Braddock (1990a), close to one fourth of middle-level schools (grades five through eight) engage in a pure form of tracking by using between-class ability grouping in all subject areas. Approximately one third of the middle schools (depending on the grade level) reported no ability grouping between classes and the remaining percentage reported ability grouping in some subjects. Ability grouping in English, math, science, and social studies increased substantially from fifth grade to eighth grade, while the percentage of schools using no ability grouping decreased substantially between these same grades. These data do not apply to ability groups that

Elementary school reading groups, based on ability, may serve as early lessons for students about who will succeed in school.

teachers might form within classrooms, only to the designation of whole classes by ability. See Table 5.1 for a complete breakdown of the national survey.

At the high school level, tracking continues to grow in scope, though not necessarily in intensity. According to another study by Braddock (1990b), who based his determinations on the 1972 National Longitudinal Study of the High School, only about 8% of the nation's comprehensive high schools used between-class ability grouping in all subject areas, but the remaining 92% used between-class ability grouping in some subjects. Course tracking was most popular in English, where 59% of the comprehensive schools used between-class ability grouping. Approximately 42% of schools engaged in ability grouping in math/science and 38% in social studies. In all the comprehensive schools, there was an overrepresentation of minority youth in remedial classes and an underrepresentation of minority youth in honors classes (Braddock, 1990b).

There are essentially two basic forms of tracking. Advocates of one form attempt to identify whole ability groups irrespective of the subject matter taught, so that so called high-level students will be taught more advanced and more accelerated courses in all subjects. Entire classes are thus marked by a high, middle, or low designation. Students in each group will, for instance, be tracked together for instruction in English, math, social studies, science, and so on. The other form of tracking reconstitutes the ability levels according to the subject matter, making it possible for one student to be placed in a high-level math course but in a low-level English course. Even this form of tracking, however, typically results in the same students being placed in the same levels across the board. A national survey, for instance, indicated that 60% to 70% of 10th graders who were enrolled in honors math were simultaneously enrolled in honors English; a similar pattern held between remedial math and remedial English (Oakes, Gamoran, & Page, 1992). Carey & others (1994) found considerable overlap between ability levels in math and English courses offered in the 10th grade.

Why is tracking used in the schools? There are several reasons typically given. First, as mentioned, tracking is expressly designed to be responsive to

TABLE 5.1

GROUPING PRACTICES IN MIDDLE-LEVEL SCHOOLS BY PERCENTAGE			
Grades	**5**	**6**	**7**	**8**
Between-Class Ability Grouping				
All subjects	23	22	22	23
Some subjects	40	44	47	50
Reading	96	86	63	54
English	24	44	54	54
Math	57	77	84	88
Science	4	5	14	16
Social studies	4	4	10	10
No subjects	37	34	31	27

Source: Braddock, J. H. (1990a). Tracking in the middle grades: National patterns of grouping for instruction. PDK, 71(6), 445–449.

the divergent instructional levels of the student. Thus, students who may not be as skilled as others in, say, math are said to be served by a slower pace and a more deliberate and detailed approach, while those who are more skilled are free to go forward without restraint. Second, it is commonly believed that when students of mixed abilities are all taught in one common classroom, the achievement of the high-ability student is lowered. The thinking is that teachers pace their teaching according to the slowest runner, and that the faster ones never get to stride fully and run far. Third, many believe that it is simply too much to expect a teacher to be responsive to a wide range of student skills in one classroom, that such an expectation is counter to good pedagogy, and that teachers can benefit from having a more precise and less wide-ranging ability target at which to aim their instruction. Teachers, it should be said, side strongly with the practice of tracking (Howe, 1993), a fact confirmed partly by its relatively widespread use in the schools.

These justifications paint tracking with a benevolent brush, suggesting that it serves high-, middle-, and low-ability students in a fair and equitable manner, but the available data demonstrate that tracking has some serious problems. Some data, in fact, point to tracking as an instrument of inequity in the classroom.

Tracking has been indicted for acting as a kind of sorting machine that provides high-quality instructional experiences for students who already have the greatest social and economic advantages and low-quality experiences for those who have the least. The problem, critics claim, is that tracking has consequences that reach well beyond the intentions of providing appropriate instructional opportunities for youth of varying ability levels. Tracking has, in effect, become a way of providing differential *qualities* of experience, in that students in high groups, when compared with their peers in low groups, benefit from higher teacher expectation, more idea-oriented learning engagements, more meaningful curriculum materials, better classroom climate, and an overall wealthier and more challenging teaching methodology. The fact that this differential in quality cuts across racial and economic lines, meaning that the low groups have a disproportionately large representation of minority and economically poor children, places tracking at the very center of the discussion on equity. Moreover, because the character of tracking usually remains frozen into its original designations of low- and high-ability levels and sees especially little movement from lower groups to higher ones, one can argue that it is a virtual institutionalized pattern of unequal education.

Much of the best work done on the inequitable nature of tracking was drawn from a national sample of schools (Oakes, 1985). Taking her data from Goodlad's landmark study of schooling, Jeanne Oakes documented the qualitative differences witnessed in the various tracks of the high school curriculum. She, for instance, reported on how the content of the curriculum varied at different track levels. Higher track levels were marked by a sharp focus on college-preparatory topics and were not likely to emphasize basic skills instruction. Generally speaking, higher track students engaged in higher cognitive work than did their counterparts in the lower tracks—making judgments, drawing inferences, and engaging in idea-oriented forms of instruction. Low track levels were dedicated primarily to rote learning and to basic skills instruction, which in English class included functional literacy skills such as filling out a job application (see the Student Voices feature in this section).

Although one would naturally expect ability tracks to vary in cognitive intensity and somewhat perhaps in content, the existing situation can be more properly distinguished as two separate cultures, one that provides high-cognitive experiences for children believed to have "higher" skills and low-cognitive experiences for those believed to have "lower" skills. This was verified also in what the teachers reported to be the desired behavioral outcomes for students in the different tracks. Teachers were more likely to describe behaviors like self-direction, critical thinking, creativity, and active involvement in learning as appropriate outcomes for the high track, while openly aiming at characteristics such as working quietly, punctuality, conforming to rules, and getting along with others for the low track (Oakes, 1985). Such disparities reflect base inequities in the way youth are educated; they cannot be justified as outcomes appropriate for varied levels of ability.

Not surprisingly, the level of teacher expectation accorded to the children in the different track levels also varied. This has resulted in a considerable instructional advantage for the high-level tracks, not only because of the obvious benefits of being marked as having ability and of being expected to fulfill the promise of one's ability, but also because of the effect that such expectations have on the teacher's instructional conduct. High-ability tracks, for instance, were reported to be less punitive in nature, less inclined to be preoccupied with discipline and control, and more environmentally friendly than the low tracks. Students in high-ability tracks observed their teachers to be more concerned with their personal needs and interests, and their own peers to be more friendly than those in the low tracks. The high track also outscored the low track on scales of teacher clarity, organization, and enthusiasm (Oakes, 1985).

In a more recently published study, Oakes (1990) examined how race and social class might affect a student's opportunity to learn math and science, asking particularly how tracking fits into matters of curriculum access. Does tracking, in other words, help to maintain inequitable access not only to curriculum programs in math and science but also to qualified teachers and to certain vital resources? Oakes again uncovered several disturbing trends.

Using a national sample of schools, Oakes (1990) found, for instance, that the basic qualification patterns of teachers were not only noticeable across schools, varying according to race and social class, but also within schools. When one looked at the qualifications of the teachers assigned to teach math and science in the various ability tracks of the secondary school, a pattern emerged. The lower tracks, when compared with the higher tracks, attracted significantly more uncertified teachers, significantly fewer teachers with bachelor of arts or bachelor of science degrees, significantly fewer teachers with master's degrees, and significantly fewer teachers carrying the endorsement or qualification of the National Science Teachers Association (see Figure 5.1). Overall, teachers working in lower tracks seemed less well prepared academically and professionally than their colleagues in higher track settings, at least in secondary math and science instruction. When one examines these same concerns across social class and race, the differences become even more exaggerated. In other words, when one compares the qualifications of teachers working in the low tracks of a low-income, largely minority, urban school against the qualifications of teachers working in the high tracks of a high-income, largely White, suburban school, the differences in teacher certification rates and levels of teacher education are eye-opening (see Table 5.2).

Not surprisingly, such clear differences in qualifications might help to manifest the differences witnessed in the instructional patterns of ability-

FIGURE 5.1

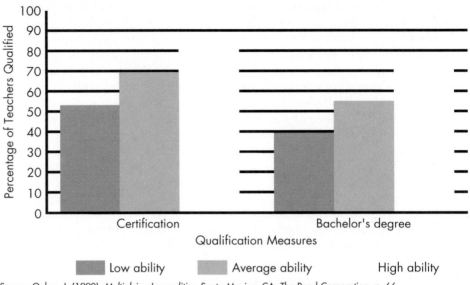

TEACHER QUALIFICATION DIFFERENCES ACROSS ABILITY TRACKS

Source: Oakes, J. (1990). *Multiplying Inequalities.* Santa Monica, CA: The Rand Corporation, p. 66.

TABLE 5.2

TEACHER QUALIFICATION DIFFERENCES ACROSS ABILITY TRACKS AND SES SCHOOL LEVELS (BY PERCENTAGE)

Teacher Qualifications	Low-Ability Classes		High-Ability Classes	
	Low-SES, Minority, Urban	High-SES, White, Suburban	Low-SES, Minority, Urban	High-SES, White, Suburban
Certified in science/math	39%	82%	73%	84%
Bachelor's in science/math	38	68	46	78
Master's in science/math	8	32	10	48
NSTA[1] qualified	11	36	5	47
NCTM[2] qualified	23	26	4	16
Computer course work	41	61	69	62

[1]National Science Teachers Association
[2]National Council of Teachers of Mathematics
Source: Oakes, J. (1990) *Multiplying Inequalities*, Santa Monica, CA: The Rand Corporation, p. 67.

based tracks. Table 5.3 depicts the differences in the pattern of instruction provided in secondary math and science classes. High-ability students in science spend less time on routine and reading and more time on hands-on activities and teacher exposition. In math, there is a tendency to spend more time on whole-group instruction in the high-ability groups. Again, if one injects social class and race into the instructional pattern, the differences in instructional treatment become even more wide. As noted in Table 5.4, the differences between the instructional emphasis in low-track/low-SES, largely minority schools and high-SES, largely White schools are startling.

Even mainstream critics have bordered on the dramatic in damning the practice of tracking. Harold Howe, Secretary of Education in the Johnson

TABLE 5.3

INSTRUCTIONAL EMPHASIS ACROSS ABILITY TRACKS IN MATH AND SCIENCE

Instructional Activity	Class Type		
	Low	Average	High
	Percentage of Time Spent on Various Activities		
All classes			
Routine	12	12	10
Science classes			
Lecture	36	36	41
Hands-on	20	20	26
Reading	12	10	5
Test or quiz	7	7	6
Other activities	13	14	12
Mathematics classes			
Class—lecture, test, etc.	48	55	59
Small groups	10	9	10
Individual	29	25	20

Source: Oakes, J. (1990). *Multiplying Inequalities*. Santa Monica, CA: The Rand Corporation, p. 97.

TABLE 5.4

INSTRUCTIONAL EMPHASIS ACROSS ABILITY TRACKS AND SES SCHOOL LEVELS IN MATH AND SCIENCE

Instructional Activity	Class and School Types	
	Low-Ability Classes in Low-SES, Minority, Urban Schools	High-Ability Classes in High-SES, White, Suburban Schools
	Percentage of Time Spent on Various Activities	
All classes		
Routine	17	9
Science classes		
Lecture	28	51
Hands-on	20	26
Reading	21	1
Test or quiz	10	4
Mathematics classes		
Class-lecture, test, etc.	48	63
Small groups	7	8
Individual	26	20

Source: Oakes, J. (1990). *Multiplying Inequalities*. Santa Monica, CA: The Rand Corporation, p. 99.

administration, has called tracking "one of the most destructive aspects of factory-model schooling," arguing that it perpetuates disadvantage, fosters racial and cultural isolation, and encourages low expectations for Black and Hispanic students (Howe, 1993, p. 144). Much of what Howe says has even caught the attention of the federal government, which is now engaged in examining the implications of ability-grouping practices as they relate to racial segregation (Armstrong, 1990). As reported in *Education Week,* the Department of Education drafted a memo to the Office of Civil Rights asking it to look into whether the use of tracking and ability grouping violated Title VI of the **Civil Rights Act of 1964,** which bars discrimination on the basis of race, color, or national origin in institutions with federally funded programs. "A prima facie case is established," read the memo, "when a racially neutral practice, such as assignment to classes on the basis of ability or achievement, has a racially disproportionate effect" (Armstrong, 1990, p. 20). Many other organizations, including the National Governors' Association, the Carnegie Corporation, and the College Board, have written reports that highlight the need to eliminate curriculum tracking (Oakes, 1992).

There is some controversy about who makes the track-placement decisions and exactly how they make them. Oakes (1985) identified the role of school counselors in making track-placement decisions, individuals who, given their workload, are often furthest removed from the student's life in school. Others have bemoaned the use of a single variable or single indicator, such as a standardized test measure, in making placement decisions. A study of curriculum tracking in middle school mathematics found that overt parental efforts to have their children placed in higher groups factored significantly into the placement decisions, and that local criteria for track placement varied so much from school to school that a student who might be viewed as fully qualified for the high track in one school might be rejected in another (Unseem, 1990). Another study, however, showed that, at least at the high school level, previous grades, teacher recommendations and prerequisite requirements are most prominent in influencing the placement of students in differentiated courses (Carey & others, 1994). If one is to accept the contention that real differences exist among students, then one must be sure that these real differences are identified honestly and properly. This currently does not seem to be the case.

The idea that tracking and ability grouping are negative phenomena in the school is not something that has gone uncontested. Several researchers have been critical of Oakes's data on tracking, arguing that she lacked good controls and made selective use of the literature to bolster her antitracking sentiments (Kulik, 1993). Two groups of researchers studying the best evidence on ability grouping claim that most forms of ability grouping (even when used at a level that might constitute tracking) do not carry the devastating effects advanced by Oakes and that, in stark contrast to Oakes's interpretation, they might be viewed as generally positive practices. Researchers at Johns Hopkins University (Slavin, 1990) and the University of Michigan (Kulik, 1993) have argued that the achievement effects of ability grouping in secondary schools have been largely positive when limited to within-class and cross-grade grouping but have been neither negative nor positive when limited to between-class grouping. Kulik (1993), in fact, claims that students in lower and middle groups have achievement scores virtually indistinguishable from similar students in mixed groups and that there are no discernable negative effects in the self-esteem of students. Part of the problem in interpreting these data is not knowing the pervasiveness and intensity of tracking in the schools tested. Children in schools where all subjects are grouped will likely have different outcomes on achievement and attitude scales than children in schools where one or two subject areas are grouped. Similarly, children assigned to low-ability groups that are small in

Student Statements About Learning in Different Curriculum Tracks

Students' written responses to the question: "What is the most important thing you have learned or done so far in this class?"

Mathematics

High-Track Students:

1. There is no one important thing I have learned. Since each new concept is built on the old ones, everything I learn is important.
   —Senior High

2. Learning to change my thought processes in dealing with higher mathematics and computers.
   —Senior High

3. Inductive Reasoning.
   —Senior High

4. Learned many new mathematical principles and concepts that can be used in a future job.
   —Senior High

5. I have proved to myself that I have the discipline to take a difficult class just for the knowledge, even though it has nothing to do with my career plans.
   —Senior High

Low-Track Students:

1. Really I have learned nothing. Only my roman numerals. I knew them, but not very good. I could do better in another class.
   —Junior High

2. I have learned just a small amount in this class. I feel that if I was in another class, that I would have a challenge to look forward to each and every time I entered the class. I feel that if I had another teacher I would work better.
   —Junior High

3. How to do income tax.
   —Senior High

Science

High-Track Students:

1. Basic concepts and theories have been most prevalent. We have learned things that are practical without taking away some in-depth studies of the subject.
   —Senior High

2. Things in nature are not always what they appear to be or what seems to be happening is not what really is happening.
   —Senior High

   —Continued

Student Statements About Learning in Different Curriculum Tracks

—Continued

3. Probably the most important thing I've learned is the understanding of the balance between man and his environment.

—Senior High

4. I have learned to do what scientists do.

—Junior High

Low-Track Students:

1. I can distinguish one type of rock from another.

—Senior High

2. How to ride motorcycles and shoot trap.

—Senior High

3. To be honest, nothing.

—Senior High

4. Nothing outstanding.

—Senior High

5. Nothing I'd use in my later life; it will take a better man than I to comprehend our world.

—Senior High

English

High-Track Students:

1. I have learned things that will get me ready for college entrance examinations. Also, many things on how to write compositions that will help me in college.

—Junior High

2. To me, there is not a most important thing I learned in this class. Everything or mostly everything I learn in here is IMPORTANT.

—Junior High

3. It teaches you how to do research in a college library.

—Senior High

4. The thing we did in class that I enjoyed the most was writing poetry, expressing my ideas. We also had a poet come and read to us.

—Senior High

Low-Track Students:

1. I learned that English is boring.

—Senior High

2. Job applications. Job interviews. Preparation for the above.

—Junior High

—Continued

Student Statements About Learning in Different Curriculum Tracks

—Continued

3. To spell words you don't know, to fill out things where you get a job.

—Junior High

4. Job training.

—Junior High

Social Science Studies

High-Track Students:

1. The most important thing is the way other countries and places govern themselves economically, socially, and politically. Also different philosophers and their theories on government and man and how their theories relate to us and now.

—Junior High

2. I have learned quite a deal about peoples of other nations, plus the ideas of creation and evolution, ideas that philosophers have puzzled over for years.

—Senior High

3. Learning political and cultural trends in relation to international and domestic events.

—Senior High

Low-Track Students:

1. I don't remember.

—Junior High

2. A few lessons which have not very much to do with history. (I enjoyed it).

—Junior High

3. To learn how to listen and follow the directions of the teacher.

—Senior High

4. I learned about being quiet when the teacher is talking.

—Junior High

5. Learned to work myself.

—Junior High

6. How to go through a cart and find a folder by myself.

—Junior High

What tentative conclusions can you draw about the effect of tracking in the lives of schoolchildren from these statements?

Source: Oakes, J. (1985). *Keeping track: How schools structure inequality.* New Haven: Yale University Press.

size, relative to the higher-ability groups, will suffer greater stigmatizing effects than if the lower group were larger (Gamoran, 1992).

Still, the disparities uncovered by Oakes paint a disturbing picture of inequity that seems structurally rooted in the school. Virtually every factor significant to the education of youth seems affected by the tracking system in

Active learning strategies, an essential part of any strong curriculum, are more likely to be used with high track students.

a way that arguably disadvantages students in the low track. One can argue that tracking has created an underclass in the school that has everything stacked against the success of students who, for varying reasons, have been identified as lacking in skill and abilities.

Given the state of tracking described, what alternatives might the school consider to tracking? All children, after all, need to be challenged at their own levels, and high-ability children need to be free to pursue their learning needs without hindrance. In thinking about this, one should be reminded that a comprehensive design of the school, which we will discuss in chapter 9, is one way to combat tracking, though in practice tracking has also flourished in comprehensive schools (Oakes, 1985; Nasaw, 1979). Although the comprehensive concept calls for an individualistic phase of the curriculum to provide children with opportunities for advanced and accelerated instruction, it tempers this call with other curriculum features, including general education (common learnings). At the high school level, high-ability students can be dealt with through elective studies, advanced placement, and individualization within heterogeneous settings. These are ways to deal with individual ability needs without resorting to tracking. Detracking a school should not necessarily mean eliminating accelerated classes for higher ability students or remedial classes for students needing help. It should mean, however, that in all grades and in all subject areas, teachers should give children time and encouragement to pursue individual learning agendas related to the scope of the course. Moreover, as Wheelock (1992) observed, to "untrack" the curriculum, the school and its teachers need to abide by a high level of expectation for all students (making high expectations the norm, not the exclusive province of the high track), to consider integrating remedial and other special services into the diversity of the heterogeneous group, to advance what is instructionally best for the "best" as best for all, and to embrace wide assessment strategies in the classroom that go beyond strict academic achievement.

 ## The Struggle for Desegregation

The struggle to desegregate the American school became most visible after the U.S. Supreme Court ruled that "separate educational institutions are inherently unequal." The Court handed this ruling down in the 1954 case of ***Brown v. Board of Education of Topeka,*** reversing the "separate but equal" doctrine that it supported 58 years earlier in another famous court case, *Plessy v. Ferguson.* In the *Brown* case, Chief Justice Earl Warren was aggressive in stating his view that separate schools were anything but equal. He opined that segregation victimized Black children with feelings of inferiority that affected their minds and hearts in ways that had long-term negative consequences.

The *Brown* ruling served notice to the schools practicing segregation. To many Southern states practicing separation by law (otherwise known as **de jure segregation**), the *Brown* ruling could not have been more clear: the "separate but equal" doctrine was dead and the dual system of schooling had to be dismantled. De jure segregation could no longer survive. The razing of the segregated school in the South would be a sign of things to come as wider challenges against segregation policies in all aspects of life were gathering speed and power. The bus boycott in Montgomery, Alabama, sit-ins at lunch counters in North Carolina, and the arrival of a new voice preaching a social philosophy of nonviolent civil disobedience all helped to lay the groundwork for Black resistance to segregation and for later federal involvement in the enforcement of desegregative edits. Over the course of a decade, Martin Luther King Jr.'s charismatic leadership would transform the question of segregation into a more expansive question of civil rights. King asked for more than just racial tolerance. He was imbued with commitment of love toward all men and women, no matter the color of their skin, which he took to be a principle of active Christianity. Peaceful or harmonious apartheid was not an acceptable answer to King. He wanted full and complete integration in the fabric of American society and demanded equal rights and opportunities under the constitutional law of the land.

Still, prosegregation forces in the South tried their best to keep the status quo, arguing that although the *Brown* case forbade discrimination in the school on the basis of race, it did not make integration mandatory. In other words, segregation was allowable as long as it was not de jure. The South was

TABLE 5.5

PERCENTAGE OF MINORITY STUDENTS ATTENDING PREDOMINANTLY MINORITY SCHOOLS (50% TO 100% MINORITY ENROLLMENT)			
	1968	**1980**	**1991**
Blacks	77	63	66
Hispanics	55	68	73

Source: Orfield, G. & others. (1993). *The growth of segregation in American schools: A Report to the National School Boards Association.* Cambridge, MA: Harvard Graduate School of Education.

The image of forced desegregation in Little Rock, Arkansas is often considered the symbol of the struggle for school desegregation.

angling at the very traditions that kept schoolchildren segregated in the North—**de facto segregation** practices that relied on segregated housing patterns and segregated school zoning. It would, in fact, take several decades, in both the South and the North, to start to see the kind of integration commanded in the *Brown* decision. Part of the problem was that the Supreme Court did not stipulate a time line for desegregation and did not explain how desegregation might take place. Instead, it granted local school districts the responsibility of formulating and implementing their own desegregation plans. Over the ensuing years, a host of initiatives followed.

Among the more popular schemes used in schools during the early stages of desegregation was **open enrollment,** which allowed families to choose the schools that they believed to be most appropriate for the education of their children. The thinking was that minority families would opt to enroll their children in White schools, but the open enrollment system was problematic because White families could use it to opt-out of schools becoming desegregated. Moreover, in the South, where an apartheid system of schooling existed for many years, there were clear psychological and social restraints to a Black parent's decision to opt for a White school.

Another option, which is still used in many urban school districts today, is known as **majority to minority transfer,** a practice that allows children to move or transfer from any school in which their race is in the majority to a school in which their race is in the minority. Over the years, the problem with this idea was that White children were not transferring, while Black children transferred at a rate lower than expected. To encourage such transfers, many school districts designed **magnet schools** that offered a special curriculum or some instructional feature that would pull students (like a magnet) to their doors. This idea, coupled with majority to minority transfer policies, served the purposes of desegregation and helped to put a halt to some of the "White flight" that many urban school districts were experiencing. At the same time, however, many magnet schools became known as elitist schools operating within the public school system (Moore & Davenport, 1990). Magnet schools

PERCENTAGE OF BLACK CHILDREN IN MAJORITY WHITE SCHOOLS IN THE SOUTH (1954–1991)			
1954	.001	1972	36.4
1960	.1	1976	37.6
1964	2.3	1980	37.1
1967	13.9	1986	42.0
1968	23.4	1988	43.5
1970	33.1	1991	39.2

Source: Orfield, G. & others. *The growth of segregation in American schools: A report to the National School Board Association.* Cambridge, MA: Harvard Graduate School of Education.

did indeed provide a more resourceful education for a few, but they did little to improve on the education of the vast number of children who did not go to them and who continued to populate the most segregated schools in the system. All in all, voluntary desegregation was usually limited to the three basic methods mentioned (Fife, 1992).

Where voluntary methods were not successful, the schools were sometimes placed under court-ordered prescriptions. In such cases, involuntary methods were used, like the gerrymandering of school zones, which sometimes involved transporting children to a school that was not in closest proximity to their homes, or the forced pairing of existing segregated schools for the purpose of swapping half the students in one school with the other for either a partial or full school day experience. Both compulsory strategies usually involved some forced busing. Although it affected a relatively small percentage of the nation's schools, busing was largely unpopular with the American public and generated much media attention in places, such as Boston, where it was claimed to have led to an enormous "White flight," a decline in educational quality, and a general crisis in the fiscal management of the city (Buell, 1982).

Despite these methods, compliance to the Court's desegregation ruling was slow in coming. In 1966, over a decade after the *Brown* ruling, the well-known **Coleman report** (1966) revealed that "the great majority of American children attend schools that are largely segregated . . . where almost all of their fellow students are from the same racial background as they are" (p. 4). The Coleman report also showed that there was a nationwide achievement gap between White and Black youngsters and that this gap widened as the students continued through the grades.

It also argued, somewhat surprisingly, that the physical facilities of the schools in America were more or less equal but that such resources were marginal to the achievement of the children. The expectation was that the study would show clear differences in the quality of the school resources used in the education of the average Black child as against those of the average White child. In fact, before the study was released, these differences were thought to be striking. But the eventual findings of Coleman's work showed that the differences in at least the school facilities of the races had not been as significant as assumed and that of the differences that did exist, the relation to achievement was not strong. Apparently, the wide disparities in achievement between White and Black youngsters could not be attributed to inequities in school facilities and instructional programs. The report instead pointed to the family background of students as the more significant factor in school achievement. It showed that school achievement among Black youth would improve if they attended schools with White youngsters who were from homes supporting education. This made the argument for integration even more compelling.

Approximately two years before the release of Coleman's *Equality of Educational Opportunity,* (1966) the federal government undertook a series of initiatives to combat poverty and racial discrimination. The federal action commenced in 1964 with the signing of the **Economic Opportunity Act,** which led to the establishment of the Office of Economic Opportunity and the support of intervention programs like Upward Bound, the Job Corps, and the widely publicized Head Start. In general, this act extended financial help to low-income students hoping to achieve a better education and sponsored instructional programs in adult education and early learning. Its ambitions were far-reaching. In summer 1965, for instance, Head Start enrolled close to half a million poor, mostly non-white children who were offered early academic experiences that would, it was hoped, translate into later academic success. The program was designed as an enhancer of equal opportunity, intended to bring disadvantaged children up to speed so that they could compete in elementary school. The irony with Head Start was that it was a compensatory program given birth during a race-conscious period that resulted in supporting the teaching of mostly non-White children in racially isolated preschools.

The year 1964 also marked the signing of the Civil Rights Act, which provided the funds and resources for various desegregative efforts. Title IV of the act gave federal financial support to school districts preparing school desegregation plans and charged the U.S. attorney general with the power to sue schools still practicing discrimination. Title VI threatened the loss of federal monies to school districts using federally sponsored programs in a racially discriminating manner.

One year later, President Johnson signed the **Elementary and Secondary Education Act of 1965** into law. The provisions of this legislation also centered on educational programs for the underprivileged. Monies justified through Title I of this act went to schools for the general purpose of advancing the educational causes of low-income children. Title II was designated for the purchasing of curriculum materials, while the other major entitlements went toward bringing the educational resources of the community and various collaborative agencies into the effort to improve the school lives of disadvantaged children. Each of these legislative mandates gave the federal government a visible role in dealing with issues of educational opportunity, racial isolation, and underachievement. The War on Poverty was on, and the public school was the main warrior.

Of course, other legislative measures were also being taken that fell outside the province of the school. The Civil Rights Act of 1968, or the Fair Housing Act, gave minority groups the right to buy and sell property

President Johnson, pictured here with his first teacher, Mrs. Kate Deadrich Looney, signs the Elementary and Secondary Education Act, irrevocably changing the federal government's role in local public schooling.

wherever they wanted. This dovetailed with the other strategies. Open access to neighborhoods would help to integrate them, which, in turn, would lead to more integrated schools.

During this period, the question of racial isolation drew forth in virtually all circles of discussion. The precipitous growth and concentration of Black populations in city ghetto areas underscored an obvious problem. In concluding its investigations on the civil upheaval and racial unrest in the cities of the country, writers of the *Report of the National Advisory Committee on Civil Disorders* (1968) warned that "our nation was moving toward two societies—one black, one white—separate and unequal" (p. 1). The committee further maintained that the corrosive forces of "white racism" were at the core of the evolving fraction. The report also supported the fundamental premise of the War on Poverty, which was that racial isolationism in schools led to isolationism outside of school on the part of both Whites and Blacks and that desegregation broke prejudices down and led to more tolerance and understanding across the races. The provision for a common and equal educational experience for all youth was presumed to be an axiom of American democracy, but in reality, quite the contrary was true.

Did the War on Poverty have a positive effect on the lives of minority children? Have the schools, almost 30 years after the release of Coleman's study, made significant inroads in desegregation and redistribution of wealth? The answer is mixed. A positive appraisal points to the widened paths of access to the middle class for minority populations and to increasing signs of academic achievement. All the national education assessment data on minority achievement, for instance, while still lower than school achievement among Whites, show an increasing movement to close the gap. Many urban schools, understanding the implications of segregation, have embraced desegregative plans unimaginable only 30 years ago. And segregation itself no longer carries the sanction of law. But a persistent culture of poverty continues to exist in the society, with large numbers of minorities living in communities marked by shocking conditions of poverty and desperation.

In many American cities and suburbs, the community populations are so imbalanced that desegregating the schools is virtually impossible. As indicated in Tables 5.6 and 5.7, the nationwide numbers on minority students attending predominantly minority schools (less than 50% White) are hardly what one might expect 40 years after *Brown v. Board of Education.* There are some small signs of improvement. From 1968, when the first national data were kept on segregated schools, to 1991, there has been a significant decline in the percentage of Blacks attending predominantly minority schools, although the number is clearly still high. The number of Blacks attending intensely segregated minority schools (90% to 100% minority enrollment), however, has fallen precipitously from 64.3% in 1968 to 33.9% in 1991 (Orfield & others, 1993). Among Hispanics, however, the opposite has occurred, with more Hispanic children attending predominantly minority schools in 1991 than in 1968. Part of the problem here is with recent immigration rates that have contributed to the number of low-income Hispanics living in concentrated areas. As observed by Gary Orfield, director of the Harvard Project on School Desegregation, "Hispanics in California and Texas are more segregated than blacks in Alabama or Mississippi in terms of educational experiences" (De Witt, 1992).

TABLE 5.6

PERCENTAGE OF MINORITY STUDENTS ATTENDING INTENSELY MINORITY SCHOOLS (90 TO 100% MINORITY ENROLLMENT)			
	1968	**1980**	**1991**
Blacks	64	33	33
Hispanics	23	28	34

Source: Orfield, G. & others. (1993). *The growth of segregation in American schools.* A Report to the National School Boards Association. Cambridge, MA: Harvard Graduate School of Education.

TABLE 5.7

PERCENTAGE OF MINORITY CHILDREN ENROLLED IN PREDOMINANTLY MINORITY SCHOOLS (50% TO 100% MINORITIES) IN CITY, SUBURBAN, AND SMALL-TOWN SETTINGS					
	Large Metro (400,000+)		**Small Metro (200,000+)**		**Town**
	City *Suburb*		*City* *Suburb*		*25,000+ small*
Blacks	92	57	62	43	45	44
Hispanics	93	63	70	51	44	60

Source: Orfield, G. & others. (1993). *The growth of segregation in American schools.* A Report to the National School Boards Association. Cambridge, MA: Harvard Graduate School of Education.

Latino students attend schools where the majority of their peers are also Latino.

A recent study done by the Harvard Project has found rising concentrations of minority students attending predominantly minority schools (Orfield & others, 1993). As of 1991, 66% of Black students and 73% of Hispanic students attend predominantly minority schools nationwide. But the conditions supporting segregation today are different from earlier times. High minority birth rates and high minority immigration rates have contributed to the isolation of these groups. Moreover, de facto segregation conditions, related mostly to housing patterns, continue to daunt desegregation efforts, arguably more so today than in the past.

Transportation remedies are typical in cases where school segregation exists because of deeply entrenched housing patterns. Over the decades, the Supreme Court has been active in setting the limits on busing as a desegregative tool. In 1971, it cleared the way for more expansive desegregation plans that included pairing noncontiguous school districts and the busing of students across school district lines. This ruling came in the case of **Swann v. Charlotte,** where de jure segregation was still being practiced in defiance of the *Brown* decision. By 1974, however, Supreme Court backpedaled slightly with its decision in the **Milliken v. Bradley** case, where it blocked efforts in Detroit to desegregate the schools by stating that suburban schools need not be included in the remedy. Detroit was a virtually all-Black school district surrounded by virtually all-White suburban schools. Its only hope for desegregation meant formulating a plan that included the involvement of the suburban district. The Court maintained that cross-district busing could not be used to cure within-district segregation. This ruling set clear limitations on the transportation remedies supported in the earlier *Swann* case.

As a result of *Milliken v. Bradley,* if one lived in the suburbs, one would likely be untouched by busing. In 1991, the Supreme Court (*Oklahoma City v.*

Dovell) retreated from the *Swann* ruling even further by making it easier for school districts to be released from court-ordered busing. Here, the Court stated that even segregated housing patterns should not compel court-ordered desegregation if such patterns existed by private choice and were not a legacy of official segregation policies. The Court also stated that any district in question would also have to demonstrate "practicable" steps toward the elimination of segregation.

In another important case, the Supreme Court eased federally-imposed desegregative measures placed on the State of Missouri and the Kansas City Public Schools because it believed that the interdistrict solutions sought by the city school district were not constitutional. The case began in 1977, when black students claimed that the state of Missouri failed to eliminate the remnants of segregation. After considerable legal haggling, the State was found in 1986 to be jointly responsible with the school district for failing to tear down a system of unconstitutional segregation. The result was a decade long effort of extra state spending on the Kansas City schools. The effect has been pay raises for school personnel, increased funds for remedial programs and considerable funding for the development and construction of state-of-the-art magnet schools (Greenhouse, 13 June, 1995). All of this was done in the interest of making the majority black district of Kansas City more attractive to white students living in the surrounding suburbs of the city. Because there were not enough white children living in the district, the courts sought a remedy that aimed to bring white children to the city district voluntarily. But in the view of the Supreme Court, interdistrict remedies, like those sought in Kansas City, could not be imposed on the State in the absence of evidence showing that the suburban schools violated the constitution. Desegregation, it argued, had to be specifically tailored to address documented discrimination within the district (Biskupic, J., 13 June, 1995). Many advocates of desegregation have viewed this ruling as a major setback, largely because it effectively removed interdistrict options.

Interestingly, Southern schools, which have historically been among the most segregated schools in the country, are now more integrated than schools in the Northeast and Midwest (Orfield & others, 1993), which still have entrenched housing patterns that keep the schools segregated. Progress in the South, in fact, has been spectacular, as demonstrated in The Historical Context feature in this section.

Still, today more than 1,200 school districts are under court mandates to desegregate (Celis, 1994). Segregation remains an enormous problem in large cities, where 15 out of 16 minority children nationwide attend segregated schools. It is also increasingly showing signs of becoming a problem in the suburbs of large cities, where 66% of Hispanic children and 60% of Black children attend predominantly minority schools (Orfield & others, 1993). These data are outlined in Tables 5.8 and 5.9.

In states with large urban populations, segregated schools continue to be the rule of thumb for Blacks and Hispanics. For instance, close to 60% of the Black children in Illinois and 60% of the Hispanic children in New York attend intensely segregated schools (90% to 100% minority). In Michigan, New York, and New Jersey, over half of the states' Black students attend intensely minority schools, and in New Jersey and Texas, approximately 40% of the states' Hispanic children attend intensely segregated schools. The most integrated states usually do not have large urban populations. In Kentucky, with a Black minority population of about 14% of the state population, and

TABLE 5.8

PERCENTAGE OF BLACK AND HISPANIC STUDENTS IN INTENSELY MINORITY SCHOOL (90% TO 100% MINORITIES) IN THE FIVE LARGEST SCHOOL DISTRICTS IN THE NATION (1988–1989)

	Percentage in Intensely Minority Schools	
	Blacks	Hispanics
New York City	74	67
Los Angeles	70	68
Chicago	81	50
Dade County (Miami)	59	41
Houston	69	53

Source: Orfield, G., & Montfort, F. (1988). *Racial change and desegregation in large school districts.* Washington, DC: National School Boards Association.

TABLE 5.9

PUBLIC OPINION ON ISSUES OF SCHOOL DESEGREGATION

Has the Quality of Education Improved for Blacks as a Result of School Integration Efforts?

	1971	1988	1994	1994 (Whites)	1994 (Blacks)
Yes	43	55	65	64	70
No	31	29	28	29	25
No opinion	26	16	7	7	5

Has the Quality of Education Improved for Whites as a Result of School Integration Efforts?

	1971	1988	1994	1994 (Whites)	1994 (Blacks)
Yes	23	35	42	39	59
No	51	47	50	52	33
No opinion	26	18	8	9	8

Do You Believe That More Should Be Done or Less Should Be Done to Integrate the Schools Throughout the Nation?

	1971	1988	1994	1994 (Whites)	1994 (Blacks)
More	30	37	56	52	84
Less	38	23	30	33	6
No change	23	31	9	9	7
No opinion	9	9	5	6	3

Source: McAneny, L., & Saad, L. (1994), May. America's public schools: Still separate? Still unequal? *The Gallup Poll Monthly*, 22–29.

Delaware, which is closer to 28%, the overwhelming majority of these children (over 90%) are enrolled in White majority schools (Orfield & others, 1993). These states accomplished integration through school consolidation efforts and through desegregation initiatives that encouraged interactions between urban and suburban districts.

Despite the uneven effects of desegregative policies, progress has been made in public opinion toward desegregation. The Gallup Poll released the results of a national survey in 1994 that indicated that 84% of the nation's population agreed with the *Brown v. Board of Education* decision and with the view that children should be allowed to go to the same schools, irrespective of their race (McAneny & Saad, 1994). This is in contrast with the views of the public in 1955, when only 55% of the population agreed with the *Brown* decision, and in 1963, when 63% of the population approved of the decision. Along similar lines, researchers for the Gallup Poll also asked whether school integration improved the quality of education received by Black students and by White students. Sixty-five percent of the respondents responded affirmatively to the former and 42% responded affirmatively to the latter. These generally positive views toward the effects of school integration were also supported with a call for more integration. Fifty-six percent of the polled public believed that more school integration is needed. In all these questions, the 1994 public response demonstrated historically high numbers (see Table 5.10).

Despite these generally positive attitudes toward the role of school integration, Americans tend not to see it as a problem that affects them locally. When asked whether they would like to see their own community more or less integrated, or whether it was just right as is, 69% of the public responded just right (71% of the Whites and 58% of the Blacks). This might not be seen as a contradictory response if most communities were integrated, but the very same opinion poll found that 74% of the Whites described their neighborhoods as all or mostly White, while only 37% of the Blacks described their neighborhoods as all or mostly Black.

The Gender of Schooling

In recent years, the question of gender discrimination has found its way into education circles. Discussions of gender in schools relate directly to school-environment concerns, most specifically to the school curriculum. To what extent, for instance, can gender discrimination be found in what is studied in the curriculum, in how knowledge and skills are taught in the curriculum, and in why there are differences in school achievement across gender in some areas.

Recently, several feminist commentators have argued that, in spite of a largely female teaching force, schools are designed for the success of males. One might ask, how can this be? Logic suggests that schools should not be places that are hostile to females. Because most schoolteachers are women (about 7 out of 10), it stands to reason that the schools should be places where females might actually be advantaged. But some critics have suggested that things do not work this way because teachers are still subordinate in the structure of school power. Their superordinates (principals and superintendents) are mostly males, and this being the case, the school seeks to promote male values in the school, which are typically seen as competition, individuality, and rationality. Meanwhile, female values, which are believed to be marked by subjectivity, empathy, and caring, do not receive their fair share of circulation in the conduct of school life. Carol Gilligan (1982), who has been at the forefront of gender research, has characterized women as more concerned with feelings and men as preoccupied with control, order, and rules. Gilligan also believes that the proclivities of men are sanctioned in the school; the values of men still hold the key to what it means to be competent and successful in life. One can, of course, criticize these conclusions as lacking in subtlety, as painting males with one broad brush and females with another. But whether one agrees with such a view, schools are clearly beginning to struggle with the question of how gender plays a role in the education of both boys and girls. Some of the early conclusions are not favorable to girls (AAUW, 1992).

During the early 1970s, Congress passed legislation under **Title IX of the Education Amendment Act** that made it illegal for any educational programs receiving federal monies to discriminate on the basis of sex or gender. For school systems, this meant that a Title IX officer needed to be appointed to coordinate compliance and to handle complaints related to sex or gender discrimination. An immediate impact was felt in athletic programs, where girls' sports were long treated as a stepchild, and in sex segregated courses in health, vocational education, physical education, and some higher levels of mathematics and science. Although Title IX received much media attention in relation to its impact on athletic programs, compliance to Title IX was slow in being met, and federal sanctions against schools that failed to follow the law have not been substantial (Hansot, 1993).

Research on gender and education has targeted various areas for investigation. In the context of the school, textbooks, classroom interactions, testing mechanisms, and subject-specific curricula have been among the more prominent areas of concern. As early as the 1970s, for instance, it was widely documented that the depiction of girls in curriculum materials was inadequate. Depictions were relatively low in frequency and tended to reinforce stereotypical traits of passivity and dependence (Stacey, Bereaud, & Daniels, 1974). Today only 1 in the 10 most commonly used books in high school English classes was written by a woman, and in both history and science textbooks, the role and place of women have been minimized. Ask children to name 10 famous women from American history and the response will not likely be impressive (Sadker & Sadker, 1994).

Even at the level of reading instruction, girls have been underrepresented in the stories used in popular basal reading programs, in widely used language arts textbooks, and in so-called award-winning literary books for children, such as the well-known Caldecott winners (Sadker & Sadker, 1994). In the actual action of the classroom, observational research has revealed the nature of student-teacher interactions (at both elementary and secondary school levels) to be favorable to boys (see the From the Editorial Page feature in this section). Teachers, for instance, tend to give boys more attention (including listening and counseling), to offer them more thought-provoking questions, and to reward them more often, though they also criticize and punish them more often (Sadker, Sadker, & Klein, 1991).

Yet girls, as a group, generally earn higher grades than boys throughout their school careers and are less likely to be placed in special education programs (AAUW, 1992). They outperform boys on National Assessment of Educational Progress (NAEP) writing-skills assessment (Mullis, & others, 1991) and have historically outscored boys in all age groups on verbal abilities (AAUW, 1992). Some researchers have trivialized the grade achievements of girls by arguing that they result from a system that rewards the quiet social behaviors of girls (Sadker & Sadker, 1994). But the school achievement of girls could well point to the possibility that boys might be shortchanged in school as well, and that gender stereotypes might be at the core of the problem.

Carol Gilligan, whose book, In a Different Voice, forced a reconsideration of gender differences in schools.

Some commentators have speculated that the disproportionately high representation of boys in special education categories might have something to do with the more aggressive and attention-commanding behaviors of boys in schools. When such behavioral problems tax the teacher's ability to keep children educationally engaged, there might be an inclination to construe the so-called behavioral problem as a learning problem (Greenberg, 1985). The paradox is that the stereotype of quiet passivity expected from girls might save them from unfair special education classifications. Similarly, the historical underperformance of boys in verbal areas again might have something to do with stereotypical views that equate reading, especially reading certain kinds of materials, with feminine behavior. The gender factor, in this sense, can work both ways, and not always to the benefit of boys.

This is not to say that these stereotypes do not victimize girls. According to Belenky and others, there is a "silence" expected from girls that exerts wide-ranging damage. In their interviews with women and girls, Belenky and others (1986) found that many women viewed their schooling experiences as sitting in classes silently, watching and listening to other students (mostly boys) talk. Because American culture tends to value girls who are polite and quietly submissive, these women and girls felt that their voices were not valued and that any effort to exercise an opinion might be construed as rude behavior. Belenky and others cite the importance of verbalizing one's thoughts in the development of crucial reasoning skills to reinforce their indictment against the school in silencing girls' voices.

Given the role of silence in the school lives of girls, Belenky and others argue that girls also tend to see themselves as receivers of knowledge in the classroom rather than as mediators of knowledge, as receptacles into which other people make "deposits" of knowledge. Receivers of knowledge tend to believe that other people have very important things to say, but that their own thoughts are unimportant. Women and girls who think of themselves as receivers of knowledge are apt to rely on authorities for what is right and wrong. They do not believe that they can develop their own facts and ideas. Again, received knowledge is an attribute that is basic to the stereotypical passivity expected from women.

Gender discrimination, however, is not always this subtle. Today increasing attention is being given to the issue of sexual harassment in school, especially as it has been conducted against female students. The problem can start in the early grades, where small boys might use sexually loaded terms to describe and taunt their female peers, often without even knowing what they are saying. In high school, it can be deliberate sexual harassment that places unhealthy pressures and anxieties on young girls. A 1993 national survey of middle school and high school students, entitled *Hostile Hallways,* demonstrated some of the problems. Eighty-one percent of girls claimed to have been subjected to some form of unwanted sexual advance and 65% of the girls said that they have been touched or grabbed in a sexual manner. Although boys also reported high levels of sexual harassment, girls reported to be more seriously affected by the harassment, with 33% of them stating that they did not want to talk in class or attend school because of it (Sadker & Sadker 1994). To make matters worse, often teachers and other school leaders tolerate these episodes of harassment, using a "boys will be boys" rationale (AAUW, 1992; Sadker & Sadker, 1994). Some girls and their families have filed sexual harassment suits against schools, arguing that the provisions of Title IX, which bars sexual discrimination in the school, should cover students against student sexual harassment. Some of these claims have been settled out of court. (Lewin, 26 June, 1995) Increasingly school boards are examining their options in trying to prevent student against student sexual harassment, lest they be found responsible for tolerating a sexually hostile environment in school.

Except for verbal and written abilities, boys outperform girls in most tested areas in the school curriculum. In mathematics and science, in particular, the achievement data are clear in showing an underperformance by girls. There is evidence that the gap is narrowing, but it still exists. Boys, for instance, still perform at much higher academic and cognitive levels in math and science, outscoring girls on NAEP testing, on Advanced Placement exams, and on the mathematical score of the Scholastic Aptitude Test. Interestingly, girls earn grades in mathematics and science that are as high as the grades earned by boys, and their participation in mathematics and science course work is not significantly less than that of boys (AAUW, 1992). This makes for an interesting question because despite a good classroom performance, girls' standardized testing results are relatively poor and their choice of career plans stays clear of the sciences and mathematics. A multitude of factors may be at play here, including a testing bias and a potential stereotypic socialization pattern in the school and in the broader society that upholds mathematics and sciences as suitable career paths for boys. According to some surveys, girls learn to think that they are not mathematically capable as early as the elementary grades (AAUW, 1992).

In regard to testing, much of the very same type of work done in revealing the stereotypic images of women in textbooks has also been done with achievement tests (Selko, 1984). Similar results indicate that references to women are low and are fashioned in stereotypic ways on achievement tests (AAUW, 1992). The disparity in test achievement that exists between boys and girls is particularly problematic because much of the standardized testing in America is tightly linked to "high-stakes" opportunities, including, most obviously, scholarships based on testing results, which under current conditions are twice as likely to go to boys (AAUW, 1992). Of course, achievement on a standardized test also carries various psychological baggage. Doing well on norm-referenced tests sanctions one's skills and abilities, while doing poorly calls one's skills and abilities into question. These effects will also likely have an impact on career choices and other life decisions.

One of the more important arguments emerging from the gender bias literature is related to the self-esteem of girls. Surveys offered in the AAUW report demonstrate lower self-esteem ratings for girls than for boys. Equally disturbing is the low sense of esteem held by boys toward girls. For instance, in one interesting study, the Sadkers asked elementary-aged boys and girls how they would feel if they suddenly found themselves to be the opposite sex. Forty-two percent of the girls managed to say something positive about being a boy, while only 5% of the boys could see some advantage in being a girl. Some of the essays written by the boys in response to the Sadkers' question used revolting images of wanting to escape from and to destroy their female bodies (Sadker & Sadker, 1994).

Still, there are encouraging trends to report for women in education. Recent annual growth rates for women enrolled in higher education have outstripped the male enrollment rates. In 1978, males earned more bach-

Shortchanging Girls

What is the essential message in Trudeau's cartoon? Is it a fair characterization? Has your own experience in schools reflected the bias conveyed in the cartoon?

elor's, master's, and doctoral degrees than females. But in subsequent years, the growth of women in higher education has been impressive. Females have now overtaken males as recipients of bachelor's and master's degrees in America, and moderate statistical projections indicate that women will continue to show a strong presence in higher education (see Figures 5.2 and 5.3). In the area of doctoral studies, women are still behind, but again, moderate statistical projections done by the National Center for Education Statistics indicate a healthy climb for women and a more fair and equal share of the conferred doctoral degrees in the future (see Figure 5.4). As of 1993, the percentage of females employed in the assistant professor ranks of America's colleges and universities was proportional to the national percentage of females in the work force. (Annual Report on the Economic Status of the Profession, 1995). Although female presence in higher education is on good ground when one looks across the university and college landscape, there is less cause for optimism when one focuses directly on the areas of science and engineering. Although the United States leads the world in the provision of access for women in the fields of science and engineering, female represen- tation in such areas is still low.

Schools clearly have to get serious about remedying any role that they might place in gender discrimination, especially because there are consider- able societal and sometimes familial trends to counter. In a review of the literature on gender equity, Olivares and Rosenthal (1992) cited several studies that pointed to the role of parents in the perpetuation of gender stereotypes. Parents, for example, still encourage sex-typed activities for their

BACHELOR'S DEGREES, BY SEX OF RECIPIENT, WITH MIDDLE ALTERNATIVE PROJECTIONS: 1980–81 TO 2005–2006

FIGURE 5.2

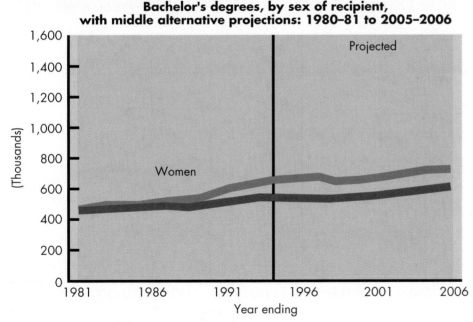

Source: Hussar W.J. & Gerald, D.E. (1995) *Projections of education statistics to 2006* Washington, DC: U.S. Department of Education. p. 56.

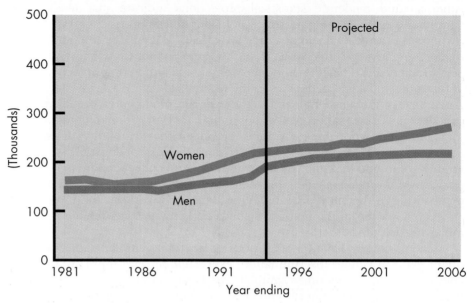

FIGURE 5.3

MASTER'S DEGREES, BY SEX OF RECIPIENT WITH MIDDLE ALTERNATIVE PROJECTIONS: 1980–81 TO 2005–2006

Source: Hussar, W.J. & Gerald, D.E. (1995). *Projections of education statistics to 2006* Washington, DC: U.S. Department of Education, p. 57.

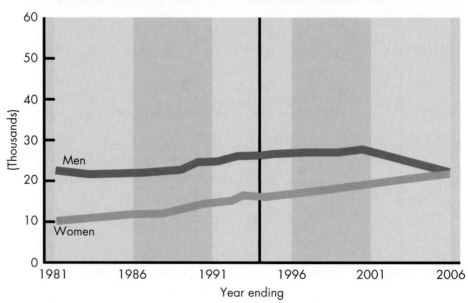

FIGURE 5.4

DOCTOR'S DEGREES, BY SEX OF RECIPIENT, WITH MIDDLE ALTERNATIVE PROJECTIONS: 1980–81 TO 2005–2006

Source: Hussar, W.J. & Gerald, D.E. (1995). *Projections of education statistics to 2006* Washington, DC: U.S. Department of Education, p. 57.

children (Lytton & Romney, 1991), continue to choose stereotyped toys and colors for infants and toddlers (Pomerleau, Boldice, & others, 1990), and frequently evaluate children negatively, especially boys, when they exhibit cross-sex play or cross-sex personality traits (Martin, 1990). Toys that might help to teach children about caring, such as dolls, have too often been seen as appropriate for only girls, while toys that might help to serve as an introduction to science, such as building blocks, have too often been seen as appropriate for only boys (Noddings, 1992). Gender discrimination is clearly a problem that transcends the school.

National public opinion polls demonstrate that the American people believe that society still favors men over women, but life in America has its ups and downs for men and women alike. Today 6 of out 10 minimum-wage earners are women. Women head 8 out of 10 single-parent households and 7 out of 10 families living below the poverty line. Ninety-four percent of all secretaries and 97% of all child-care workers are women, while 82% of all lawyers, physicians, and judges are men, and 94% of all engineers are men (Scollay, 1994). Of course, boys are more likely to be expelled from school, to drop out of school, to be held back, to be punished, and eventually to land in jail. They are more likely to be victims of homicides, suicides, and accidents.

Gender inequities have led some schools to consider the idea of gender-segregated classes. The presumption here is that boys undermine the education of girls through their attention-getting and competitive behaviors and through the preferential treatment given to them by teachers. As indicated, some thinkers also believe that girls simply learn differently from boys and are best taught away from boys.

Gender-segregated classes, however, are problematic in several respects. One could argue that they violate a basic principle of the public school mandate, which is to provide integrated experiences for all youth irrespective of race, ethnicity, social class and gender. In fact, a legal argument has recently emerged against gender-segregated classes. At a federal level, such classes are being examined as violations of Title IX. Some states, such as Iowa, have openly declared that gender-segregated classes are illegal and cannot be sustained without an official exemption.

But there are public schools that have experimented with the idea, especially in the area of math and science instruction. Some anecdotal evidence seems to support the fact that these classes improve the achievement, elevate the self-esteem, and encourage more active learning behaviors among girls (Wee, 1 May, 1995). There is little word on their effect on the education of the boys.

Critics of gender segregation have argued that all-girl classes seem to be a peculiar response to the gender-based criticisms against the school, because they imply that girls cannot perform in an integrated classroom and because they potentially set the conditions for the legitimization of stereotyping and the widening of gender-based schisms. Other critics maintain that making gender the salient factor in classroom enrollment comes at the expense of broader experiences that go beyond and are arguably more important than gender (Powlishta, 1995).

Given these criticisms, school leaders might want to ask if gender bias can be addressed without resorting to segregated classes? If boys are ridiculing girls, can a method be found to prevent such episodes? If teachers are unwittingly providing advantages to boys, can the school seek a remedy that keeps the classroom integrated? And if segregation by gender finds a compelling argument in terms of enhancing the school performance of girls, can similar arguments then be made for ethnic or race-based education?

Some thinkers observe that the problems that boys (and men) have can be blamed, at least partly, on the absence of men in the socialization of boys. Women still perform the largest share of work in the early familial care of boys and in the early school development of boys. The postindustrial rage to keep parents, especially men, at work and the continuing collapse of the nuclear family, which often results in single-parent households headed by females, likely militates against the healthy development of girls and boys. The fact that so many fathers fail to exhibit responsible paternal behaviors also contributes to the problem. But in the end, it will be the school, as much as any other agency, that must be at the forefront of proposing remedies that will facilitate communication across the sexes, provide equal opportunities for quality learning, and ultimately help create a new generation inspired by a concern for the common good.

KEY TERMS

Title IX of the Education Amendment Act
Open enrollment
Majority to minority transfer
Curriculum tracking
Civil Rights Act of 1964

Elementary and Secondary Act of 1965
Magnet schools
Brown v. Board of Education of Topeka
Milliken v. Bradley

Swann v. Charlotte
Coleman report
De jure segregation
De facto segregation
Economic Opportunity Act

KEY QUESTIONS

1. What are the typical justifications given for curriculum tracks in schools?

2. How have critics argued that curriculum tracking practices are inequitable and unfair to poor and minority students?

3. What is the difference between curriculum tracking and ability grouping?

4. What are some of the ways that schools might offer differentiated instruction without resorting to tracking?

5. In what ways did school districts voluntarily cope with the mandate to desegregate?

6. What were the essential findings of the Coleman report, and how did the report contribute to the call for desegregation?

7. What were some of the strategies embraced by the federal government during the 1960s as it dealt with issues of race and class in the public schools?

8. What are the national trends in the area of school segregation and where has there been the most progress?

9. Where is school segregation most intractable and why?

10. What have been the views of the Supreme Court in the area of transportation remedies (busing) for school segregation?

11. What do the national opinion polls have to say about the American people's views toward school segregation and school integration?

12. How do schools shortchange girls?

13. How do schools shortchange boys?

14. How does the school expectation of silence presumably victimize girls?

15. How can one explain the strong classroom performance of girls in math and science against their underperformance on standardized tests in math and science?

16. What are the general arguments for and against gender-segregated classes? What are your personal views on the matter?

REFERENCES

American Association of University Women. The report of (1992). *How schools shortchange girls*. Washington, DC: National Education Association.

Annual Report on the Economic Status of the Profession (1995). *Academe,* 81(2): 8–87.

Armstrong, L. S. (1990, February 20). Draft O.C.R. memo outlines ground probing ability grouping. *Education Week, 10*(22), 21–22.

Belenky, M., Clinchy, B., Goldberger, N., & Tarule, J. (1986). *Women's way of knowing*. New York: Basic Books.

Biskopic, J. (13 June 1995) Desegregation remedies rejected. *Washington Post,* p. 1.

Braddock, J. H. (1990a). Tracking in the middle grades: National patterns of grouping for instruction. *PDK, 71*(6), 445–449.

Braddock, J. H. (1990b). *Tracking: Implications for student race ethnic subgroups* (Report No. 1). Baltimore: Center for Research on Effective Schooling for Disadvantaged Students.

Buell, E. H. (1982). *School desegregation and defended neighborhoods*. Lexington, MA: Lexington Books.

Carey, N. & others (1994) Curricular differentiation in public high schools, Washington, DC: Nat'l Center for Education Statistics ED, 379–338.

Carson, C. C., Huelskamp, R.M., & Woodall, T.D. 1993, May/June. Perspectives on education in America. *Journal of Educational Research,* 259–310.

Celis, W. (1994, May 18). 40 years after Brown, segregation persists. *New York Times,* Sec. A, p. 1.

Coleman, J.S & others (1966). *Equality of Educational Opportunity*. Washington, DC: Office of Education, Department of Health, Education and Welfare.

Cremin, L. A. (1965). *The genius of American education*. New York: Random House—Vintage Books.

De Witt, K. (1992, January 9). Rising segregation is found for Hispanic students. *New York Times,* Sec. A, p. 15.

Fife, B. L. (1992). *Desegregation in American schools: Comparative intervention strategies*. New York: Praeger.

Gamoran, A. (1992). The variable effects of high school tracking. *American Sociological Review, 57*(6), 812–828.

Gilligan, C. (1982). *In a different voice*. Cambridge: Harvard University Press.

Greenberg, S. (1985). Educational equity in early education environments. In S. Klien (Ed.), *Handbook in achieving sex equity through education*. Baltimore: Johns Hopkins University Press.

Greenhouse, L. (13 June, 1995). Justices Say Making State Pay in Desegregation Case was an Error *New York Times,* p. 1.

Hansot, E. (1993). Historical and contemporary views of gender and education. In S. K. Biklen & D. Pollard (Eds.), *Gender and education* (Part 1: Ninety-second yearbook of the National Society for the Study of Education). Chicago: NSSE.

Howe, H. (1993). *Thinking about our kids*. New York: The Free Press.

Husen, T. (1983, March). Are standards in the U.S. schools really lagging behind those in other countries? *Phi Delta Kappan.* 64(7): 455–61.

Kozol, J. (1991). *Savage inequalities*. New York: Crown Publishing.

Kulik, J. (1993, Spring). An analysis of the research on ability grouping. *National Research Center on the Gifted and Talented Newsletter,* 8–9. (ED 367-095)

Lewin, T. (26 June, 1995). Students use law on discrimination in sex-abuse suits, *New York Times,* p. 1.

Lytton, H., & Romney, D. (1991). Parents' differential socialization of boys and girls. *Psychological Bulletin, 109,* 267–296.

McAneny, L., & Saad, L. (1994, May). America's public schools: Still separate? Still unequal? *The Gallup Poll Monthly,* 22–29.

Martin, C. L. (1990). Attitudes and expectations about children with non-traditional and traditional gender roles. *Sex Roles, 22*(3/4), 131–165.

Moore, D. & Davenport, S. School Choice: The new improved sorting machine. In W. Boyd & H. Walberg (Eds.) *Choice in education Berkeley, Ca: McCutehan Publishing Corp.*

Mullis, & other. (1991). *Trends in academic progress*. Prepared by Educational Testing Service Washington, DC: U.S. Government Printing Office ED#338–720.

Nasaw, D. (1979). *Schooled to order*. New York: Oxford University Press.

National Advisory Committee on Civil Disorders. (1968). *Report of the National Advisory Committee on Civil Disorders*. Washington, DC: U.S. Government Printing Office.

Noddings, N. (1992). Gender and the curriculum. In P. W. Jackson (Ed.), *Handbook of research on curriculum*. New York: Macmillan.

Oakes, J. (1985). *Keeping track: How schools structure inequality*. New Haven: Yale University Press.

Oakes, J. (1990). *Multiplying inequalities*. Santa Monica, Ca: The Rand Corporation.

Oakes, J. (1992). Detracking schools: Early lessons from the field. *PDK, 73*(6), 448–454.

Oakes, J., Gamoran, A., & Page, R. (1992). Curriculum differentiation: Opportunities, outcomes, and meanings. In P. W. Jackson (Ed.), *Handbook of research on curriculum*. New York: Macmillan.

Olivares, R. A. & Rosenthal, N. (1992). Gender equity and classroom experiences: A review of research. ED# 366–701.

Orfield, G., & Monfort, F. (1988). *Racial change and desegregation in large school districts*. Washington, DC: National School Boards Association.

Orfield, G. & others. (1993). *The growth of segregation in American schools*. A Report to the National School Boards Association. Cambridge, MA: Harvard Graduate School of Education.

Pomerleau, A., Boldice, D., & others. (1990). Pink or blue: Environmental stereotyping in the first two years of life. *Sex Roles, 22*(5/6), 359–67.

Powlishta, K. K. (1995). Gender segregation among children: Understanding the "Cootie Phenomenon," *Young Children,* 50(4): 61–73.

Sadker, M., & Sadker, D. (1994). *Failing at fairness*. New York: Charles Scribner and Sons.

Sadker, M., Sadker, D., & Klien, S. (1991). The issue of gender in elementary and secondary education. In G. Grant (Ed.), *Review of research in education*. Washington, DC: American Educational Research Association.

Scollay, S. J. (1994). The forgotten half. *The American School Board Journal,* 181(4), 46–48.

Selko, P. (1984). *Assessing sex bias in testing*. New York: Greenwood Press.

Slavin, R. (1987). Ability grouping and student achievement in elementary schools. *Review of Educational Research,* 57 (3), 293–336.

Slavin, R. (1990). Achievement effects in ability grouping in secondary schools. *Review of Educational Research, 60*(3), 471–499.

Stacey, M., Bereaud, S., & Daniels, J. (Eds.). (1974). *And Jill came tumbling down.* New York: Dell Books.

Tanner, D., & Tanner, L. N. (1995). *Curriculum development: Theory into practice* (2nd ed.). New York: Macmillan.

Tyler, R. W. (1981, January). The United States and the world: A comparison of educational performance. *Phi Delta Kappan.* 62(5): 307–18.

Unseem, E. L. (1990). *Getting on the fast track in mathematics.* Paper presented at the American Educational Research Association, April 16–20, Boston.

Wee, E. (1 May, 1995). A lesson in confidence. *Washington Post* p. 1.

Wheelock, A. (1992). *Untracking the school.* New York: The New Press.

6

THE QUESTION OF SCHOOL ACHIEVEMENT

Sister Pauline Lemaire helps her preschoolers in Portland, Oregon, spell words with preformed letters. Like all teachers, she asks questions about her students' progress. Are they making progress toward recognizing letters? Are they learning the role of numbers? Are they learning to work cooperatively? Are they understanding the idea of community?

The task of reporting the academic success or failure of U.S. students is now largely left to standardized tests. Of course, there is nothing wrong with standardized tests, but do they tell the whole story? Student test scores are now used to make thousands of comparisons. For instance, how are U.S. students doing in comparison to students in other industrialized countries? This chapter challenges our common understanding in this area and reports that U.S. schools are not doing as poorly as some would have us believe.

One does not have to go very far or dig very deep to encounter less-than-complimentary commentary on the public schools. SAT scores are declining, comparative cross-national achievement scores are less than encouraging, dropout rates in the urban schools are embarrassingly high, and complaints about the lack of quality in American education are well represented in the news media. The American schools, like all the society's institutions, are beset with serious problems. Obviously much needs to be done to make the school a safer and more enlightened place. As documented in Kozol's *Savage Inequalities* (1991), the nature of school life for many children of poverty is utterly shameful.

But the American public schools have not always been evaluated fairly by their critics. In fact, much of the portrayal of the public school in the media and in the rhetoric of politicians has been committed to negativity, often conveyed with attention-commanding language about crisis, calamity, and catastrophe. Remarkably, this kind of hysteria over a "crisis in education" has been with us for at least half a century (Passow, 1984), a fact that calls each so-called crisis into question. Indignant about the barrage of negativity mounted against the school, some commentators have tried to correct "the big lie" that they believe has been told about public education (Bracey, 1991, 1993; Schneider, 1994).

One hardly needs to be reminded of the various charges standing against the school. Over the years, the schools have been blamed for virtually every perceived failure or decline in the nation's industrial, commercial, military, and technological markets. In 1983, a presidentially appointed commission even declared the nation "at risk" because of the alleged low state of achievement in public education (NCEE, 1983). Thirty years ago, the Soviet Union was believed to be holding a supreme militaristic advantage over

America because the U.S. public schools evidently could not produce enough scientists, mathematicians, and engineers to meet the Soviet challenge; 10 years ago, the Japanese were known to be better at producing high-quality cars and microchip technologies, again because of American school failings. What is so striking about such criticisms is that the public school always seems central to any sign of failure in the society but is somehow insignificant or incidental to signs of societal progress and success. Where there have been economic, technological, and military successes (and there have been many), the schools have escaped receiving credit. In truth, if one were to judge the schools according to the nation's success on various nationalistic and techno-industrial scales, one would necessarily have to make a positive judgment because the United States is now largely viewed as the world's only superpower.

American Education in the International Context

The characteristics of the educational systems across the world vary at the most basic levels. Many advanced nations are ethnically homogeneous and are organizationally centralized with national curricula. In centralized systems, there is usually little debate over what should constitute the common culture of the school and few complications related to church and state concerns as well as to parental relations. In decentralized systems, there are inevitably concerns about diversity and local prerogative. In a pluralistic society, such as in America, there are matters of second-language learning and second-culture assimilation that also have to be considered. But the differences only start here. There is, for instance, much variance in the instructional commitment of time to school education in different countries—in the actual lengths of school days and school years. These data are often held against the United States because its school year is among the shortest in the world. Few commentators, however, consider the instructional commitment of time over an average student's career in America, which is quite high because of the open access to the educational system (Hlebowitsh, 1989), and few acknowledge that some countries that mandate more days in schools actually provide fewer instructional hours in school. Japan, for instance, has a 220-day school year and Korea, 222 days, but both provide significantly fewer instructional hours in school than does the United States, where the school year is 180 days long (Griffith & others, 1994).

When engaging in cross-national comparisons, it is also important to note the sociological problems that the schools inherit from their societies. One way or another, poverty, crime, and the social conditions that lead to problems such as teenage pregnancies, single-parent families, and racism will all militate against the development of healthy schools. Furthermore, teacher salaries and teacher prestige vary across national systems of education. In Japan, for instance, the average teacher's salary is about 50% higher than in the United States, after adjustments are made for the relative incomes of the countries. This is despite the fact that U.S. teachers, on the average, have much higher levels of education. The average Japanese teacher has a bachelor's degree or less, while the average American teacher has a master's degree or more (Carson, Huelskamp, & Woodall, 1993). In Japan, the very word for "teacher" has overtones of reverence, while in the United States the teacher is still struggling for professional status.

Obviously, there are also vital differences in school-investment strategies and legislative restraints across the schools of the world. U.S. schools, for instance, are influenced by legislative edicts related to the education of disabled children and to the education of non-English-speaking children, issues that may not be as vital in other countries. Native language instruction to nonnative speakers is a major undertaking in the American public school, while in culturally homogeneous countries, such as Japan, such instructional concerns largely do not exist.

Even the home activities of schoolchildren vary in ways that might influence education. Rates of recreational reading, school homework, community involvement, and television viewing all vary considerably across the world. In Japan, private "after school schools" provide instruction to many children in English and in the tested areas of the national curriculum. In China, grandparents play a vital role in the home life of children, while in America, extended families are more likely to be separated by distance. Belief systems related to effort, interest, expectation, and ability are also mediated by cultural and ethnic conditions (Stevenson & Stigler, 1992). These factors should give us pause when we compare schools on an international basis. They demonstrate the complicated and dynamic context in which each school system operates.

There have been, of course, ways of examining American schools on an international basis (see Table 6.1). The best data are drawn from the results of tests administered by the International Association for the Evaluation of Educational Achievement (IEA), a group of international researchers interested in examining cross-national school achievement as it relates to school organization, student selection, grouping practices, curricula, and socioeconomic factors (Tanner, 1972). For many years now, the association has offered a glimpse of education across national systems through its international assessments. Another valuable source for data on international comparisons is the International Assessment of Educational Progress (IAEP), an assessment sponsored by Educational Testing Service and the U.S. Department of Education. Both associations have cautioned against the tendency to use cross-national achievement in the context of an international contest.

In 1988, the director of the National Center for Education Statistics expressed his agency's views on this very matter. He underscored the importance of IEA and IAEP studies toward helping to inform American judgments about schooling, but he made it clear that such data were not to be used for competitive purposes. "We find a keen interest in information that places American measures side by side with other nations not because we want to hold someone accountable, or want to run an international academic olympics, but because we expect to find differences that give us something to ponder, that enable us to question our actions, and that let us assess whether a practice in another country might fit here" (Suter, 1988, p. 2). Unfortunately, the cautions mentioned about the use of IEA and IAEP studies have been largely ignored by the news media, which continue to use international test data to declare the global ranking of U.S. schools, and by politicians bent on describing the schools in their worst light.

The work done by the IEA has historically shown that American schools rank among those having the lowest socioeconomic bias and the highest educational yield. This has essentially meant that, relative to other advanced nations, the United States has had a fairer and more open system of schooling. Naturally, this openness has affected the average achievement in various academic areas, and in comparison with other nations, the United States has tended to be on the lower end of the achievement ratings, especially at the high school level. But because the lower scores are partly a function of a wider representation of students from lower socioeconomic settings and diverse cultural backgrounds, one could arguably construe the lower mean scores in a positive light. Sanguine pronouncements about U.S.

TABLE 6.1

CHARACTERISTICS OF EDUCATIONAL SYSTEMS (1991)						
Country	Ethnic Homo-geneity[1]	Age for Starting School	Average Days in School Year[2]	Average Minutes of Instruction in School Day[2]	National Curriculum[3]	Percent of Schools With One or More Problems
1	2	3	4	5	6	7
Populations (comprehensive)						
Canada[4]	No	6	188 (0.2)	304 (0.8)	No	13 (1.3)
France	Yes	6	174 (1.7)	370 (3.4)	Yes	29 (4.9)
Hungary	Yes	6	177 (1.5)	223 (1.3)	Yes	32 (4.2)
Ireland	Yes	6	173 (0.9)	323 (4.4)	Yes	39 (5.8)
Israel[5]	No	6	215 (2.2)	278 (6.5)	Yes	46 (6.7)
Jordon	Yes	6	191 (0.9)	260 (2.9)	Yes	63 (5.3)
Korea	Yes	6	222 (2.5)	264 (2.4)	Yes	24 (4.9)
Scotland	Yes	5	191 (0.9)	324 (2.3)	Yes	23 (4.0)
Slovenia	Yes	7	190 (1.5)	248 (2.5)	Yes	50 (5.3)
Spain[6]	No	6	188 (2.3)	285 (3.2)	Yes	33 (5.0)
(Former) Soviet Union[7]	No	6 or 7	198 (2.1)	243 (2.6)	Yes	72 (5.1)
Switzerland[8]	No	6 or 7	207 (3.2)	305 (7.4)	No	11 (3.5)
Taiwan	No	6	222 (2.5)	318 (6.9)	Yes	10 (2.8)
United States	No	6	178 (0.4)	338 (5.0)	No	5 (2.2)
Populations (with exclusions or low participation)						
Brazil, Fortaleza	No	7	183 (1.1)	223 (9.8)	No	62 (5.3)
Brazil, Sao Paulo	No	7	181 (0.2)	271 (9.3)	No	60 (4.6)
China	Yes	6.5 or 7	251 (2.1)	305 (7.1)	Yes	43 (6.3)
England	Yes	5	192 (1.8)	300 (4.4)	Yes	24 (8.3)
Italy[9]	Yes	6	204 (0.5)	289 (5.0)	Yes	18 (5.1)
Mozambique, Maputo, and Beira	No	7	193 (0.0)	272 (0.0)	Yes	92 (0.0)
Portugal	Yes	6	172 (1.1)	334 (6.5)	Yes	56 (7.9)

[1]90 percent of entire population from one ethnic group.
[2]For 13-year-olds.
[3]Problems included: overcrowded classrooms, inadequate facilities and maintenance, shortages of textbooks and other educational materials, student absenteeism, lack of discipline, and vandalism of school property.
[4]Four provinces assessed 9-year-olds. Nine provinces assessed 13-year-olds.
[5]Schools where instruction is in Hebrew.
[6]Schools where instruction is in Spanish, in all regions except Cataluna.
[7]Schools in 14 republics, where instruction is in Russian.
[8]Fifteen Cantons.
[9]Emilia-Romagna province only.
NOTE.—Standard errors appear in parentheses.
Source: National Center for Education Statistics. (1995). *The digest of education statistics* (p. 429). Washington, DC: U.S. Department of Education.

schools have existed in the writings of Ralph Tyler and Torsten Husen for many years, both highly respected scholars in educational evaluation. In 1993, a report from the National Center for Education Statistics declared U.S. citizens the most educated population in the world, noting that the United States has the highest percentage of adults attending college and graduating with college degrees (NCES, 1992a).

Cross-National Outcomes

In 1991, IAEP released the latest rounds of math test scores for 9-year-old and 13-year-old students. Among the countries with comprehensive elementary schools, American 9-year-olds scored relatively low, with a mean score that was significantly lower than Korea, Hungary, Taiwan, the former USSR, and Israel (see Table 6.2). Among the 13-year-olds, U.S. math scores were lower than every nation except Jordan (see Table 6.3). The home activities of American 9-year-olds indicated that although American students were prodigious TV watchers, they were in good company. Israel, Canada, and Ireland also posted very high TV-viewer ratings. The recreational reading rates and homework rates of American 9-year-olds, on the other hand, were about average. But as it turned out, the relation between homework and average performance on international tests among 9-year-olds was weak. Countries with higher average performance levels in math did not always have the highest homework rates and those with the lowest average performance did not always have the lowest homework rates (Griffith & others, 1994).

The 1991 IAEP findings in math are similar to the ones found two years earlier in a study conducted by the Educational Testing Service (ETS). The ETS report, titled *A World of Differences,* examined mathematics and science achievement among 13-year-olds in five countries and in four provinces of

TABLE 6.2

IAEP MATH ACHIEVEMENT AND HOME ACTIVITIES AMONG 9-YEAR-OLDS (1991)				
	Average Percentage Correct on Math Test	**Percentage of Students Who Read for Fun Every Day**	**Percentage of Students With Two or More Hours of Homework Daily**	**Percentage of Students Who Watch Five or More Hours of TV Daily**
Korea	75	25	22	9
Hungary	68	50	25	16
Taiwan	68	29	31	8
Former USSR	66	63	31	18
Israel	64	57	35	24
Spain	62	55	29	17
Ireland	60	45	18	23
Canada	60	48	13	22
USA	58	45	20	26
Slovenia	56	63	15	8

Source: National Center for Education Statistics. (1995). *The digest of education statistics* (p. 429). Washington, DC: U.S. Department of Education.

TABLE 6.3

MATHEMATICS TEST SCORES OF 13-YEAR-OLDS IN THE EDUCATIONAL SYSTEMS PARTICIPATING IN THE IAEP (1991)

	Average Percentage Correct
Korea	73.4
Taiwan	72.7
Switzerland	70.8
Former USSR	70.2
Hungary	68.4
France	64.2
Israel	63.1
Canada	62.0
Scotland	60.6
Ireland	60.5
Slovenia	57.1
Spain	55.4
USA	55.3
Jordan	40.4

Source: National Center for Education Statistics. (1995). *The digest of education statistics* (p. 432). Washington, DC: U.S. Department of Education.

Canada (LaPoint, Mead, & Phillips, 1989). The findings are listed as they referred to countries only and do not include the provinces of Canada because such subpopulations represent comparatively small regional groups, not unlike, for instance, comparing achievement in the state of Iowa, which is quite high on most measures, to overall achievement in Canada, which, internationally speaking, is relatively low. The ETS study found that the overall math and science achievement of 13-year-olds in the United States was low relative to other countries (see Figures 6.1 and 6.2).

Why do such differences exist? They cannot be explained with the claim that the United States tests a higher proportion of the student-age population because the percentage of 13-year-olds in school among the nations was more or less equal. There are, however, a few other factors that could be at work.

One of the more interesting things that the ETS researchers did was to ask teachers to indicate the percentage of seventh- and eighth-grade students who had an opportunity to learn the concepts tested on each question in the mathematics and science assessment. The effort was to determine whether children had been instructionally exposed to the very ideas and concepts against which they were being tested. A lower **opportunity-to-learn** scale meant a less wide exposure to the tested items. We scaled these opportunity-to-learn (OTL) percentages against the overall mean achievement and found that in some areas of mathematics and science, the mean achievement was essentially proportional to the OTL. In other words, a lower OTL usually meant a lower mean score, a higher OTL meant a higher mean score. This is something to consider when contemplating international scores. Schools with lower OTLs, such as those in the United States, cannot necessarily be faulted for low achievement if the actual items are not being as widely taught. In the United States there can never be very strong linkage between the school curriculum and the actual international testing mechanism because the educational system is decentralized and manages its mathematical and science curriculum content in varied ways. Moreover, given the openness of

FIGURE 6.1

AVERAGE SCIENCE PROFICIENCY, AGE 13

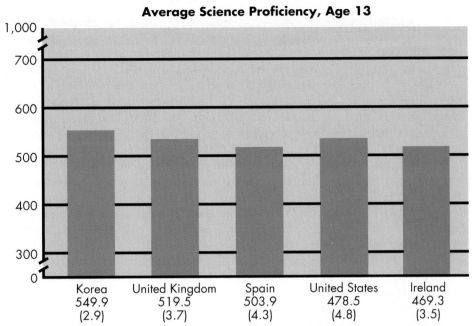

Average Science Proficiency, Age 13

Source: Lapointe A.E., & others. (1989). A *world of differences* (p.36). Prepared by Educational Testing Service. Washington DC: U.S. Department of Education and the National Science Foundation.

FIGURE 6.2

AVERAGE MATHEMATICS PROFICIENCY, AGE 13

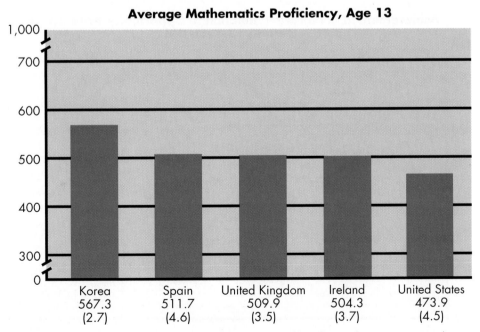

Average Mathematics Proficiency, Age 13

Source: Lapointe A.E., & others. A *world of differences* (p.14). Prepared by Educational Testing Service. Washington DC: U.S. Department of Education and the National Science Foundation.

the U.S. system, many of the very items not taught to 13-year-olds might very well be taught at a later date, whereas such a luxury may not exist in Korea, for instance, where only 38% of the population will go to academic high school. The important point is that curriculum timing and curriculum content are essential concerns in understanding single-point international comparisons. Not all areas of achievement managed to show a proportional relation to OTL, but Figures 6.3 to 6.6 represent findings in a few areas.

This very problem has also been discussed in the context of other international studies. Sloane, O'Rafferty, and Westbury (1996) contend that opportunity-to-learn measures can also be computed by examining the degree of commonality between what is covered in the content of a textbook and what is tested on an international test. In math and science especially, the content of the text very much dictates what will be taught during the school year. Thus, discrepancies between what is in the text and what is on the test attest to a coverage or opportunity-to-learn factor that might negatively influence the performance of students. Sloane, O'Rafferty, and Westbury (1996) cite the work of others in claiming that considerable differences exist in the content of science texts used by students taking the IEA test in science achievement and the content of the IEA exam. In math, a similar condition seemed to prevail. American eighth graders spend 20% of their time on algebra, compared with 37% for similar students in Japan. In the United States, the math curriculum focuses mostly on algebra, whereas in many other countries the curricular focus is calculus (Griffith & others, 1994). All these issues speak to differences in opportunity-to-learn. Much of this

FIGURE 6.3 ACHIEVEMENT IN CHEMISTRY IN RELATION TO OPPORTUNITY-TO-LEARN (OTL) AMONG 13-YEAR-OLDS

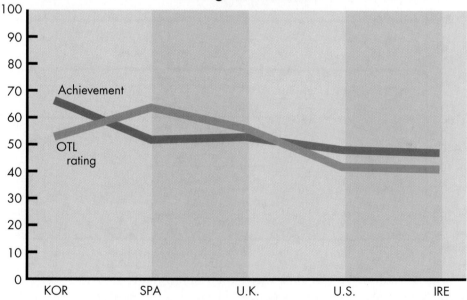

Achievement in Chemistry in Relation to Opportunity–to–Learn (OTL) Among 13–Year–Olds

PART TWO: THE SCHOOL AND SOCIETY

FIGURE 6.4

ACHIEVEMENT IN PHYSICS IN RELATION TO OPPORTUNITY-TO-LEARN (OTL) AMONG 13-YEAR-OLDS

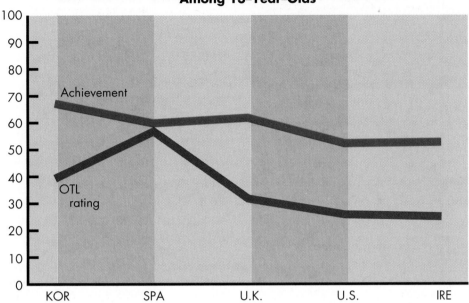

Achievement in Physics in Relation to Opportunity–to–Learn (OTL) Among 13–Year–Olds

FIGURE 6.5

ACHIEVEMENT IN GEOMETRY IN RELATION TO OPPORTUNITY-TO-LEARN (OTL) AMONG 13-YEAR-OLDS

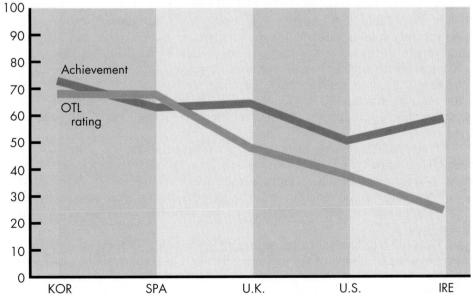

Achievement in Geometry in Relation to Opportunity–to–Learn (OTL) Among 13–Year–Olds

FIGURE 6.6

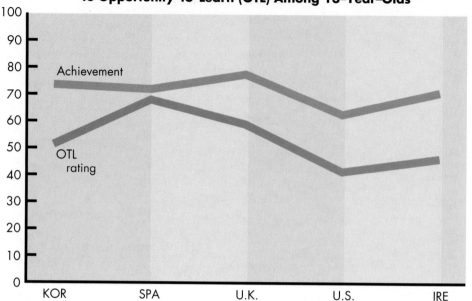

Achievement in Logic and Problem Solving in Relation to Opportunity-to-Learn (OTL) Among 13-Year-Olds

type of interpretation is based on the earlier work of Ian Westbury (1992), who showed how IEA achievement is affected by how tightly linked the curricula used in different nations are to the actual items on the IEA examinations. Given the decentralized nature of its schooling system, the United States cannot bring its curriculum to be strongly aligned with IEA tests, while centralized systems, such as Japan's, have less trouble.

The latest IAEP data on science achievement for 9- and 13-year-olds were slightly more encouraging for the United States than those found in the ETS study (See Table 6.4). Among 9-year-olds, only Korea and Taiwan had a significantly higher science achievement score than the United States, but among the 13-year-olds, the United States again sank to a lower place on the list, with six countries posting numbers *significantly* better. Remembering that the raw IAEP data are not ranked is important, largely because there might not be a significant difference between the rankings. For instance, there might not be a statistically significant difference between first and, say, ninth place.

There has, however, been much good news about the achievement of American students on the IAEP measures taken on reading skills among 9- and 14-year-olds. In a 31-nation study, American 9-year-olds outperformed every nation except Finland, and the 14-year-olds scored eighth, although their distance to the first-ranking nation was almost as close as the 9-year-olds (see Table 6.5).

Remarkably, the news of American high achievement in reading was simply not taken up by the national media. No major media outlets gave substantive coverage to the event, and the few that provided some coverage were not on top of the story and came at it quite slowly (Hlebowitsh, 1994).

TABLE 6.4

IAEP SCIENCE ACHIEVEMENT AMONG 9-YEAR-OLDS AND 13-YEAR-OLDS (1991)

	Average Percentage Correct on Science Test	
	9-Year-Olds	*13-Year-Olds*
Korea	67.9	77.5
Taiwan	66.7	75.6
Switzerland	–	73.7
USA	64.7	67.0
Canada	62.8	68.8
Hungary	62.5	73.4
Spain	61.7	67.5
Former USSR	61.5	71.3
Israel	61.2	71.6
Slovenia	57.7	70.3
Ireland	56.5	63.3
France	–	68.6
Scotland	–	67.9
Jordan	–	56.6

Source: National Center for Education Statistics. (1995). *The digest of education statistics* (pp. 433–435). Washington, DC: U.S. Department of Education.

Again, curriculum timing issues came into play with the IAEP reading scores, but this time in a way that favored the United States. Part of the early reading achievement in the United States might be explained by the fact that, on the average, U.S. schools introduce reading instruction at an earlier age than do the schools of many other nations. Generally speaking, 9-year-olds in the United States spend more time learning and studying languages than do 9-year-old students in many other nations (Griffith & others, 1994). Denmark,

Japanese students learning math at a prestigious school. Many Americans equate Japanese teenagers with intelligence and hard work while showing little respect for US high school students.

TABLE 6.5

READING LITERACY SCORES OF 9-YEAR-OLDS AND 14-YEAR-OLDS: SELECTED COUNTRIES (1992)

Scores	Age 9	Rank	Age 14	Rank
Finland	569	1	560	1
United States	547	2	535	8
Sweden	539	3	546	3
France	531	4	549	2
Italy	529	5	515	18
New Zealand	528	6	545	4
Norway	524	7	516	17
Iceland	518	8	536	5
Hong Kong	517	9	535	8
Singapore	515	10	534	10
Switzerland	511	11	536	5
Ireland	509	12	511	20
Belgium	507	13	481	24
Greece	504	14	509	21
Spain	504	15	490	23
W. Germany	503	16	522	15
Canada	500	17	522	15
E. Germany	499	18	526	12
Hungary	499	19	536	5
Slovenia	498	20	532	11
Netherlands	485	21	514	19
Cyprus	481	22	497	22
Portugal	478	23	523	14
Denmark	475	24	525	13
Trinidad/Tobago	451	25	479	25
Venezuela	383	26	417	26

Source: National Center for Education Statistics. (1995). *The digest of education statistics* (pp. 436–7). Washington, DC: U.S. Department of Education.

which is known for its high adult literacy, scored quite poorly on the IAEP reading test for 9-year-olds but rose on the list with the achievement of its 13-year-olds. Denmark generally does not introduce reading instruction into the curriculum until about the third grade (Elkind, 1987).

At the secondary school level, the overall achievement of students in the United States was quite low in almost all the tested areas. In the specialized disciplines of science, the American performance was particularly low. In the 1991 IEA *Study of Science* (Postlethwaite & Wiley, 1991), the United States scored last in biology and at the very bottom level in both chemistry and physics (see Table 6.6).

These scores, however, are affected by sampling and OTL factors. The high numbers of students continuing to advance in the schools of America bring a high percentage of the age cohort into the testing arena. For instance, as shown in Table 6.6, some countries, such as Ghana, have a comparatively high mean achievement drawn from tests given to about 1% of the student population, whereas the United States' mean is drawn from closer to 80% of the population. To give an idea of the relation between achievement and the percentage of the population tested, several line graphs (Figures 6.7, 6.8, and 6.9) depict the relation between achievement in some areas of science and

TABLE 6.6

BIOLOGY, CHEMISTRY, AND PHYSICS ACHIEVEMENT FOR SENIORS IN HIGH SCHOOL

	Biology Mean	Chem- istry Mean	Physics Mean	Percent- age in School	Average Number of Science Subjects Studied
Australia	46.6	49.1	48.7	39	5
Canada (Eng.)	43.7	39.6	41.7	68	6
Canada (Fr.)	39.3	27.9	26.7	67	6
England	62.4	69.3	58.4	20	3
Finland	50.2	35.9	37.9	41	9+
Ghana	57.6	60.2	50.5	1.2	3
Hong Kong	55.2	68.2	61.2	27	6
Hungary	59.9	50.2	58.7	18	9+
Israel	51.6	45.1	54.5	65	7
Italy	42.3	38.2	29.2	34	7
Japan	45.5	55.5	58.5	63	7+
Korea	40.1	30.9	39.8	38	9+
Norway	55.4	44.3	54.1	40	7
Poland	56.3	46.5	53.2	28	9+
Singapore	66.1	65.7	55.0	17	6
Sweden	53.4	43.9	46.0	28	9+
Thailand	42.6	35.8	34.3	14	6
U.S.A.	38.1	37.7	45.3	83	5

Source: Postlethwaite, T.N. & Wiley, D.E. (1991). *The IEA Study of Science II.* Oxford, U.K.: Pergamon Press.

FIGURE 6.7

IEA ACHIEVEMENT IN CHEMISTRY IN RELATION TO THE PERCENTAGE OF THE STUDENT POPULATION TESTED IN THE LAST YEAR OF HIGH SCHOOL (1991)

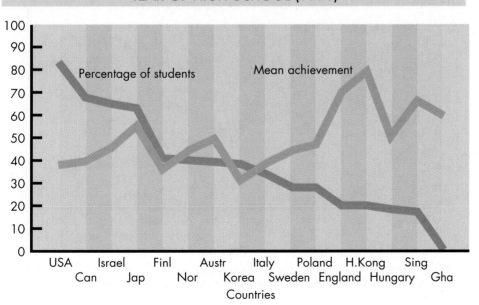

FIGURE 6.8

IEA ACHIEVEMENT IN BIOLOGY IN RELATION TO THE PERCENTAGE OF THE SCHOOL POPULATION TESTED IN THE LAST YEAR OF HIGH SCHOOL (1991)

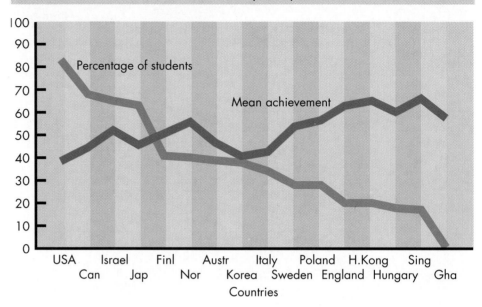

FIGURE 6.9

IEA ACHIEVEMENT IN PHYSICS IN RELATION TO THE PERCENTAGE OF THE STUDENT POPULATION TESTED IN THE LAST YEAR OF HIGH SCHOOL (1991)

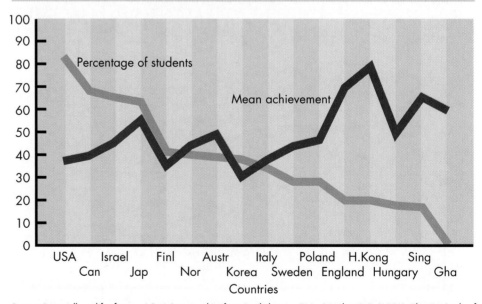

Source: Data collected for figures 6.3-6.9 were taken from Postlethwaite, T.N., & Wiley, D.E. (1991). *The IEA Study of Science II.* Oxford, U.K.: Pergamon Press. The actual data were collected between 1983 and 1985.

the percentage of students tested. It is not a perfect relation, but it does clearly show a trend. Again, it seems as though the quality of U.S. achievement is in some ways a casualty of its democratizing tradition. Note that in certain countries, such as Japan, Korea, Canada, Hungary, Finland, and Sweden, the percentage of students is larger than is indicated on the graph. In Japan, for instance, the actual number is 89% and in Korea it is 83%. The IEA tests, however, did not use high school age youth enrolled in vocational schools. The graphs in the figures presented here indicated the percentage of the student population actually being tested by IEA (Postlethwaite & Wiley, 1991).

There are other issues to consider in weighing the low performance of the United States in science. For instance, the percentage of the students studying a science subject in the final year of secondary schooling ranges widely with each discipline in each country: from 3% to 41% in biology, 1% to 37% in chemistry, and 1% to 35% in physics (Sloane, O'Rafferty, & Westbury, 1994). This curriculum timing factor will likely influence the results of the test. Moreover, the issue of how the science curriculum is arranged and how certain topics and skills are introduced is significant. In most major systems, science subjects are taught simultaneously (physics, chemistry, and biology). In the United States, science, more often than not, is taught one discipline at a time: biology for grade 10, chemistry for grade 11, and physics for grade 12. In Japan, science is taught as a single subject up to grade 11, and in countries such as Hungary, the three major disciplines of science are taught simultaneously as early as seventh grade. Before students graduate from a Hungarian high school, they will see up to nine subject area exposures in science. The actual classroom time devoted to science also varies across the nations, from about 10% of the total instructional time in some countries to close to 50% of the instructional time in others. (Sloane, O'Rafferty, & Westbury, 1994). Only 6% of all high school students in the United States will take advanced courses in biology, compared with about 45 % in Finland and 28% in English-speaking Canada. Similarly, students studying advanced chemistry and physics in America represent a very small percentage of the age cohort, while by comparison, other advanced nations might offer advanced instruction in these disciplines for up to one fourth of the enrolled student population (Mullis & Jenkins, 1988). All these matters complicate the answers to questions of international school comparisons.

Unlike many other countries, students in the United States enjoy relatively open access to postsecondary education. Carson, Huelskamp, and Woodall (1993) have examined data taken from the National Center for Education Statistics and found that, in both technical and nontechnical fields, a very high percentage of youth obtain bachelor's degrees in the United States (see Figure 6.10). In fact, for the past 20 years the United States had led the world in this particular statistic. Education in the United States, especially when one looks through an international lens, has grown upward and outward. The universalization of secondary schooling in the United States seems to have created a population hungry for postsecondary schooling. In only the past two decades, the proportion of high school graduates going directly to college has increased from about 47% to 63%. High school graduates from low-income families (defined as the bottom 20% of all family incomes) are now twice as likely to go to college than they were 20 years ago, though they are still under-represented. In 1993, 62% of White high school

FIGURE 6.10

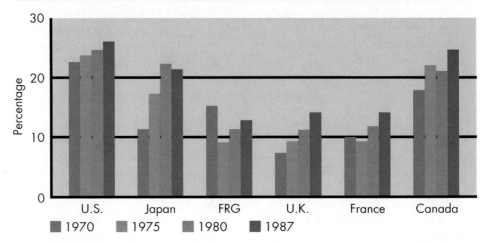

PERCENT OF 22-YEAR-OLDS OBTAINING A BACHELOR'S DEGREE—ALL FIELDS

Source: Carson, C. C., Huelskamp, R. M., & Woodall, T. D. (1993). Perspectives on education in America. *Journal of Educational Research*, 86(5), 286.

graduates and 55% of Black high school graduates were enrolled in either a two- or four-year college in the fall following graduation. The increases in enrollment in higher education are likely a reflection not only of its relative accessibility but also of its value in relation to other postsecondary options available to high school graduates (National Center for Education Statistics, 1995).

Using the SAT to Measure Successful Schools

The use of the SAT as a barometer of school failure is another example of how the U.S. schools have been unfairly treated. Much has been said and written about the clear three decade decline in the SAT score (Table 6.7). To the minds of many, such a decline suggests a debility in the public schools. However, the SAT was never designed to be used as a school evaluation instrument—it only measures the aptitude of those going to college, and it is limited largely to verbal and mathematical skills. The SAT's purpose is to predict college achievement so that college admissions offices can better evaluate prospective students, and it does not even do that very well.

But even if one were to accept the validity of the SAT as a yardstick of strength or weakness in the school, one would still have to account for the demographic changes in the test-taking population to make any judgments. Minority students and students from low-income settings have historically scored lower on the SAT than White and middle/upper-income populations. Figure 6.11 shows the relation between income and SAT achievement. One could argue that the gradual decline of the SAT score is partly a function of a larger proportional representation of minority and low-income groups in the test-taking population, an effect that should actually be a source of satisfaction. As reported by Carson, Huelskamp, and Woodall (1993), if one were to control for the demographics of the population in evaluating the 1990 age

TABLE 6.7

SAT SCORE AVERAGES FOR COLLEGE-BOUND SENIORS

SAT Score (Math and Verbal)

School Year	Score	School Year	Score
1966–67	958	1980–81	890
1967–68	958	1981–82	893
1968–69	956	1982–83	893
1969–70	948	1983–84	897
1970–71	943	1984–85	906
1971–72	937	1985–86	906
1972–73	926	1986–87	906
1973–74	924	1987–88	904
1974–75	906	1988–89	903
1975–76	903	1989–90	900
1976–77	899	1990–91	896
1977–78	897	1991–92	899
1978–79	894	1992–93	902
1979–80	890	1993–94	902

Source: National Center for Education Statistics. (1995). *Digest of education statistics (p. 127).* Washington, DC: U.S. Department of Education.

FIGURE 6.11

AVERAGE SAT BY FAMILY INCOME

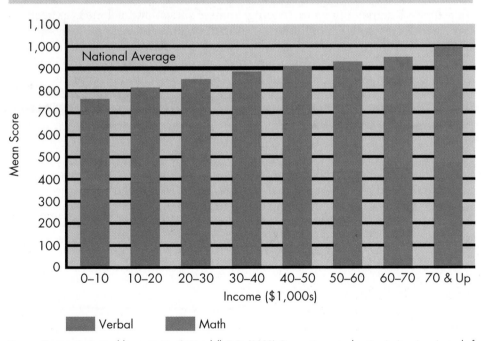

Source: Carson, C. C., Huelskamp, R. M., & Woodall, T. D. (1993). Perspectives on education in America. *Journal of Educational Research,* 86(5), 269.

cohort against the 1975 age cohort, the SAT score would actually go up. In other words, if one were statistically to make the 1990 test-taking population look like the 1975 test-taking population, in terms of race and income, the SAT score could be projected to be on the rise.

One of the more interesting phenomena related to the SAT is that all the racial subgroups (Whites, Blacks, and Hispanics) in the testing population have shown an increase in the SAT scores while the general or overall average has continued to drop. If all the subgroups have scores that are on the rise, how could the overall score continue to fall? The answer has to do with the changing nature of the testing population. Sloane, O'Rafferty, and Westbury (1994) provide the explanation. If the majority population (Group A), which is made up of, say, 100 test takers, achieves a score of 50 on an exam and the minority (Group B), which is made up of 20 test takers, achieves a score of 40, the overall mean for the groups combined is 48.3. If, over the next year, Group A increases its mean to 51, but still has 100 test takers, and Group B increases its mean to 41, but has twice the number of test takers (40 test takers), the overall mean drops slightly to 48.1. The point is that both groups improved their scores but because of a larger representation of the lower-performing group in the test-taking pool, the overall mean dropped. This is, in essence, what is at work with the SAT. Historically low-performing populations are taking the test in increasing number, thereby pulling down the overall average despite showing a subgroup increase in the score.

 ## The National Assessment of Educational Progress

Since the 1960s, the United States has also been engaged in criterion-based measures of achievement in reading, mathematics, and science, as well as more recent tests in writing, literature, history, and civics. Such tests are not made to compare the U.S. schools to other schools, although they are sometimes used in such a manner, but are designed to track longitudinal achievement on a set of skills and knowledge in various subject areas. These tests, known as the tests of the **National Assessment of Educational Progress** (NAEP), track achievement across several different variables, including gender and race. They are administered to a national sample of students, usually in fourth, eighth, and twelfth grades. They also are sometimes accompanied with survey data that deal with attitudinal views toward certain subject matter and home-learning conditions. The NAEP assessments are ongoing and are congressionally mandated. Virtually all the recent NAEP assessments (in science, mathematics, and reading and writing) demonstrate not only growth in academic achievement over the past two decades but also a closing of the proficiency gap between White and non-White groups, as well as between males and females.

Reading Proficiency

The NAEP reading proficiency exam, which has been in operation for more than two decades, is a comprehensive measure of reading ability. The test, which is given to 9-, 13-, and 17-year-olds, is based on a wide range of reading assessments, from simple narrative passages to complex articles dealing with specialized topics. Reading selections in the NAEP test include poems, essays, reports, passages from selected texts, and stories. Comprehension is judged with multiple-choice measures and with some open-ended questioning (Mullis & Jenkins, 1990).

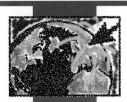

The Clearinghouse on Assessment and Evaluation

The Educational Resources Information Center, or ERIC, is the primary source of educational literature in the United States. Among the services and components supported by ERIC are 17 Clearinghouses for information on specific topics. The ERIC Clearinghouses collect, abstract, and index education materials for the ERIC database; respond to requests for information in their subject specific areas; and produce special publications on current research, programs, and practices. The Clearinghouse that is most directly related to this chapter is the Clearinghouse on Assessment and Evaluation.

The Clearinghouse on Assessment and Evaluation web site, located at

http://www.cua.edu/www/eric_ae/

contains full-text documents on traditional assessment programs and alternative assessments such as portfolios. Perhaps the most useful part of the site is the test-locator service, a joint venture between ERIC and the Educational Testing Service.

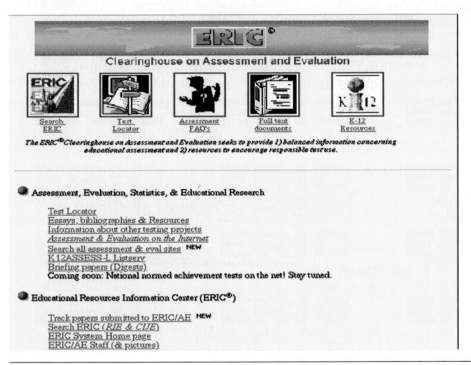

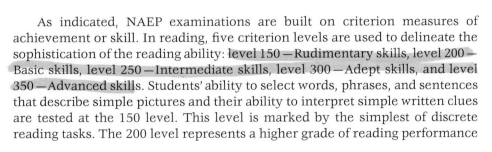

As indicated, NAEP examinations are built on criterion measures of achievement or skill. In reading, five criterion levels are used to delineate the sophistication of the reading ability: level 150 — Rudimentary skills, level 200 — Basic skills, level 250 — Intermediate skills, level 300 — Adept skills, and level 350 — Advanced skills. Students' ability to select words, phrases, and sentences that describe simple pictures and their ability to interpret simple written clues are tested at the 150 level. This level is marked by the simplest of discrete reading tasks. The 200 level represents a higher grade of reading performance that includes the ability to locate and identify facts from simple paragraphs and articles, as well as the ability to make inferences from short, uncomplicated reading passages. This Basic level is generally marked by the skills needed to understand specific and sequentially related written information.

The Intermediate level of performance, which is notched at the 250 mark, asks students to search for and locate information that they read in relatively lengthy passages. Intermediate skills demand that students recognize paraphrasing and make inferences and generalizations based on the main idea of an article and the author's purpose. The Adept level (300 level) demands understanding of complicated literary and informational passages. Students must be able to analyze the text and provide reactions and explanations of the readings. Here the abilities to find, understand, summarize, and explain relatively complicated materials are tested. The Advanced reading level (350 level) asks students to extend and restructure ideas from their reading and to make generalizations about subtly styled reading passages. Here the learner is asked to synthesize and learn from highly complicated and specialized learning materials (Mullis & Jenkins, 1990).

The general two-decade trend in reading proficiency found on the NAEP exams demonstrates rising abilities across all ages (see Figure 6.12), though there has not been much progress since 1980. Older students are significantly more competent readers today than in 1971, when the first NAEP tests in reading were conducted. Nine-year-old and 13-year-old students are also significantly better than their 1971 counterparts. The NAEP reading data clearly demonstrate progress, though an argument can be made that the current averages are still too low. The average 17-year-old reader, for instance, has not quite achieved the criterion standard for an Adept reader.

Interesting, many of the gains in the reading proficiency scores have come from the minority student populations, particularly from Black students

FIGURE 6.12

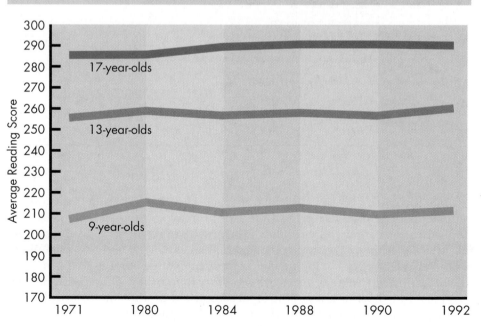

AVERAGE READING PROFICIENCY BY AGE

PART TWO: THE SCHOOL AND SOCIETY

(see Figures 6.13A, 6.13B, and 6.13C). Reading proficiency levels have remained rather steady for White students, but for both Black and Hispanic populations, the gains have been strong. In 1990, the general climb in minority scores was broken, but the overall picture from 1971 still shows considerable growth in minority reading achievement. The reading proficiency gap

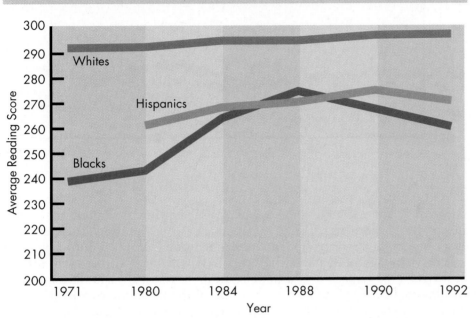

FIGURE 6.13A

AVERAGE READING PROFICIENCY BY RACE/ETHNICITY
(17-YEAR-OLDS)

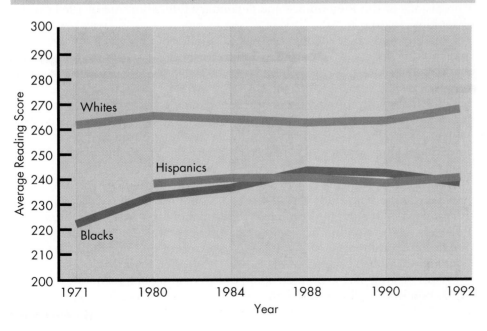

FIGURE 6.13B

AVERAGE READING PROFICIENCY BY RACE/ETHNICITY
(13-YEAR-OLDS)

FIGURE 6.13C

AVERAGE READING PROFICIENCY BY RACE/ETHNICITY (9-YEAR-OLDS)

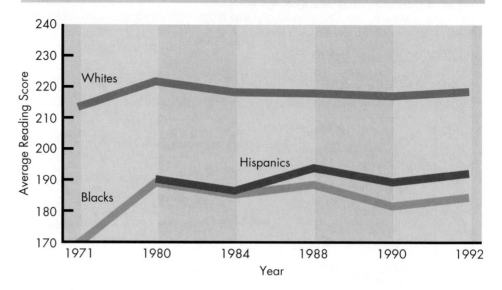

between White and non-White populations has been slowly closing, a fact made all the more remarkable by the decrease in the dropout rate among Black students. Minority students who might have dropped out in previous school years are now staying in school. This being the case, the average score might be expected to drop, but until 1988 the opposite has occurred, making the gains by the minority groups all the more impressive (Mullis & Jenkins, 1990). Some commentators have speculated that the gains in reading achievement among 9-year-old minority children from 1971 to 1980 resulted, at least in part, from the academic support provided to disadvantaged youth from federal programs such as Head Start and the Title 1 provisions of the Elementary and Secondary Education Act of 1965 (Mullis & Jenkins, 1990).

Reading proficiency along the scale of gender has received less attention than race and ethnicity. The NAEP trends clearly show a female advantage. At each age level, the advantage thinned in 1980s only to open up again in the 1990s (see Figures 6.14A, 6.14B, 6.14C). Among 13-year-olds, there has virtually been no improvement in the proficiency differences between males and females from 1971, but among 17-year-olds and 9-year-olds, there has been a very slight closing of the gap. Interestingly, the underperformance of boys on reading proficiency has not drawn the attention of gender-bias researchers.

Overall it appears that a two-decade effort to strengthen reading proficiencies of American students has worked. There has definitely been a rise in the proportion of students reading at the Rudimentary, Basic, and Intermediate levels, but the nation has yet to see significant positive movement in the proportion of students reading at the highest criterion levels, the 300 Adept level and the 350 Advanced level.

NAEP testing also examined some of the reading behaviors of the adults in the homes of children and compared these results to reading proficiency scores. The results confirm the long-standing belief that the home-reading

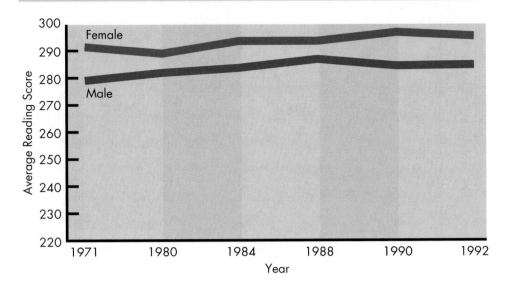

FIGURE 6.14A

AVERAGE READING PROFICIENCY BY GENDER (17-YEAR-OLDS)

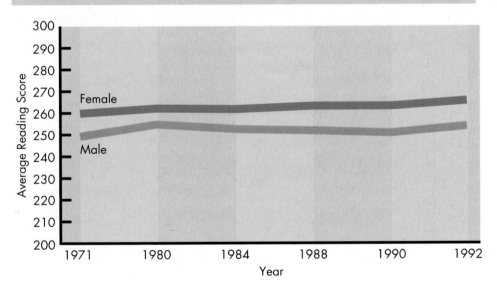

FIGURE 6.14B

AVERAGE READING PROFICIENCY BY GENDER (13-YEAR-OLDS)

environment of a child is associated with a child's reading proficiency. Students were asked to report how often the people in their homes actually read a newspaper, magazine, or book. Five levels were assigned to their responses: daily, weekly, monthly, yearly, and never. The proficiency scores of the students who responded to this question were then computed and compared to their response on the home-reading survey. As indicated in Figure 6.15, at all age levels, higher frequencies of reading in the home were consistently associated with higher NAEP scores.

A similar correlation existed in relation to how much homework a student did every day. The NAEP asked students to report on the amount of time they

FIGURE 6.14C

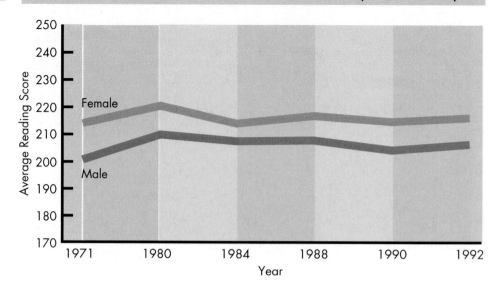

AVERAGE READING PROFICIENCY BY GENDER (9-YEAR-OLDS)

FIGURE 6.15

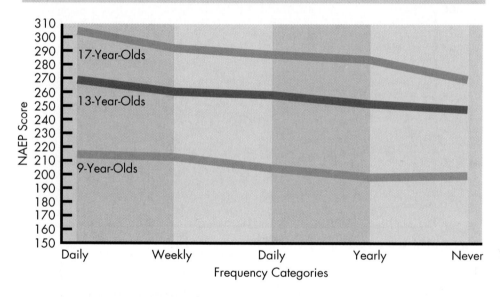

EXTENT OF READING IN THE HOME VERSUS READING PROFICIENCY (1992)

devote to homework each day, again using five scales: none, did not do assignment, less than 1 hour, 1 to 2 hours, and more than 2 hours. The reported level of time dedicated to homework was then compared with the average reading proficiency score of the students. For both 13- and 17-year-olds, there was a positive relation between daily time expended on homework and reading proficiency level. This, however, was not the case among 9-year-olds. It very well might turn out that 9-year-olds, who likely get to bed earlier than 17-year-olds, need more time for recreational events that might include reading for pleasure. A ponderous amount of homework for a

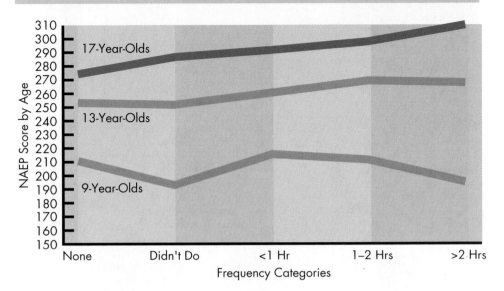

9-year-old (2 hours or more) might backfire because it might eliminate opportunities to pursue recreational reading and other activities that might serve reading proficiency levels (see Figure 6.16).

Science Proficiency

The NAEP has also been involved in testing science proficiency for the past two decades. It has based its assessments on a range of science-content areas, including the life sciences, the physical sciences, and earth and space science. The test has also set out to determine a student's ability to solve problems in scientific contexts; to conduct, design, and interpret scientific experiments; and to read tables and graphs of varying difficulty.

As with the reading exam, the NAEP science proficiency exam is criterion based and gauges the skills of students according to five levels of science knowledge and understanding. The most rudimentary 150 level of proficiency (Knowledge of Everyday Science Facts) deals with the knowledge of some general science facts that could be learned from everyday experiences. The 200 level (Understanding Simple Scientific Principles) asks students to demonstrate knowledge of simple scientific principles, particularly in the life sciences. The 250 level (Applying Scientific Information) asks students to interpret data from simple tables, to draw inferences from experimental results, and to exhibit some understanding of the life and physical sciences. The 300 level of performance (Analyzing Scientific Procedures and Data) demands that students evaluate the appropriate usage of an experimental design, use scientific knowledge to interpret new information, and demonstrate an understanding of more advanced principles in the physical sciences. The highest level of skill performance (the 350 level—Integrating Specialized Scientific Information) tests students on their ability to make inferences and draw conclusions from detailed knowledge taken from the physical sciences, particularly chemistry. Students at this level should also be able to apply

The NAEP science exam invites students to solve real science problems. Experiences in labs no doubt improve scores.

principles of genetics and interpret the societal implications of scientific work in genetics.

The national trends in the NAEP data demonstrate an improving condition in science education, especially since 1977 (see Figure 6.17). Although the average science proficiency of 17-year-olds in 1992 has dropped since 1970, there have been small gains in the achievement of 9- and 13-year-olds since 1970. Most of the declines in all of the age groups, however, occurred during the 1970s. During the 1980s, the scores rebounded and have continued to improve into the early 1990s. Since 1977, the proficiency levels of all age groups have improved markedly. Among 9- and 13-year-olds, there has been an uninterrupted line of improvement since 1977, a phenomenon that should have positive carryover effects for the achievement of 17-year-olds in the years to come.

In the area of race and ethnicity, the NAEP science proficiency scores are down slightly for both 17-year-old Whites and Blacks since 1970 (Figure 6.18A). They are up significantly, however, for 9- and 13-year-old Whites and Blacks, and up quite noticeably for Hispanic students at all ages (Figures 6.18B and 6.18C). The overall growth in proficiency among 9- and 13-year-olds has been mostly a function of the proficiency levels achieved by the minority groups at these ages. Although the scores for 13- and 9-year-old students have, more or less, remained stable since 1970, the scores of the minority groups at the same age levels have risen significantly. Again there is a clear sign of a closing of the gap in achievement, though the gap is still quite wide. White and Black 17-year-olds still stand at two fundamentally different

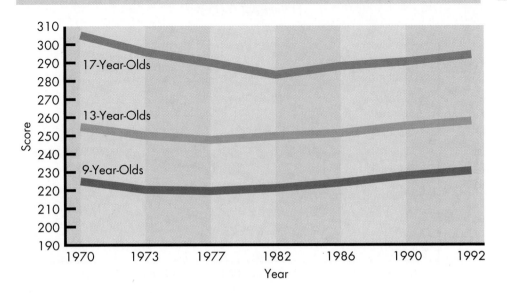

AVERAGE SCIENCE PROFICIENCY BY AGE

FIGURE 6.17

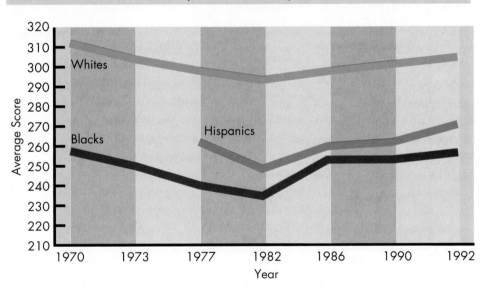

AVERAGE SCIENCE PROFICIENCY BY RACE/ETHNICITY
(17-YEAR-OLDS)

FIGURE 6.18A

levels of average proficiency (the 300 versus 250 level). But the growth in proficiency for Black students seems well rooted because Black 9-year-old children continue to show a slow, steady, and substantive line of growth in proficiency. It should again be emphasized that because high proportions of Black and Hispanic children come from lower socioeconomic settings, the disparities in performance likely have something to do with the lower education level of parents, differences in reading materials and other learning resources available in the home, and general conditions of deprivation that often accompany the home lives of poor children.

FIGURE 6.18B

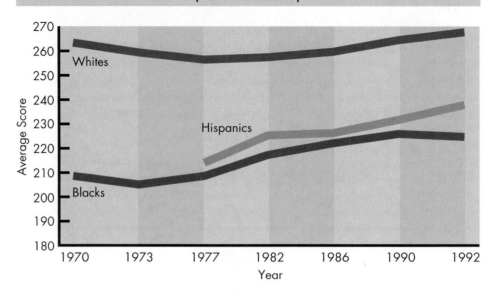

AVERAGE SCIENCE PROFICIENCY BY RACE/ETHNICITY
(13-YEAR-OLDS)

FIGURE 6.18C

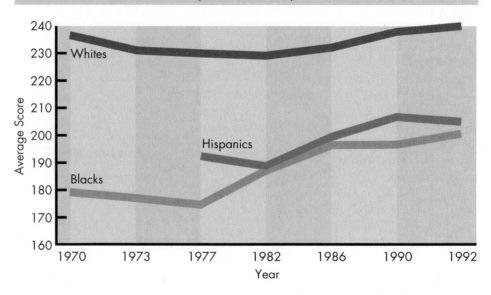

AVERAGE SCIENCE PROFICIENCY BY RACE/ETHNICITY
(9-YEAR-OLDS)

   The gap in science performance between boys and girls at ages 9 and 13 has been small and has favored the boys (Figures 6.19B and 6.19C). Over the years, the distance between the scores of the boys and the scores of the girls in these age groups has been consistent. The scores declined and recovered virtually in parallel. Among 17-year-olds, however, the performance of the boys has been significantly better than that of the girls (Figure 6.19A). Since 1970, the average scores have gone down for 17-year-olds for boys and girls alike, but the girls' scores have declined less, and hence the gap in performance has closed a bit. The depth of this decline reached it lowest point in

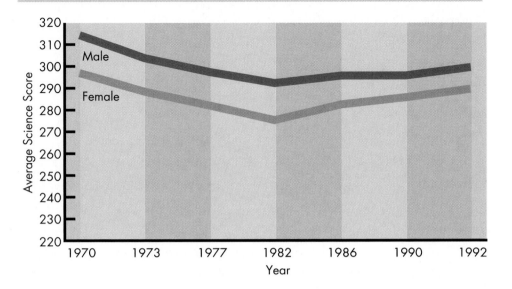

FIGURE 6.19A

AVERAGE SCIENCE PROFICIENCY BY GENDER (17-YEAR-OLDS)

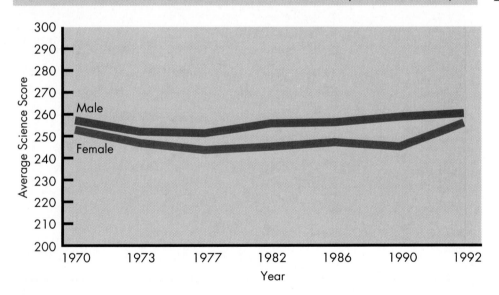

FIGURE 6.19B

AVERAGE SCIENCE PROFICIENCY BY GENDER (13-YEAR-OLDS)

1982. Since then, the average science proficiency scores for 17-year-old boys and girls have been on the rise.

As indicated earlier, the differences in achievement could depend on gender-bias factors such as differences in teacher expectation in science, differences in the instructional methods used for boys in science as opposed to girls, and the widespread use of textbooks that send the message that science is a good field of study for boys but not for girls. It could also be that the home environment supports more science-related activities for boys than for girls. Increasingly, there have also been discussions about brain-sex differences between boys and girls that might make one gender more predisposed toward certain studies. It has also been speculated that the

FIGURE 6.19C

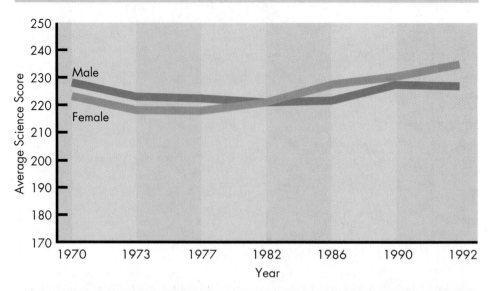

AVERAGE SCIENCE PROFICIENCY BY GENDER (9-YEAR-OLDS)

TABLE 6.8

	Male	Female
SCIENCE COURSE TAKING AT AGE 17—THE PERCENTAGE OF 17-YEAR-OLDS WHO STUDIED DIFFERENT SCIENCE SUBJECTS FOR ONE YEAR OR MORE		
General Science		
1992	86	83
1990	84	81
1986	84	82
Biology		
1992	91	93
1990	87	91
1986	84	82
Chemistry		
1992	47	51
1990	45	45
1986	42	39
Physics		
1992	15	12
1990	16	13
1986	14	8

Source: National Center for Education Statistics. (1994). NAEP 1992 *trends in academic progress* (p. 64). Washington, DC: U.S. Department of Education.

differences in the achievement levels of 17-year-old boys and girls might be explained by differential course taking patterns. The NAEP data indicate, however, that this is not the case (Table 6.8). Girls have been very slightly underrepresented in the broad field science courses (general science, physical science, and life sciences) but have also been slightly overrepresented, with the exception of physics, in the more discipline-centered science courses (biology and chemistry). Generally speaking, there is no evidence of significant underrepresentation of girls in science courses.

Math Proficiency

The math assessment materials used by the NAEP also entail a comprehensive set of skills, ranging, at the simplest level, from knowledge of number facts, simple measurement instruments, and simple problem solving, to skills of increasing complexity in the areas of fractions, percents, geometric figures, exponents, square roots, algebraic expressions, linear equations, functions, and coordinate systems. Again five criterion levels are used: level 150—Simple Arithmetic Facts, level 200—Beginning Skills and Understandings, level 250—Basic Operations and Beginning Problem Solving, level 300—Moderately Complex Procedures and Reasoning, and level 350—Multistep Problem Solving and Algebra. The 150 level encompasses basic additions and subtraction facts, two-digit addition, and simple word problems in which addition and subtraction are used. The 200 level moves into regrouping procedures in subtraction, basic multiplication and division facts, the manipulation of coins, and simple tables and charts. The 250 level entails the application of whole numbers in word problems, finding the product of two-digit and one-digit multiplication, and comparing data on tables and graphs. The 300 level covers computations with decimals, simple fractions, and percents. Students at this level are also expected to evaluate formulas, operate signed numbers, exponents, and square roots, find averages, and solve linear equations. The 350 level of performance expects students to display reasoning skills in the solving of multistep problems using functions, percents, geometric forms, exponents, and square roots.

The academic performance trends in mathematics are again quite positive. There has been an improved average level of proficiency in all age groups from 1973 to 1992 (Figure 6.20). The gains from 1978 are particularly impressive. There has been a steady rate of improvement in the scores of 9- and 13-year-olds since 1978 and a steady rate of progress among 17-year-olds since 1982. The 1992 scores for 17- and 13-year-olds represent all-time high points, and for 9-year-olds, the 1992 scores equaled an all-time high score achieved in 1990.

NAEP math trends in relation to race and ethnicity are also positive (Figures 6.21A, 6.21B and 6.21C). All race and ethnic groups, at all age groups, earned higher scores in 1992 than in 1973. Among 13-year-olds, the gains in the Black and Hispanic populations have been particularly strong, while among Whites the improvements have been less positive. Following a decline during the 1970s, the proficiency levels of 17-year-old Whites increased and now stands at an all-time high in 1992. The proficiency level of 17-year-old Blacks also dipped slightly during the 1970s but has since grown steadily into 1990 before falling slightly in 1992. Whites still have a significantly higher level of proficiency, in all age groups, than non-Whites, but the gap has narrowed considerably among 9- and 13-year-olds and slightly among 17-year-olds. The consistent easing of the differences between the races in proficiency in the earlier grades should serve future outcome measures for non-White 17-year-olds.

FIGURE 6.20

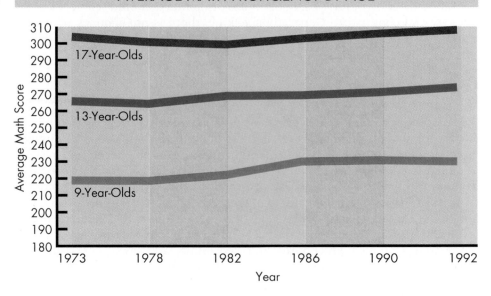

AVERAGE MATH PROFICIENCY BY AGE

FIGURE 6.21A

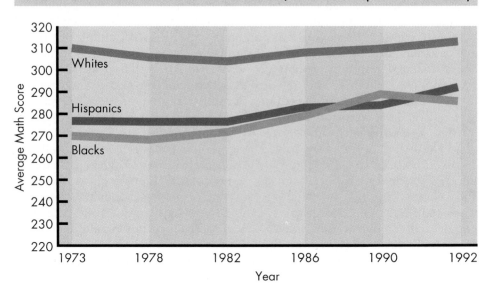

AVERAGE MATH PROFICIENCY BY RACE/ETHNICITY (17-YEAR-OLDS)

The NAEP proficiencies in math for both boys and girls have indicated significant progress among 9- and 13-year-olds (Figures 6.22B and 6.22C). Among girls, the 1992 scores are better in all age groups from the 1973 scores. Most of the improvement occurred during the 1980s. There is very little difference between the scores of boys and girls at ages 9 and 13, though the boys carry a slight advantage. There has been a significant difference in proficiency among 17-year-old boys and girls, but this difference has been slowly eroding (Figure 6.22A).

There are also some interesting data to report on the relation between math proficiency and television viewing. The data from 1990 and 1992 show

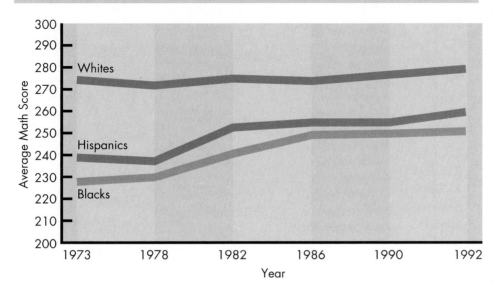

AVERAGE MATH PROFICIENCY BY RACE/ETHNICITY (13-YEAR-OLDS) **FIGURE 6.21B**

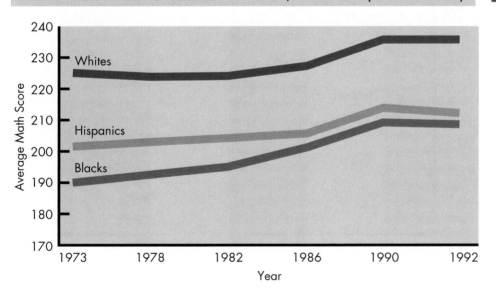

AVERAGE MATH PROFICIENCY BY RACE/ETHNICITY (9-YEAR-OLDS) **FIGURE 6.21C**

that there is a negative association between mathematical proficiency and reported levels of television viewing as it applied to 13- and 17-year-olds, but that such a relation is less clear among 9-year-olds. Among 17-year-olds reporting to watch between zero and 2 hours of television per day and those reporting to watch 6 or more hours of daily television, there was about a 30 point difference in average math proficiency (virtually an entire criterion level). The same condition applied to the 13-year-olds. Among the 9-year-olds, however, differences in the proficiency scores were not as great between those who watched a little television and those who watched a lot. Moreover, there was very little difference between those who watched

FIGURE 6.22A

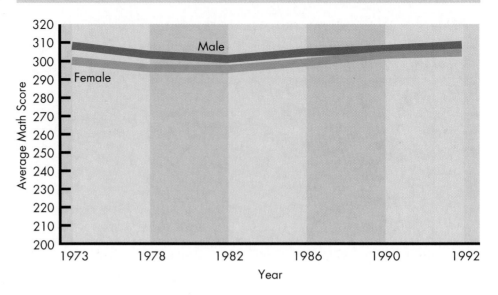

AVERAGE MATH PROFICIENCY BY GENDER (17-YEAR-OLDS)

FIGURE 6.22B

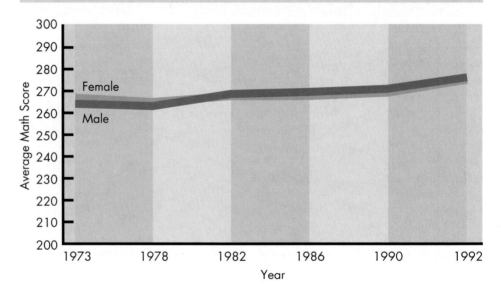

AVERAGE MATH PROFICIENCY BY GENDER (13-YEAR-OLDS)

infrequently (0 to 2 hours) and those who were in the midrange of viewers (3 to 5 hours per day). It is again important to note that these associations might be disguising other factors such as poverty levels or parental education level. Homes where 6 or more hours of TV is watched per day, for instance, might carry associational sociological conditions, such as lower parental education levels, that are not accounted for in Table 6.9.

Again the role of course taking has proved to be essential to mathematical proficiency. The average proficiency scores of a student may be very much a function of the highest mathematical course taken (Figure 6.23). The difference between students taking precalculus as their highest math course and those taking Algebra I as their highest math course is over 50 points. There

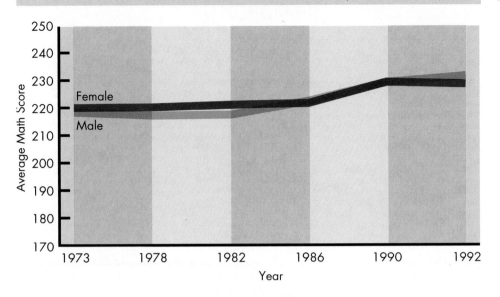

FIGURE 6.22C

AVERAGE MATH PROFICIENCY BY GENDER (9-YEAR-OLDS)

TABLE 6.9

AVERAGE MATH PROFICIENCY VERSUS DAILY TELEVISION WATCHING (1990 AND 1992)

Television Watched per Day:	Average Math Proficiency					
	9-Year-Olds		13-Year-Olds		17-Year-Olds	
	1990	1992	1990	1992	1990	1992
0 to 2 hours	231	231	277	280	312	314
3 to 5 hours	234	233	271	273	300	300
6 or more hours	221	219	258	255	287	285

Source: National Center for Education Statistics. (1995). *Digest of education statistics. (p. 121).* Washington, DC: U.S. Department of Education.

may, in fact, be wisdom in some of the recent calls to increase graduation requirements and to include more academic courses. The data suggest that simply taking the course might contribute to overall proficiency, though one cannot take this too far. Still, this issue again raises the question of OTL. The fact that some students gained a limited exposure to math while others received an extended exposure speaks to opportunity-to-learn factors. Some research suggests that the course-taking pattern between 8th grade and 10th grade in mathematics explains differences in proficiency. After controlling for 8th-grade proficiencies in math, researchers have found that higher math gains are associated with a course-taking pattern that reflects more advanced math course work (Rock & others, 1994). Although many school districts have examined student achievement against race, ethnic, and gender variables, few have attempted to disaggregate the data by OTL (Steven & Grymes, 1993). It could very well be that curriculum tracking, special education placements, certain remedial courses, and general counseling initiatives conspire to keep certain students from a full academic exposure in disciplines like mathematics.

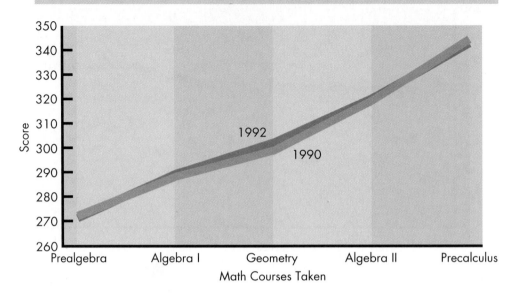

Writing Proficiency

The NAEP writing assessment accounts for three basic forms of writing: informative, persuasive, and imaginative. Students are asked to complete brief informative descriptions, reports, and analyses, to write persuasive letters and arguments, and to invent their own stories (Applebee & others, 1994). An assessment is made of their writing by accounting for the appropriateness of the writing response to the charge, by scoring the holistic fluency of the writing, and by assessing the mastery of the conventions of written English (spelling, punctuation, and grammar). Seven criterion levels were used. The first level is a "not rated" level. This level includes indecipherable papers and blank responses. The second level (Response to Topic) represents some kind of response but one that completely misunderstands the assignment. The third level (Undeveloped Response to Task) includes papers judged to be abbreviated, disjointed, or circular in their reasoning and unresponsive to the writing task. The fourth level (Minimally Developed) includes papers that contain the information and ideas needed but are brief, vague, and confusing. The fifth level (Developed) includes papers that not only included the necessary information to complete the assignment but also achieved the writing purpose. The sixth level (Elaborated) is papers that provided elaborate responses to the writing charge and that offered a coherent response. The highest level (Extensively Elaborated) is papers similar to the sixth level but better organized, more clear, and generally less flawed (Applebee & others, 1994). Unlike the other NAEP tests, the writing assessment does not allow for much cross-grade comparisons because the scaling of the criterion levels varies with each grade level. Roughly speaking, Minimally Developed levels were scaled at the 150 level, Developed ratings, at the 250 level, and Elaborated, at the 350 level.

Average writing proficiency skills have shown the greatest improvement among 8th graders, whose 1992 scores have reached a new high point and whose improvement from 1984 has been most impressive. The proficiency ratings of 11th graders, however, have not changed significantly over the years, while the ratings of the 4th graders have improved only slightly. Among all age groups there was a considerable drop in the scores in 1990, so much so that they represented low points on the NAEP writing scores. Since 1990, the performance of the two lower grades has bounced back (Figure 6.24).

The writing proficiency scores are in many ways disappointing when one examines them in relation to race and ethnicity (Figures 6.25A, 6.25B, and 6.25C). Although Hispanic children at all age levels, especially at the two higher

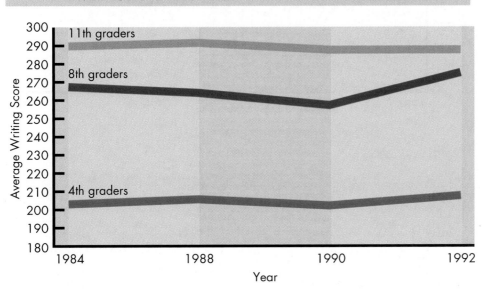

FIGURE 6.24

AVERAGE WRITING PROFICIENCY BY GRADE LEVEL

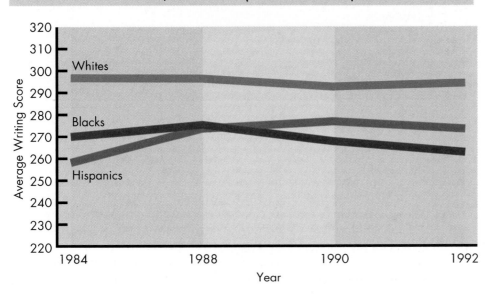

FIGURE 6.25A

AVERAGE WRITING PROFICIENCY BY RACE/ETHNICITY (11TH GRADERS)

FIGURE 6.25B

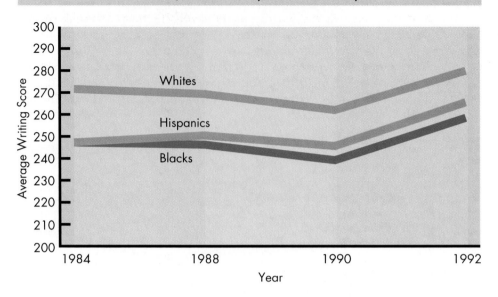

AVERAGE WRITING PROFICIENCY BY
RACE/ETHNICITY (8TH GRADERS)

FIGURE 6.25C

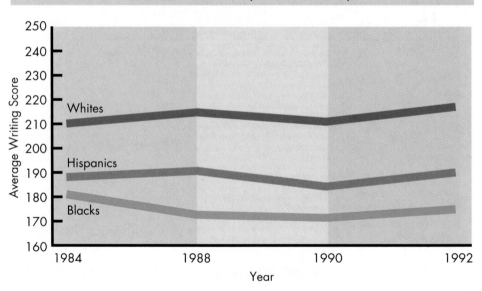

AVERAGE WRITING PROFICIENCY BY
RACE/ETHNICITY (4TH GRADERS)

grades, have improved their scores from 1984, the scores of White and Black 11th graders have declined since 1984. Because 11th graders represent the end product of the school system, this is a considerable disappointment. The scores of Black children have suffered the most over the years. The difference in average proficiency scores have actually widened and Hispanics in 8th and 11th grades, who were once scoring lower than Black children, are now better performers on the NAEP. The scores in the two lower grades in all the races seemed to have bottomed out in 1990, but for 11th-grade Blacks, the 1992 scores represented an all-time low, and for 11th-grade Hispanics, the 1992 scores represented a return to the 1988 levels.

The average scores attained on the NAEP writing assessment demonstrate the largest performance gaps between the sexes (Figures 6.26A, 6.26B and 6.26C). Females hold a wide advantage over males in all age groups. This advantage has held steady for the past eight years and has even, in the case of 4th graders, widened. In 1990, the writing proficiency scores for males at all grade levels reached their lowest levels. Two years later, they recovered, and in the case of 8th-grade males, the scores jumped up to their highest levels.

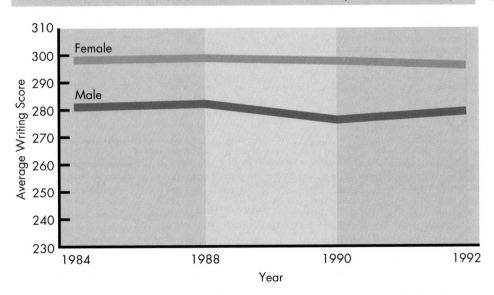

FIGURE 6.26A

AVERAGE WRITING PROFICIENCY BY GENDER (11TH GRADERS)

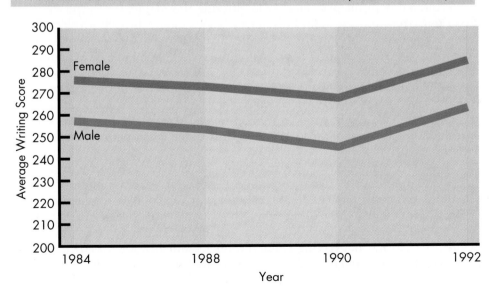

FIGURE 6.26B

AVERAGE WRITING PROFICIENCY BY GENDER (8TH GRADERS)

FIGURE 6.26C

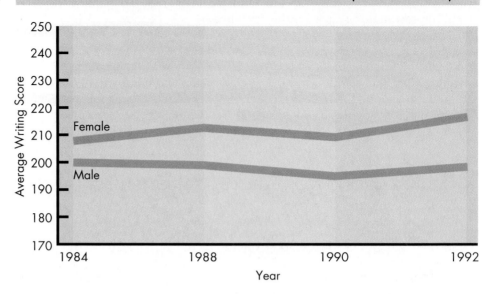

AVERAGE WRITING PROFICIENCY BY GENDER (4TH GRADERS)

History Proficiency

The first NAEP assessment of historical knowledge was taken in 1986 and was restricted to juniors in high school. Another followed in 1988 that accounted for the proficiency levels of 4th, 8th, and 12th graders. Unlike other assessments, the history test had only four criterion or proficiency levels: 200 level—Simple Historical Facts, 250 level—Beginning Historical Information and Interpretation, 300 level—Basic Historical Information and Ideas, and 350 level—Interpretation of Historical Information and Ideas. The 200 level included knowledge of simple historical facts that might be learned from everyday experiences, such as knowing why national holidays like Thanksgiving and the Fourth of July are celebrated. The 250 level included knowledge of a wider variety of historical facts that would more likely be learned from the study of history, such as identifying the *Mayflower* as the Pilgrims' first ship and knowing how President Lincoln died. The 300 level included broad knowledge of historical terms, facts, regions, and ideas, such as knowing the content of major documents that influenced the country's political, economic, and social life. The most advanced level (350 level) included a detailed understanding of historical vocabulary, facts, regions, and ideas, as well as the relation of social science concepts to historical events and themes. Students might be asked, for instance, to compare the powers of the president today against those of President George Washington (Hammack & others, 1990).

Results from the 1988 test indicated that students held an inadequate understanding of U.S. history (see the Objects of Teaching feature in this section). Although the vast majority of 4th graders (76%) attained the 200 level of proficiency, only 16% of the 4th graders were able to rate at the 250 level. There could also be OTL issues at work here. Many of the 4th-grade students reported not having studied more recent historical knowledge and less than half reported having social studies instruction every day. Among the

OBJECTS OF TEACHING

Items from the NAEP Test on Historical Knowledge

Here are the 40 lowest-scoring items on the 1988 national assessment of history. The number indicates the percentage of students who correctly answered the question that was asked about the item. Do you find these results to be distressing, or do you find that such results are not indicative of anything important?

Description	Total
"Nullification" related to states' rights	42.4
Hoover, Franklin Roosevelt were presidents during Depression	41.1
Jane Addams founded settlement houses to help the poor	41.0
"Reconstruction" occurred between 1850–1900	40.2
The Federalist advocated adoption of Constitution	40.1
Dred Scott decision: slave who moved to free state was not free	39.5
D-Day occurred between 1943–1947	39.5
Renaissance was characterized by cultural, technological advances	39.3
Paine's *Common Sense* argues for colonial independence	38.3
Emancipation Proclamation freed slaves in Confederacy	38.2
Union membership grew in the 1930s because of new laws	38.2
Jamestown founded before 1750	38.0
Restrictions on immigration were not part of New Deal	37.8
"Three-fifths compromise" in Constitution defined status of slaves	37.7
Immigration from southern and eastern Europe grew, 1890–1910	37.6
Immigration restriction in 1921, 1924 aimed at SE Europeans	37.3
Scopes trial was about teaching evolution	37.2
Upton Sinclair, Lincoln Steffens, Ida Tarbell known as muckrakers	37.1
Theodore Roosevelt was president between 1895–1912	36.9
Articles of Confederation failed to provide adequate taxing power	36.8
Find region on US map acquired from Mexico in war	36.2
Religious toleration in colonies due to common interest of many groups	36.0
Jonas Salk invented polio vaccine	34.3
Spanish-American War made US an international power	33.0
American foreign policy after World War I known as isolationist	32.3
The Civil War occurred between 1850–1900	32.2
US foreign policy in early 1900s: "Speak softly, carry a big stick"	31.6
Purpose of Jim Crow laws was to enforce racial segregation	30.7
Magna Carta is foundation of British parliamentary system	30.6
Andrew Jackson was president between 1820–1840	29.9
Reformation led to establishment of Protestant sects	29.8
The United Nations was founded between 1943–1947	25.9
The Seneca Falls Declaration concerned women's rights	25.8
Abraham Lincoln was president between 1860–1880	24.7
Lyndon Johnson's term included Medicare and Voting Rights Act	23.9
Betty Friedan and Gloria Steinem led women's movement in 1970s	22.8
"Progressive movement" refers to reforms before World War I	22.6
"Reconstruction" refers to readmission of Confederate states	21.4
John Winthrop and the Puritans founded a colony in Boston	19.5

Source: Ravitch, D., & Finn, C.E. (1987). *What do our 17-year-olds know?* (pp. 268–269). New York: Harper and Row.

8th graders, 96% reached the 200 level and close to 70% reached the 250 level, leaving only about 13% at the 300 mark. Again in reference to opportunity-to-learn, about half the 8th graders noted having never studied the period from 1945 to the present. Almost all the 12th graders had achieved the 200 level and close to 90% reached the 250 level, but less than half were able to gain 300 level mastery and a measly 4.6% reached the highest level.

In examining the scores, the male scores in all grades were higher, though not dramatically so, and the difference in proficiency between the sexes widened with the older students. Similarly, White scores were significantly higher than non-White scores, with the proficiency difference starting in the early grades and growing wider in the later grades. The scores between Blacks and Hispanics were comparable (Table 6.10).

As with other NAEP studies, the history assessment also examined the relation of proficiency to home factors, such as TV viewing and amounts of daily homework, as well as opportunity-to-learn factors, such as the frequency of classes that the students had in subjects like social studies and history (Tables 6.11 and 6.12). Although the amount of homework done daily was positively associated with achievement among 8th and 11th graders, the association was much less clear, as it usually seems to be, with 4th graders. Among the 4th graders, the highest proficiency scores were made by students reporting no daily homework, but among the later grades the exact opposite was the case. The students reporting 2 or more hours of homework per day did best on the NAEP.

In a similar manner, daily TV viewing rates were clearly negatively associated with proficiency scores among 8th and 11th graders—the less TV viewed, the better the achievement score. But among 4th graders, the relation between TV watching and performance on the NAEP was confused. The frequency that one was taught historical knowledge was also a factor in NAEP proficiency ratings. The data indicated that more frequent exposures to social studies instruction in 4th grade pays an achievement dividend, but only up to a certain point. The proficiency differences between students reporting to have social studies classes three to four times a week and students who reported having hardly ever had social studies classes are striking. At the high school level, a similar condition prevails, with course work clearly demonstrating a positive effect on achievement, up to a certain point.

TABLE 6.10

AVERAGE PROFICIENCY ON THE NAEP U.S. HISTORY ASSESSMENT		
1988 4th Grade	**1988 8th Grade**	**1988 12th Grade**
Total 220.6	263.9	295.0
Male 222.9	266.7	298.5
Female 218.2	261.6	291.8
White 227.5	270.4	301.4
Black 199.5	246.0	274.4
Hispanic 202.7	244.3	273.9

Source: National Center for Education Statistics. (1995). *Digest of education statistics* (p. 120). Washington, DC: U.S. Department of Education.

AVERAGE PROFICIENCY VERSUS TV AND HOMEWORK RATES

TABLE 6.11

Rate of Daily TV Viewing:	4th Grade	8th Grade	11th Grade
0–2 hours	222.6	269.6	299.0
3–5 hours	225.6	265.0	293.3
6 or more hours	210.8	251.1	276.7
Time Spent on Daily Homework:			
None	223.6	253.4	280.7
Didn't do it	209.0	247.2	291.6
½ hour or less	221.6	262.2	295.4
1 hour	223.2	265.7	295.6
1 hour and more	214	–	–
2 hours	–	267.9	299.4
More than 2 hours	–	267.2	302.4

Source: National Center for Education Statistics. (1995). *Digest of education statistics* (p. 120). Washington, DC: U.S. Department of Education.

AVERAGE PROFICIENCY SCORES VERSUS FREQUENCY OF COURSE WORK

TABLE 6.12

Frequency of Social Studies Classes:	Percentage Responding	4th-Grade Scores
Every day	45	220.7
3 to 4 times a week	25	225.9
1 to 2 times a week	16	219.2
Less than once a week	5	209.0
Never or hardly ever	8.5	208.0

Years of U.S. History Course Work:	Percentage Responding	11th-Grade Scores
None	1.8	255.9
½ year	2.3	269.1
Between ½ and 1 year	3.2	274.5
1 Year	42.2	300.8
More than one year	50.5	292.7

Source: Hammack, D.C., & others. (1990, April). The *U.S. history report card* (pp. 74 and 78). Prepared by Educational Testing Service. Washington, DC: U.S. Department of Education.

 Societal Problems and School Benefits

Changes in demographics, families, crime rates, drug-use rates, and the overall pervasiveness of poverty in America reflect new challenges for the schools. Some of these changes point to a troubled America. Each year, for instance, an average of 350,000 children are born to cocaine-addicted mothers. Today, about 20 million children have not received their proper vaccinations, another 20 million return home from school each day without adult supervision in the home, and yet another 20 million are abused or neglected at home (Hodgkinson, 1991). Infant mortality in America is virtually at third-world levels. Young males in the United States are about five times more likely to be murdered than are their peers in other developed nations, and the incarceration rate in the United States is the highest in the world (Hodgkinson, 1991). On the other hand, the national dropout rate has declined significantly in recent decades, and the number of college graduates in the country continues to increase. Moreover, the NAEP indices of school achievement document national progress, the overall teacher-to-student ratio in schools has never been lower, and the average per pupil expenditures are at their zenith.

The public school opens its doors each morning and embraces its constituency. It does not screen for admission or suitability. It works with the larger society and absorbs all its problems as part of its own makeup. Thus, an examination of societal changes is, in effect, an examination of the sociological conditions that dwell in the school.

For a look at some of the parental and societal issues that relate to education, see the Contemporary Debate feature in this section.

Poverty and Families

One of the more overlooked issues in the discussion of the status of American education is the ever-increasing number of children who are living below the poverty line. As demonstrated in Table 6.13, the United States is a leader among advanced nations in the percentage of children living below the poverty line. The impediments of poverty are not incidental to the functioning of the school. The American school inherits from its society a greater proportion of students living with the deprivations of poverty than in many other developed nations. Approximately 30 million American children lived below the poverty line in 1990. Over half of these children were either Hispanic or Black (60%) and a very large share lived in single-parent/female-headed households (Synder & Fromboluti, 1993).

The issues, however, go even further than economics. The demographics of the family and the home in America have also posed new problems for the public school. Over the past several decades, for instance, there has been a dramatic rise in the number of children living in homes where both parents

TABLE 6.13

PERCENTAGE OF CHILDREN LIVING IN POVERTY IN INDUSTRIALIZED NATIONS, 1991 (BEFORE AND AFTER TAX AND TRANSFER ADJUSTMENTS)		
	Before	**After**
Sweden	7.9	1.6
West Germany	8.4	2.8
Netherlands	14.1	3.8
France	21.2	4.6
United Kingdom	27.9	6.4
Australia	16.4	9.0
Canada	15.7	9.3
United States	22.3	20.4

work and in homes led by a single parent. The United States has had a higher divorce rate than most other developed nations (although it also has a higher marriage rate), and only Denmark has had significantly higher rates of out-of-wedlock births (see Tables 6.14 and 6.15). The growth of births to unwed mothers and the rising divorce rate have resulted in a significantly large proportion of children in fatherless homes in America (Synder & Fromboluti, 1993). In 1992, 24% of all children lived in single-parent homes. These are clearly factors that influence school education.

The disintegration of the traditional family in America has yet to be fully understood in terms of its consequences to the education of children. But the American family of the late 1990s is clearly different from the American family of the 1950s and 1960s. Since 1950, the number of divorces in America and the number of children involved (under age 18) in a divorce increased by over 200% (Synder & Fromboluti, 1993). This has simultaneously occurred with a threefold increase in the rise of single-parent homes in America (see Figure 6.27 for data since 1970).

Of course, the traditional nuclear family does not have a monopoly on providing an enlightened and loving experience for children. Against difficult

TABLE 6.14

MARRIAGE AND DIVORCE RATES IN SELECTED NATIONS, 1988 (PER 1,000 PERSONS)		
	Marriages	**Divorces**
USA	9.7	20.7
France	4.9	8.4
Germany	6.5	8.8
UK	6.9	12.3
Netherlands	6.0	8.1
Italy	5.5	2.1

Source: Synder, T.D., & Fromboluti, C.S. (1993). *Youth indicators*, 1993 (p. 20). Washington, DC: U.S. Department of Education.

TABLE 6.15

BIRTHS TO UNMARRIED WOMEN AS A PERCENTAGE OF ALL LIVE BIRTHS IN SELECTED NATIONS, 1988 AND 1960		
	1960	**1988**
USA	5.3	25.7
Denmark	7.8	44.7
France	7.8	26.3
Germany	6.1	10.0
Greece	1.2	2.1
Ireland	1.6	11.7
Italy	2.4	5.8
Netherlands	1.3	10.2
Portugal	9.5	13.7
UK	5.2	25.1

Source: Synder, T.D., & Fromboluti, C.S. (1993). *Youth indicators, 1993* (p. 27). Washington, DC: U.S. Department of Education.

FIGURE 6.27

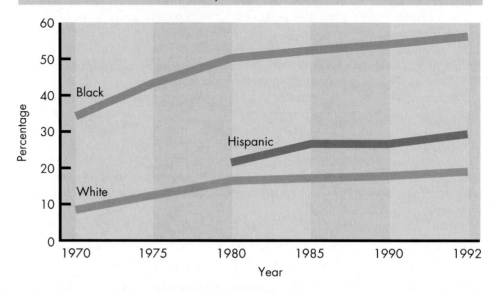

PERCENTAGE OF CHILDREN LIVING WITH A SINGLE PARENT BY RACE, 1970 TO 1992

FIGURE 6.28

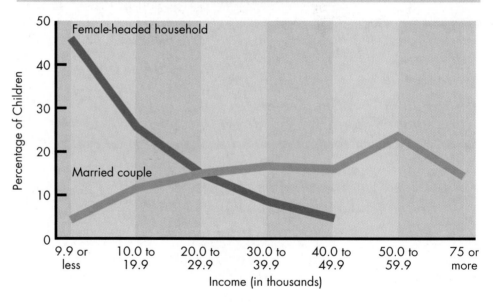

PERCENTAGE OF CHILDREN (UNDER 18) BY FAMILY TYPE AND INCOME (IN THOUSANDS), 1991

odds, many single-parent families give children a healthy upbringing. However, the data indicate that many single-parent families live at the lowest income levels (see Figure 6.28). The material deprivations of poverty work hand in hand with the deprivations posed by the difficulties of running a household singlehandedly. Again this is a phenomenon that has grown by considerable proportions in the nation. In 1991, about 70% of the children living in female-headed households lived in either absolute or relative poverty. In 1992, the percentage of children living in single-parent homes in

School Readiness

The following represents the results of a national survey given to parents. What is the essential message? Do you agree with it?

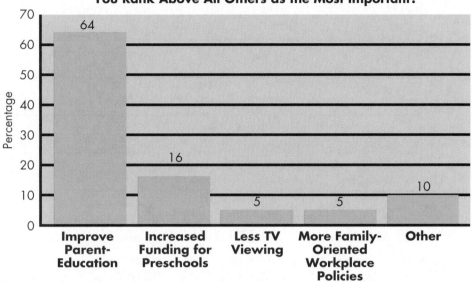

Which One of the Following Goals Would You Rank Above All Others as the Most Important?

Note: Other suggestions equaled 10 percent.
Source: Boyer, E. L. (1991). *Ready to learn* (p. 42). Princeton, N.J.: Carnegie Foundation for the Advancement of Teaching.

America had never been higher. It has risen among all the races, but has gone from bad to worse among Black Americans.

Another factor playing into school performance is the changing role of women in the workforce. In 1950, only 11.8% of married women with children under the age of 6 were employed or actively seeking employment. In 1992, the number was up to 58.9%. In 1950, only about 28% of women with children between the ages of 6 and 17 were employed or seeking employment, while in 1992, the percentage stood at 73.6%. Divorced and separated women with children have always been much more likely to be employed than married women. The percentage of divorced or separated women participating in the workforce has more or less held steady over the years, but there are more of them today than ever before. The implied message here is not that women should stay home to raise children, but that familial conditions for the raising of healthy children have changed in ways that reflect on schools.

Dropouts

A high school diploma has long symbolized an achievement in America. And for good reasons. For young adults, there are documented lifetime benefits that accrue from staying in school. The lifetime earning powers of an

Parental Involvement With Children

What message do you derive from the two figures? Are these positive or negative data? What might be needed to improve family life?

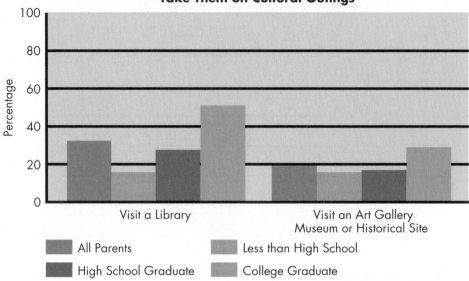

Three-to-Five Year Olds Whose Parents Frequently Take Them on Cultural Outings

- All Parents
- Less than High School
- High School Graduate
- College Graduate

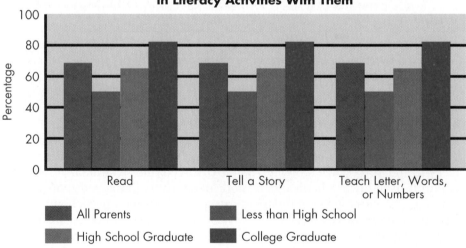

Three-to-Five Year Olds Whose Parents Regularly Engage in Literacy Activities With Them

- All Parents
- Less than High School
- High School Graduate
- College Graduate

Source: Boyer, E. L. (1991). *Ready to learn* (p. 36). Princeton, NJ: Carnegie Foundation for the Advancement of Teaching.

individual and the general indices of quality in an individual's life are profoundly tied to education levels. It has been estimated, for instance, that the average dropout will, over a lifetime, earn about $212,000 less than a high school graduate and $812,000 less than a college graduate (Schwartz, 1995). Those who stay in school are less likely to be unemployed, less likely to land in jail, and less likely to be the victims of poverty and crime.

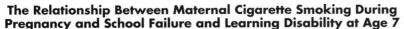

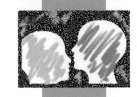

School Achievement and Prenatal Care

What are some of the main conclusions that can be drawn from these figures? What factors are implicated in the results displayed here?

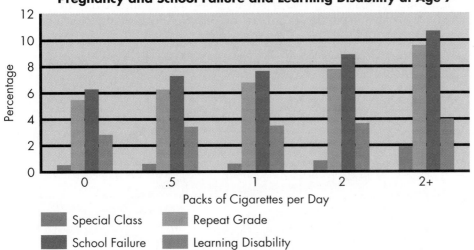

The Relationship Between Maternal Cigarette Smoking During Pregnancy and School Failure and Learning Disability at Age 7

Legend: Special Class, Repeat Grade, School Failure, Learning Disability

X-axis: Packs of Cigarettes per Day (0, .5, 1, 2, 2+)
Y-axis: Percentage

Source: Newman, L., & Buka, S. L. (1990). *Every child a learner: Reducing risks of learning impairment during pregnancy and infancy* (p. 7). Denver: Education Commission of the States.

The Relationship Between Birthweight and School Failure

Legend: Special Education, Repeat Grade, School Failure

X-axis: Very Low Birthweight, Low Birthweight, Normal Birthweight
Y-axis: Percentage

Source: Boyer, E. L. (1991). *Ready to learn* (pp. 17 and 18). Princeton, N.J.: Carnegie Foundation for the Advancement of Teaching.

In many places, especially in the cities of America, the dropout rate is often tragically high, indicative perhaps of the failure of the school to keep youth interested and meaningfully engaged in learning. But understanding the meaning of the dropout rates is not as cut-and-dried as it might seem. Dropping out of school, for example, is not always a final condition. Students who drop out sometimes return to school or decide to pursue a GED. Accounting for the GED brings the traditional dropout rate down by a considerable measure. A recent study that used a national sample of longitudinal data showed that 84% of the high school sophomore class graduated on time in 1982, but that two thirds of the remaining 16% completed high school over the next 10 years, the vast majority over the first four years. Over a 10-year period, the graduation or completion rate of the class of 1982 went up to 93.7% (National Center for Education Statistics, 1995a).

The National Center for Education Statistics measures the dropout rate in three ways. It tracks those who leave high school each year; the proportion of people in the population who have not completed high school, regardless of when they dropped out; and a single group of students over time (NCES, 1993). We have used the numbers of the National Center for Education

FIGURE 6.29

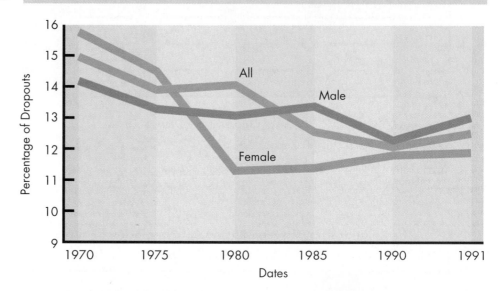

PERCENTAGE OF HIGH SCHOOL DROPOUTS BY GENDER*

FIGURE 6.30

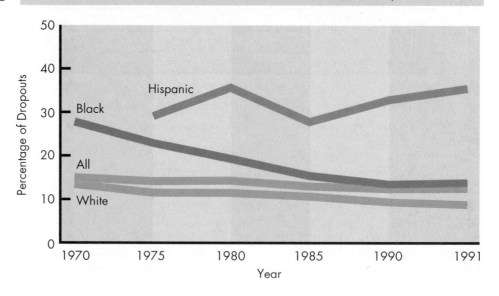

PERCENTAGE OF HIGH SCHOOL DROPOUTS BY RACE/ETHNICITY

PART TWO: THE SCHOOL AND SOCIETY

Statistics to report on dropout trends. These dropout rates account for students who later earn a Graduate Equivalency Diploma (GED). In Figures 6.29 and 6.30, dropouts are persons who are not enrolled in school or who have not completed high school, either traditionally or through a GED (Synder & Fromboluti, 1993).

As each Figure demonstrates, the national dropout rate in America has declined significantly since 1970. The overall decline from a 15% dropout rate to a 12.1% dropout rate amounts to about a 20% decrease. Most of the decline has been accounted for by the precipitous fall in the dropout rate among Black children, which had gone from about 28% in 1970 to about 13% in 1990, which is better than a 50% fall. Although not as dramatic, similar progress has been made with girls, where the dropout rate has fallen from 15.7% to 11.8%. The data, in fact, are encouraging on virtually all the subsets of race, gender, and ethnicity. The Hispanic dropout rate, of course, is the exception.

It is encouraging to note that the 1992 dropout rate for Black children in middle-income families was slightly lower than that of their White peers in middle-income families (McMillen and others, 1993). This points to the powerful role that income likely plays in school performance. Most dropouts, irrespective of race, emerge from low-income settings. An analysis of dropout trends done by Carson, Huelskamp, and Woodall (1993) lends further credibility to this view. After disaggregating the dropout data by ethnicity and community type, they found that the dropout rate for Blacks living in suburban communities to be significantly lower than the dropout rate for Whites living in the suburbs. Similarly, the dropout rate of Whites living in central city settings was about equal to the dropout rate of Blacks living in central city settings. The dropout rate among Hispanics, however, was not similarly influenced.

Students rarely cite job opportunities as a reason for dropping out of school.

The Hispanic dropout rate represents an anomaly in the national trends. Hispanic dropout rates have fluctuated over the years but have remained quite high and have not followed the downward trend seen among White and Black students. Researchers in the National Center for Education Statistics, however, found that a significant share of the Hispanic dropout rate is composed of immigrant youth who are sometimes not even educated in their own native language. They found that the reported national dropout rate for Hispanic youth is a figure clearly affected by immigration patterns and can likely be cut in half if limited to U.S.-born Hispanics. About 43% of all Hispanic children born outside the United States were dropouts and about 63% of all Hispanic dropouts were born outside the country (NCES, 1992b). These are dramatic numbers. Accounting for the immigration factors brings the Hispanic dropout number down considerably, as evidenced in the way that the numbers improve when one examines the dropout rate of students from first and second generation families (Figure 6.31).

Are there characteristics that many dropouts hold in common? Much research, of course, has tried to find the variables around which dropouts might cluster and to ask why the choice to leave school seemed attractive.

When asked why they dropped out, the students often paint a picture of a nonresponsive and frustrating school experience. The reasons that they cite could be viewed as the factors that might help to push students out of school. Generally speaking, it comes down to the fact that such students do not like school very much and often report not being able to keep up with the work. They also cite problems with getting along with peers and teachers and with discipline problems. In some cases they also say that they feel unsafe in school (Schwartz, 1995).

These school-related factors, of course, do not tell the whole story. There are variables outside of the school that pull students out. Foremost among

FIGURE 6.31

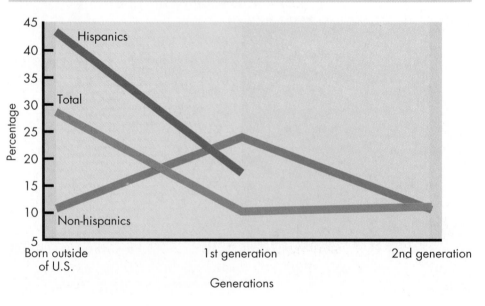

PERCENTAGE OF DROPOUTS (16- TO 24-YEAR-OLDS) BY GENERATIONS, 1989

PART TWO: THE SCHOOL AND SOCIETY

these is the fact that students who leave school often do so because they have become a parent and sometimes feel compelled to try to get married and support their family. On a national level, researchers have found that about one fifth of all dropouts were married, living with someone, or divorced, with females more likely to be married than males. Forty percent had a child or were expecting one. Dropouts were also more likely to move during their high school years than graduates. One fourth changed schools two or more times. Twelve percent, twice as many as graduates, ran away from home. One half were enrolled in a general high school program; very few were in college preparatory studies. One third were either suspended or put on probation. Students who repeated one or more grades were twice as likely to drop out than those who had never been held back (Schwartz, 1995).

Drug Abuse and Crime

Another area of sociological examination that is important to the school is the issue of drug abuse among older schoolchildren. Here there seems to have been some progress. The 1990 rates of "regular" usage of cigarettes, alcohol, marijuana, and cocaine have dropped considerably among high school seniors since 1975 (see Figure 6.32). Regular cigarette smoking has dropped about 20% since 1975 and regular marijuana usage has dropped by over 50%. The use of alcohol, the most popular drug among high school seniors, has also dropped by about 20% since 1975. The 1992 regular cocaine usage rates are at about the same level as in 1975 but are down considerably from the enormous increases in usage seen during the 1980s. In 1992, for the first time since about 1986, the Gallup Poll data indicated that the public no longer pointed to "use of drugs" as the most frequently cited problem facing local public schools (Elam, Rose, & Gallup, 1993). By 1994, the Gallup Poll showed that "drug

FIGURE 6.32

PERCENTAGE OF HIGH SCHOOL SENIORS REPORTING TO HAVE USED CIGARETTES, ALCOHOL, MARIJUANA, OR COCAINE DURING THE PREVIOUS 30 DAYS

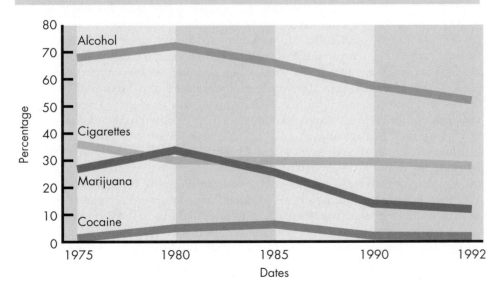

FIGURE 6.33A

NUMBER OF HOMICIDES AND SUICIDES OF 5- TO 14-YEAR-OLDS (PER 1,000 PERSONS IN THE AGE COHORT)

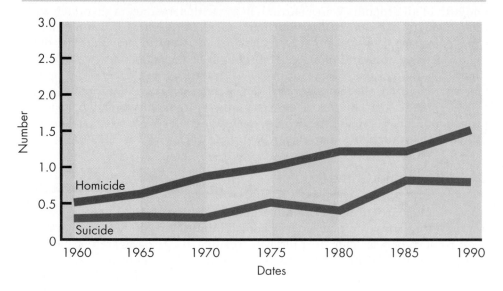

abuse" fell behind three other "bigger" problems in the public schools (Elam, Rose, & Gallup, 1994). But drug use among students is an ongoing struggle. In 1995, federal surveys showed that marijuana use doubled from the levels recorded in 1992, though cocaine and alcohol use remained stable ("Use of Marijuana Soars," 1995). Other national surveys show that despite the progress made in student drug use, many adolescents still see drugs as the greatest problem they face, much more so than even crime, social pressures, sex, or school grades (Lewin, 1995).

At the same time, there has been an unabated rise of violence and crime by and toward young people. The 1990 homicide rates of children ages 5 to 14 have increased by threefold since 1960 and suicide rates have doubled (Figure 6.33A). Among young people ages 15 to 24, the homicide rate has similarly tripled since 1960 while the suicide rates have more than doubled (Figure 6.33B). The 1990 criminal arrest rates of young people ages 14 to 17 have tripled since 1960 and have increased by thirtyfold since 1950 (Synder & Fromboluti, 1993). During the 1987–88 academic year, 6% of the nation's 10th graders reported being robbed and being attacked at least once in school. Close to 2% of the nation's 10th-grade males claimed to have brought a gun to school on more than a monthly basis. Among 8th graders, 11% stated that they did not feel safe at school, and another 10% claimed to have been offered the purchase of drugs in school (NCES, 1994). When one examines these numbers, one has to be drawn to the fact that many children live in a less safe world today than in the 1950s and early 1960s. One also has to be cognizant of the limiting negative effects that such conditions impose on public education. Where the security and safety of children are compromised, as it is in so many communities across America, public education is itself compromised. The most recent Gallup Poll on this subject indicated that "fighting/violence/gangs" was the number one problem facing the American schools (Elam, Rose, & Gallup, 1994).

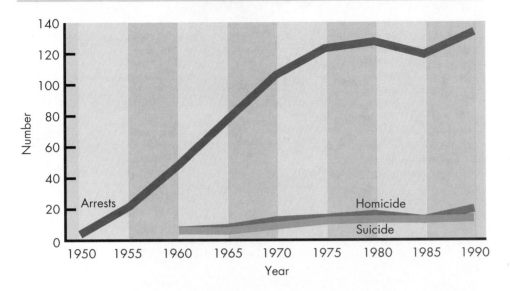

FIGURE 6.33B

NUMBER OF HOMICIDES AND SUICIDES OF 15- TO 24-YEAR-OLDS AND ARRESTS OF 14- TO 17-YEAR-OLDS (PER 1,000 PERSONS IN THE AGE COHORT)

Rooted in poverty and desperation, violence has a disproportionate effect on the lives of minorities and minority children. A Black person is now seven times more likely to be a victim of homicide than a White person and is at considerably more risk of harm by assault, robbery, and rape (Elders, 1994). A school that sits in the middle of a community of violence and poverty often has its educational senses dulled by anxieties over safety and stability. Where violence is an issue in the school, it is particularly an issue among minority schools. These are precisely the kind of sociological circumstances that militate against the school achievement of many minority students.

The school has a relationship with crime in another way also. There is a strong association between those who carry out crime and those who drop out of school. More than 80% of today's prisoners are high school dropouts; the states in the nation that have the fewest dropouts also have the fewest prisoners (Howe, 1993). In a manner of speaking, secondary school retention among adolescents actually pays a dividend to the society by helping to curb crime. Although there is not a cause-and-effect relationship between dropping out and going to jail, there is an association that points to the constructive role of the school in helping to keep youth out of trouble with the law.

Economic School Benefits

The benefits of schooling in America manifest in several ways. The school-effects literature, for instance, demonstrates that schools clearly make a difference in the area of student achievement (Rutter & others, 1979; Teddlie & Stringfield, 1993). Even the NAEP data tend to show that longer instructional exposures to different subject areas provide proficiency gains in those areas. At the same time, it has long been believed that schools help to

Participation in gang life is associated with dropping out, which is in turn related to crime rates. Schools are challenged to find a place where gang members can participate in the educational experience.

promote a common culture, a common discourse, and a common understanding; that they help to stabilize neighborhoods and bring the diverse elements of society together in ways that no other public institution can. School is where literacy and academic knowledge are taught, but it also a place that aims to make good citizens, good family members, good workers, and self-actualized individuals.

But the benefits of schooling can also be found in the areas of employment and individual earning power. As indicated in Figure 6.34, the medium annual earning of a worker is highly associated with the number of years of schooling completed. There are notable differences in the salaries earned by men as opposed to women, but association between the growth of salaries and years of schooling applies to both sexes. In a similar manner, the advantages of education also seem to help protect against unemployment, as indicated in Table 6.16. Among adults at ages 25 and over, unemployment trends have an inverse relationship with years of schooling. The odds of being unemployed as a high school dropout are virtually two times greater than that of a high school graduate and almost four times greater than that of a college graduate.

The People's Grade

Ask any number of American citizens to pass judgment on the quality of public education and they will likely say that the schools are less than adequate on virtually every important scale of performance. They might support such a conclusion with familiar arguments about poor test results on various achievement and aptitude tests, high dropout rates, a lack of academic rigor in the curriculum, poorly trained teachers, and an increasingly growing sense of crisis in the moral character of the student population—to

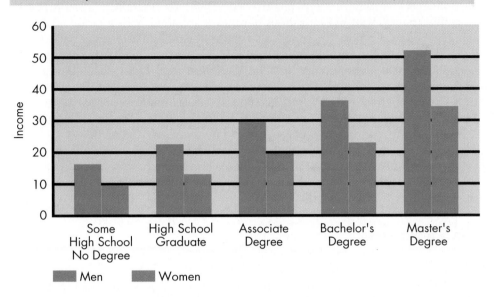

FIGURE 6.34

MEDIAN ANNUAL EARNINGS OF WORKERS 25-YEARS-OLD AND OVER, BY YEARS OF SCHOOL COMPLETED AND SEX, 1991

■ Men ■ Women

TABLE 6.16

UNEMPLOYMENT RATE BY EDUCATION LEVELS (1992)

Sex, race/ethnicity, and highest degree attained	Percent unemployed			
	Persons 16 to 24 years old			
	Total	16 to 19 years	20 to 24 years	25 years and over
1	2	3	4	5
All persons				
All education levels	14.3	21.7	12.0	6.1
Less than a high school graduate	24.9	27.3	22.3	11.4
High school graduate, no college	13.9	18.8	12.5	6.8
Some college, no degree	9.6	11.5	9.3	6.0
Associate degree	6.0	14.6	5.3	4.7
Bachelor's degree or higher	6.5	–	6.5	3.2

Source: National Center for Education Statistics. (1995). *Digest of education statistics* (p. 405). Washington, DC: U.S. Department of Education.

name just a few. They might also add that the public schools in the United States simply do not measure up to the standards of academic performance in the public schools of other advanced nations.

But when these same citizens are asked what they think about their neighborhood schools, more likely than not their judgment of public education will take on a very different tone. As the annual Gallup survey has long demonstrated, the American people hold their local schools in high regard (Elam, Rose, & Gallup, 1994). When local data on academic performance, teacher competence, resource commitment, and other factors are weighed, the American public rates its local schools quite favorably. When these ratings are limited to the views of parents with children in public school, the response is overwhelmingly positive. In 1994, for instance, a Gallup Poll revealed that 70% of public school parents responded with a grade of A or B when asked to evaluate the school that their oldest child attends, a percentage more than three times greater than the A/B rating given to the nation's schools. In 1994, the Annual Phi Delta Kappan Gallup Poll indicated that 44% of those asked to grade their local schools offered a grade of A or B, while only 22% gave a grade of A or B when asked to assess the nation's schools. A similar trend occurred in 1993: 47 percent graded their local schools A or B, while 19% grade the nation's schools A or B (Elam, Rose, & Gallup, 1993). This is significant because the impressions of public school parents are staked into what is actually happening in the schools to their children, as opposed to what someone might be telling them about the schools. To know the school, it seems, is to appreciate it.

The Sandia Report

Although there is a history of debasing the public school, in recent years the effort to shortchange the achievements of the schools has taken on new dramatic proportions. Such deliberate negativism may in fact have something to do with the emerging strategy to reform schools through privatization, an idea that will be explored later. The veracity of the argument for privatization, which would loosen public monies to be used by parents to educate their children in either a public or a private school setting, depends on the belief that schooling is in need of a basic restructuring or reconfiguration. If the current structure leads to inevitable failure, the thinking might go, then it follows that a reconstruction is in order. And this, of course, leads to proposals for privatization.

When the Bush administration appointed a third-party laboratory to conduct an evaluation of public schooling in the United States, the expectation must have been that the finding would complement all the rhetoric regarding privatization. The report that followed, written by three authors from the Sandia Laboratories in New Mexico, concluded that the American schools were performing at desirable and adequate levels in many areas, a finding that likely led to the later the suppression of the document from the American public. The Sandia researchers essentially argued that no fundamental reconfiguration of the public school was in order, that the present structure was sound, and that the achievement and sociological gains in the schools were, in their own way, impressive. The report, however, was withheld from the American public, largely because officials in the federal government stated that its statistics were lacking and that its recommendations did not pass the review process. Daniel Tanner (1993) has documented the story of the Sandia report, focusing on the politics tied in to its suppression. The report has since been published in the *Journal of Educational Research,* which has a circulation of approximately 1,000 readers. Interestingly, a much less systematically developed document published in 1983, now well known as the *A Nation at Risk,* report, had no problem finding a public audience and widespread media dissemination to promote its highly negative impressions about public schooling. *A Nation at Risk* used highly inflammatory language to criticize the schools and failed to make balanced judgments based on the very data that its committee sponsored (Hlebowitsh, 1990).

KEY TERMS

National Assessment of
   Educational Progress

Opportunity-to-learn

KEY QUESTIONS

1. Why are cross-national school comparisons often hazardous?

2. How do curriculum timing and opportunity-to-learn (OTL) factor into national school performance?

3. Why might it be unfair to criticize U.S. schools for their low mean performance in certain subject areas?

4. Is the SAT an effective barometer for school achievement in the United States? Why or why not?

5. Explain how the SAT score can improve for all race and ethnic subgroups but still decline overall.

6. Some commentators have explained that the drop in the SAT score should be celebrated. Explain.

7. What is the NAEP?

8. What are the overall trends to report on NAEP reading proficiency?

9. What makes the recent rise in minority reading proficiency particularly remarkable?

10. What is the general relationship between reading proficiency and home conditions, such as home-reading environment?

11. What are the overall trends to report on NAEP science proficiency?

12. How might one explain the differences in NAEP science proficiency between boys and girls?

13. What are the overall trends to report on NAEP math proficiency?

14. What is the general trend between math proficiency and TV viewing/math proficiency and homework rates?

15. How might you explain the fact that homework rates do not correlate well with achievement among 9-year-olds?

16. What are the overall trends to report on NAEP writing proficiency?

17. What are the overall trends to report on NAEP history proficiency?

18. What is the two-decade national trend on dropouts?

19. In what way is the national Hispanic dropout rate an anomaly?

20. How has the landscape for American families changed since the 1950s and 1960s? How have these changes affected public education?

21. Explain the contradiction in the Gallup Poll over the public's grading of public education.

22. What is the Sandia report and how is it relevant to discussions of American school performance?

REFERENCES

Applebee, A. N., & others. (1994). *NAEP 1992 writing report card.* Washington, DC: NCES and U.S. Department of Education.

Bracey, G. W. (1991). Why can't they be like we were? *Phi Delta Kappan, 73*(2), 104–117.

Bracey, G. W. (1993). The third Bracey Report. *Phi Delta Kappan, 75*(2), 104–117.

Carson, C. C., Huelskamp, R. M., & Woodall, T. D. (1993, May/June). Perspectives on education in America. *Journal of Educational Research,* 259–310.

Elam, S., Rose, L., & Gallup, A. (1993). The 25th annual PDK Gallup Poll. *PDK, 75*(2), 137–152.

Elam, S., Rose, L., & Gallup, A. (1994). The 26th annual PDK Gallup Poll. *PDK, 76*(1), 41–56.

Elders, J. (1994). Violence as a public health issue for children. *Childhood Education, 70*(5), 260–262.

Elkind, D. (1987). *Miseducation: Preschoolers at risk.* New York: Alfred Knopf.

Griffith, J. E., & others. (1994). *Understanding the performance of US students on international assessments.* Washington, DC: NCES and U.S. Department of Education.

Hammack, D. C., & others. (1990). *The U.S. history report card.* Washington, DC: U.S. Department of Education.

Hlebowitsh, P. S. (1989). International school comparisons and the linkage to school reform. *The High School Journal, 72*(2), 54–59.

Hlebowitsh, P. S. (1990, Winter). Playing power politics: How *A Nation at Risk* achieved its national stature. *Journal of Research and Development in Education,* 82–88.

Hlebowitsh, P. S. (1994). Cries of crisis: Assessment of the public school in the national newsprint. In P. S. Hlebowitsh & W. G. Wraga (Eds.), *Annual Review of Research for Middle and Secondary School Principals.* New York: Scholastic.

Hodgkinson, H. (1991). Reform versus reality. *Phi Delta Kappan, 73*(1), 9–16.

Howe, H. (1993). *Thinking about our kids.* New York: The Free Press.

Kozol, J. (1991). *Savage inequalities.* New York: Crown Publishing.

Lapoint, A., Mead, N., & Phillips, G. (1989). *World of differences.* Princeton, NJ: Educational Testing Service.

Lewin, T. (1995). Adolescents say drugs are biggest worry. *The New York Times,* p. 8.

McMillen, M. M., & others. (1993). *Dropout rates in the United States.* Washington, DC: Department of Education.

Mullis, I. V. S., & Jenkins, L. B. (1988). *Science learning matters.* Princeton, NJ: Educational Testing Service.

Mullis, I. V. S., & Jenkins, L. B. (1990). *The reading report card.* Washington, DC: U.S. Department of Education.

National Center for Education Statistics. (1993). *Dropout rates in the United States.* Washington, DC: U.S. Department of Education.

National Center for Education Statistics. (1992a). *International assessment of educational progress, learning mathematics.* Washington, DC: U.S. Department of Education.

National Center for Education Statistics. (1992b). *Are Hispanic dropout rates related to migration?* Washington, DC: U.S. Department of Education.

National Center for Education Statistics. (1994). *Digest of education statistics.* Washington, DC: U.S. Department of Education.

National Center for Education Statistics. (1995). *The condition of education.* Washington, DC: U.S. Department of Education.

National Center for Education Statistics. (1995a). *Dropouts and late comers.* Washington, DC: U.S. Department of Education (ED # 382-756).

National Commission on Excellence in Education. (1983). *A nation at risk.* Washington, DC: U.S. Department of Education.

Passow, A. H. (1984). Tackling the reform reports of the 1980s. *Phi Delta Kappan, 65*(10), 674–83.

Postlethwaite, T. N., & Wiley, D. E. (1991). *The IEA study of science II: Science achievement in twenty-three countries.* New York: Pergamon Press.

Rock, D., & others. (1994). *Changes in math proficiency between 8th and 10th grade.* Washington, DC: NCES and U.S. Department of Education.

Rutter, M., & others. (1979). *Fifteen thousand hours: Secondary schools and their effect on children.* Cambridge, MA: Harvard University Press.

Schneider, J. (1994). Battling the big lie. In P. S. Hlebowitsh & W. G. Wraga (Eds.), *Annual Review of Research for Middle and Secondary School Principals.* New York: Scholastic.

Schwartz, W. (1995). *School dropouts: New information about an old problem.* Washington, DC: OERI. (ERIC Clearinghouse in Urban Education ED# 386-515).

Sloane, F. C., O'Rafferty, M. O., & Westbury, I. A. (1996). National and international studies of mathematics and science: What have we learned? In P. S. Hlebowitsh & W. G. Wraga (Eds.), *Annual Review of Research for Middle and Secondary School Principals.* New York: Scholastic.

Steven, F. I., & Grymes, J. (1993). *OTL: Issues of equity for poor and minority children.* Washington, DC: NCES and U.S. Department of Education.

Stevenson, H. W., & Stigler, J. W. (1992). *The learning gap.* New York: Summit Books.

Suter, L. (1988). *International conference on cross-national education, conference report.* Washington, DC: NCES and U.S. Department of Education.

Synder, T. D., & Fromboluti, C. S. (1993). *Youth indicators, 1993.* Washington, DC: U.S. Department of Education.

Tanner, D. (1972). *Secondary education.* New York: Macmillan.

Tanner, D. (1993). A nation truly at risk. *Phi Delta Kappan, 75*(4), 288–297.

Teddlie, C., & Stringfield, S. (1993). *Schools make a difference.* New York: Teachers College Press.

Use of Marijuana Soars. (1995, September 13). *The New York Times,* p. 16.

Westbury, I. (1992). Comparing American and Japanese achievement: Is the United States really a low achiever? *Educational Researcher, 21*(5), 18–24.

7

**THE CULTURE AND THE
LANGUAGE OF SCHOOLING**

Teresa R. de Garza teaches in Colorado. Her students participate in bilingual education, in which they learn to read and write first in Spanish, their native language. Is such an education a sound idea in a public school system? Many Americans are surprised to learn that the goal of bilingual education is literacy in English.

This chapter examines the exciting diversity in public schools. Children of many languages, cultures, and religions have taken full advantage of the public school's offerings. It is also true that schools have failed many students whose cultural background is different. The balance between helping students become "Americans" and helping them retain their own heritage is a major theme of both this chapter and the history of public schooling in the U.S.

In 1908, Jane Addams wrote a short essay titled "The Public School and the Immigrant Child" in which she argued that immigrant traditions were fundamental to the process of assimilating foreign-born children into American culture through the school. To Addams, the differences among Americans were at the very heart of their commonalities; who they were individually had everything to do with creating who they were collectively. She believed that, at some level, these differences had to be circulated, fostered, and accommodated into a community of common concerns, common principles, and common dialogue. Hence, Addams had little tolerance for those who aimed to educate children in a manner that ignored the cultural dynamics of children's lives. She wanted to use these dynamics to give children a global and multiethnic view of life in a way that related to the problems, issues, and values of American democracy. She expressed this idea clearly in her 1908 essay:

> Can we say, perhaps, that the schools ought to do more to connect these [immigrant] children with the best things of the past, to make them realize something of the beauty and charm of the language, the history, and the traditions which their parents represent. It is easy to cut them loose from their parents, it requires cultivation to tie them up in sympathy and understanding. The ignorant teacher cuts them off because he himself cannot understand the situation, the cultivated teacher fastens them because his own mind is open to the charm and beauty of that old country life. In short, it is the business of the school to give to each child the beginnings of a culture so wide and deep and universal that he can interpret his own parents and countrymen by a standard which is worldwide and not provincial. (Addams, 1908/1985, p. 138)

Addams, of course, was unique for her time, but the problem of forging a common culture without disrupting the pluralistic elements of American society continues to be debated by policymakers and practitioners alike. How is it possible, after all, for the school to acculturate schoolchildren (whose identification with an ethnicity, class, language, religion, and politics is overwhelmingly varied) into an American culture without destroying the very essence of diversity that makes democracy so vital and interesting? Students of various ethnic and language traditions have always needed to learn how to reconcile their own culture with a broader culture. But does this mean that certain youth will need to reject their own culture in the interests of assimilating into a larger or more dominant culture?

The forces of assimilation and diversity have been both the torment and the blessing of the American school. The idea that a widely diverse population can be formed into a unified whole has stabilized the American population and made it better prepared to work in the interests of the public good. When one looks across the world and sees how issues of ethnic diversity have wreaked havoc in parts of Eastern Europe, the former Soviet Union, and the Mideast (just to name a few places), one appreciates the unifying aspects of society in the United States. The by-product of unity, however, can sometimes

Jane Addams worked tirelessly to help teachers see the value of immigrant children and their families.

lead to the severing of community or family-based cultural connections for some groups, which, in the context of the school, could mean that students might give up a language or lose some identification with cultural traditions in the home. It could also mean that students might suffer from psychical distress over not being able to use their original language or over the prospect of altogether rejecting one set of priorities that reside with the family or community while embracing another set residing with the school. These are not necessary trade-offs, but they do sometimes occur to children in schools.

Students come to school with distinct value systems, some of which are not typically associated with what might be seen as American culture and some of which may even seem at odds with the overall goals of democratic schooling. Educators make decisions daily about whether they will encourage or even make attempts to understand the culture of their students. When students come to school speaking a different language, educators have to decide whether their classroom and school will support the students' first language (and with what degree of intensity). The same concerns apply to the cultural traditions and gender roles that children bring to school. How should various cultural issues be treated in the curriculum? Is sponsoring an international food day or celebrating Black History Month adequate? What about the many students from multigenerational American families who do not have a strong ethnic identification? Should the school honor cultural differences between what might be considered best for boys and for girls? If so, how does one protect against stereotyping? These are difficult questions that do not always have definitive answers.

The Culture of Schooling

The idea of culture is complicated. Acceptable definitions are hard to frame. For purposes here, the notion of culture will be examined in terms of the forces that it exerts in binding people together and establishing rules, norms, and customs for behavior. In other words, how does the school contribute to the formation of a larger American culture, to the making of rules, knowledge, and traditions to which everyone can identify? The "culture" of the school should clearly reflect the wider culture, but how can the school apprehend this culture and give it life in its daily operations?

Toward a Common Culture

In *The Interpretation of Cultures,* Clifford Geortz (1973) writes that "cultural patterns are programs: they provide a 'template' or 'blueprint' for the organization of social and psychological processes" (p. 216). The use of the words template or blueprint as analogies for the way a culture guides a group of people suggests that, despite individual variations, those who share a culture are guided by a set of underlying "directions" for living. This so-called set of directions depends on a foundation of commonality—a common language, common problems and concerns, and common values and principles. Dewey (1916) stated that humans live in communities by virtue of the things that they have in common, and they communicate as a way to share and eventually possess things in common. Thus, without a sense of commonality, there can be no communication, and without communication, there can be no community. The conceptual anchor for community is the idea of commonality.

Language, of course, is the best way of ensuring some basis of commonality, though obviously it is not always enough. Although nearly everyone is endowed with the capacity to speak, the kind of language that people speak is obviously culturally derived—it includes a person in one culture, but it might also exclude that person from another. People consistently use language and other cultural commonalities to help define who they are and, equally importantly, who they are not. Thus, societies always have some semblance of a common language. If this is the case, where does this leave the pluralistic democracy in the United States, which clearly upholds English as a common language (essential to the maintenance of some sense of commonality) but which also supports diversity in language, thought, and values as part of its very essence of commonality? Can a society sustain both its commonality and its diversity?

The answer to these questions has everything to do with using the school to paint a comprehensive and dynamic picture of American culture that is couched in constitutional principles and social democratic theory but that also supports ethnic, racial, political, and religious diversity. Simply having a sense of association or commonality in the school and the society is not enough. As Dewey (1916) explained it, there is, after all, "honor among thieves . . . a band of robbers has a common interest as respects its members [and] Gangs are marked by fraternal feelings, and narrow cliques by intense loyalty to their codes" (p. 95). One has to know the character of the commonality being perpetuated in the school and know whether the sense of cultural community is, at its very essence, inclusive or exclusive, democratic or fascist, uniform or varied, rigid or open.

The things held in common in the American schools must abide by a social democratic standard, which means that the makeup of the people and of the ideas in the school must be cosmopolitan (not few and constricted) and must encourage free forms of social interactions with other modes of association or community (Dewey, 1916). The implication is that the common culture of the school must in fact be intercultural. To be vital, common culture has to be formed and reformed through an interplay of social insight, through the taking and receiving of insight brought forth by all members of the group (Dewey, 1916). At the same time, it must also be marked by democratic principles of tolerance, dissent, and conversation. A common school culture, then, should comprise a variety of shared undertakings and experiences relevant to the livelihood of all, precisely the kind of experiences that the school has arguably been derelict in providing.

In most cases, the thinking on the making of a common culture in the school embraces either of two frameworks. One view conceives the school's role in the acculturation of youth as providing the heat for a "melting pot" society, where differences are dissolved into a uniform mold. Under such conditions, exclusive immersion in the English language is required, and finding ways for children to fit into one cultural design is the very purpose of schooling. Such a perspective, of course, leads to a common culture, but it fails to meet the standards discussed here. In other words, the things held in common are not "numerous and varied," and they do not necessarily lead to open and fruitful interactions.

In principle, the "melting pot" conception of acculturation might be viewed as inappropriate for schooling in a democratic society. Critics argue that the problem with the "melting pot" metaphor is that diversity is deliberately erased in the interest of unity. In fact, the very idea of unity in the context of such a metaphor can actually be construed as having imperialistic qualities because all diversity is washed away and rebuilt in the image of only one culture, which, historically speaking, has been one that resides in the traditional liberal arts (with its attendant emphasis on so-called Western thinking and Western literature). Critics have also found the "melting pot" metaphor is wanting in another respect. Because American schools are organized according to a decentralized pattern of governance that aims to reflect local prerogatives in concert with state-mandated directives, the school has some obligation to capture the unique dimensions of local school priorities, which, of course, might include reflecting a panoply of local cultural and community traditions. Such an obligation works against the "melting pot." The school, as indicated, needs to be careful with these matters because it should also provide a cosmopolitan experience that goes beyond local desires. To many thinkers the "melting pot" metaphor fails because it provides limited room for the exercise of local uniquenesses. Howe (1993) goes even farther and observes that the "melting pot" ideal actually creates the conditions for ethnic divisiveness, not unity, because it forces certain groups to huddle together in order to protect their cultural uniquenesses from dominant forces.

Another way of looking at acculturation is to frame it as a process that cultivates a dual identity—one with the larger American tradition, and the other with the more community-based or familial tradition. This has been expressed by some as the "salad bowl" metaphor, where differences are

Diversity in schools is manifested in each and every child. This young boy will write best about what he knows, whether or not that knowledge mirrors the teacher's knowledge.

essential to the overall quality of the whole. Thus, national identity does not come at the expense of an ethnic identity but is vested in a multitude of ethnic identities, an idea that stresses democratic principles of tolerance and understanding. To be different, then, is to be normal, as long as these differences have some center of gravity. This is probably a more appropriate way of seeing the acculturation process in the American schools, though there are potential dangers here as well. The question is, How do educators make the "salad bowl" metaphor work in the conduct of the school? Clearly it is easier said than done.

Proposals for a Common Curriculum

Among the functions of curriculum design that could lend some stability and direction to the common school experience in the United States is the idea of **general education,** which can be defined as "that part of the student's whole education which looks first to his life as a responsible human being and citizen" (Report of Harvard Committee, 1945, p. 51). Its main purpose is to engage youth in a common universe of discourse, understanding, and competence that promotes the development of socially responsible citizens (Tanner & Tanner, 1995, p. 352). As the facet of the curriculum that deals with the knowledge that all citizens must share, general education necessitates an outlook on knowledge and teaching that is principally different from the knowledge and teaching employed in specialized or college preparatory settings. Generally speaking, all education justified under general education emphasizes a sociocivic content focus that promotes problem-centered inquiry and group cooperation. General education is also marked by interdisciplinary subject matter schemes, heterogeneous classroom settings, and a curricular commitment to the educability of all youth.

The idea behind general education does not necessarily lead to a preidentified body of knowledge that the teacher might be asked to transmit. The nature of the knowledge brought forth in general education has everything to do with the nature of the issues and problems embraced in the local school, which, as discussed, is limited only by a general commitment to collective sociocivic themes as they relate to the life of the learner and the life of the society. Chapter 9 explores how general education might be integrated into the school curriculum.

What should be the common knowledge base perpetuated in general education? The nature of the knowledge should, of course, vary somewhat. But generally speaking, students in the general education phase of the curriculum should learn something about themselves in relation to the problems in their homes, communities, and society—problems, for instance, related to the long-term sustenance of the environment, to the disruptions of crime, to poverty, civil strife, and violence, as well as to various emergent social and political events. These types of problems are broached through various disciplines of science, social science, literature, history, and mathematics. Students in general education should also learn something about the development of the institutions in their society—the economic, governmental, and legal systems; the governing constitutional principles of society; and the wealth of historical events that have tested these principles. A premium should also be placed on understanding the cultural diversity of the United States, with an interest in examining the social forces that have led many

Maya Angelou, poet laureate, is a gifted writer whose works may be omitted in the effort to create core readings.

groups to struggle for the very freedoms that attracted them to this country or, in the case of Black Americans, in examining the long and painful journey of coming out from under the yoke of slavery and discrimination.

Also central to general education is the effort to inquire into how knowledge is constructed, revealing the various twists that "facts" and "truth" can take when they are in the hands of various special interest groups. Students learn to question common sense and to reveal, as best as possible, the ways in which knowledge is made. They might, for instance, examine issues related to the distribution of knowledge in the society, tensions related to the freedom of press and the freedom of speech, and case events related to censorship and government control of knowledge, as well as issues related to the media manipulation of events and to the advertising propaganda perpetrated daily on the American people.

General education is also dedicated to showing the historical struggle of the nation and its people to achieve its highest ideals of justice, equity, freedom, and tolerance, and to understanding the factors that have stood in the way of these achievements. The common curriculum aims to create a common culture that deals with society's democratic principles, institutions, and diverse peoples. The knowledge used in the common curriculum adjudicates these issues and cannot be fully known ahead of time. This essentially means that the common curriculum is constantly in flux, rooted in principle but not program, consisting of a public or constitutional faith that includes a commitment to cultural diversity and an openness to differences. As Barber (1991) has stated, "Americans have no faith in common other than a faith in the commons, no shared faith but their public faith" (p. 43).

Such a view of the common curriculum, however, is opposed to the kind of common curriculum that various conservative commentators advanced during the 1980s. The more conservative position has essentially embraced the "melting pot" metaphor and has argued that the school socialization of youth should be immersed in a view of culture laden with classical Euro-Western biases. The justification for this thinking is that the United States is historically built on a Euro-Western cultural ground. In 1987, for instance, William Bennett, the secretary of education in the Reagan administration, advanced a model for high school education that required course work in, among other things, British Literature and Western Civilization. Nothing about Bennett's proposal acknowledged the diversifying factors within the nation's commonalities; rather, his focus was to build the school on a foundation of Western traditions. His document, in fact, bore quite a resemblance to the Committee of Ten report. Similarly, E. D. Hirsch, in a best-selling book titled *Cultural Literacy*, put forth a list of what every American child needs to know to be "culturally literate." His list has been widely criticized as arbitrary and as failing to capture the diverse elements of the nation's society.

Both Bennett and Hirsch tried to capitalize on the notion that a shared base of common knowledge is essential to generating the quality of social discussion and sense of community required to educate good citizens. Such an ideal, as indicated, has long been established. What makes Bennett's and Hirsch's proposals different is not the idea of common learnings for social discourse and community cohesiveness, but rather the curricular means that they believe are necessary for achieving these ends. The progressive view of general education is one that deals with pervading sociocivic problems framed with the intention of developing competencies for effective citizenship. This includes understandings related to the values and aims of society, the pervading problems of society, the institutions of society, the cultural pluralism of society, and the manner in which truth is constructed and conveyed in society. Such issues stand at the center of a social discourse that develops the critical thinking skills and the democratic attitudes essential to the sustenance of democracy in the United States.

The conservative positions taken by Bennett and Hirsch, on the other hand, center on specifying to the schools the precise elements of knowledge to be studied in the common curriculum. In this regard, the role of the curriculum is to transmit a preidentified body of knowledge to students for the purpose of engaging them in later conversation and debate. In Hirsch's case, the recipe-like approach toward cultural literacy is underscored by the fact that he has published cultural-literacy dictionaries, cultural-literacy workbooks, and cultural-literacy tests. Rather than valuing student dialogue, the common curriculum posed by Hirsch (1987) seems to value the acquisition of facts, which inevitably leads to reductive forms of teaching and assessment that contradict the general education spirit of problem-focused inquiry for social insight. Different conceptions of common learning are depicted in Figure 7.1.

Hirsch (1987), moreover, has taken an aggressive position against what he views as "contentless" teaching in the public schools. He bemoans the loss of influence that the Committee of Ten once had and faults the Cardinals Principles Report (as well as John Dewey) for scorning the profound importance of the subject matter and for choosing to emphase a pedagogy dedicated exclusively to the life interests of the learner. This is obviously a controversial interpretation, but it underscores the fact that the debate over the common curriculum continues to be one that centers around the question of what knowledge is most worthwhile.

In the reality of public school life, the common curriculum looks very much more like what Bennett and Hirsch desire than not. From the standpoint of state-mandated graduation requirements, the common curriculum typically includes 3 or 4 courses in English, 2 or 3 in social studies, 2 in math, 2 or 3 in science, 1 in physical education and a remaining array of miscella-

FIGURE 7.1

TWO OUTLOOKS ON COMMON LEARNING			
Overarching Metaphor	**Basis of Commonality**	**Organization of Knowledge**	**Cultural Function**
"Salad bowl"—Commonality is vested in society's differences, in creating a common discourse, and in understanding and appreciating democratic values and principles	*Social problems *Social institutions *Democratic principles *cultural dynamics of population	*Issue centered *Problem focused *Interdisciplinary	*Transmit democratic values *Create social discourse *Renegotiate cultural traditions and norms
"Melting pot"—Commonality is invested in a Euro-Western view of knowledge and reason as revealed in the study of the liberal arts	*The academic disciplines in the liberal arts	*Discipline centered *Strict academic studies *Emphasis on Euro-Western traditions	*Transmit Western culture

neous courses (Coley, 1994). Such courses are operationally convenient. They are neatly categorized and departmentalized, and easily scheduled and inventoried. However, as an integrated offering designed to illumine social intelligence and to sharpen the skills and competencies of democratic living, the common curriculum (general education) has fallen into deep neglect. It has become, de facto, a subject curriculum influenced by what one needs to graduate or to go to college.

Culture and Critical Theory

Over the past decade, a new line of radical scholars in education has examined schools from the standpoint of socioeconomic and minority-group interest (Apple, 1990; Giroux, 1983; McLaren, 1994). These scholars have tried to disclose the injustices and inequities of public school practice, focusing on practices such as "low-ability" curriculum tracks and special education that affect disproportionately large numbers of minority children and children living in poverty. They have also examined the nature of culture being perpetuated in the schools and have accused the public school of practicing **cultural hegemony,** which is the enthroning and imposing of one cultural tradition on the diverse ethnic and cultural groups within the American public school. The style of their criticism has been overtly ideological, supportive of predetermined beliefs about the oppressive functioning of schooling. Overall, their thinking has also been committed to providing a sociological critique of the school. This critique is designed to protect society from reasoning that might lead to a status quo condition or to the erection of rigid cultural conventions based in Western civilization.

Such an outlook can be said to be informed by **critical theory,** which is, in essence, a neo-Marxist view of schooling in America that holds to the belief that schools reproduce, rather than ameliorate, socioeconomic conditions (Gibson, 1986). Schools, in this way, are believed to be instruments of oppression, designed to keep certain groups down while lifting a few others up. This process of reproduction is said to occur in various ways, including differential access to knowledge, differential opportunities to think and use language, and the basic privileging of different subject matter. The decision, for instance, to teach literature in a high school English class with a list of readings drawn from Western traditions suggests an open privileging of one set of writings over another and the concomitant privileging of one cultural perspective over another. A critical theorist, for instance, will ask why Shakespeare should have a prominent place in the curriculum and also ask whose interests are being served by such a phenomenon (see the Objects of Teaching feature, which presents the results of two reading-list surveys). A critical theorist will also ask why certain types of students seem to find their way into low-ability curriculum tracks, again wanting to know why and how certain groups are affected.

Critical theorists see politically conservative thinkers as the main villains in the story of the school's oppression. Conservatives are the ones, they claim, who want to build the curriculum on Western texts and traditions; they are the ones who want to convey a narrow set of values and knowledge to schoolchildren. Even the notion of conservation itself is seen as dangerous because it begs the question of what should be conserved, which in the eyes of the critical theorist always advantages those in power.

The Most Popular Literature in High School English

THE MOST POPULAR LITERATURE IN ENGLISH CLASS, GRADE 7-12

Percentage of Public Schools Assigning Each Book in English Class, Grades 7-12, 1988

1.	Romeo and Juliet	Shakespeare	90%
2.	Macbeth	Shakespeare	81
3.	Huckleberry Finn	Twain	78
4.	To Kill a Mockingbird	Lee	74
5.	Julius Caesar	Shakespeare	71
6.	The Pearl	Steinbeck	64
7.	The Scarlet Letter	Hawthorne	62
8.	Of Mice and Men	Steinbeck	60
9.	Lord of Flies	Golding	56
9.	The Diary of a Young Girl	Anne Frank	56
9.	Hamlet	Shakespeare	56
12.	The Great Gatsby	Fitzgerald	54
13.	Animal Farm	Orwell	51
13.	Call of the Wild	London	51
15.	A Separate Peace	Knowles	48
16.	The Crucible	Miller	47
16.	The Red Badge of Courage	Crane	47
18.	Great Expectations	Dickens	44
18.	Our Town	Wilder	44
20.	A Tale of Two Cities	Dickens	41

What does the above list of books have to say about what American teachers choose for reading materials in English classes between Grades 7 and 12? What do the above books have in common? Do they fail to pass the multicultural test?

Source: Applebee, A. (1989). A study of book-length works taught in high school English. Report Series 1.2. Albany, NY: Center for the Learning and Teaching of Literature, State University of New York.

One of the ways that critical theorists seek to slay the so-called cultural hegemony in the school is to question the role of common sense in school rationalizations. The criticism against common sense is actually a criticism against accepting any "truth" without a deliberate analysis. Common sense, in the eyes of the critical theorist, is typically seen as truth verified by various rationalist tools, often statistical judgments. Thus, when a school determines whether a student should be designated for "special education," there is often wholehearted agreement in the school that such a category is "in truth" viable and that school personnel are capable of determining who belongs and who does not.

Critical theorists say that special education is not real in nature but is artificial and vulnerable to all kinds of problems and prejudices in judgment. They state that special education, while legitimated by a science of test scores and research findings, is not only not effective at serving special-needs students but actually leads to the further deterioration of their academic competence and life skills. The problem is that once given the label, students become the label, despite whether they really fit the label. The label might provide access to various special instructional services, but at the same time it also sends a psychical message to the students about their own low skills and about the school's low expectations.

In this way, scientific explanations of social phenomena in the schools are met with considerable skepticism by critical theorists. Science, as the argument goes, is a weapon of control. It uses a technical and often dazzling numerical method to hide the social realities of oppression and inequities. It is not the neutral/nonpolitical method that its advocates believe it to be, but it is a highly ideological method that imposes rational solutions to social problems, that disguises socially repressive conditions with technical showmanship, and that rejects imaginative and more subjective judgments as essentially unworkable. These alleged effects play into the radical belief that science itself is responsible for creating an amenable social arrangement for dominant economic groups. The role of standardized examinations in the school is a good example. Standardized exams often hold the key to unlocking the doors to scholarships, to being admitted to well-known universities, and to various certifications. They are supported by a technical science of reliability and validity that reminds everyone of their fairness and that creates the impression of a level playing field. But the exam itself and the system in which it operates rarely get interrogated for their role in blocking access to knowledge for certain children and for their prejudicial powers against certain groups.

Along these same lines, schools are also viewed by critical theorists as places that indoctrinate youth into political compliance and into acceptance of their place in the economic social order. Children are taught through the school that their worth can be literally measured through testing devices and that their success is dependent on the merit of their work. Therefore, those who fail in school can only blame themselves, making it more difficult for the oppressed to understand their oppression and eventually to exercise a call for revolution. Interestingly, teachers become the unwitting accomplices in the process of alienating and oppressing certain groups.

Some leftist commentators also believe that the repressive force of the school is also exercised in the economic arena. In fact, much has been written about the alleged correspondence between the needs of capitalism and the methods of public schooling. The school, in the context of such an argument, exists to serve capitalism. It acts to stratify the labor force, to create low-level and high-level workers, and to socialize youth into the acceptance and inevitability of a class-based economic system. It not only produces the needed variance of skills for the workforce, including nonskilled workers, but it also inculcates habits and personality traits to accompany such skills—docility for the low worker and self-direction for the high worker. The school, in this sense, should not be perceived to be creating inequities but to be involved in their reproduction. Such a position is sometimes known as **reproduction theory.** As noted by Bowles and Gintis (1976), the heart of this reproduction is found in the social encounters of the school, encounters that "correspond closely to the social relations of dominance, subordination, and motivation in the economic sphere" (p. 265). Bowles and Gintis are confident that the school teaches youth their place in the capitalistic working order.

One of the more interesting and popular commentators on the topic of how schools might provide handicapping experiences to certain students is Brazilian scholar Paulo Friere. As a social activist with Marxist leanings, Friere has helped historically oppressed people in Latin America rise up

Paulo Freire's writings have affected the way many educators view the relationship among culture, power, and schooling.

against the system that has been holding them down. It was through this process that Friere (1982) formulated a theory that took a direct look at how schools tend to fix their instruction on the transmission of facts and information that, at least in Freire's eyes, prevented young children from learning how to think and live.

Friere has argued that many schools abide by what he calls **banking education,** which represents an instructional preoccupation with conveying facts and information to students in ways that stunt their thinking capacity. To learn through banking education means to memorize information and to be the uncritical recipient of someone else's knowledge and words. Such a bias in learning gives the teacher dominance over the student, making the teacher "the teller" and the student "the receiver." Banking education keeps the students passive and quiet. It does not encourage dialogue or any use of language in the action of learning. It also blunts the opportunity for students to develop their own consciousness and to form the skills and dispositions needed to become socially responsible and critically minded citizens. Banking education, as Friere (1982) stated it, is "an act of depositing, in which the students are recipients and the teacher the depositor. Instead of communicating, the teacher issues communiques and makes deposits which the students patiently receive, memorize and repeat" (p. 58).

Although Friere was speaking of the manner in which children are socialized in oppressive Latin American conditions, his idea can also be used as a critique against some ways that children in the United States are taught, especially minority and economically disadvantaged children. Cummins (1986), for instance, found that a preoccupation with a transmissive model of learning has had particularly negative effects in the education of minority children in the United States. Such instruction might value the centrality of skill-drill manipulations, the memorization of facts, and an expository style of dealing with information in the classroom. One study found that the philosophical underpinnings for more conservative and transmissive agendas in the classroom were more likely to be supported by principals working in minority-school settings as opposed to predominantly White settings (Hlebowitsh, 1993). Some researchers have openly stated the need for the instruction of disadvantaged youth to be less supportive of dialogue, to be less pupil-initiated, and to be more concerned with low-level questions (Medley, 1979; Rosenshine, 1979). Low-track curriculum experiences, which affect disproportionately high numbers of minority children, can themselves be construed as banking education.

The Hidden Curriculum

Much of what occurs in the school occurs without intention, in ways that are subtle and often difficult to understand. The tone of one's voice, the style of one's body language, the character of the subject matter used in class, and hundreds of other nuances contribute to what and how children learn. Each is part of what is known as the covert or **hidden curriculum.**

Educators typically acknowledge their actions in relation to a student's performance in areas of knowledge acquisition, skill development, and cognitive facility. Teachers might believe that improved student test scores were due to certain instructional behaviors. They might believe that higher-level thinking skills were in evidence in a student's work because thoughtful questions were asked in the classroom that demanded students to engage in analytical exercises. But what educators often overlook are the hidden effects of classroom behaviors, rarely acknowledging that the very actions that led to higher test scores also taught children something about liking or disliking school or perhaps something about what it means to work hard and to abide by some standard of ethics.

The hidden curriculum raises important questions for educators: What effect do schools have on the disposition to enjoy learning, to derive pleasure from inquiry and from the world of knowledge brought to bear in the school? What do schools do to construct the positive or negative self-esteem of youth, to influence their leisure-time habits, and to sway their attitudes and actions toward community, society, and government?

Dewey (1938) captured the notion of the hidden curriculum by referring to the process of collateral learning. He observed:

> Perhaps the greatest of all pedagogical fallacies is the notion that a person learns only the particular thing he is studying at the time. Collateral learning in the way of formation of enduring attitudes, of likes and dislikes, may be and often is much more important than the spelling lesson or lesson in geography or history that is learned. (p. 48)

The hidden curriculum can also explain how various cultural values and norms might be conveyed or transmitted in the school. Philip Jackson (1968), who was among the first to develop the idea of the hidden curriculum, showed how traits like conformity, docility, patience, obedience, perseverance and discipline can become formed in the hidden curriculum in ways that directly influence students' successes in school and their future successes in society. A lesson is not likely to be dedicated to teaching patience, for instance, but it might covertly teach students about patience. Understanding how such things get taught helps educators to be more clear on how cultural values and norms are erected in the school. In other words, the idea of the hidden curriculum forces teachers to take a sharper and more deliberate look at how their actions influence the formation of various attitudes and dispositions. Something as innocuous and trivial as teaching children their multiplication tables necessarily takes on more grand terms when accounting for the hidden-curriculum effects.

As Kilpatrick (1923) stated it: "Whether we like it or not, whether we know it or not, a child learning multiplication combinations is also at the same time learning something about dawdling and not dawdling" (p. 289). Kilpatrick also described how such a student also learns something about liking or disliking arithmetic and liking or disliking school and the teacher. The student also learns something about self-esteem and self-ability, whether it pays to try hard, whether books or schooling have anything to do with life, whether minimal efforts derive maximal rewards or vice versa, and whether a student's own voice and own ideas are believed to be significant contributions to the conduct of the classroom. Kilpatrick believed that all this occurs, at a minimum, with the simple act of learning multiplication combinations.

Multicultural Education

The call for multicultural education has been reverberating in the discussions on public education for at least three decades. The strength of the current

I recall the 1956 presidential campaign. Adlai Stevenson, for whom I was working, had a weak record on civil rights in America but a strong record on nationalism in Africa. I suggested to a group of sympathetic black leaders that maybe if Stevenson talked to black audiences about Africa for the Africans, he could make up for his deficiencies on civil rights. My friends laughed and said that American blacks couldn't care less about Africa.

"Nor can the American Negro," wrote Abram L. Harris, the radical black economist, "be considered in any logical way African." The black educator Horace Mann Bond spoke in 1959 of "the American Negro's traditional aversion to Africa and things African." In 1964 the sociologist Milton Gordon wrote about black Americans, "Their sense of identification with ancestral African national cultures is virtually nonexistent." "The Negro is an American," Martin Luther King Jr. told Robert Penn Warren. "We know nothing of Africa."

How do you react to Arthur Schlesinger's narrative? Would America be a healthier place if its immigrants and first-generation citizens dropped their ethnic affiliations?

movement to bring multicultural education into the curriculum is, in some ways, indicative of the problem that the school has had with diversifying its experiences.

Various commentators have argued that the systematic bias toward a so-called European culture in the school has damaged the ability of minority youth to succeed in schools. Not many years ago, the treatment of non-White groups in the curriculum materials and textbooks of the American schools not only was infrequent, but also was often negligent with the truth and sometimes outright offensive toward minority groups. These kinds of abuses have led to a call for the dislodging of Western dominance in the school curriculum and for the widening of school experiences along different cultural lines.

Some advocates of multicultural education have argued for ethnocentric forms of instruction, meaning that Black youth should receive an Afrocentric education, Latino youth a Latino-centered education, and so on. Their critics say that this is not multicultural education but is a kind of ethnic separatism that assumes the worst from the so-called Western tradition and inevitably sets the wheels of divisiveness into motion in society. Arthur Schlesinger's *The Disuniting of America* shows how the multicultural argument has spawned ethno-centric curricula marked by distorted histories and distorted pedagogies (just as some past White historians provided bad histories to both White and non-White children). Ethnic separatists often treat non-Western cultures in the most felicitous terms, ignore any of the virtues of the West, and ultimately ask minority children to study their ethnicity with more intensity than their own common American culture. Thus, African-American youth are claimed to be able to learn more by studying African culture, which is itself impossibly variegated, than by studying American culture (see the Scholarly Voices feature on a narrative of Black Americans' relationship to Africa).

Ravitch (1990) has called to this perspective on the role of culture in learning **particularistic multiculturalism.** Rather than focusing on the broadest interpretation of the common culture in America in the interests of seeking a more enriching common discourse, particularistic multicultaralists reject the very idea of an American common culture and advise an empathetic identification with ancestral culture. Ravitch argues that, if taken seriously, **particularistic multiculturalism** can lead to a proliferation of culturalized or ethnicized versions of what gets taught in school and how it gets taught. Such a development would undermine the very purpose of public schooling, which is to provide a common experience in the values, principles, problems and pluralistic dimensions of American culture. Progressive educators have long argued that the school curriculum should provide countervailing experiences to the more parochial (particularistic, if you will) experiences of the home, widening the common basis for ethnicity, social class, religion and political orientation, all in the interests of a greater homogeneity vested in pluralism.

It goes without saying, that multicultural education has an important place in the school. As indicated, America's common culture *is* multicultural, and any effort to celebrate its differences should contribute to the whole of the American experience. Thus, the study of U.S. history, for instance, cannot be properly managed unless it reflects the nation's many multicultural aspects, including stories about the considerable hardships that a wide range of ethnic groups had to endure over the years and stories of discrimination, xenophobia, and bigotry, as well as stories of assimilation and of the legal, political, and social struggles to make America the pluralistic democracy that it is. A good multicultural education finds the teacher in dialogue with all students in an effort to explore their social, political, and historical place in modern America. Through the creation of a culturally democratic classroom, in which all students feel as though their cultural heritage is respected, students can learn to examine the dynamic problems and possibilities of growing up in America.

The purpose of multicultural education is to prevent and reduce prejudice and stereotyping, to promote a better understanding of many different ethnic groups in society, and to find a center of gravity. Multicultural education allows teachers to infuse the curriculum with a strong sense of identification and understanding of America's pluralistic society (see The School Experience in Literature for an example of poetry by Tomás Rivera).

What are the racial and ethnic attitudes of youth in America? Kenneth and Margaret Clark (1947) were among the first to gain some visibility for their research in this area when they examined racial awareness and racial preference among black nursery school children. Some of the findings pointed to the fact that these children not only were fully aware of racial differences but were actually inclined to express a preference to be white. This was taken to be a highly unhealthy sign, suggesting the possibility that the children were suffering from the self-denial of their race and from the accompanying distress of low self-esteem. The Clark's work eventually helped to inform the legal argument that was later made to the Supreme Court in the 1954 Brown versus Topeka case.

More recent evidence on racial attitudes among youth is a mixed bag. In 1992, the People for the American Way released a study, based on a national survey, about the racial attitudes of American youth between the ages of 15 and 24. When asked whether race relations in the nation were more good than bad, 42% of all youth said race relations were good and 50% characterized them as bad. Among White and Hispanic youth, the response was very

THE SCHOOL EXPERIENCE IN LITERATURE

Searching at Leal Middle School

Tomás Rivera was recognized as one of America's finest contemporary poets. A migrant farmworker for over 20 years, he earned his doctorate in literature and eventually became the chancellor at the University of California at Riverside. After his death in 1984, several fine collections of his poetry were printed. In his "Searching at Leal Middle School," he describes his Chicano students and his passion for teaching them. His style of switching from Spanish to English is common among Chicano writers.

> At first I saw only
> the backs of black hair heads
> Cabezas de pelo negro, negro era [heads of black hair, black they were]
> Cabezas de pelo negro, [heads of black hair]
> brillante, de brillo, brillo era [brilliant, coarse, coarse they were]
> and as
> I went to the front of the room
> to face them
> I saw their limitless eyes
> ojos sin límites [eyes without limits]
> ojos oscuros [dark eyes]
> ojos sonrientes [smiling eyes]
> juguetones [playful] . . .
> And
> We talked of thinking
> > of inventing ourselves
> > of love for others
> > of love to be
> > of searching
> > for ourselves

Source: Rivera, T. (1990) *The searchers*. Houston, TX: Arte Publico Press.

similar to the overall percentages, but among Black youth the response was decidedly more negative—35% believed race relations were good, while 57% said they were bad. Among young White Americans, there was evidence of continued negative stereotyping of Black America (People for the American Way, 1992). Some recent national surveys of adult Americans show that sharply racist views are not only held by Whites against minorities but also by minorities against Whites and minorities against other minorities (Holmes, 3 March, 1994). Clearly, the multicultural aspect of the common curriculum has an important purpose to fulfill in combating prejudice.

Although the report by the People for the American Way offered some gloomy news, it also uncovered some highly positive developments. It found, for instance, that most young people in America have significant personal contact with people of other races, including friendships. It also found a widespread consensus among all youth on core values, including the significance of the family, the importance of personal responsibility and the belief in equity. It also showed, rather definitively, that the school is still the one place where youth have regular contact with people of other races and ethnicities—more so than work, the neighborhood, sports activities, church/synogogue activities, and in most cases, social activities (People for the American Way, 1992). Given this reality, schooling is, by the very composition of the student population, a diversifying event.

There are several forms of multicultural education (Banks, 1988; Cornbleth & Waugh, 1995). One form is known as **additive multicultural education.** Here the thinking is that multicultural efforts can be dealt with by simply trying to append a multicultural piece onto the existing curriculum. Thus, a high school might develop a long list of elective studies that deals with minority cultures and groups. In the classroom, a teacher using an additive approach might add a feature onto a conventional unit in an effort to be more attendant to diversity needs or might make a classroom event of presenting students with the food, language, and music of a particular culture. With the use of an additive approach, multiculturalism becomes periodically plugged into the curriculum. Such a plug-in tactic sometimes leads the teacher to try to use the limited time accorded to multiculturalism by focusing on heroic contributions (Cornbleth & Waugh, 1995). This sometimes results in denying the stories of failed efforts and of the obstacles that continue to stand in the way of many minority groups.

Another form is known as **multiperspective multicultural education.** This approach, aims at a wider and more integrated mark. Here the thinking is that multiple perspectives need to be folded into the historical narrative and the general study of society. Schoolbooks, for instance, should not shy away from providing alternate viewpoints on various histories and events. In the context of the Civil War, the North and the South perspectives would be viewed, and in the context of World War II, the perspectives of each participating country would be provided. Native American views toward the White westward movement and toward their fellow native groups would have to be understood. Multiple perspectives are provided in the interest of spawning discussion and critical examination of the issues.

How might a multiple perspective approach toward multicultural education look in the classroom? First, each classroom or school would find a way to represent different cultural elements through books, artwork, and other artifacts in its everyday surroundings. These could grow out of multiple perspective learnings. Second, where appropriate, cultural pluralism would be integrated into the historical, political, and social educations of youth. One, for instance, could not understand the Civil War without acknowledging the role of the Black soldiers fighting for the Union or without accounting for the cultural life of slaves, to name two obvious examples. One could not understand the political landscape of the country without broaching the question of the overwhelming minority representation in the Democratic Party, which, of course, leads to historical questions as well. One could not understand the history of the New World without knowing how native populations were mistreated and without understanding the Hispanic legacy of language and religion in Latin America. In the context of history, every effort would be made to share stories about life in other times and places. World War II could be studied from the eyes of Japanese-Americans, Germans, American GIs, European Jews, Russians, and women working in American factories.

The curriculum implication here is that a multiple-perspective approach to multicultural education is probably best placed in the function of general

Generations of immigrants have viewed the public schools as important pathways for social and economic mobility.

education, dealing with common sociocivic problems without disciplinary pressures. If the common culture is multicultural, then the mandate for multicultural education is to also help establish working commonalities.

As Figure 7.2 shows, multicultural education can be viewed as part of the common learnings tradition. A study of social problems and social institutions is one leg of the conceptual tripod. There are many common social problems that are wrapped up with cultural frictions. Current-day examples, such as the poverty, crime, and racism, are by-products of various social ills between the races, between economic groups, and between social institutions and people. These considerations can lead to broader explorations in areas related to philosophies of government, the role of business in people's lives, societal attitudes toward the poor, and the role of the courts, unions, the media, the schools, churches, and families in the problems of society. All these open doors to multicultural education. Another leg used in building a framework for the convergence of common and multicultural issues is broadly associated with a treatment of constitutional and democratic principles, in particular with how various groups (past and present) have struggled to gain their rights and how such struggles have affected social institutions and the overall way

FIGURE 7.2

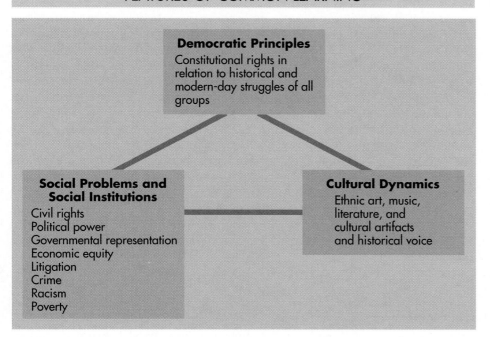

FEATURES OF COMMON LEARNING

Democratic Principles
Constitutional rights in relation to historical and modern-day struggles of all groups

Social Problems and Social Institutions
Civil rights
Political power
Governmental representation
Economic equity
Litigation
Crime
Racism
Poverty

Cultural Dynamics
Ethnic art, music, literature, and cultural artifacts and historical voice

of life. The direct study of the various cultural dynamics of society is the last foundation of the framework, underscoring the theme of ethnic differences (music, art, literature) in relation to common social struggles. Thus, it is possible to understand the cultural artifacts of a group (its art and music) in the light of its historical and present-day problems.

 ## *The Language of Schooling*

The function of language in the classroom seems, on the surface, to be a simple matter. Teachers usually teach using verbal language, and students typically are asked or required to respond verbally or in writing. The choice of language in the classroom seems simple as well. Because English is the most commonly spoken language in the United States, it is usually considered wise to conduct class in that language. But language also has a broader function that cannot be overlooked. Cazden (1988) has studied the nature of language in the classroom and has pointed out three very distinct features of classroom language. The first feature is obvious; language in the classroom communicates manifest messages. The second feature of language in the classroom, however, speaks to the effects of the manifest messages and how they establish and maintain social relationships, while the third feature is associated with the process by which individuals gain their self-identity. Cazden contends that this last feature of language is the least recognizable but perhaps the most important. Individuals are all defined in large measure by the specific language they use. Language clearly contributes to who individuals are, how others see them, and inevitably how they see themselves.

If one acknowledges that language carries at least three basic purposes (the communication of information, the establishment and maintenance of relationships with others, and the expression of one's identity), then one also has to admit that what is said, how it is said, what others say, and how one reacts to it all relate prominently not only to the function of communication but also to the construction of social relations and self-identities. Language in this sense is more than communicating; language always communicates something that will influence the social environment. How, then, do educators respond to the clear need to teach youth Standard English in the school? If students use a different style of English (for instance, Black English), what should be the teacher's response? If teachers "correct" it, are they doing damage to the student's self-identity and to the social relationship with the student? If they privilege it, are they contributing to the marginalization of the youth's language skills in a society where advancement depends on the use of Standard English? The question should not be framed in binary terms—it is not a question of either teaching Standard English or teaching non-Standard English, either teaching English or teaching a foreign language. Rather the question should be how educators can teach children Standard English *and* all the other forms of language beneficial to the life experiences of youth.

Bilingual Education

Bilingual education is perhaps the most misunderstood feature of modern schooling. Vitriolic letters to editors printed in major newspapers argue "Why are my tax dollars being spent to teach children in America a foreign language? These children should be learning English. That's the only way that they will make it in this country." Such letters have drawn support from various politicians and even from various officials in the Department of Education, including, most prominently, William Bennett, who as secretary of education during the Reagan administration proclaimed the federal sponsorship of bilingual education a wholesale failure. Conservative politicians often speak of the dangers of bilingualism, of the linguistic schisms that it is likely to create in the nation, of the centrality of English to the doors of opportunity in the society, and of the historic decision to teach immigrant children in English. Legislation in the House and Senate, generated largely by political conservatives, has aimed to find support for the declaration of English as the official language of the country. Depending on the specifics of the various bills pending, this could result in all government business being conducted in English and all public documents, with the likely exception of documents dealing with public health and public safety, being written in English. It could also result in the actual banning of bilingual education and bilingual ballots. (Broder, 5 Sept. 1995)

Such sentiments are typically driven by an assimilationist view that embraces monolingual instruction in English. The American schools, the argument might follow, have historically aimed to ignore the native language of immigrant children in the interests of furthering the integration of such children into the society. Although there were some accommodations made by some schools toward dual language instruction in earlier times, especially during the late decades of the 19th century among German immigrants living in the Midwest, such instances were eventually smited by 20th-century assimilationist impulses. Some states even drafted laws prohibiting the teaching of a foreign language in private and public schools for the first eight grade levels, laws that were eventually struck down as unconstitutional (Ravitch, 1985). Many assimilationists point to this history and argue that the same conditions should apply to language-minority children today. They draw further evidence for their argument by claiming that the federal data on bilingual instruction fail to document improvements on the test scores and on dropout rates of language-minority students and fail to support the superiority of bilingual programs over structured immersion programs (Hearings on Bilingual Education, 22 July, 1993).

Federal legislation enacting bilingual education in America was passed in 1968. Federal monies for bilingual education were first authorized through Title VII of the Elementary and Secondary School Act of 1968, which is also known as the **Bilingual Education Act.** The bilingual programs emerging from this legislation were compensatory in nature, serving poor students born to families in which English was not the dominant language. The idea was to assist low-income children who were believed to be at an instructional disadvantage because of their limited English. The design of the program was not intended to develop or strengthen the native cultural and linguistic background of the language-minority student but to compensate for it. Part of the rationale for bilingual education also appealed to the view that non-English-speaking children were suffering from low self-esteem caused by the absence of their native language in the classroom.

The scope of Title VII has expanded since 1968. It now not only provides money for a variety of bilingual-education programs, but it is also involved in bilingual research and bilingual teacher training (Aleman, 1993). In 1969, the federal government funneled $7.5 million through Title VII. In 1992, the annual federal commitment of monies for Title VII grew to $195 million (U.S. Department of Education, 1992).

Despite the presence of Title VII funds, the legal responsibility of school districts to offer bilingual programs was not formally resolved until 1974, in the Supreme Court ruling of *Lau v. Nichols,* 414 U.S. 563 (1974). This case originated in 1970 as a class-action suit that was brought by Chinese public school students against the San Francisco Unified School District. The essential complaint was that the school district had failed to provide bilingual education to Chinese pupils and that such a neglect represented a violation of the students' right to an equal educational opportunity. How could the Chinese students have an equal opportunity to learn, asserted the complainants, when the language used in the school was completely foreign to them? The school district openly admitted that only half of close to 3,000 limited-English-proficient (LEP) students were receiving second-language assistance but that the right to an equal-educational opportunity was not violated because all the students were receiving the same curriculum, though some in a language foreign to them. Every student, it was argued, comes to school with some advantages and some disadvantages, including linguistic ones, and the school cannot be legally bound to provide special programs because of such differences.

The Supreme Court disagreed with this line of reasoning, believing that the Chinese students were effectively shut off from meaningful education because of their lack of English speaking skills. Basing part of its decision on the Civil Rights Act of 1964, which bars discrimination because of race, color, or national origin in any program sponsored by the federal government, the Supreme Court stated that there is no equality of treatment merely by providing students with the same facilities, textbooks, teachers and curricu-

Learning to read and write in the early grades is critical. These students learn to read and write in Chinese. Their foundation in Chinese literacy will make learning a second language easier.

lum. The lesson of the ruling was straightforward: If students arrive at school speaking a language other than English, it makes little sense to attempt to teach them to read and write in a language that they do not yet speak. In elementary education, the clear implication was that instruction in children's first or native languages for the initial years of their education lays a foundation for learning to read and write in a second language. This would become the rationale for a national movement in bilingual education (see the Web Points feature in this section).

Diane Ravitch (1985) has criticized the Bilingual Education Act of 1968 as "the first time that Congress has ever legislated a given pedagogical method" (p. 244). She has argued that the ruling in the Lau v. Nichols case which obviously influenced federal legislation, did not necessarily mean that schools had to embrace bilingual education. All that it meant was that schools had to find some educationally sound way to deal with the English language deficits of their students and that various instructional approaches that did not emphasize instruction in a student's native language and culture could be used.

Bilingual instruction for limited-English-proficient students can take on different forms (Malakoff & Hakuta, 1990). The most popular form is known as **transitional bilingual education,** in which students are subjected to dual-language instruction and grade-appropriate materials before being mainstreamed in English-speaking classrooms. In the United States, the bilingual classroom is most often applied to Spanish-speaking children whose frequency in the school population allows entire classrooms to be designed with bilingual materials and activities. Contrary to popular opinion, the transitional model of bilingual education actually aims at assimilationist goals—it seeks to use the student's native language to teach English and eventually to

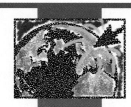
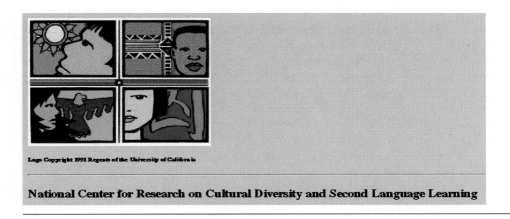
make English the dominant language. In other words, transitional bilingual education uses bilingual means to carry out a monolingual result. The transitional bilingual program is not interested, for instance, in teaching the continued maintenance or the advancement of the native language. Usually transitional programs are divided into two types—early exit transitions and late exit transitions. The early exit program limits the exposure to bilingual instruction to about two years, while the late exit programs allow bilingual instruction to continue until sixth grade (Baker, 1993).

Another popular instructional approach used with limited-English-proficient students is the **English as a Second Language (ESL)** model. ESL is used mostly in settings where LEP students are from a wide range of linguistic backgrounds. A school, for instance, that has non-native-speaking students who come from a very wide range of nations will likely employ an ESL strategy. Under such conditions, there would not be enough students from one particular language to justify a transitional bilingual program. In an ESL model, LEP students are pulled out of their mainstream settings for special instruction in English for part of the school day. This instruction takes on what is known as a "sheltered English" approach, in which the vocabulary and language of the special instruction are managed carefully. But ESL students will actually spend a greater part of the day with their English-speaking peers in a mainstream setting. Thus, ESL operates in an English-only context that offers limited supplemental experiences in sheltered English. The aim of both transitional bilingual and ESL education is to take students who are in most cases monolingual in a foreign language and help them obtain proficiency in English. In this sense, both transitional bilingual and ESL programs are known as taking a **subtractive bilingual education** programs because they see the native language as a bridge to English proficiency and are not concerned with maintaining the native language once the student becomes an English speaker.

Other less popular approaches to bilingual education take an "additive" perspective by aiming to teach students proficiency in two languages. **Additive bilingual education** programs teach everything in two languages and are appropriate for both language-minority and language-majority youth. One additive approach, known as **"two-way" bilingual education,** teaches both the majority and minority language in a school to both language-majority and language-minority children. For instance, a two-way program in Spanish and English might teach in each language on alternate days or in alternate instructional periods to all the children in the school. The objective is for both language-majority and language-minority students to "add" a language to their communicative repertoire. Of course, such a program requires completely fluent bilingual teachers. In states such as Texas, California, Florida, and New York, where Spanish may be spoken widely in numerous communities and where one can encounter the language in various contexts, including in the popular culture, "two-way" bilingual education makes quite a bit of sense. The overwhelming majority of two-way bilingual programs in the United States, in fact, can be found in California and New York. Most of these programs serve elementary school-aged children and over 90% provide instruction in Spanish and English (Christian & Whitcher, 1995).

If the reasoning behind bilingual education seems sound, why does there continue to be so much resistance to it? Part of the problem turns on an argument about the "melting pot" versus "salad bowl" metaphors. The assimilationist impulses of the "melting pot" advocates call for an immersion approach that says it is best to teach youth exclusively in English, as has been done historically with a wide range of immigrant populations (where the loss of the mother tongue has been the norm). "Salad bowl" advocates, on the other hand, claim that initial instruction in a native language will not only assist in the eventual development of English but also grant the student skills in another language and another social or cultural context (see The Contemporary Debate feature in this section).

Although the research on the effects of bilingual education is conflicting, there is an overall belief, supported by the federal government and the courts, that children should be initially instructed in their native languages as a way to assist their development in English. It is clear that bilingual education carries obvious social and cognitive advantages for the individual (Cummins, 1976; Hakuta & Diaz, 1985) and potential nationalistic advantages

THE CONTEMPORARY DEBATE

English Only?

Many people in the United States view their nation as a melting pot. Whereas immigrants have generally been welcomed, many believe that the cultural and linguistic differences they bring with them must be melted down into a unified culture—U.S. culture. Scholars have argued which of these traditions, cultural or linguistic, is more difficult to modify. For example, is it more difficult for immigrants to learn English or to adopt U.S. customs? Or are culture and language tied closely together? Whatever the answer, the United States holds the unique distinction as one of the few democracies in the world in which the use of foreign languages is discouraged. Many European countries, for example, promote foreign-language learning in early elementary school and view bilingual citizens as national assets.

Perhaps this is the reason why the "English-only movement" in the United States makes no sense to the rest of the world. Not only does the United States fail to promote bilingualism, but also there appears to be an effort to suppress other languages while promoting English as the "official" language (Commission on Excellence, 1983). By the mid-1980s, the English-only movement had helped pass official-language legislation in 14 states, and new initiatives appear each year. Supporters of English only argue that many immigrants refuse to learn English, leaving them isolated from mainstream society and dependent on social services. In their view, bilingual education encourages such tendencies among immigrants. As a testimony to English-only and antiforeign sentiment, California voters on November 8, 1994, voted 59% to 41% to approve Proposition 187, the "Save Our State" Initiative. The first section of the proposition restricts "illegal aliens" from the state's public education system from kindergarten through university, and requires public educational institutions to begin verifying the legal status of both students and their parents. Never before in the history of the United States has a voting group delivered such an indictment on immigrants. In spite of its sweeping reforms, a federal judge blocked the implementation of virtually all sections of Proposition 187.

The group targeted by the proponents of 187 are the Mexican-American immigrants, whose population in the United States continues to grow. One public policy group has projected that by the year 2000, over 34,818,000 Latinos will live in the United States. The growing population of Latinos suggests that an increasing number of people do not speak English. Yet despite public opinion to the contrary, the data suggest that native-born and immigrant Latinos learn English. In addition, they want their children to speak English. After 10 to 15 years in the United States, nearly 75% of all Hispanic immigrants are speaking English regularly, and virtually all their children will speak English and have abandoned the use of Spanish as a daily language (Veltman, 1988).

Source: Hispanic Policy Development Project. (1988). *Closing the gap for U.S. Hispanic youth: Public/private strategies.* Washington, DC: Hispanic Policy Development Project. (ERIC Document Reproduction Service No. ED 298 242) National Commission on Excellence in Education. (1983). *A nation at risk.* Washington, DC: U.S. Department of Education. Veltman, C. (1983). *Language shift in the United States.* Amsterdam: Mouton Publishers.

for the society, especially in relation to international markets where multilingual competence is important (Simon, 1980). Much of the debate revolving around the effects of bilingual education is complicated by the need to control income, parent education, and immigration factors, and by the penchant to limit the judgment of bilingual education to achievement in the English language, while ignoring important data on self-esteem, moral development, social adjustment, and employability.

KEY TERMS

Additive bilingual education
Additive multicultural education
Banking education
Bilingual Education Act
Critical theory
Cultural hegemony
English as a Second Language (ESL)

General education
Hidden curriculum
Lau v. Nichols
Multiperspective multicultural education

Particularistic multiculturalism
Reproduction theory
Subtractive bilingual education
Transitional bilingual education
"Two-way" bilingual education

KEY QUESTIONS

1. Why is it important for the school to involve itself with common learnings?

2. What are the curricular consequences of a "melting pot" outlook on common learning?

3. What is general education?

4. How might you address the need to deal with common issues in a diverse classroom environment?

5. How can banking education result in the oppression of youth?

6. What are the essential assumptions of critical theory?

7. Why do critical theorists rail against common sense?

8. Why might a critical theorist criticize the dominance of Shakespearean readings in a high school English class?

9. What are your views on reproduction theory?

10. Do you believe that Afrocentric or Latino-centered schools serve the causes of multicultural education?

11. Why is multicultural education well suited for general education?

12. What kind of teaching might result in multicultural education if it followed the model outlined in Figure 7.2?

13. Explain how a multiple-perspective approach to multicultural education might be used to teach the westward movement in America.

14. What is the hidden curriculum, and how can it lead to positive and negative outcomes in the curriculum?

15. What might be some of the hidden curriculum effects of teaching 8-year-olds the multiplication tables strictly through flash cards?

16. In your view, how should the school handle the education of language-minority children? Are you partial to an assimilationist view? Why or why not?

17. What is the difference between an additive and a substractive approach to bilingual education?

18. What are the potential advantages and disadvantages of a "two-way" bilingual program?

19. Explain the issues involved in the *Lau v. Nichols* case.

20. What are the potential hidden curriculum effects in a school that abides by an assimilationist attitude toward the education of language-minority children?

REFERENCES

Addams, J. (1985). Immigrants and their children. In E. C. Lagemann (Ed.), *Jane Addams on education.* New York: Teachers College Press. (Original work published in 1908)

Aleman, S. R. (1993). *Bilingual Education Act: Background and reauthorization issues.* Washington, DC: Congressional Research Service.

Apple, M. (1990). *Ideology and curriculum.* London: Routledge and Kegan Paul.

Banks, J. (1988). Approaches to multicultural curriculum reform. *Multicultural Leader, 1*(2), 1–3.

Baker, C. (1993). *Foundations of bilingual education and bilingualism.* Philadelphia: Multilingual Matters, Ltd.

Barber, B. (1991). *An aristocracy for everyone.* New York: Ballentine Books.

Bennett, W. (1987). *James Madison High School.* Washington, DC: Office of Education.

Broder, D. S. (5 Sept, 1995) Dole backs official language; English is needed to unify nation. *Washington Post* p. 1.

Bowles, S., & Gintis, H. (1976). *Schooling in capitalist America.* New York: Basic Books.

Cazden, C. (1988). *Classroom discourse.* Portsmouth, NH: Hinemann.

Christian, D., & Whitcher, A. (1995). *Directory of two-way bilingual programs in the United States.* Washington, DC: Department of Education ED# 384–342

Clark, K. B. & Clark, M. P. (1947). Racial identification and preference in Negro children. In Newcomb, T. M., & Hartley, E. L. (Eds.). *Readings in Psychology* New York: Holt, Rinehart & Winston.

Coley, R. J. (1994) What Americans study revisited. Princeton, NJ: Educational Testing Service. ED#: 373–095.

Cornbleth, C., & Waugh, D. (1995). *The great speckled bird.* New York: St. Martins Press.

Cummins, J. (1976). The influence of bilingualism on cognitive growth: A synthesis of research findings and explanatory hypotheses. *Working Papers in Bilingualism, 9,* 1–43.

Cummins, J. (1986). Empowering Minority Students. *Harvard Educational Review, 1,* 18–36.

Dewey, J. (1916). *Democracy and education.* New York: The Free Press.

Dewey, J. (1938). *Experience and education.* New York: Collier Books.

Friere, P. (1982). *The pedagogy of the oppressed.* New York: The Continuum Publishing Co.

Geortz, C. (1973). *The interpretation of cultures.* New York: Basic Books.

Gibson, R. (1986). *Critical theory and education.* London: Hodder and Stoughton.

Giroux, H. (1983). *Theory and resistance: A pedagogy for the opposition.* New York: Bergin Garvey.

Hakuta, K., & Diaz, R. M. (1985). The relationship between degree of bilingualism and cognitive ability: A critical discussion and some new longitudinal data. In K. Nelson (Ed.), *Children's language* (pp. 319–344). Hillsdale, NJ: Lawrence Erlbaum.

Hearings on Bilingual Education (22 July; 1993). Hearings before the Subcommittee on Elementary, secondary and vocational education of the Committee on Education and Labor. Congress of the United States. Washington, DC: U.S. Government Printing Office.

Hirsch, E. D. (1987). *Cultural literacy.* Boston: Houghton-Mifflin Co.

Hlebowitsh, P. S. (1993). Philosophical orientations on the school curriculum. *NASSP Bulletin, 77*(557), 92–104.

Holmes, S. A. (3 March, 1994). Study finds minorities resent one another almost as much as they do whites. *The New York Times,* p. 8.

Howe, H. (1993). *Thinking about our kids.* New York, NY: The Free Press.

Jackson, P. (1968). *Life in classrooms.* New York: Holt, Rinehart and Winston.

Kilpatrick, W. (1923). *Source book in the philosophy of education.* New York: Macmillan.

Malakoff, M., & Hakuta, K. (1990). History of language minority education in the United States. In A. Padilla, H. H.

Fairchild, & C. M. Valadez (Eds.), *Bilingual education.* Newbury, CA: Sage Publications.

McLaren, P. (1994). *Life in schools.* New York: Longman.

Medley, D. (1979). The effectiveness of teachers. In P. L. Peterson & H. J. Walberg, (Eds.). *Research on teaching.* Berkeley, CA: McCutchan.

People for the American Way (1992). *Democracy's next generation II: A study of American youth on race.* Washington, DC: People for the American Way. ED 344–965.

Ravitch, D. (1985). Politicalization and the schools: The case of bilingual education. In J. W. Noll, (Ed.). *Taking sides.* Guilford, CT: Dushkin Publishing Group.

Ravitch, D. (1990). Multiculturalism: E. pluribus plures. In Ryan, K. & Cooper, J. M. (Eds.). *Kaleidoscope: Readings in Education.* Boston: Houghton-Mifflin Co.

Report of Harvard Committee. (1945). *General education in a free society.* Cambridge: Harvard University Press.

Rosenshine, B. (1979). Content, time and direct instruction. In P. L. Peterson & H. J. Walberg, (Eds.). *Research on teaching.* Berkeley, CA: McCutchan.

Schlesinger, A. (1992). *The disuniting of America.* New York: W. W. Norton.

Simon, P. (1980). *The tongue-tied American.* New York: The Continuum Publishing Co.

Tanner, D., & Tanner, L. N. (1995). *Curriculum development: Theory into practice* (3rd ed.). New York: Macmillan.

U.S. Department of Education. (1992). *The condition of bilingual education in the nation.* Washington, DC: U.S. Department of Education.

8

SCHOOL REFORM AND THE
SOCIOPOLITICAL CONTEXT

Sandy Jernberg, pilot teacher for Higher Order Thinking Skills program, stands in a field with some of her students. As an innovative teacher, Jernberg recognizes that as her students and society change, she, too, must change the way she teaches. Some features of good teaching remain the same, but others require modification based on a changing world.

This chapter explores the idea of school reform in America. Everyone agrees that schools cannot stand still in time, but the direction of school reform is usually contested. Interestingly, school-reform advocates rarely learn from the past and often favor changes driven by sociopolitical pressures. This chapter examines some of these changes and pays particular attention to the current rage of school choice.

Throughout the 20th century, various commissions, committees, and individuals have studied the problems of U.S. education with the intention of proposing reforms. The result has been a historical succession of reform movements. In fact, over the past five decades or so, schools have been beset by changes that have led to confounding swings from one end of the reform pendulum to the other (Tanner, 1986; Goodlad, 1966). Events have gone on like this because each era along the reform time line has been marked by a curriculum emphasis that reflected the sociopolitical temper of its time. School-reform ideas believed to be most vital during the cold war, for instance, were fundamentally different from, if not at odds with, school-reform ideas believed to be most vital in succeeding periods, especially during the social strife of the mid- and late 1960s.

When educational reform is moved by prevailing political winds, the school runs the risk of repeating past mistakes and of embracing a reform logic tied to narrow nationalistic causes as opposed to broadly conceived professional ones. Such a situation also sets the conditions for reactionary change. Thus, when the dominant sociopolitical bias of a particular period runs its course and the changes that it wrought lose their appeal, the school is left vulnerable to new fashions that might follow new sociopolitical imperatives. To complicate matters further, the change that one period represents, when driven by sociopolitical causes, is often extreme enough to catalyze an equal and opposite reaction in a subsequent period. Hence, school reform tends to proceed like a seesaw, with a back-and-forth action that does little to advance the education of children. One extreme is undone by a counterextreme that itself is undone (in time) by yet another counterextreme. This principle, in fact, is demonstrated in the story of American curriculum reform from midcentury to the 1980s.

In the 1990s, however, the debate on school reform turned toward a very different orientation, one that looked to honor family wishes through school-choice initiatives. Neighborhood elementary schools and regional comprehensive high schools have been slowly giving way to a wide range of special theme schools that allows parents to select an education that best approximates what they perceive to be most appropriate for their child or children. Such actions are driven by the belief that parental choice could invigorate new levels of responsiveness, variety, and flexibility in the schools. The thinking is that when parents are given "consumer power" to determine the character of education for their children, the public schools will flourish with alternative approaches responsive to a wide range of student needs and interests.

Historical Epochs of Reform Since Midcentury

The nature of school reform in America has followed general sociopolitical trends. This was most obvious during the post-Sputnik era, but it has occurred with consistency well into the 1990s. School reform in this discussion refers to national movements that have led to practical changes in the ways that teachers dealt with their students in classrooms. All the major trends that will be discussed received quite a bit of support from external agencies (the government or private foundations) and received headline treatment in the news media. In almost all cases, the reforms were practical movements that had a constituency in the school and a lively presence in the professional literature. They were not simply chalkboard ideas.

Education During the Cold War and Space-Race Crisis

In the early 1950s, curriculum reform was shaped by a "back-to-basics" retrenchment that surfaced mainly from conservative forces that gained strength during the early stages of the cold war. Although there were many influential thinkers at the time, the work of Professor Arthur Bestor (1953;1956) and Admiral Hyman Rickover (1959) was especially instrumental in getting the schools to accept this reductionist plan. Bestor was a professor of history who argued for the restoration of a strict academic curriculum, and Rickover was an admiral in the U.S. Navy who wrote extensively about the failing of American education in relation to the academic achievement evidenced in other advanced countries.

Buoyed by a nationalistic fervor to compete with the Soviets in all realms of global domination, both Bestor and Rickover submitted what they viewed as a no-nonsense reform directive for the schools. The approach they advocated was straightforward: focus the schools' program on the singular goal of disciplined intellectual training; reduce the course work in the high school to the core academic disciplines; relegate the role of vocational studies, art, music, and physical education in the unified school setting to an inferior status; and focus the early years of schooling on the inculcation of basic skills. In many ways, this was a retrogradation to the traditional humanist times of the early century.

Bestor and Rickover represented a very strong conservative reaction against the progressivism of an earlier decade. During the 1940s, the public schools had embraced a wide range of progressive initiatives, including a new spirit for curriculum experimentation and a new regard for life activities

The small Soviet satellite that launched an education reform in the United States. Soviet success in space was interpreted as a failure of U.S. schools

in teaching and learning. Bestor and Rickover were dismayed by these events and believed that the time had come for the school to recover its subject-centered core, to fulfill its overtly academic function, and to cease its practice of attempting to build learning experiences around children's needs and interests. They were convinced that the schools were engaging in an anti-intellectualism that would eventually destroy America. It was the soft pedagogy of an earlier period, they claimed, that had already eroded at America's status as a world power. Their solution was to restore rigorous intellectual training in the school. In Rickover's (1959) words, "The educational process must be one of collecting factual knowledge to the limit of the [learner's] capacity. . . . Nothing can really make it fun" (p. 61). This was clearly a movement that aimed to revitalize the role of disciplinary knowledge in the curriculum. The stakes were high because Bestor and Rickover did their best to remind everyone that the very sustenance of the nation was dependent on a no-nonsense approach to basic-skills education for young children and a no-nonsense academic education for high school children.

This regard for basic skills and strict academic training continued to hold sway into the late 1950s and early 1960s. Galvanized by the Soviets' success with Sputnik 1—the first artificial satellite—in 1957, U.S. educators inaugurated a new discipline-centered reform, highlighting an unprecedented curriculum-revision effort in the national-security-related areas of mathematics and science. A general "get-tough" attitude pervaded the emerging reform direction. The major changes included the strengthening of graduation and curriculum standards, the provision of special services for the gifted and talented, and the elevation of the doctrine of curriculum disciplinary as the centerpiece of school reform. Jerome Bruner's *The Process of Education* (1960) played an enormous role in setting the conceptual framework for the new

Jerome Bruner in 1965. His ideas on cognition and the disciplines fit well into reform mandates of the 50s and 60s.

discipline-centered curriculum programs. James Conant's *The American High School Today* (1960) also helped to push the curriculum in the direction of disciplinarity by formulating new requirements for "academic excellence."

Clearly the changes wrought in the schools during the post-Sputnik era period were partly shaped by the demands that Bestor and Rickover raised during the early 1950s. The nature of the new reform was palpably subject or discipline centered. Through the monetary assistance of the National Science Foundation (NSF) and theoretical work of Bruner, several national curriculum programs were developed by university-based scholar-specialists. Given the Soviet achievements in space, the American schools were faced with a national mandate to improve mathematics and science education and to sharpen the emphasis on the education of the nation's most gifted children. This gave the NSF an entrée into educational reform. The NSF, for instance, not only sponsored the development of actual curricula in high school biology, chemistry, physics, and math, but it also financed a nationwide network of teacher training institutes used to immerse teachers into the methodology of teaching these new curricula.

The NSF-sponsored programs and the wider effort to move the school toward subject-centered traditions took their conceptual lead from Bruner's *The Process of Education,* a report partly funded by the NSF (Tanner & Tanner, 1995). Bruner's work espoused a new manifesto for curriculum reform, an idea known as the **"structure of a discipline"** doctrine. To Bruner (1960), the term "structure" represented all the fundamental ideas and generalizations that comprised subject matter. "To learn structure," he contended, "is to learn how things are related" (p. 7). Unfortunately, the "structure" to which Bruner referred was discipline specific; it was all about finding the structure within disciplinary lines rather than across them. Bruner, however, promoted something even more provocative; he asserted that each discipline included a concentration of ideas that could be taught in some intellectually honest way to any age group. As stated by Bruner (1960) himself: "Intellectual activity is anywhere the same, whether at the frontier of knowledge or in a third-grade classroom" (p. 14).

This kind of thinking, coming from one of America's most distinguished psychologists, helped to widen the path of access to the school curriculum for scientists and other scholar-specialists. The "structure of a discipline" put a great premium on discipline-specific skills and reconstructed the nature of the learner in the image of the scholar-specialist. The learner could now be treated as a miniature scholar. When teaching math, for instance, the teacher was now justified in treating the learner as a miniature mathematician. This tended to aggrandize the abstract and the technical and to deemphasize learning tied to life experiences. This logic applied to all the disciplines.

Another development central to the curriculum initiatives of the post-Sputnik climate was the passage of the **National Defense Education Act of 1958.** The purpose of the legislation was to "ensure trained manpower of sufficient quantity and quality to meet the national defense needs of the United States." During the first four years of its operations, the act authorized more than $1 billion worth of aid to the schools, funneling it through 10 title grants. Title three (a financial assistance program for science, mathematics, and foreign-language instruction) received the lion's share of the appropriations. The bulk of this money went toward the purchase of large amounts of equipment and materials for mathematics and science instruction, as well as toward the purchase of the new teaching technology in language instruction.

No money went toward the funding of education in the arts or the humanities. These areas of the curriculum simply did not fit into the war-preparedness mode that characterized the act's mission.

Another significant statement on school reform was written by one of the most influential advocates of education of the time, James B. Conant. Conant, who had achieved national visibility as president of Harvard University and U.S. ambassador to Germany, had a long history of involvement in education. After leaving his post as ambassador, Conant was commissioned by the Carnegie Corporation to oversee a study of the American high school. The fruit of his labor was the *American High School Today,* a work that outlined several basic recommendations for public school reform. Essentially, his report was friendly to the American comprehensive high school design. Although there were considerable pressures at the time to adopt the dual model of schooling used in Europe, which separated academic students from vocational students at preadolescence, Conant (1960) stood by the American model of education and maintained that a unified school should give all youth a general academic education, an individualized elective program, an accelerated academic training for the college bound, and a first-rate vocational education program for the noncollege bound. In this sense, one could argue that Conant saved the American school from falling prey to the dual system used in Europe, a change that was being promoted vigorously by Rickover and that even found its way to the floor of debate in Congress (Tanner & Tanner, 1995).

But the success of Conant's proposal had to do with the manner in which he layered his thinking about the comprehensive high school with a concern for academics and the most academically inclined. He put a strong conservative edge to his proposal by recommending that the general education core of studies in the high school consist of traditional academic studies. There was no talk about interdisciplinary insight or sociocivic traditions in the core, although Conant did promote a senior-level course in Problems of Democracy. As for the academically inclined, Conant wanted to see advanced-placement work available and more widespread use of ability groups on a subject-by-subject basis. In English class, for example, Conant advocated at least three types of classes: one for the most able, another for the middle ground, and yet another for the so-called slowest learners. Besides endorsing ability groups, Conant recommended that aptitude tests be used more often, that class ranking of students and academic honors lists be kept, and that special counseling be provided for the most academically skilled.

Clearly the sociopolitical climate of the cold war and space race affected the nature of school reform. This climate helped to highlight the need for the school to be attentive to the education of the academically able, to stress the importance of reform in the defense-sensitive areas of math and science, and to maintain that the most empowering forms of learning were conducted in subject-centered contexts.

The nationalistic urges to use the school for the purposes of military and technological domination, however, eventually gave way to a new set of priorities, anchored in a new sociopolitical condition. Within a decade's time, a shift was witnessed away from the discipline-centered curricula of the cold war period to the "humanizing" reforms of the late 1960s. The change was supported by a political climate that called attention to society's most pervasive problems (poverty, crime, civil rights, and drug abuse). These new conditions would call for new reforms in the schools.

Humanizing the Schools in a Period of Social Protest

As the international crisis that surrounded the Sputnik spectacle abated, public interest took little time turning to the domestic front. Among the items at the top of the agenda was the question of racial separatism in the schools and its association with lost educational opportunity for minority groups. The federal government inaugurated a War on Poverty that marshaled an array of legislative and financial strategies designed to break the back of racial isolation in the society. The main tool for the government's plan was the public school. Thus, the emphasis in the school was no longer placed on the academically talented; the new educational gospel being preached spoke to the needs of the educationally disadvantaged. Moreover, the threat to the nation was no longer seen as coming from the outside, in the form of imperialist Soviet Union, but was seen as coming from the inside, in the form of civil strife, urban violence, abject poverty, and student protest. The school could not reasonably stand on the belief in a subject-centered curriculum. The times were calling for new levels of sensitivity to learners' needs and interests, and new child-centered approaches were gaining ground.

This new period of reform had its share of unconventional views. Radical critics of education, whose proposals ranged from abolishing compulsory education to framing a more humanistic pedagogy, garnered an impressive readership in the popular press and in the popular bookseller markets. Many of these thinkers abided by a romantic view of the world, taking their lead from the work of Rousseau and espousing the need for the classroom and school to be more sensitive to the felt needs and interests of the individual child. In 1970, the passions of this romantic fire were further fanned with the publication of Charles Silberman's *Crisis in the Classroom.* Receiving headline treatment in major newspapers and journals, Silberman's study portrayed the American schools as mindless, joyless, and oppressive. Silberman's solutions to the school's problems, however, were emblematic of the day: make education more interesting, joyful, and humane (see the Scholarly Voices feature in this section).

The appearance of a new radical/romantic confederacy in American education was very clearly a sign of the times. The abstract discipline-centered initiatives that grew out of the space race left a lingering foul taste on the American educational palate. A counterreform was now in order, one marked by the reassertion of humanity, openness, social purpose, and individual relevance in the school.

The major figures emerging from the romantic Left in American education included A. S. Neill (in England), John Holt, George Dennison, Herbert Kohl, Paul Goodman, Edgar Friedenberg, and Ivan Illich. Originating from literary circles, this radical/romantic group built its message with rather bitter tones of social protest. Two main themes provided the common ground. One theme maintained a deep hostility toward what was viewed as a profligate society and grim educational establishment. The other major theme was expressed as romantic faith in the self-educating forces of a free and unhampered childhood and adolescence. Because the school, in the language of this genre, *crippled* the process of learning, *destroyed* the dignity of students, and *mutilated* the natural instincts for curiosity, a "do your own thing" ideology emerged.

The titles of the books and articles published by the radical/romantic element emphasized the dehumanizing and iniquitous nature of the educa-

The Romantics

"Abolish authority. Let the child be himself. Don't push him around. Don't teach him. Don't lecture him. Don't elevate him. Don't force him to do anything." A. S. Neill

"In the tender grades, the schools are a babysitting service during a period of collapse of the old-type family and during a time of extreme urbanization and urban mobility. In the junior and senior high school grades, they are an arm of the police, providing cops and concentration camps paid for under the heading 'Board of Education.' " P. Goodman

In *Crisis in the Classroom,* Silberman provided a concrete example of an open classroom setting: "At any one moment, some children may be hammering and sawing at a workbench, some may be playing musical instruments or painting, others may be reading aloud to the teacher or to a friend, still others may be curled up on a cot or a piece of carpet, reading in solitary absorption, oblivious to the sounds around them."

Do you agree with the ideas expressed by some of these writers? How is their rhetoric representative of the time during which they wrote?

---

tional establishment. Consider the following: Jonathan Kozol's *Death at an Early Age: The Destruction of the Hearts and Minds of Negro Children in the Boston Public Schools* (1967), Paul Goodman's *Compulsory Mis-education* (1964), and Nat Hentoff's *Our Children Are Dying* (1966). Charles Silberman (1970a; 1970b) published several critical essays of schooling in the *Atlantic Monthly* under the titles "How the Public Schools Kill Dreams and Mutilate Minds" and "Murder in the Schoolroom." These writings were mostly about how the American school system had lost its humanizing soul.

As far as the school was concerned, the humanizing backlash of the 1960s manifested mainly as emotional protest. Unlike the Sputnik period, there was no systematically developed curriculum-reform proposal. In fact, it was not until 1967 that the first signs of a movement built on practical action began to make its way into American educational thinking. These ideas were imported from England, drawn from the British Plowden Committee's *Children and Their Primary Schools* report (Central Advisory Council for Education, 1967). The report drew much attention because it led to more child-centered schemes in British education, but unlike the American movement, it endorsed an undifferentiated integrated curriculum as a way to relate what was learned in school to wider life experiences. The lesson that the American schools would draw from the Plowden report, however, had less to do with an integrated day and an interdisciplinary curriculum than with the effort to find happy and open experiences for children. Education in America offered rhetoric about freedom, individuality, and self-directed action and brought it together under a blanket cover known as **open education.**

In its application, open education clearly meant different things to different people. It did not have well-articulated goals and never commanded the kind of foundational and governmental support that had characterized many reform initiatives 10 years earlier. In attempting to define the open-education phenomenon, Charles Silberman (1973) maintained that it was "not a model or set of techniques to be slavishly imitated or followed" but an approach to instruction that encompassed a "set of attitudes and convictions about the nature and purposes of teaching and learning . . ." (p. xix). Others were willing to try to outline the principles central to the operation of open education:

> First, the room . . . is decentralized. Second, the children are free. . . . Third, the environment is rich in learning resources. . . . Fourth, the teacher and his aides work most of the time with individual children. (Gross & Gross, 1970, p. 71)

Such a characterization described some of the more common manifestations of open education, but like Silberman's account, it failed to point to specific curriculum goals and procedures. Not surprisingly, the open classroom came to be considered "open" according to any number of criteria. A school could promote its commitment to openness by abolishing ability groups, by encouraging children to move about the classroom at will, by knocking down classroom walls to foster more physical freedom, by designing self-initiated learning units in a departmentalized classroom, by reorganizing the curriculum into more integrated units, or by using any combination of these. The open classroom sadly had little more to offer than the idea of openness; this made it vulnerable to some of the laissez-faire romanticism expressed at the time. The overall practical effect in the classroom was a recognition of the child in the teaching/learning equation and a proliferation of child-centered views that supported the place of unplanned experiences in the school that made a virtue of virtually any experience that the child was committed to perform. At the secondary school and university levels, this mentality led to a multiplicity of electives in the curriculum justified as relevant to the student's interests.

Clearly, the late 1960s represented an effort to bring the learner back into the discourse on the school curriculum. Years of neglect during the early cold war period, which glorified the subject matter and framed the learner as the passive recipient of the knowledge inherent in the subject matter, made such a movement virtually inevitable. Similarly, the earlier stress placed on math and science led to later concerns over the humanities, while the earlier emphasis on the academically inclined led to new concerns about the disadvantaged. In other words, the excesses of the earlier period of reform set the conditions for a subsequent correction. Unfortunately, this correction generated its own set of new excesses. It would only be a matter of time before the child-centered themes of the late 1960s would be undone by a new counterreform. On the horizon was a new wave of reform designed to bring the school "back to basics," back to the familiar ground of the subject-centered curriculum; open classrooms, open schools, and alternative education would soon become anachronisms.

Educational Retrenchment in the 1970s

The problems that beset the American economy during the 1970s created a conservative financial climate that threatened the fiscal budgets of several social institutions, including public education. Encumbered with a growing inflation and unemployment rate, the U.S. economy showed few optimistic signs. The taxpaying public responded to these circumstances by displaying an increasing reluctance to support financially the programs of their local public schools. This air of conservatism led to the promotion of cost-saving measures in public education. Efficiency values and productivity models were embraced as appropriate responses to the challenges of classroom instruction.

It was in this climate that the "back-to-basics" movement was launched. The renewed effort to devote the school curriculum to a strict education in the basics was accompanied by a new regard for accountability, performance assessment, and **competency-based instruction.** Back to basics also meant that the curriculum would be reduced to its least common denominator, that fundamental literacy and mathematics would take priority, and that other aspects of the curriculum, notably the arts, writing, and more interdisciplinary approaches to learning, would take a backseat. Back to basics also valued whatever was most easily measured. It set its sights on minimum standards and advanced a skill-drill instructional mentality to achieve these standards. In some cases, the back-to-basics movement influenced grade-promotion guidelines based on the results of standardized tests.

Basic skill achievement was essentially a cost-saving idea. With back to basics, the schools would have to worry less about providing a comprehensive and resourceful education. Competency-based strategies toward instruction seemed ideally suited for this because they could itemize exactly what needed to be taught and evaluate each component of the curriculum concerning whether or not each student achieved mastery. Competency-based reading programs, for instance, created a highly specific set of competencies, sequenced the competencies according to grade levels, directed the teacher to teach specifically to each competency, and regulated each student's movement through the curriculum with mastery tests. The result was a highly skill-based school experience marked by rather low-level activities. What could not be effectively measured was not taught. Skills in oral communication, in writing, in argumentation, in problem solving, in cross-disciplinary insight, and in research (to name just a few) were simply not part of the instructional picture. A price would naturally have to be paid for this neglect. During the early 1980s, the National Assessment of Educational Progress showed nationwide deficiencies in writing skills, inferential reasoning, and problem-solving skills among publicly educated 17-year-olds. Given the nature of the back-to-basics movement, these findings should have come as no surprise.

This period of reform also did not do much to advance the professional development of educators. Given the prevalence of competency-based systems of teaching, teachers had little room to exercise their intelligence and creativity. The most important judgments were already made for them; all they had to do was to follow directions and issue the work sheets and skill-based activities already developed for them. It was in this climate, in fact, that **"teacher-proof" materials** came into favor. These materials consisted of programmed learning workbooks, some varieties of computer-assisted instruction, and highly prescriptive learning packages that scripted what teachers should say and do. Their orientation was to find a way to protect the curriculum from the teacher; hence, the term "teacher proof."

Much of this retrenchment mentality was also fueled by nationally visible studies that looked at the limits rather than at the possibilities of schooling. Christopher Jencks's *Inequality* (1972) was perhaps the most widely read. The focus of his report was to question whether school significantly affected economic differences and cognitive differences among schoolchildren. The central finding was that schools did not help to equalize the incomes of school graduates, and that any effort to use the school for this end would be wasted.

Jencks further maintained that family background characteristics of the students were far more important in the development of cognitive skill than anything that the school did. This last proposition led to the popular conclusion that schools made no difference, which itself turned out to be a virtual command for educational divestiture. Because the public school was believed to be marginal to the economic and cognitive life of children, alternative school options and earlier work opportunities were given more consideration and weight.

Many of the alternative school ideas were discussed and promoted in a series of federally sponsored **commission reports of the 1970s,** including the report of the National Commission on the Reform of Secondary Education (1973), the report of the President's Science Advisory Committee (1974), and the report of the National Panel on High School and Adolescent Education (1976). Each work sought to narrow the responsibilities of the high school by advocating the workplace and other nonschool settings as viable alternatives for education. To the panels and commissions of the 1970s, the reform emphasis was on reduction. An earlier compulsory school-leaving age, a shortened school day and year, a narrowed curriculum offering, and a commitment to sundry alternative-schooling arrangements were among the salient recommendations coming from the national reports.

Like the basic-skills education initiative pushed during the early 1950s, the retrenchment period of the 1970s eventually evolved into a pursuit of academic excellence and an effort to structure the goals of schooling according to the wishes and demands of the military-industrial complex. In 1983, influenced by the **A Nation at Risk** report, public education was again subjected to a spate of charges that resembled many of the conditions witnessed during the post-Sputnik period. As a strongly worded statement with considerable political backing, *A Nation at Risk* was effective at catching the public ear and lighting the fuse for an explosion of another round of reform ideas.

Education in a Period of Technological and Industrial Mobilization

The 1980s brought the schools full circle, back to the subject-centered traditions that were popular during the 1950s. Generally speaking, the times called for a "get-tough" approach to the curriculum modeled along familiar cold war themes. The school, for instance, was asked to take on tougher graduate standards, to reaffirm the importance of the traditional academic curriculum, to renew its concern for the so-called gifted and talented, to examine itself in relation to schooling in other advanced nations, to stress the importance of mathematics and science education, and in direct contrast to what was valued only one decade earlier, to emphasize the importance of a longer school day and longer school year. Replace past fears over the military prowess of the Soviet Union with new fears over the technological and economic prowess of the Japanese and the parallel is virtually complete.

The report of the National Commission on Excellence in Education (NCEE), otherwise known as *A Nation at Risk,* was undoubtedly the most influential document of the 1980s. Appointed by President Reagan, the NCEE engaged in a yearlong study of the American school that culminated in the writing of its report. A significant portion of the report was dedicated to dramatizing the school's alleged low state, often with the use of strident and attention-commanding language:

> If an unfriendly foreign power had attempted to impose on America the mediocre educational performance that exists today, we might well have viewed it as an act of war. As it stands, we have allowed this to happen to ourselves. . . . We have, in effect, been committing an act of unthinking, unilateral educational disarmament. (p. 5)

By describing a nationwide educational calamity and influencing various media outlets to promulgate its message, the NCEE had set the stage for its own reform recommendations. The nature of these recommendations embraced the timeworn discipline-centered curriculum. It promoted the importance of the "basics" and the resolidification of the subject curriculum, aimed to increase and strengthen graduation requirements, placed a new emphasis on the importance of math and science education, and advanced the idea of tying evaluation standards into exit and promotion decisions. The NCEE report also called for new alternative ways to educate teachers, aiming to make it easier for someone with a college degree to teach without necessarily going through teacher-preparation courses. Lastly, it supported merit pay for teachers, recommended increased course loads for students, and proposed to lengthen the school day and year.

The onus for these so-called reforms fell squarely on the shoulders of state government. President Reagan repeatedly used the NCEE report as evidence that reform could be accomplished without any increase in federal monies and federal presence in education. It was not long after the release of *A Nation at Risk* that all 50 states established task forces that followed the reforms suggested by the NCEE. Within 10 months of the report's introduction to the public, 44 states claimed to have raised their graduation requirements, 20 were considering a longer school day, and 42 were reexamining the way that they certified and prepared teachers, especially in math and science (U.S. Department of Education, 1984).

The NCEE report was not alone. During the 1980s, a raft of education reform reports focused on the reformulation of the school curriculum. Included in the reform discussion were proposals that advanced a monolithic, one-track academic curriculum (Adler, 1982; Bennett, 1987; Sizer, 1984), proposals that called for a reconceived commitment to general education (minus the placement of vocational education) in a comprehensive school program (Boyer, 1983; Goodlad, 1984), and proposals that recast the educational mission of the school in language that was responsive to techno-industrial goals (National Commission on Excellence in Education, 1983; National Science Board Commission, 1983; Task Force on Education for Economic Growth, 1983).

As the school moved toward a new decade, much of the reform thinking began to take on a new rhetoric that highlighted the need for variety and choice in the school curriculum. Rather than working to influence a particular type of school reform, proponents called for the opening up of new school alternatives and choices as a way to improve public education. To some, this also meant allowing private schools to enter into competition with public schools, as parents exercised their consumer right of choice. During the 1990s, the main themes for reform did not have a particular nationalistic anchor but were influenced by a new regard and a faith in the powers of the marketplace to make schools better.

The Idea of School Choice in the 1990s

Today most children in the United States are educated in the public school assigned to their residential community. **Neighborhood schools,** as they are known, are convenient to attend and are central to the functioning of communities that they serve. Because they are charged with the responsibility of educating the neighborhood's children, they often become centers for community deliberation and community understanding. A working community is virtually assured when children who live together go to school together. Neighborhood parents become acquainted through their connection to the school, and the life of the school (homework, athletic events, extracurricular activities) often becomes shared in the homes of the neighborhood. In this sense, the neighborhood school is not only a place where one goes to class, but it is also a place where community prerogatives are exercised and where the general spirit of people living together can be found. This is the very principle founded in the early Puritan efforts to keep the school close to the local people.

The necessity of a neighborhood school arrangement, however, has been questioned by school reformers who believe that there is a need to broaden the menu of school choices available to parents. They ask: Why should parents be content with the choice of only one school for the education of their children? What if such a school was believed to be inadequate in the eyes of the parent? Should not a mechanism be available to parents to choose a school that best approximates what they want in the education of their children, without necessarily resorting to private schooling? These questions have brought the idea of school choice into the center of educational debate. Today there is a growing public acceptance of the right for parents to be able to exercise greater choice over where their children should go to school (see The Contemporary Debate feature on school choice).

Public School Choice

Many parents, of course, have always had the option of exercising choice over their children's education. For parents who could afford private education and for parents whose public school districts provide intradistrict options, a variety of school options is available. School districts throughout the country, in fact, have been testing a wide range of choice strategies within their district lines for some time. Many districts, for instance, have controlled choice programs that allow parents to select from a limited list of district public schools, including magnet schools, **charter schools,** and various open-enrollment options. This is known as **intradistrict choice,** meaning school options available to parents *within* the boundaries of a school district. In several states, including Colorado, Ohio and Washington, intradistrict choice is mandatory (Bierlein & others, 1993). Another form of school choice gaining some attention is **interdistrict choice,** which allows parents to select a school for their child outside of their residential school district. The receiving school district can only deny the request for transfer if it is oversubscribed or if the enrollment option students create racial imbalances in the school population. In most cases, parents have to provide their own transportation, but exemptions are often given to disabled and low income students.

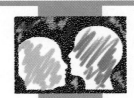

School Choice

#1   In Jackson Heights section of Queens (in New York City), the parent association of a local school filed suit to have a nearby magnet school put under the local district's control, as opposed to the central board of education. The reason was that the local neighborhood school was overcrowded, operating at 139 percent capacity, while only 13 blocks away, a city-run magnet school (populated by students all over the city) was operating at 88 percent capacity. "The city is paying for lots of yellow buses to bring children from all over Queens," a parent complained, "while denying children next door admission." (Hevesi, 1995, p. 20) Hevesi, D. (March 26, 1995). Neighborhood schools: Louis Armstrong to remain a magnet school. *The New York Times,* Sec 13, p. 20.

What do you think about such a situation? Is this the price that has to be paid to bring more school-choice opportunities into city school districts? How might such a situation be remedied?

#2   In many city school systems, zoned schools have become, in a manner of speaking, pauper schools, worthy only for those who do not care about or cannot manage a better school option. In a *New York Times* article, one New York City student explained the situation. "No one wants to go to a zoned school," he observed. "It explains itself. It's like a last option. You want to try for other options. If you don't get accepted anywhere else, you just automatically go there." (Richardson, 1994, p. 23) Richardson, L. (June 19, 1994). Being anonymous and going truant. *The New York Times,* Sec 1, p. 23.

Here, as the student makes quite clear, where one lives is exactly where one should not, and often does not, go to school, a complete inversion of the American tradition of local schooling. Is this the only way to salvage the education of serious and responsible students living in poverty? Can we realistically expect to build healthy neighborhoods without building healthy neighborhood schools?

Interdistrict choice is supported in Iowa, Minnesota, Nebraska, Utah and Washington (Bierlein and others, 1993).

Advocates of choice often cite evidence from national surveys that testify to the popularity of public school choice among parents. Few parents, in fact, are likely to deny an interest in exercising some choice or authority over the character of their child's education. When the Gallup Organization asked parents if they favor or oppose allowing students and their parents to choose which public schools students can attend, regardless of where they live, the response was solidly in favor of choice. The power to choose is, undeniably, not something that is taken lightly by Americans. But choices have consequences, and school choices necessarily have societal consequences. To get at this bigger picture, the Carnegie Foundation for the Advancement of Teaching (1992) conducted a national survey that turned the question about choice into one that reflected a broader public mandate, not simply a personal desire to exercise a preference for a school. The survey asked parents to state whether American education could be best improved by giving neighborhood schools the resources that they need to achieve excellence or by letting schools compete for students with the understanding that good schools would flourish while weak ones would improve or close. More than 80% of the parents surveyed chose the former response, favoring the neighborhood school response.

Despite media rhetoric about widespread dissatisfaction with public schooling, the vast majority of parents, in fact, express satisfaction with the education that their children receive in the public schools (Elam and others, 1994; Carnegie Foundation for the Advancement of Teaching, 1992) and are actually hesitant to switch schools even when options are available. Table 8.1 shows that the participation rate among parents in statewide interdistrict options is less than overwhelming. Although the rates are increasing, at their best they affect about 1.5% of the school population.

Parents who opt for interdistrict choice sometimes based their decision on convenience factors, often wanting a school for their child close to their workplace (Carnegie Foundation for the Advancement of Teaching, 1992). A national survey (NCES, 1995) showed that parents who sent their children to public schools of choice, rather than to the neighborhood or assigned school, usually cited three major reasons for their action–a better academic environment (26%), special academic courses (23%) and school convenience (23%). The fact that so many parents were willing to base their decision on location is troubling to advocates of school choice because it means that the effectiveness of a school's curriculum and its teachers is not necessarily a primary consideration in the exercise of choice. This, of course, undermines an important rationale for choice.

Interestingly, the findings on satisfaction levels between neighborhood schools and chosen public schools (magnet schools, schools chosen in open enrollment districts, and interdistrict choices) do not show any great advantage for choice. As Table 8.2 shows, the positive perceptions of parents toward assigned and chosen public schools are comparable. These data should be viewed in light of the fact that about one third of the nation's magnet schools maintain requirements for admissions (Blank & others, 1996) and that many neighborhoods lose some of their best students and most supportive families to the magnet schools and other "choice" mechanisms. The ratings for private schools are, of course, higher than either assigned or chosen public schools. This likely has something to do with the financial commitment that the family makes to the private school and with the association that the private school might have with certain religious views.

TABLE 8.1

PARTICIPATION RATES IN INTERDISTRICT CHOICE IN STATES MANDATING INTERDISTRICT CHOICE			
States	**1990-91**	**1991-92**	**1992-93**
Iowa	.3	1	1.4
Minnesota	.8	1.3	NA
Nebraska	.2	1	1.7
Utah	NA	NA	1.5
Washington	1.1	1.2	1.3

Adapted from: Beirlein, L. & others (1993). *A national review of open enrollment/choices: Debates and descriptions.* Tempe, AR: Morrison Institute of Public Policy.

PART TWO: THE SCHOOL AND SOCIETY

The new publicly-controlled school choice option that is on the minds of many educators and parents today is the charter school. Many see the idea as an effective compromise between those who want to limit choice to public schools and those who lobby for the full participation of both public and private schools in choice mechanisms.

Charter schools are public schools usually operated by licensed teachers, in contract (or in charter) with a local school board. They are designed to be unconventional innovative schools that would not likely be supported in the normal policy climate of a school district. Under charter school laws, various groups of educators and parents can ask for approval to operate their own unique approach to schooling without having to worry about administrative authority and control. The idea here is to try to allow a school to perform as it might in a free market, by essentially leaving it alone, allowing it to grow out of the local desires of teachers and parents, but ultimately holding it accountable to the school district or state performance standards.

In most states with charter school laws, proposals for charter school approval require a comprehensive design that includes information on evaluation and the measurement or demonstration of pupil progress. Students in charter schools, in fact, will usually be tested in accordance with state standards and state performance measures. If a charter school cannot demonstrate progress toward state or district outcomes or objectives, it can eventually be shut down.

As of 1995, eleven states passed charter school legislation, including Arizona, California, Colorado, Georgia, Hawaii, Kansas, Massachusetts, Michigan, Minnesota, New Mexico and Wisconsin. California has been at the forefront of the movement, with more than 70 charter schools currently authorized in the state (General Accounting Office, 1995). The nature of the charter school legislation points to some interesting differences, but most states are in agreement over limiting the number of charter school authorizations and most also require some level of support from or participation of licensed school teachers in the charter school. See Table 8.3.

Because they use public monies, charter schools must be nonsectarian, nondiscriminatory and tuition-free. Advocates claim that these conditions allow charter schools to maintain the common school ideal (Bierlein and

TABLE 8.2

PARENTS' PERCEPTIONS OF THE SCHOOLS THEIR CHILDREN ATTEND BY TYPE OF SCHOOL: 1993 (CHILDREN IN GRADES 3 TO 12)			
Agree or strongly agree that:	**Public, Assigned**	**Public, Chosen**	**Private**
Child challenged at school	83%	85%	97%
Child enjoys school	87	91	94
Teachers maintain discipline	89	92	98
Students and teachers respect each other	86	90	98
Principal maintains discipline	91	93	98

Source: National Center for Education Statistics. (1995). *Use of school choice* Washington, D.C.: U.S. Department of Education, p. 2.

TABLE 8.3

LEGISLATIVE REGULATION OF CHARTER SCHOOLS AMONG SELECTIVE STATES

	MINNESOTA	CALIFORNIA	COLORADO	GEORGIA	MASSACHUSETTS
How many charter schools are allowed in the state?	20	100	50	no limit	25
How many charter schools are allowed in a school district?	5	10	–	no limit	<5 in Boston/Springfield <2 in other cities
Are preferences given to certain schools?	no	schools targeting low achievers	schools targeting "at risk" students	no	no
Are private schools eligible?	yes	no	no	no	no
Can nonlicensed personnel teach in charter schools?	no	yes	with a waiver	with a waiver	no
Can the charter school set admissions standards?	no	yes	no	no	yes
Who can apply for a charter school?	licensed teachers	any individual, with specified support from teachers	any individual or group, with specified support from teachers	licensed teachers	any individual or group
How long is the charter given	up to 3 years	up to 5 years	up to 5 years	3 years	5 years

Source: Adapted from: Williams, S. & Buechler, M. (January, 1993). *Charter schools.* Policy Brief. Bloomington, IN: Indiana Education Policy Center, and Beierlein, L. & Mulholland, L. (1993) *Charter school update: Expansion of a viable reform initiative* Tempe, AR: Morrison Institute for Public Policy.

Mulholland, 1994). Critics, however, have wondered if the public school mandate can be served when one allows a school to operate around virtually any odd gathering of ideas that someone might want to try (Hlebowitsh, 1995). Some states, it should be said, require some level of approval from licensed educators before the charter school application can even go forward, but the fact that many states limit the authorization of charter schools points to some caution or fear over their proliferation. Some of the charter schools already approved and in operation seem somewhat out of the current of the common school experience. Williams and Buechler (1993), for instance, described a charter school where students from ages 12-20 design, build, market and sell wooden toys and crafts, in the interests of learning basic skills and business skills. In the end, parents, educators, and school leaders will have to ask themselves if a common public school experience is important and if it will ever be recognizable if charter schools evolve into the new state of affairs in the governance of public education.

But the real controversy related to school choice centers on the question of whether private-school options should be included in the program or menu of school choices. This is where the discussion heats up and where the very rationale for public schooling in a democracy hangs in the balance. The question is: Should parents be allowed to use public monies to fund private-school choices for their children?

Vouchers, Privatization, and the Rationale for Choice

Private schools might eventually be able to procure public funds in a school-choice program through something known as an education **voucher.** An education voucher is, in essence, a government certificate that represents a designated amount of money to be used in the purchase of all or some part of a child's schooling. The government would likely issue a redeemable voucher or certificate to all parents with school-age children. Once in receipt of the voucher, parents would function as consumers and would be free to enroll their children in a participating school of their choice. If they later found that the school they chose was not appropriate, they could opt for another. Whether certain regulations might be in place regarding the participation of certain private schools would, of course, depend on the legislative framework from which the voucher certificate was authorized.

In the United States, the first systematic effort to develop a voucher plan was articulated by the economist Milton Friedman (1962). During the post-Sputnik period, he was among the first to cast a dissenting vote against the then-popular trend toward national uniformity in the schools. It should be recalled that during the mid to late 1950s and early 1960s few questioned the character and extent of governmental responsibility in the affairs of the public schools. Given the space race, the school was resolutely dedicated to meeting narrow nationalistic needs. The educational leadership fell in line with this overarching priority and helped to develop educational policies committed to securing nationally consolidated educational outcomes.

Friedman, however, believed that the ultimate source of school control should be with the individual consumer (the parent). In seeking to develop a framework to secure this goal, Friedman advanced the now-familiar argument for "schools of choice." American education, he claimed, could best be improved by changing the financial and governance structure of public education in directions that encouraged schools to compete for students and that helped parents to exercise consumer choice in deciding where their children would be educated. The idea was fairly simple: Provide parents with redeemable vouchers, which would be roughly equivalent to the per-pupil expenditures of the local public school, and permit them to spend their vouchers at any school of their choice. Friedman advocated no substantive restrictions on the participating "voucher" schools, stating that each school need only be approved by the government much in the way, to use his analogy, that the government inspects restaurants to ensure minimum sanitary standards.

The funding mechanism for vouchers differs radically from the usual method of funding and operating American schools. Under present conditions, school districts are financed directly through monies garnered from local, state, and federal sources channeled into the school through a governance structure that is empowered at both the state and the local levels. In contrast, vouchers would probably rely on a central directorate, likely operating at the state level, that would issue monies directly to the family. Each school, public and private alike, would then be placed in the position of trying to convince parents that it merits their patronage.

To many parents there is a surface appeal to such a concept because it provides them and their children with an avenue of access to both the public and the private school. But before any judgment can be passed on vouchers, the essential details regarding the ways in which vouchers are regulated in areas such as admissions, school administration, and curriculum development need to be articulated. Marked differences of opinion exist over the size of vouchers, the eligibility requirements, and the character of the evaluation and information systems used to judge and disseminate school performance (Catterall, 1985). These variations make it difficult to speak for or against the pure idea of vouchers. Still, there are general keynotes to the idea that could help clarify whether education by voucher is appropriate in the United States.

By encouraging parents to take an active hand in the selection of their children's school, all voucher systems claim to put a series of salutary educational changes into motion. First, there is the claim that vouchers will infuse the current system of schooling with an attractive assortment of school programs. In essence, the claim is that vouchers will "break the back" of an entrenched system of schooling marked by widespread curriculum uniformity and staleness. The mechanism of market accountability is at the center of this belief because only the "best" schools will presumably survive in the competitive climate that vouchers will generate. Second, the education by voucher concept claims to provide new decision-making authority to the underclass, giving this neglected population a means of access to better schools. It also claims to induce new openness in the area of school administration, to build new circles of interaction among socioeconomic classes, to prompt sorely needed community support for education, and ultimately to liberate the teacher from the tethers of an imposing school bureaucracy. These claims cut across specific voucher proposals. They are advanced for the general idea of vouchers.

Opponents have argued that vouchers, in any form, will lead to a divided school system that fails to reaffirm the historical commitment to common learnings. This viewpoint sees the rise of an open school marketplace as a sign of abandonment of the public school ideal. Publicly funded private schools, for instance, might sap the system of the best students, leaving the public schools with the hard to educate. Even with regulations, natural divisions in the population could result in theme schools developed along religious, racial, cultural, political, or philosophical lines. This could lead to a proliferation of school extremes and the consequential problem of further segregating and deepening the class and racial divisions in society.

Opponents also warn that the financial stakes for private education could simply be raised incrementally with tuition add-ons, that the so-called best private schools will still be inaccessible to minority and underclass clientele. Where parochial schools come into play, opponents raise the issue of church and state, and where for-profit schools are advanced, they caution against the conceivable rise of hucksterism by a profit-making mind-set. Others feel that the level of government monitoring required to certify that the voucher system is operating according to approved rules and regulations will prove to be a bureaucratic monstrosity. Concern is also raised over whether parents would be supplied with enough information about schools to make informed choices. Providing this kind of information is obviously difficult because educational methods and outcomes are complex constructs that are multidimensional in orientation and long range in outlook.

Critics have also maintained that arguments for vouchers and **privatization,** while hinting at ideals of equity and justice, possess no systemic commitment to democratizing principles. Schools in the marketplace, they assert, are customized in a way that aim to capture a market. Schools for the athletically gifted, schools stressing a particular ethnic or cultural tradition, premedical elementary schools, Great Books schools, foreign-language immersion schools, technology schools, back-to-basics schools, open education schools, quasi-military schools, schools run by fast-food industries, and schools stressing the virtues of capitalism could emerge in such an arrangement. Parents would have more choice, but the interests of the individual and the society would be left to the quixotic adjustment of the school to consumer demand (Hlebowitsh, 1994).

There are already a few fledgling educational corporations in the United States looking to make a profit by designing and operating schools. Of particular note is the role that the Whittle Corporation has been playing to bring "choice" to the schools. The Whittle Corporation, which has achieved some fame for its success at bringing commercial television into the classroom (through its Channel One program), has plans of building a corporation devoted to offering relatively inexpensive private-school education to Americans, an initiative known as the Edison Project. The founder of the Edison Project, Christopher Whittle, has been forthright in stating his belief that private schools deserve public funding and in stating his desire to procure these monies for his own schools.

In some states, the public purse has already been opened to private corporations. Charter school laws have allowed private organizations to seek approval from local or state boards of education (depending on the state) to run or to open public schools, with public monies. In 1994, the state of Massachusetts awarded the Edison Project with three school charters (Celis, 19 March, 1994). Another "school for-profit" firm, known as Education Alternatives, Inc. (EAI), was hired to run some public schools in the cities of Baltimore and Hartford. In Baltimore, EAI promised to clean up the schools given to them, to install computers and to raise test scores, all without any extra cost to the district. In Hartford, a similar promise was given. EAI was convinced that it could make its profits from public monies that were at current per pupil expenditure levels while providing the children at EAI-managed schools with a better education. The results told a different story. In 1995, Baltimore canceled its contract with EAI. The test results from the schools managed by EAI in Baltimore were uneven and accusations were made that EAI was being paid more than the city average (Judson, 7 Dec, 1995). Moreover, there were budgetary cuts that EAI was not prepared to accept. In Hartford, EAI never received full payment for its services because of the manner in which the financial arrangements were structured. It is estimated that EAI lost close to 8 million dollars in Hartford. These early examples of for-profit schooling provide some glimpse into the complexity of trying to make profits in a public institution that carries a weighty public agenda and that often inherits weighty social problems.

Although school choice has been resonating in discussions about school reform for some time now, the open commitment to privatization in the Bush Administration's *America 2000* (U.S. Department of Education, 1990) was likely influential in giving the idea of choice more political visibility. The report was developed out of the 1989 Governor's Conference on Education. The main outcome of the conference was the *America 2000* report, which supplied six simple objectives for the public schools to meet by the year 2000: 1) all children in America will start school ready to learn; 2) the high school graduation rate will increase to at least 90%; 3) American students will leave grades 4, 8, and 12 having demonstrated competency in challenging subject matter; 4) American students will be first in the world in mathematics and science achievement; 5) every American will be literate and will possess the skills necessary to compete in a global economy and to exercise the rights and responsibilities of citizenship; and 6) every school in America will be free of drugs and violence and will offer a disciplined environment conducive to learning. These goals were formally drafted and adopted by the governors.

The report, however, also discussed how such goals might be met. On this front, it discussed the possibility of voluntary national standards and voluntary national testing. It also touched on the possibility of examining alternative certification programs for teachers and openly embraced the need to employ a school-choice strategy that included private schools in the mix. Because the state governors endorsed the report, there will likely be a series of state-based referenda that will ask voters whether a formal choice mechanism, which includes private options, should be enacted in their states. California has already faced the question, asking its voters in November 1994 to decide whether public monies ($2,600 per student) should be used to gain open access to either a private or a public school education. The voters, it should be noted, overwhelmingly defeated the proposal.

Adding compelling evidence to the argument for privatization was the release of a much-celebrated empirical study that examined the achievement differences between private and public schools. In 1990, Chubb and Moe claimed to have discerned superior student achievement effects among private schools and asserted that such effects were mostly related to the fact that private schools were less bureaucratized and less controlled by centralized authority than were public schools. Supported by these findings, Chubb and Moe (1990) argued that school-improvement efforts would best be served by extricating the public school from its heavy-handed governance structure. They claimed that public schools were naturally bureaucratic and hierarchical and that layers of public authority and public regulations in the school resulted in stifling teacher intelligence and administrative leadership. Chubb and Moe felt that the only way to release the intelligence, creativity, and leadership of educators in the interest of improving public schooling was to situate the public school in the context of the free marketplace, where ideas are tested against the ever-powerful mechanism of consumerism. This would make public schools more like private ones—free from a centralized authority, free to respond openly to their clientele, free to exercise their own vision of enlightening schooling, and ultimately accountable to the judgments of the marketplace.

Chubb and Moe (1990) spiced their analysis with rhetoric about the failings of the current system of schooling, with cross-national comparisons that were uncomplimentary to the United States and with a clear preference in believing that school organization affects student achievement (and not the opposite). Of course, critics have indicated that the very national systems that are allegedly outperforming those in the United States are highly bureaucratized and centralized systems, such as Japan and Germany, and that the inefficiency of public schooling is an inefficiency born out of an effort to educate a population democratically and widely (Fowler, 1991). The fact that achievement advantages were found in private schools with fewer layers of bureaucracy and public control might speak to the fact such schools simply do not carry the weight of troubles that accompany public democratic institutions. In other words, the organizational structure of the public school (a key point to Chubb and Moe) is influenced by sociological conditions that are absent in private schools. Along these same lines, Chubb and Moe apparently also failed to account for the fact that most of the private schools that displayed an advantage in their study were also religious schools that might possess associational sociological conditions favorable to student achievement in the private schools (Fowler, 1991).

In 1992, the Carnegie Foundation for the Advancement of Teaching released its own report on school choice as a counterargument to the Chubb and Moe book. The findings in the Carnegie report, which were part of a yearlong examination, hit at some of the foundational marketplace arguments. For example, the report found that better-educated parents were most likely to derive the benefits of choice, that school performance did not necessarily improve from choice, and that funding inequities between rich and poor districts could potentially be worsened through choice. It also dealt with the successful examples of school choice in places such as East Harlem but emphasized that the success of these schools had as much to do with the large financial investments made in such districts and with the considerable intelligence of the school leadership as with parents' freedom to choose schools. The Milwaukee schools' small-scale experiment with vouchers, which allowed a small group of inner-city youth to attend private schools at public expense, also came in for some criticism. The report noted that test scores did not improve among the children involved in the experiment and that attrition rates were very high (Carnegie Foundation for the Advancement of Teaching, 1992).

Despite such criticism, school choice has become the darling of bipartisan support in Washington, although Republican advocates have been much more willing to consider choice proposals that cut across both public and private sectors. Much of the enthusiasm started in the 1980s when spokespersons in the Department of Education voiced ardent support for a wide range of choice mechanisms, largely because they felt that the guiding conception of parental sovereignty in a competitive climate would improve the school's responsiveness and accountability. As secretary of education, William Bennett (1988) was particularly active in his support, prominently displaying "choice" as one of the main conceptual threads of his administration. Much of this early support was followed by limited efforts to test "choice" in school districts and by ever-increasing acceptance and use of the magnet school alternative, which in some urban districts is still a foil against court-ordered busing.

To conservative commentators like Chester Finn (1991), the reform of the school absolutely depends on a wholesale reconstruction of schooling that has public and private school choices at its center, a view that he rightly outlines as radical and that has him likening himself to a revolutionary. Finn is not simply engaging in hyperbole. Both right-wing and left-wing forces are actually in agreement on the idea of eradicating the current system (Hlebowitsh, 1993). Conservative economic critics, for instance, have contended that public schooling in America operates as a kind of monopoly that generates pervasive levels of school complacency and stagnancy, while radical critics have argued along similar lines, maintaining that the public school exercises cultural monopoly and social control over the student population with the effect of institutionalizing the inequitable treatment of underclass youth. In both cases, the public school is portrayed as a monolith marked by extraordinary uniformity, dreary learning conditions, and pervading anti-intellectualism. In both cases, the call for reform entails establishing better sensitivity to parental expressions of choice. Civil libertarians and evangelists, free marketers and socialists, civil rights advocates and ethnic separatists all see their particular agendas served by school choice.

The Marketplace Priority

In 1972, Sizer wrote that "competition is the newest old panacea for the reform of American schools" (p. 24). In the 1990s, this old panacea once again became new, as advocates from inside and outside the school called for competition among schools as a way to foster their improvement.

Part of the fascination with the competition priority is associated with the accusation of a public school monopoly. This accusation is the logical first step in demanding that free-market principles guide school development. The belief is that market pressures will neutralize the monopolistic position of the public schools by placing all schools (private and public) on the same competitive ground. This will effectively recast the idea of a public school by opening up the school market to a plethora of new school arrangements. Private schools currently operate with few public funds. As a result, they demand tuition fees that are typically beyond the financial reach of many families. Because the private schools are not able to reach out to all segments of society, the public schools stand incriminated for possessing singular control over the service of education.

The notion of a public school monopoly is also used to explain the monolithic pattern in which youth are supposedly educated across the nation. Goodlad (1984) and Cuban (1984) confirmed the continued dominance of the basic whole-class instruction/recitation/seatwork model in public school teaching. Such a finding helps to paint the picture of a school monopoly because it creates the image of educational uniformity. Adding fuel to the fire is the perceptible loss of community responsiveness in local school policy making. As documented earlier, state and local efforts have always had to struggle against powerful nationalizing forces.

One, of course, could counter by noting that the schools in the United States are decentralized and that the locus of policy-making control is in the hands of the state and the local school boards which represent widely disparate communities. This being the case, the argument of monopoly loses some of its vigor. One should keep in mind that American public schools are highly decentralized agencies that carry a historic association with local prerogatives. Fifty different states represent 50 different measures of school governance, each containing independent local school districts that range in size, curriculum emphasis, climate, and philosophical direction. Each school district, moreover, incorporates some variety of local schools, and each local school itself includes a variety of different classroom teachers. Some works, such as Powell, Farrar, and Cohen's *The Shopping Mall High School* (1985) and Pauley's *The Classroom Crucible* (1991) demonstrate a wide range of differences in classroom teaching styles in the public schools. Put simply, the argument of a school monopoly is simply not an easy one to make against the highly decentralized American school system (Cookson, 1994).

By describing a school system that is lacking in variety and responsiveness, voucher advocates set the conditions for a view of education that places marketplace priorities at the center of all school-improvement initiatives. Under such circumstances, individual families could then dictate the substance of the school offering. But the emergence of quality under this scheme presumes a fit between consumer preferences (the kinds of schools that parents seek) and professional judgments (the kinds of schools that school professionals support as fundamentally sound). Such a presumption, however, does not necessarily apply to the voucher scene. As Raywid (1987) observed, a voucher plan "is a plan for financing schools, not for improving them" (p. 764). The point is that there is nothing in the voucher concept that expresses a design for school improvement. The improvement of the school is left to the winds of the marketplace.

The current faith put in competition is part of a wider faith that school critics and reformers have placed in the application of business priorities and principles to the design of the school curriculum. In 1983, the rising success of foreign business competitors (especially the Japanese markets) captured the thinking of both the corporate and the political leadership in ways that generated new levels of dialogue between the world of public education and the world of business. Unfortunately, the relationship was one-sided with most of the emphasis being placed on what business and industry perceived as their needs. A document drawn up by a subgroup of the Education Commission of the States, titled *Action for Excellence* (Task Force on Education for Economic Growth, 1983), demonstrated the problem. Here the school was called on to take up a larger share of participation in a plan to bring lasting economic vitality to the United States. With the backing of state governors and national corporate leaders, this document specifically alluded to the need to bring business elements into the process of setting goals for education. Direct references were made to creating a curriculum that "made sense for economic education" and to linking education initiatives to economic objectives (p. 22). The broader dimensions of schooling were lost in the consuming passion to gear the school to the needs of the corporate world.

In 1962, Raymond Callahan documented the incompatibilities that exist between the institutions of education and business in a book titled *Education and the Cult of Efficiency.* Callahan underlined the dangers of seeing educational value in terms of dollars and cents. He was very careful to show that the idea of cost-effectiveness (efficiency) was often at odds with the idea of educational effectiveness. Cost-effective thinking, for example, frequently gave justification to reducing the curriculum to its most basic and narrow elements and to lowering the role of the teacher to that of a pedagogical technician or functionary. In this way, cost-effective thinking testified to a basic misdirection of thinking about schooling.

Contemporary critics of vouchers fear that a cult of efficiency could be reawakened in a system where for-profit schools would be allowed to compete for students. Guided by the profit motive, voucher schools might opt for low-level approaches to teaching like programmed instruction, "teacher-proof" materials, performance contracting, accountability formulas, and different types of competency-based learning systems. To those who seek financial profit in school development, these are alluring strategies because

Margaret Brown of Schreveport, Louisiana, is a teacher at the J.B. Harville School Away from School for pregnant high school girls. School reforms have created many alternative settings for students, but restructured schools are not always in the image of those who call for school choice.

they are relatively cheap and easy. These are also strategies that are well suited for teaching to the test, which, as will be discussed, makes them even more attractive to the profit-making mentality.

Ironically, providing evidence of quality in a competitive market is a process that could actually result in a narrowing of the school offering. As consumers, parents are liable to fix their sights on demonstrable signs of school success, like, in the case of a secondary school, achievement on the SAT, ACT, or some state competency exam. The problem is that parents are also likely to believe that these test scores are valid indicators of the school's overall health. This, in turn, could compel schools to gear their curriculum to the all-important test. In a marketplace atmosphere where the schools are competing for clients, an obvious premium would be placed on this kind of activity. In pursuing the status associated with a high-achievement ranking, however, the school runs the risk of limiting the curriculum to the narrow dimensions of information and skill covered on the external test. As a result, the claim of greater diversity among voucher schools might not be realized at all and might actually backfire into a more standardized system (Wise & Darling-Hammond, 1984).

This is not a problem that can be taken lightly. Standardized testing is already influencing the school curriculum in undesirable ways (Madaus, 1988). It has almost become accepted practice among public schools to use standardized tests as concrete measures of prominence and rank. Outside pressures have helped to institutionalize this narrow method. Real estate agencies, for instance, have been known to use narrow test data to sell homes in areas where the school scores are favorable.

It could very well be that marketplace competition will exacerbate these conditions and pressures. In Baltimore, for instance, Educational Alternatives, Inc. (EAI), the private firm hired to try to improve on the education of youth in nine city schools, has resorted to a computer drilling system to raise the test scores on basic skills ("Selling the Schools," 1994). Drilling for skill, of course, is among the most timeworn and least innovative pedagogical methods known to educators and is very much a part of the very monopolistic structure that choice advocates see in public education.

One of the arguments of pro-voucher advocates is that the school will show new levels of respect and responsiveness to parents and their children. Fearing the loss of a paying customer, the school will be much more sensitive to the needs and interests of its clients. But schools may not be as responsive as claimed, particularly if the nature of the parent-school relationship is not good for business. There is a distinct possibility that the school, when faced with a rather intractable problem, might fail to show a commitment to proposing a solution because it knows that the parents could simply seek another school. Another way of saying this is that the parent might choose a school, but the school might not choose the student. This is not a hypothetical problem. Currently, over 70% of Catholic high schools require an entrance exam. In Milwaukee, where a program exists that allows some poor families to receive a voucher for private education, 40% of the children designated for the program could not find a private school that would accept them (AFT, 1993).

The idea of a working school community could also be lost under these circumstances because parents would be implicitly encouraged to walk away from the school if matters do not go their way. Hirschman (1970) calls this phenomenon an example of the economist's bias for exit as opposed to voice.

The decision to voice one's views and help make them prevail in a democratic process goes by the wayside when exit options are encouraged. Rather than seek improvements in the neighborhood school, the parent is persuaded to shop around for another choice. Because the school is often the centerpiece of the community, this willingness to exit could well have negative social effects. As Raywid (1987) put it:

> to assign parents full and unfettered responsibility for choosing their children's education in an open market is to telegraph the message that the matter is solely their affair and not the community's concern. . . . Thus I fear that vouchers would bring in their wake a further downplaying of education on the public agenda and a further waning of public commitment to the enterprise. (p. 763)

The school could also find itself in the vulnerable position of responding to parental whim rather than standing by a professional rationale. This could lead to the rise and fall of many educational fads, as schools attempt to quell parental pressure by staying on top of the latest breaking fads and fashions. Kliebard (1988) theorized that the notorious cycles of school reform are partly due to the schools' failure to practice an art of exclusion. In his view, there is a kind of "anything goes" mentality that gives every aspiring school claimant an undeserved equal standing on the school landscape (p. 18). Privatization and vouchers are likely to contribute to this problem.

The recent effort by public school districts to permit the development of special charter schools is a good example of how the very coherence of the American system of schooling could be lost through an ever-proliferating range of school alternatives. Charter schools are public schools usually operated by licensed teachers, in contract with a local school board, who want to try something different and innovative without the worries of administrative authority and control. The idea is to try to allow a school to operate as it might in a free market, by essentially leaving it alone and allowing it to grow out of local parental desires and by ultimately holding it accountable to the district's judgment of its performance. But the question will be, To what extent will charter schools contribute to the relativization of the essential core purposes and functions of public education? Will charter schools, for instance, lead to any odd gathering of ideas that someone might want to try?

Lastly, if free enterprise for public education is advocated, the question of who is in control of the school must be broached. The state will not relinquish its interest in the way the school conducts itself. The very concept of compulsory education is in fact an indication that the state has chosen to remove certain choices.

The Public Interest

The call for choice obviously places great value in giving parents the freedom to select a school that best approximates what they desire in an education for their children; it pins its faith on the belief that parents are the most suitable agents in determining how and where their children should be educated.

A large part of the debate over vouchers revolves around a dualism that frames the main purpose of the school to be in either the best interest of the individual (the child) or the best interest of the society. Some advocates of choice, like Coons and Sugarman (1978), contend that the school's main objective should be devoted to the individual and that the family is, therefore, the most effective agent in shaping the school experience. To Coons and Sugarman, maximizing the individual welfare is perceived as maximizing the welfare of the society. This view has been criticized by those who see the objective of the school in broader and more collective terms. Antivoucher sentiment sees family choice as basically selfish and antisocial because it focuses on the wants of a single family rather than the needs of society. Public education, the reasoning might go, must be protected from the prevailing orthodoxies of parents and must be influenced instead by the general values and aims of democratic living. Wise and Darling-Hammond (1984) serve notice of the very thin line that voucher proponents walk: "If parents' choices of schools reinforce social class stratification and socialization," they state, "[then] we must accept the outcomes as justified by choice and as in the child's best interests" (p. 43). Coons and Sugarman oppose this by maintaining that family initiative is not inherently selfish and destructive and that such a suggestion belies the free-thinking principles of society. They also find it hypocritical that family choice is tolerated when exercised by the rich and disputed when even considered for any other group, especially the so-called underclass.

Critics of vouchers see several other problems with the idea of handing school decision-making power over to parents. First, there is the view that parents should not be empowered to make school decisions because of inherent conflicts between private interest and schooling for the common good. Second, there is the view that all parents or families cannot make such decisions because they are not all equally informed or equally committed to the education of their children. The idea of a benevolent, caring family acting as the sole benefactor of the child in school matters is, in many ways, dangerously one-sided. Others scoff at this point. West (1984), for instance, stated that it is a paradox to say that the very individuals who are seen as frequently being misinformed or incapable of making judgments on education (parents) are allowed to influence (with votes) a system called the state that is to provide their education for them (p. 52). Wagner (1977) stated the problem another way. "If parents (citizens) cannot be trusted to make educational choices," he declared, "one might wonder why they should be trusted to make political choices" (p. 116).

Regarding the public interest, there is a concern about the effects that vouchers might have in dismantling the public schools and leaving a fragmented and segregated society in its wake. Jencks (1972a), however, has attacked this idea as implausible. His contention is that a properly regulated voucher system will enhance accessibility to good schools for everyone, thereby expanding and enhancing the public school's main mission. Interestingly, many of those who are proponents of vouchers claim that the common school concept of public education has long been lost, and that the fear of its demise is no longer an important consideration. Coleman, Hoffer, and Kilgore's (1982) *High School Achievement* is the work upon which this claim is frequently based. In this study, Coleman, Hoffer, and Kilgore argued that private schools demonstrate lower levels of internal segregation than do public schools. The three authors believe that residential stratification has produced a public school system that no longer integrates the various segments of the population. The public school does indeed serve a cross section of American children, they claim, but it does so in highly segregated and stratified ways. To argue, then, that vouchers will destroy the integrative spirit of the public school is, according to Coleman, Hoffer, and Kilgore, not compelling.

If vouchers were eventually granted to parents, the private and parochial schools that may eventually profit under such a system will probably have to face the prospect of dealing with state regulation and authority. As mentioned earlier, it is extremely unlikely that the government will not exert a role in areas like personnel, admissions, and financial administration. The government is also likely to be involved in helping to define and monitor the character of school initiatives. Ironically, this regulation could turn against the private school to the extent that it saps it of its distinctive qualities. Certainly, a fundamentalist school that uses the first chapter of Genesis as a text for instruction in biology might find state regulation onerous and unreasonable. Thus, in the face of some kind of regulation, private schools will run the risk of losing a part of their uniquenesses, which absolutely contravenes the spirit and intent of the choice argument. In fact, in the 1970s, Catholic schools did not support vouchers precisely for this reason (Catterall, 1985). As Wise and Darling-Hammond (1984) put it: "To the extent that the regulation of vouchers seeks to counteract preferences for private association, the very foundation of the voucher concept is weakened" (p. 38).

Choice and National Standards

School reform discussions in the 1990s have also yielded practical proposals for national education standards. In a period strongly associated with school choice, this, at first glance, looks to be an unusual, if not paradoxical, occurrence. National standards, especially if they manifest as national curricula or national testing, necessarily contradict the fundamental rationale for choice, which is to encourage schools to proliferate in multiple varieties as they respond to parental (consumer) desires. For this reason, the national standards movement has been criticized by those who believe in the power of the free market and by those who want to keep the place of federal agendas out of school policy. But other commentators see a symbiotic relationship between standards and choice. Believing that pure and unregulated school choice is a practical impossibility, advocates of standards see a need for school choice to be circumscribed by and accountable to a core set of standards that all schools, irrespective of their pedagogical style and curriculum emphasis, must recognize.

The effort to simultaneously embrace school choice and national standards started with the *America 2000* report, which, besides encouraging the adoption of choice mechanisms, implied the need for national standards of academic achievement in several of its major goals. The legislative consequences of *America 2000* were later embodied in Goals 2000, which was a law designed to make the major goals of *America 2000* a reality. Because Goals 2000 was adopted under the Clinton Administration, the emphasis was more on standards than on choice. Title I and Title II of the legislation were devoted to providing monies to encourage the development of academic standards at state and national levels. The federal government cannot, of course, dictate standards to the states, but it can encourage their development and adoption. Thus, Goals 2000 provided monies to states interested in developing and implementing standards. Forty states have since applied for the monies (Lewis, 1995).

In recent years, several academic subject areas have been formulated into standards that describe what students should know and be able to do.

The United States Department of Education funded some of these projects, but others, like the standards established by the National Council of Teachers of Mathematics, started well before the passage of Goals 2000 legislation. Advocates claim that such standards are empowering, in that they allow teachers and local school leaders to be liberated from the unintentional national curriculum found in school textbooks and testing systems (Allen and Brinton, 1995) and establish a framework that better ensures equal access to content and courses of study (Ravitch, 1995). Critics counter by arguing that, far from liberating teachers, standards chain them down with test driven instruction geared specifically to the standards and with formulaic textbooks. Eisner (1995) has argued that the uniformity in curriculum content implied by standards is neither necessary nor desirable in the school curriculum because it undermines the emphasis that should be paid to processual goals in areas like thinking, communication, and social democratic attitudes, while enthroning content goals.

In the end, the reconciliation of national standards with school choice will likely be difficult to achieve because it will mean that some choices will not be acceptable. This outcome runs against the grain of the free market and brings us closer, as some critics might add, to recognizing the need to fashion a common comprehensive school experience, rather than an overwhelmingly varied one.

KEY TERMS

'A Nation at Risk
America 2000
Charter schools
Commission reports of the 1970s
Competency-based instruction

Interdistrict choice
Intradistrict choice
National Defense Education Act
  of 1958
Neighborhood schools

Open education
Privatization
'Structure of a discipline"
"Teacher-proof" materials
Voucher

KEY QUESTIONS

1. Describe the pendulumlike nature of school reform since midcentury.

2. Why are reactionary changes likely when schools respond to narrow nationalistic pressures?

3. What was the fundamental reform message preached by Arthur Bestor and Admiral Rickover during the 1950s?

4. What were some of the things that occurred in the school curriculum because of the forces unleashed by the Soviet launching of Sputnik?

5. What was Bruner's essential contribution to the nature of school reform during the post-Sputnik period?

6. How did James Conant save the American school system from embracing the dual, or bipartite, model popular in Europe during the post-Sputnik period?

7. How did the excesses of the post-Sputnik era lead to counterreform measures that generated their own set of new excesses?

8. What was the main message emerging from the romantic left during the 1960s?

9. How did open education lead to a laissez-faire attitude in the curriculum?

10. What was competency-based instruction, and why was it an attractive idea during the 1970s?

11. What is right or wrong with the idea of "back to basics"?

12. Why was the idea of alternative schools popular with the commission reports of the 1970s?

13. What was the essential finding of Jencks's well-known *Inequality*, and what were the main implications for the school curriculum?

14. Compare the nature of reform in the 1980s to the reforms undertaken during the post-Sputnik period.

15. What were the main recommendations of the *A Nation at Risk* report?

16. What are the basic arguments supporting school choice, with and without the inclusion of private schools?

17. What are the basic arguments against school choice?

18. What were the main goals of the *America 2000* report, and how did the report support the idea of school choice?

19. What was the essential finding and the main implication of the Chubb and Moe study?

20. Why are both right-wing and left-wing forces openly supportive of the idea of school choice?

21. What are some of the problems with subjecting schools to marketplace conditions?

22. How would you respond to someone who says: "It is a free society. If we are free to choose our own doctors and plumbers, why should we not also be free to choose our own child's school?"

23. Explain some of the public school choice options available to many parents today.

24. What is a charter school, and what are the essential advantages and disadvantages of supporting it?

25. Do you see the advocacy of school choice *and* national education standards as necessarily contradictory?

REFERENCES

Adler, M. J. (1982). *The Paideia proposal.* New York: Macmillan.

Allen, D. W. & Brinton, R. C. (1996) Improving our unacknowledged national curriculum *The Clearinghouse* 169(3):140–145.

American Federation of Teachers, AFT. (1993). Myths and facts about private school choice. *American Educator, 17*(3), 26A–26H. In F. Shultz, *Education* (22nd ed.). Guildford, CT: Dushkin Publishing Group.

Bennett, W. (1987). *Our children and our country.* New York: Simon and Schuster.

Bierlien, L. & Mulholland, L. A. (1994). *Comparing charter school laws: The issue of autonomy* (Policy brief) Tempe, AR: Morrison Institute of Public Policy.

Bierlien, L. & Mulholland, L. A. (1993). *Chapter school update: Expansion of a viable reform.* Tempe, AR: Morrison Institute of Public Policy.

Bestor, A. E. (1953). *Educational wastelands.* Urbana, IL: University of Illinois Press.

Bestor, A. E. (1956). *The restoration of learning.* New York: Alfred A. Knopf.

Blank, R. K. & others (1996). After 15 years: Magnet schools in urban education. In Fuller B. & Elmore, R. F. (Eds.) *Who Chooses? Who Loses?* New York, NY: Teachers College Press.

Boyer, E. (1983). *High school.* New York: Harper and Row.

Bruner, J. S. (1960). *The process of education.* Cambridge: Harvard University Press.

Callahan, R. E. (1962). *Education and the cult of efficiency.* Chicago: Phoenix Books, The University of Chicago Press.

Carnegie Foundation for the Advancement of Teaching. (1992). *School choice: A special report.* Princeton, NJ: Carnegie Foundation for the Advancement of Teaching.

Catterall, J. S. (1985). *Education vouchers.* Fastback 210. Bloomington, IN: Phi Delta Kappan Educational Foundation.

Chubb, J. E., & Moe, T. (1990). *Politics, markets and America's schools.* Washington, DC: The Brookings Institution.

Coleman, J. S., Hoffer, T., & Kilgore, S. (1982). *High school achievement.* New York: Basic Books, Inc.

Conant, J. B. (1960). *The American high school today.* New York: McGraw-Hill Book Co.

Cookson, P. W. (1994). *School choice.* New Haven: Yale University Press.

Coons, J. E., & Sugarman, S. D. (1978). *Education by choice.* Berkeley, CA: University of California Press.

Celis, W. (19 Mar, 1994) 15 Massachusetts Public Schools are entrusted to private managers *The New York Times* Sec:1 p. 1.

Cuban, L. (1984). *How teachers taught.* New York: Longman Press.

Eisner, E. W. (1995). Standards for American schools *PDK* 76(10): 758–764.

Elam, S. & others (1994). The 25th Annual *PDK* Gallup Poll, *PDK* 76(1): 41–56.

Finn, C. (1991). *We must take charge.* New York: The Free Press.

Fowler, F. C. (1991). The shocking ideological integrity of Chubb and Moe. *Journal of Education, 173*(3).

Freidman, M. (1962). *Capitalism and freedom.* Chicago: University of Chicago Press.

General Accounting Office (1995). *Charter schools: New model for public school provides opportunities and challenges.* Washington, DC: Health, Education and Human Services Division.

Goodlad, J. I. (1966). *The changing school curriculum.* New York: Fund for the Advancement of Education.

Goodlad, J. I. (1984). *A place called school.* New York: McGraw-Hill.

Goodman, P. (1964). *Compulsory mis-education.* New York, NY: Horizon Press.

Gross, R., & Gross, B. (1970, May 16). A little bit of chaos. *Saturday Review.*

Hentoff, N. (1966). *Our children are dying.* New York: Viking Press.

Hirschman, A. O. (1970). *Exit, voice and loyalty.* Cambridge: Harvard University Press.

Hlebowitsh, P. S. (1993). *Radical curriculum theory reconsidered.* New York: Teachers College Press.

Hlebowitsh, P. S. (1994). Choice and the splitting-up of the American school. In D. Tanner & J. W. Keefe, (Eds.). *Curriculum issues and the new century.* Alexandria, VA: National Association of Secondary School Principals.

Hlebowitsh, P. S. (1995). Can we find the traditional American school in the idea of choice? *NASSP Bulletin* 79(572): 1–11.

Jencks, C. (1972). *Inequality.* New York: Basic Books, Inc.

Jencks, C. (1972a). Giving parents money for schooling: Education vouchers. In J. A. Mecklenburger & R. W. Hostrop, (Eds.) *Education vouchers: From theory to alum rock.* Homewood, IL: ETC Publications.

Judson, G. (7 Dec, 1995). Bad times for education company force a shift in vision. *The New York Times* Sec:B p. 1.

Kliebard, H. M. (1988). Fads, fashions, and rituals: The instability of curriculum change. In L. N. Tanner (Ed.), *Critical issues in curriculum. Eighty-seventh yearbook of the National Society for the Study of Education, Part 1.* Chicago: The University of Chicago Press.

Kozol, J. (1967). *Death at an early age.* Boston: Houghton-Mifflin Co.

Lewis, A. C. (1995). An overview of the Standards Movement. *PDK* 76(10):745–750.

Madaus, G. E. (1988). The influence of testing on the curriculum. In L. N. Tanner (Ed.), *Critical issues in curriculum. Eighty-seventh yearbook of the National Society for the Study of Education, Part 1* (pp. 83–121). Chicago: The University of Chicago Press.

National Center for Education Statistics (1995). *Use of school choice.* Washington, DC: U.S. Department of Education ED1.336:SCH6.

National Commission on Excellence in Education. (1983). *A nation at risk.* Washington, DC: U.S. Department of Education.

National Commission on the Reform of Secondary Education. (1973). *The reform of secondary education.* New York: McGraw-Hill Book Co.

National Panel on High School and Adolescent Education. (1976). *The education of adolescents.* Washington, DC: U.S. Government Printing Office.

National Science Board Commission. (1983). *Educating Americans for the twenty-first century.* Washington, DC: National Science Foundation.

Panel on Youth of the President's Science Advisory Committee. (1974). *Youth: Transition to adulthood.* Chicago: The University of Chicago Press.

Pauley, E. (1991). *The classroom crucible.* New York: Basic Books.

Powell, A. G., Farrar, E., & Cohen, D. K. (1985). *The shopping mall high school.* Boston: Houghton-Mifflin Co.

Raywid, M. A. (1987, June). Public choice, yes; vouchers, no! *Phi Delta Kappan.* 68(10):762–69.

Ravitch, D. (1996). The case for national standards and assessment. *The Clearinghouse* 169(3): 134–135.

Report of the Central Advisory Council for Education. (1967). *Children and their primary schools.* London: Her Majesty's Stationary Office.

Rickover, H. G. (1959). *Education and freedom.* New York: E. P. Dutton and Co., Inc.

Selling the Schools. (1994, May 2). *U.S. News and World Report,* 61–65.

Silberman, C. E. (1970). *Crisis in the classroom.* New York: Random House.

Silberman, C. E. (1970a, June). How the public schools kill dreams and mutilate minds. *Atlantic Monthly, 226.*

Silberman, C. E. (1970b, July/August). Murder in the schoolroom. *Atlantic Monthly, 226.*

Silberman, C. E. (1973). *The open classroom reader.* New York: Random House.

Sizer, T. R. (1972). The case for a free market. In J. A. Mecklenburger & R. W. Hostrop (Eds.) *Education vouchers.* Homewood, IL: ETC Publications.

Sizer, T. R. (1984). *Horace's compromise.* Boston: Houghton-Mifflin Co.

Tanner, D. (1986). Are reforms like swinging pendulums? In H. J. Walberg & J. W. Keefe (Eds.) *Rethinking reform: The principal's dilemma.* Reston, VA: NASSP.

Tanner, D., & Tanner, L. (1995). *Curriculum development.* New York: Macmillan.

Task Force on Education for Economic Growth. (1983). *Action for excellence.* Washington, DC: Education Commission of the States.

U.S. Department of Education (1984). *A nation responds.* Washington, DC: Department of Education.

U.S. Department of Education. (1990). *America 2000.* Washington, DC: U.S. Department of Education.

Wagner, R. E. (1977). American education and the economics of caring. In J. S. Coleman (Ed.), *Parents, teachers and children.* San Francisco: Institute of Contemporary Studies.

West, E. G. (1984, Winter). Parental versus state goals in education. *Educational Theory, 34.* (1):81.

Williams, S. & Buechler, M. (1993). *Charter schools: Policy Bulletin.* Bloomington, IN: Indiana Education Policy Center.

Wise, A. E., & Darling-Hammond, L. (1984, Winter). Education by voucher: Private choice and the public interest. *Educational Theory, 34.* (1):29–53.

PART THREE

THE PRACTICE OF SCHOOLING

It is the office of the school environment to balance the various elements in the social environment, and to see to it that each individual gets an opportunity to escape from the limitations of the social group in which he was born, and to come into living contact with a broader environment.

John Dewey

9

**THE COMPREHENSIVE CONCEPT OF
AMERICAN EDUCATION**

Louis Algaze, a general science teacher in Miami, Florida, shows off the admiration of his students. As a science teacher, he is part of a curricular tradition dating back several decades. His responsibilities likely include offering course work designed for common, elective and advanced studies in science. His pedagogy likely reflects individual, social, academic and vocational priorities.

Schools in America have a mandate to offer a comprehensive curriculum. Yet many schools fail to offer a comprehensive curriculum. For instance, many high schools have closed wood and metal shops in favor of a more academic curriculum. What are the consequences of abandoning these "non-college" subjects? What if such studies returned and were required of all students, not just those not planning on college? A school that claims to offer comprehensive education must provide a broad range of learning experiences.

The American public school has always carried a heavy burden of responsibility. Its mandate has been inclusive of learning experiences that underscore the importance of personal, social, vocational, and intellectual growth, even though its curriculum has often been dominated by the intellectual obligations of an academic education. The public has always held the public school to a comprehensive charge. Today, for instance, publicly financed schools are expected to socialize the rising generation of youth in the principles of democracy; to instill in youth the skills of competence needed to advance the interests of business and industry; to play a direct role in the psychological, social, intellectual, and physical development of each child; to have a hand in curbing virtually every social ill that prevails in the society; and to be the ultimate weapon in the military defense of the nation.

The notion that popular education exists to serve society is, of course, not new. One could see these very connections being made centuries ago by prominent thinkers. In Plato's *Republic*, for instance, the very essence of a good society implied a set of educational policies and practices that would give life to the highest ideals of the society. To Plato, societies were not created by whim or accident but by a deliberate and conscious socialization process that occurred at the level of the community. In the early history of the United States, the core of Plato's idea was maintained and applied, at least at the level of rhetoric, to the popularization of the common public school (Cremin, 1965). To Thomas Jefferson, the universalization of public schooling was essential to the enlightenment of a vital citizenry. To his mind, there could be no democracy unless the upcoming generation had the skills of intelligence and the ethical conviction to preserve such a complex social arrangement. He believed that such a mission could only be carried out through the agency of mass public schooling.

285

American Versus European Traditions of Schooling

James Mitchner's celebratory description of American education focuses on the level of opportunity provided in American schools. Do you agree with him?

Let me summarize my attitude toward American education by explaining what one suffers when he talks with European critics. They badger him with observations like this: "Everyone knows that a high-school degree from France or Germany or Israel is superior to the average college degree in America. Professor Klumper taught at Upper Oklahoma State Teachers one year and told us that most of his students barely knew how to read."

I used to argue with such critics but have lately developed a different tactic. I confess everything: "You're right, the European high school does teach more than our second-class college. You're right, we do have students who can barely read. You're right, discipline in our schools is deplorable." And I admit to all other weaknesses. Only then do I make my point: "But you must not judge your system against ours because we're trying to do something never before attempted. We're trying to educate an entire people. For every young Frenchman or German who can wangle a place in one of your colleges, we provide places for seventeen young Americans. When we try to educate so many, some are bound to be poor risks, so naturally, if you compare your best students with our worst, your system is superior. But if you put your top against our top, ours do not suffer. And we produce seventeen times as many. Our gamble is to educate everyone who looks as if he could absorb an education, and that's why our society moves ahead. That's why we draw down so many more Nobel Prizes than our population would warrant."

Source: Mitchner, J. A. (1970). *The quality of life.* Philadelphia, PA: J. B. Lippencott Co. pp. 54–55.

This line of thought continued into the 19th century with the work of Horace Mann, who used his position of superintendent of schools in Massachusetts to make common schooling mandatory through the elementary grades (Butts, 1989), as well as with the work of Lester Ward (1883) and John Dewey (1916), who both held that schools were essential to building the dispositions, skills, and general insights needed to conduct a democratic community. Dewey (1916), in fact, observed that the role of the school was to provide an enlarging experience that went beyond the less encompassing nature of education in the home, church, and community. Under these circumstances, the school was framed in the broad role that it serves today. Thus, in a manner of speaking, one could see the concept of comprehensive schooling as an American tradition, though not one without its share of detractors (see the From the Editorial Page feature and Scholarly Voices feature in this section).

The question today is whether the public schools still need to carry the burdens of trying to be all things to all youth. Is it unreasonable and unworkable for the public school to fulfill simultaneous agendas in academic and vocational training, in citizenship education, in areas of self-satisfaction and self-realization, and in sundry community-related projects? Does the effort to be comprehensive lead to widespread compromises in vital intellectual and academic arenas? Is the historic purpose behind the comprehensive

Counts on the Genius of American Education

In this statement, George Counts discusses the difference between the old dual system of schooling and the single system. The unified or single system, he states, expresses the genius of the American people. What do you think he means by this?

> America transformed the dual educational system of the Old World into a single system. This achievement constitutes a major contribution to the evolution of educational institutions and to the growth of civilization. In no other social institution has the genius of the American people more fully expressed itself.

Source: Counts, G.S., (1926) The senior high school curriculum. Supplementary Educational Monographs, No. 29, Chicago, IL: University of Chicago, p. 1.

concept outdated? The answers to these questions are basic to fashioning the role of the school in the society and to framing the actions of the teacher in the classroom (see The Contemporary Debate feature on full-service schools).

 ## The Design of a Comprehensive School

The idea of educating all youth in one unified setting, as opposed to separate academic and vocational schools, has been fundamental to the history of schooling in the United States (Cremin, 1961; Wraga, 1993). This concept has led to the development of **the comprehensive high school,** a uniquely American invention that aims to offer a wide-ranging education to all youth. The curriculum of the comprehensive high school endeavors to provide an education in citizenship (common learnings), to offer elective and exploratory courses for individual improvement, and to support strong specialized programs for both academic and vocational learning. In the ideal, the comprehensive high school is designed to be an instrument of democracy, to militate against social stratification, and to be a place where all youth receive a well-rounded education. It has long come under attack by those who want to see the most intellectually able attend separate academic high schools (Bestor, 1953; Rickover, 1959).

In outlining the design of a comprehensive school, Tanner and Tanner (1995) pointed to four complementary functions in the organization of the curriculum. These include: 1) **general education,** otherwise known as common learnings; 2) **specialized education,** which deals with both specialized academic and vocational knowledge; 3) **exploratory and special interest education,** which is designed to meet and broaden individual interests; and 4) **enrichment education,** which aims to offer advanced course work for students with particular talents. The Tanners see these four functions as interacting in the center of the school, providing youth with opportunities to pursue personal, sociocivic, intellectual, and vocational goals.

What these four functions represent is a rationale for a school or classroom experience that goes beyond traditional models of academic education. Under such a rationale, academic education is not ignored but is supplemented with a broader curriculum strategy. For example, with such a

The Full-Service School

The ongoing debate on welfare and public assistance in the United States elicits a wide range of reactions. Social conservatives argue that programs should be dramatically cut. Liberals argue that children of the poor deserve help to improve their condition. However, everyone agrees that the system could be made more efficient. In addition, there is wide agreement that medical and social services should be accessible to those families who need them.

As it now stands, families with school-age children who require governmental assistance must negotiate a confusing patchwork of services that may be located at opposite ends of the city, have vastly different procedures, and often deliver overlapping programs. What if, instead, the family could schedule dental checkups and receive social services at the school where the children attend? Schools are the most common organized social setting in the United States. Schools, it seems, are everywhere.

The interdisciplinary approach, which places medical and social services in schools, is gaining attention as a way to cut costs and improve access. Social analysts suggest that if the schools served as the primary access point for medical and social services, needy families would be better served and costs could be trimmed. Several innovations are currently under way in several states. For instance, First, Curcio, and Young (1993) outline a New Jersey initiative in which a minimum of 30 schools will receive grants to establish full-service schools. In New Jersey's full-service schools, parents will be able to take parent training classes, receive mental health services, and even schedule a doctor's appointment for their children.

Although the concept of a full-service school is attractive to many educators, some believe that such schools compromise the educational mission of schools. Schools, they argue, are for teaching youth and should not, for example, be in the business of mental health services for adults. Nor, they argue, should families perceive the school as a social service agency. The general opposition to full-service schools is that they encourage in needy families an unhealthy dependence on public assistance. Proponents argue that full-service schools are needed to improve families' ability to provide for themselves. Keep watch on this debate, which will surely grow in the next decade.

What are your thoughts on this issue? What are the advantages and disadvantages of a full-service school? Would you like to work in such an environment?

Source: First, P. F., Curcio, J. L., & Young, D. L. (1993). State full-service school initiative: New notions of policy development. In L. Adler & S. Gardner (Eds.), The politics of linking schools and social services (pp. 63–64). Washington, DC: The Fulmer Press.

design there must be an effort made in the curriculum to offer youth opportunities to deal with social issues and problems related to their growth as citizens in a democracy. There must also be some effort made to fulfill the obligations inherent in the exploratory, special interest and enrichment functions of the curriculum, which are meant to reflect individual desires and needs in the school experience. These are not separate functions, but overlapping and complementary ones. Thus, exploratory courses could fulfill academic or vocational purposes, vocational courses could be merged with

The comprehensive school provides students with comprehensive opportunities.

sociocivic issues, academic course work could be fundamental to vocational programs, and so on.

These functions can be used to explain the concept of comprehensive schooling. Figure 9.1 provides one organizational picture of a school curriculum that aims to fulfill a comprehensive education mandate. The purpose of the diagram is to show how the school aims to fulfill simultaneous responsibilities over all the grade levels. In the elementary school, the relation between common learning and the academic curriculum should be flexible. The nature of academic learning need not be specialized in elementary school and should be free to broach vital social issues that can be dealt with through interdisciplinary units of teaching. Because there are influences even in the elementary school that militate against interdisciplinary forms of academic instruction, such a shift may not be as easy as it might seem. In the middle school, specialized studies and prevocational studies enter the picture, though in the case of the former, the course work that will apply to college admissions usually does not become a factor until the ninth grade. In the secondary school, interdisciplinary studies move into the common curriculum and specialized course work begins to apply to students as determined by their chosen academic or vocational program. The overlapping character of the curriculum should be stressed because, depending on the school, academic subjects can play a vital role in the education of certain broad vocational fields, while common learnings, though interdisciplinary in nature, can draw from certain vocational and academic studies.

The Comprehensive Needs of All Youth

The notion of a comprehensive curriculum is greatly served by articulating a basic perspective on what one expects from the school for the education of all youth. In other words, what should be the education goals for all youth in the American public schools? Interestingly, this question was answered directly

FIGURE 9.1

THE INTERACTIVE FUNCTIONS OF A COMPREHENSIVE CURRICULUM

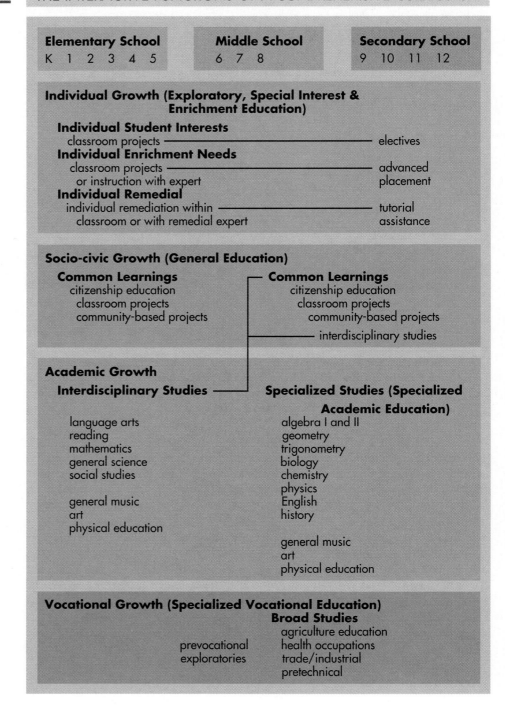

during earlier times in documents such as the Educational Policies Commission reports titled *Education for ALL American Youth* (1944) and *Education for ALL American Children* (1948). The effort at the time was to establish a foundation of objectives for all youth. To establish a working framework for a comprehensive education today, one could revisit this issue by asking exactly what skills and competencies all American youth need to manage their lives in a free society. The needs to be discussed in this section are adapted from *Education for ALL American Youth* (1944). With some exceptions, they apply generally to all ages and grade levels, though the time and resources devoted to each need will vary across grade levels. Exactly how each need might be developed will also differ across grade levels, classrooms, and schools. Each goal, with varying degrees of emphasis, has some role to play in the academic, social, vocational, and individual growth of the student.

The following is a list of essential education needs. It is offered as an initial attempt at identifying a comprehensive education for all American youth.

1. All youth need to be able to think rationally, to deal with persuasion deftly, to express written and verbal thoughts clearly, to learn how to question truth and common sense, and to understand and live with complexity and ambiguity.

2. All youth need to develop the skills of social tolerance and social cooperation and to grow in their understanding and use of ethical principles and values.

3. All youth need to understand the rights and duties of citizenship and to embrace democratic attitudes and values in their actions.

4. All youth need to develop a realistic sense of self-confidence and self-esteem and to understand their own inner selves.

5. All youth need to understand the communicative power of literature, art, and music and to appreciate the importance of aesthetics in life and nature.

6. All youth need to understand the role of science in relation to contemporary society, to be aware of the limitations of scientific thought, and to understand the basic scientific knowledge related to humankind and the environment.

7. All youth need to develop the skills and understandings needed to become productive and critically minded workers.

8. All youth need to have a critical understanding of a capitalist economy and of the skills needed to be an intelligent consumer of goods and services.

9. All youth need to develop and maintain good health and physical fitness.

10. All youth need to command the fundamental processes of reading, writing, and arithmetic.

The remainder of this chapter will examine how the comprehensive objectives discussed here can be integrated into a design that accounts for individual, sociocivic, academic, and vocational growth. In the Appendix following Chapter 11, the 10 needs of youth are cross-referenced against the 4 curriculum functions, highlighting points of emphasis for each function.

🐦 *Individual Growth*

The individual aspects of the school curriculum should emphasize the development of individual responsibility, seek to cultivate individual talents and skills, aim at assisting youth in their emotional, cognitive, and physical

WEB POINTS

ERIC

Perhaps the most comprehensive web site for classroom teachers is the AskERIC page developed by the Educational Resources Information Center (ERIC). The main address is

http://ericir.syr.edu/

but many links to other resources are also available. For example, the key areas include ERIC's Lesson Plan archive. This link provides the browser with access to several hundred lesson plans created by teachers across the United States.

Another important link allows the browser to conduct ERIC searches of research over the web. For instance, a search using the key term "cooperative learning" will yield hundreds of study citations along with an abstract of each study. Of course, the full text of the articles must be found in the original journals. This feature makes searching much easier.

Also included in the ERIC web site are links to other ERIC documents, some of which are full-text articles on important topics in education. In addition, the site also offers a question and answer service where browsers can inquire about education-related resources and receive an answer through e-mail from one of ERIC's on-line professionals.

The ERIC main web site has won many awards from various Internet reviewers and may prove to be the best location for practicing educators.

A Pocket Guide to ERIC

What is ERIC?

The Educational Resources Information Center (ERIC) is a national information system designed to provide users with ready access to an extensive body of education-related literature. Established in 1966, ERIC is supported by the U.S. Department of Education, Office of Educational Research and Improvement.

The ERIC database, the world's largest source of education information, contains over 850,000 abstracts of documents and journal articles on education research and practice. This information is available to you at about 3,000 locations worldwide.

You can access the ERIC database online, on CD-ROM, through the printed abstract journals, Resources in Education and Current Index to Journals in Education, or through cumulated microfiche indexes. The database is updated monthly (quarterly on CD-ROM), ensuring that the information you receive is timely and accurate.

—Continued

development, and generally serve the objectives of self-understanding and self-expression.

Individual goals in the curriculum typically stress the differences between youth for the purpose of instructionally targeting individual uniquenesses. For instance, where there are assumed differences in specific skills and talents, the school might provide special curriculum options, such as advanced placement courses, various enrichment offerings, or remedial course work. Various personal preferences could lead to extra-classroom experiences (school clubs or cooperative initiatives with community-based agencies) or to a more formal display of elective studies devoted to advancing individualistic goals.

The following section will deal with individual or personal goals that need to be broached in the school curriculum. Outlining the manner in which the individual phase of the curriculum can be structured in the school and the classroom is also included.

Individual Growth and the Curriculum

Attending to the particularities of children is what individualization in the curriculum is all about. Individualization is supposed to pertain not only to how one teaches but also, commonly, to what one teaches. Many initiatives in the individualization of learning are centered only on the instructional question of how to teach. This might lead to pacing differences or to differences in the structure of the teaching strategy (as influenced by, say, developmental processes or by an understanding of multiple forms of intelligence). But individualization should deal with more than purely instructional strategies and should support a differential approach pertaining not only to how certain things are taught but also to what is taught. This could have bad effects in the curriculum, not unlike those documented by Oakes in her research on tracking, but it could also lead to very vital and healthy instructional practices. What cannot be denied is the need for some phase of the classroom or curriculum to be dedicated to the exploration of personal abilities and individual interest and to the pursuit and further development of particular talents.

The Individualized Phase of the Curriculum

Most schools make some effort to represent individual interests in the design of their curriculum. In most elementary schools, individualization is the responsibility of a teacher who tries to find some way to deal with individual concerns within a self-contained classroom, although it is not unusual to find pullout programs for remedial education or for the education of the so-called gifted and talented. At the middle and high school levels, however, individualization usually takes shape through systematically designed course work that might be promoted as elective study, advanced placement, or remedial/foundations education. Classroom teachers, of course, continue to do their part as well.

In the classroom, individualization can be accomplished through individual and group projects and through various extra-classroom activities. All this means is that certain students will have the opportunity to participate in certain projects on their own (or in some small groups) for the purpose of pursuing a question or an interest that they personally find worthwhile. The teacher, of course, has to spark this initiative by providing possibilities and options for extended and exploratory education. Ideas for a project can occur spontaneously from the students, but most projects should be deliberately designed in the classroom as opportunities to pursue issues raised in the classroom and as opportunities to develop new interests.

A teacher might, for example, list ways to extend and further develop interests related to the classroom. To the mathematics educator, this might mean getting students involved in a math club or in other extra-classroom initiatives requiring numeracy. In high school, extra-classroom activities or even classroom-based activities such as a schoolwide group dedicated to polling student views on various social issues, a consumer advocacy group interested in discerning the best local buys for various items typically purchased by students, or a computer group interested in exploring fractals could all be possibilities for cultivating student interest in mathematics. If a student shows a particular aptitude and keen interest in highly advanced mathematics, the teacher's role is usually limited, but curriculum options for elective study or study outside the school should be available.

To the elementary school teacher, the idea of grooming and initiating student interests is usually broader than it might be to a subject-centered high school teacher. It might include a desire to involve students in group activities, such as choral singing, dramatics, student government, and community-outreach programs. It might also be related to the desire to instill in each student a passion for recreational reading, an intrinsic desire to pursue intellectual problems in various academic areas, or an interest in various school or community-based problems.

Time can be reserved each day for an individualized program of studies related to a student's own interests. During this period, small groups might meet to work on their projects, some individuals might go to the library to conduct research, other students might sit with their favorite books for a quiet reading session, and yet others might pursue an interest in an area like computers.

It should be stressed, however, that a classroom period devoted to individual interests does not translate into a laissez-faire "do-your-own-thing" classroom climate. The teacher must be an active participant in each student's work and should have a fundamental sense of what each student intends to do during these sessions. This could be accomplished by requiring all projects to be approved before they can be pursued in class and by establishing a list of generic activities that all students could do during the so-called individual period. Each individual period might, for example, allow any reasonable number of children to read or research in the library (or another quiet area), to read the local newspaper and associated magazines for children, to work in the computer lab or on classroom computers, or to work on approved ongoing projects.

This should also be a time when students with particular talents and aptitudes might arrange for special instruction outside the classroom. A child with particular gifts in the visual arts might arrange to work with the art teacher during this period; children with an aptitude for writing, when not using this time to work on their short stories or other writing projects, could arrange for opportunities to read their work to other classrooms. At the high school level, these concerns need to be broached through advanced place-

A child's success in school depends greatly on lessons learned outside the school.

ment courses, though the same type of classroom-based opportunities should be available in the secondary school as well.

It is important for all teachers to realize that the role of individualizing the curriculum is designed not only for students to pursue preexisting interests, which is undoubtedly important, but also for students to widen and explore new interests. Thus, educators should try to keep an inventory of what each student is doing in the individualized phase of the curriculum. It is probably not in the student's interest to devote all his time to one area of interest during the course of an academic year. A student who only works on the computer, or who only reads to herself all the time, needs to be encouraged, if not required, to widen her areas or bases of participation.

It is also important to stress that concerns over individualization need not always be reserved for a period devoted to such concerns. Students typically will have time in school when their work in the other phases of the curriculum is completed or is made an optional homework assignment. In such a situation, students should be allowed and encouraged to pursue other projects and assignments, including those often reserved for the "individual interest" period. Often, teachers do not have the luxury of isolating a period devoted to individual interests, thereby forcing such projects to be conducted between the time spaces of other classroom-based experiences or during times outside the classroom. Also, some elementary school teachers no longer work in self-contained settings where they are expected to teach all the broad subject areas. Even departmentalized elementary school teachers, however, should aim to develop an individualized component in the curriculum that deals with the convergence of student interest upon their particular subject area. Table 9.1 itemizes some activities that might play a central role in the individualized phase of the curriculum.

TABLE 9.1	INDIVIDUAL GROWTH AND THE CURRICULUM

Curricular Objective

To provide the experiences that attend to individual interests, individual enrichment needs, and individual remedial needs

Potential Activities

A. Library research related to any topic, interest, or pending school assignment.
B. Recreational reading, which might include the daily newspaper, various magazines, or any book of interest.
C. Ongoing individual or small group projects. Examples might include the following. Right Writers: A Standing Student Editing Committee (Language Arts); Problems in Our School: An Advisory Committee to the Student Government and the Principal (Social Studies); The Hazards of Smoking: A Report to the Classroom and School (Science); The Poetry of Me: Ways of Showing Who I Am (Language Arts).
D. Hobby or club activity that reflects student interests.
E. Advanced study in an area in which the student shows a strong aptitude. Most likely, the student will need to have an experience by arrangement with an expert in a particular area.
F. Remedial assistance within the classroom in a particular area or with a particular skill or outside the classroom with a remedial expert.

Instructional Methodology and the Nature of the Learner

Individualization exists to deal with personal and unique interests and to expand the horizons of interest and skill of each student. It also is a reminder of the need for all educational decisions to be responsive to the nature of the individual learner. Teachers have much to gain not only by getting a sense of the learner's interests and concerns but also by having a fundamental idea of maturational growth, learning style, cultural background, and other personal characteristics. When teachers abide by these priorities, they are more inclined to see schooling as an agency that is not restricted to the development or command of facts and skills associated with basic literacy and subject-matter competence. Teachers ignore attitudes, student character, developmental factors, and the like at the expense of their own teaching and ultimately at the expense of the education of the child. To know the nature of the learner is to commit oneself to the education of the whole child—accounting for attitudes, skills, behaviors, strengths, weaknesses, maturation, and overall personality.

In recent years, researchers have offered new conceptions about intelligence and learning to assist the teacher's chances of educating the whole child. The work of Howard Gardner (1983), for instance, has allowed teachers and administrators to expand their notions of intelligence to include actions and processes not typically situated in traditional versions of intelligence. These include a range of intelligences that accounts for linguistic, musical, logical-mathematical, spatial, bodily kinesthetic, interpersonal, and intrapersonal competence. This is important because it puts a broad scope of intelligence on an equal ground, which in turn points to the need for schools to attend to all the abilities implied by these multiple intelligences, as opposed to the linguistic and mathematical traditions that are typically stressed in the schools.

Howard Gardner's work reminds educators that children and youth have abilities beyond reading, writing, and mathematics. Musical abilities, along with interpersonal skills, must also be nourished.

This new range of intelligence also presents new possibilities in the individualized curriculum by calling for new contexts or learning environments that are expressly designed to be responsive to the formation of intelligence embodied in each individual. Although it would be impossible and arguably undesirable to design a specific environment for each child in all phases of the curriculum, programs situated in the individualized component of the curriculum can easily gear their efforts to the specific intelligence of a child. Thus, in the remedial or enrichment setting, teachers can target their instruction to the particular skills of intelligence held by the student. To a student with a high degree of spatial intelligence, for instance, there would likely be many new ways to go about the teaching of reading or the teaching of any skill or competence required in the curriculum.

Similarly, some work has been done to reveal the so-called learning styles of human beings. The idea behind this is to help teachers to complement their own instruction with materials and tactics attuned to an individual's learning style. Torrence and Rockenstein (1988), for instance, have been able to associate learning strengths with brain hemisphericity. They assert that persons with "right brain" dominance are inclined to have skills in nonverbal, spatial, analogic, creative, and aesthetic functions, while those with "left brain" dominance are predisposed to have skills in logical activities, language, and linear thought. Exploring the "learning styles" literature to get a basic grasp of the various cognitive styles can help in the development of instructional methods.

There are dangers in developing the abilities inherent in one learning style at the expense of the abilities inherent in another. To be sure, traditional teaching typically stresses logical and sequential problem-solving activities, with which "left-brain" dominant persons are presumably most comfortable. Such a bias obviously points to the need to represent right-brain styles of thinking. A learning-style assessment, however, should never lead to the pigeonholing of a student's learning style. Both the dominance and the nondominance of certain thinking styles in a student can be used to justify certain teaching methods. A particular learning style can and should be tapped to assist in problematic and individualistic situations, but all children should encounter a variety of learning styles and strategies.

 ## *Sociocivic Growth*

Public schools have long been viewed as fundamental agencies in the social development of children. Most public schools, after all, try to stress the highest ideals of the society in their policy and in their practice. They may be utterly inadequate in fulfilling such ideals and may be committed to the values and aims of the society in word only, but most schools believe that they are carrying out, in one way or another, a sociocivic mandate. In recent years, however, this aspect of the school curriculum has been dealt with rather dismally in the practice of teaching. Often the mission of sociocivic learning has been relegated to extra-classroom experiences and to the belief that sociocivic issues are served naturally in the ebb and flow of school life (i.e., team sports, classroom and cafeteria conversations). In a democracy, the public schools need consciously to abide by civic virtues like social responsibility, cooperation, tolerance, and equity, preferably within a social context that is characteristic of the society's population. Schools should support experiences that promote the development of interpersonal relations that speak directly to the roles and responsibilities of democratic citizenship, that enculturate the student population into a common heritage (without extinguishing the diversity inherent to this heritage), and that teach students to develop a critical moral perspective on their conduct.

The Neglect of Civic Education

Measuring or otherwise understanding the civic skills of American youth has not been a very popular line of inquiry for educational researchers. The National Assessment of Educational Progress, for instance, has labored mightily to perform exhaustive and ongoing gauges of math and reading performance in American schools, but has only taken a sporadic interest in civic knowledge. Very few studies are currently available on topics related to the sociocivic function of schooling. Research on the democratic attitudes of children, on their knowledge of politics and government, their skills as citizens and their general levels of civic consciousness have not been at the top of the research agenda. Few public schools take an interest in evaluating students in these areas.

Part of the problem is that civic education is struggling for identification in the school curriculum. It surfaces in the high school within history, social studies or government courses, and finds its way through various outlets in the elementary and middle schools, but it has not gotten the kind of attention that it demands in a comprehensive schooling framework.

The last NAEP assessment of civic knowledge was published in 1990 and was based on 1988 data. As is NAEP's tradition, students in the fourth, eighth, and twelfth grades were tested. The principal findings are subject to wide interpretation but are generally less than encouraging. The NAEP assessment design identified four criterion levels of civic knowledge. The rudimentary 200 level (Recognizes the Existence of Civic Life) shows that students can discern the types of services provided by the government and understand some basic rules of law and some of the basic rights provided to individuals. The intermediate 250 level (Understands the Nature Political Institutions and the Relationship Between Citizen and Government) shows that students are aware of particular democratic rights, such as freedom of speech, the right to a fair trial, the right to be treated equally and so on. Students at this level can also command basic civic vocabulary, knowing the definition and general usage of words such as legislation, governor, and constitutional right. The advanced 300 level (Understands Government Structure and Functions) shows that students have a knowledge of the structures and functions of government and have a nuanced understanding of the various principles underlying American government, such as separation of powers. Finally, the most advanced 350 level (Understands a Variety of Political Institutions and Processes) shows that students have a complex understanding of government. They know, for instance, the subtleties of governmental processes, have a historical basis of government understanding, and can apply or transfer knowledge of civics to problem contexts (Anderson & other, 1990).

Table 9.2 outlines the results of the NAEP assessment along these four levels. The age-appropriate level for fourth grade is about the 200 level, yet almost 30% of fourth graders did not meet the achievement index for this level. Similarly, less than half of eighth graders scored at their appropriate

TABLE 9.2

PERCENTAGE OF STUDENT SCORING AT EACH OF THE LEVELS OF CIVIC UNDERSTANDING BY GRADE, 1988			
	4th grade	**8th grade**	**12th grade**
200 level Recognizes the Existence of Civic Life	71.2	94.4	96.8
250 level Understands the Nature of Political Institutions and the Relationship Between Citizen and Government	9.6	61.4	89.2
300 level Understands Government Structure and Functions	.1	12.7	49
350 level Understands a Variety of Political Institutions and Processes	0	.3	6

Source: Anderson, L. (1990). *The civics report card.* Washington, DC: U.S. Department of Education.

age-level. Thirty-eight percent of eighth graders, for instance, did not know that Congress makes laws and more than half didn't know the meaning of the "separation of powers." Not even half the seniors in high school could achieve the index for the 300 level. About one half, for instance, did not recognize the presidential veto, the Congressional override, or Supreme Court decisions as examples of the federal system of checks and balances. Only a select few (6%) could achieve the 350 level.

When one couples these finding with other gauges of civic knowledge and civic action, one could argue that the sociocivic function of schooling has fallen into deep neglect. Census Bureau data show that in 1992, only 53% of all citizens between the ages of 18 and 20 were registered to vote and that only 42% of those registered actually voted (People for the American Way, 1992). The Center for Civic Education has surveyed civic knowledge among adults and found some signs of an uninformed public. Only one third of adults, for example, knew that the Bill of Rights was the first ten amendments to the Constitution and about one third believed that the purpose of the U.S. Constitution was to declare independence from England. Surveys gauging the participation of youth in community service show that less than half of high school seniors performed any unpaid community service during the 1990–1992 period. This includes service that was both required and voluntary. If one limits the participation rate to just voluntary service, only 33% of public school seniors were involved. Half of the seniors reporting to be involved in community service were connected to church-related activities and events, showing perhaps the influence of the church rather than the school in the area of community service. Students in parochial schools, particularly Catholic parochial schools, were much more likely to perform required service activities than public school youth (NCES, 1995).

The course taking pattern and the actual topics covered in civic education also indicate that the sociocivic learning of schooling has been slighted. In fourth grade social studies classes, 23% of students reported never being exposed to topics dealing with the rights and responsibilities of citizenship; 34% were never exposed to topics dealing with elections and voting, and 12% were never exposed to topics dealing with their community. In the eighth and twelfth grades, the exposure levels improved but 27% of eighth graders reported never being exposed to topics dealing with the principles of government and 20% were never exposed to topics dealing with other forms of government. Table 9.3 displays the exposure levels to various topics relevant to the sociocivic function of schooling. These data show that the sociocivic purpose of school education is certainly not enjoying the notice that is accorded in the design of a comprehensive school.

Concern over the rather incoherent and inconsistent status of civic education in the school curriculum has moved some groups to design and develop curriculum standards for civic education. By setting national parameters for what should be taught and what should be known in the area of civics education, groups such as the Center for Civic Education (1991) and The National Council for the Social Studies (1994) hope to rehabilitate the place and the influence of civic learning in public education. The most comprehensive effort to date at setting civic education standards was completed by the Center for Civic Education and published in a document titled *Civitas*. Although the document makes no endorsement of general education per se, it does plow the ground for civic education by outlining a framework

TABLE 9.3

TOPICS COVERED IN CIVIC EDUCATION IN GRADES 8 AND 12, 1988.

Percentage of students responding to the following: "How much have you studied the following topics in American government or civics?"

		A LOT	SOME	NONE
U.S. Constitution	8th	55.7	39.9	4.4
	12th	55.0	42.5	2.5
Congress	8th	41.7	42.5	7.9
	12th	45.3	50.8	3.9
How Laws Are Made	8th	38.2	51.8	10.0
	12th	42.6	52.6	4.7
Court System	8th	29.6	52.7	17.6
	12th	38.8	55.0	6.2
President & Cabinet	8th	39.3	48.5	12.2
	12th	39.6	55.8	4.6
Political Parties, Elections & Voting	8th	44.3	46.9	8.8
	12th	45.0	51.1	3.9
State & Local Government	8th	30.0	55.0	15.0
	12th	36.4	57.4	6.2
Principles of Democratic Government	8th	20.4	52.2	27.5
	12th	32.0	59.2	8.8
Other Forms of Government	8th	20.5	59.5	20.0
	12th	26.2	66.2	7.6
Rights & Responsibilities of Citizenship	8th	42.8	44.7	12.5
	12th	44.6	50.6	4.8

Source: Anderson, L. (1990). *The civics report card.* Washington, D.C.: U.S. Department of Education, p. 79.

that is both extensive (ranging from elementary to high school education) and specific to particular grade levels.

Citizenship and the Common Curriculum

As indicated, in high school, citizenship education is often seen as belonging to the disciplines of social studies and history or to extra-classroom activities like student government. In lower schools, it is believed to be served by interactions in the classroom, in the lunchroom, and on the playground. Few schools devote an actual block of time to citizenship education.

If one considers citizenship education in more deliberate terms, a basic agreement on its objectives has to be negotiated. The following are some possibilities. First, citizenship education needs to center directly on under-standing and interpreting constitutional rights and liberties. This means that youth should not only have a basic grasp of the tenets in the Constitution and the Bill of Rights, but they should also have an operational idea of how these rights and liberties have been interpreted and how they apply to one's own actions and attitudes. Citizenship education also needs to deal with current social problems (crime, the environment, economic conditions, social injus-tice, and all forms of social tensions and disaffection) and should be con-ducted in a climate that models democratic attitudes and principles. It must be required of all students and be organized instructionally with heterogeneous groups. It must also develop skills of political and community action and offer a forum for ongoing conversation and public debate. Furthermore, citizenship education should cultivate critics of the state, whose loyalties are with the causes of democracy.

This is obviously a tall order for any single course or for a single discipline or broad field like social studies. The idea of citizenship education, at nearly all levels, is probably best realized in a common curriculum arrangement. The common curriculum of the school, which has been frequently equated with a liberal arts education for all youth, could be conceived as the ground where issues common to youth are examined and where the pervading problems of the society are probed. Its purpose is expressly civic in orientation. It is not beholden to any discipline and is usually organized through integrated schemes because the kinds of problems that are the focus in common learnings typically transcend traditional subject-matter lines.

Over the years, the idea of common learning has been in and out of favor with school leaders. During the progressive period after World War II, the notion of general education was held in great esteem in the educational literature. The well-known Educational Policies Commission report *Education for ALL American Youth* (1944) stressed the significance of common learnings by highlighting a comprehensive range of needs that applied to the education of all youth and by describing how these needs might be integrated into the design of the curriculum. The concept advanced in the commission report was dedicated to the idea of helping students develop personal and social competencies in areas like consumer economics, family and community life, aesthetics, health, leisure, scientific understanding, ethical values, and democratic citizenship, the very same elements that went into the earlier description of learner needs. One third of the entire secondary school curriculum was organized along these lines, which, as provinces of common learnings, were justified as fundamental areas of proficiency for democratic living. The emphasis on citizenship competencies was a signal theme in the progressive educational thought of the time and was supported in some practical settings, including the curriculum frameworks of various experimental schools.

Another notable statement on common learnings popularized during the post–World War II period was the Harvard report *General Education in a Free Society* (1945). The report shared a kinship with *Education for ALL American Youth* by promoting a general education program attuned to the contemporary needs of the young citizen. The Harvard report, however, departed from the progressive tradition of general education by preserving an academic subject curriculum (while asking teachers to provide interdisciplinary connections in their respective classrooms) and by allowing ability groups to be constituted in the general education curriculum. These provisos violated the citizenship focus that is basic to common learnings.

During the two decades following the release of the Educational Policies Commission and the Harvard Committee reports, the idea of common learnings lost much of its support. The emergence of the cold war and the increasing effort to use the school as an instrument in the space race curtailed the common learnings function of the curriculum and overemphasized the specialized function of the curriculum (which was tied to the nationalistic urge to produce more scientists, mathematicians, and engineers). During the cold war, school critics like Bestor (1953) and Rickover (1959) sought to alter schooling in the United States by recasting it in the image of the dual system model used in Europe. Both Bestor and Rickover wanted the American public schools to embrace a separate system of schooling that routed the vast majority of children into apprentice and vocational programs at a young age, while keeping the remaining few in academic schools that eventually led to enrollment in college. Under such conditions, common learnings would, of course, be quite impossible, except perhaps at the earliest grade levels, and the entire ideal of comprehensive education, which is so unique to the American schools, would be lost to a fragmented and separate system.

The cold war, however, was only the beginning of a long slide for common learnings in the curriculum. During the humanizing initiatives of the late 1960s, common learnings remained a distant idea, overwhelmed by the high regard placed on the design of school alternatives. The prevailing belief was that the public schools were entirely too bland and too closely wedded to a traditional rote and recitation model of teaching and learning. School alternatives and school variety became the darlings of the day. This left the common curriculum as an optional factor in the plans of a school curriculum. The comprehensive notion of schooling, in fact, was on equal ground with all other potential school alternatives.

The Common Curriculum in Practice

The common phase of the curriculum is not intended to provide an academic education in the specialized disciplines; nor is it intended to deal exclusively with areas of inquiry related to individual interest. The common curriculum is decidedly civic in orientation, meaning that it deals with those issues related most closely to the development of the citizen.

How does one operationalize common learnings throughout the grades? What might the common curriculum look like in an elementary, a middle, or a secondary school, and how might it be operationalized in a school long accustomed to departmentalized subject-area requirements?

One could argue that at the elementary school level, virtually all the curriculum should be devoted to common learnings. Important fundamental skills in reading, writing, communicating, thinking, and calculating can be dealt with in a common learnings context; subject-matter departmentalization would be obviated in the interests of advancing interdisciplinary schemes. Given the high priority placed on academic learning these days, however, it is not likely that many teachers, principals, or parents would likely embrace a common learnings block, organized along social focal points, to fulfill the perceived needs to teach the traditional disciplines. Academic features (mathematics, science, reading, and so on) can, of course, be treated substantively in such an arrangement, but many state and district curriculum content guidelines call for a more direct and departmentalized treatment of the subject.

At all grade levels, common learnings are best accomplished by putting an entire block of time aside for common learning experiences. In the earliest grades, the basic issues would relate to family and school community; at later grades, the focus would expand to include neighborhood, town, city, and state issues. Eventually wider societal issues could be integrated. In some schools, such a block might be justified as social studies. Although the label is less important than the idea of conducting common learnings, it should be clear that common learnings are not social studies in the formal sense because the curriculum is not influenced by content guidelines in the social studies but by emerging problems and issues related to the children's school, community, and society.

Depending on the organizational structure of the school curriculum, elementary teachers can operationalize common learnings in any number of ways. The first step would be to recognize a time in the classroom schedule that deals specifically with sociocivic issues in the school and community. During the common learnings session, for instance, children in first grade could be taught a unit on the people who provide important services to their homes, neighborhood, and town; in third grade, the session can be used to prepare a formal presentation of a news hour that deals with vital social concerns in the school and community; in later grades, students might use the period to develop a monthly classroom newsletter, to invite guests from the community in for discussion, to prepare interview questions to be asked of authorities in the community or to prepare survey questions to be asked of students, to engage in letter-writing campaigns to public officials, or to develop a series of occasional reports that deal with issues like AIDS, propaganda in advertising, the gun-control debate, or more local matters such as how to curb graffiti in the neighborhood.

Each of these initiatives is difficult to contain in subject areas; however, depending on the project, vital subject-area skills in reading, language arts, social studies, and science are developed. Thus, common learnings can also be organized along subject-area streams that each raise sociocivic questions. The science stream in elementary school, for instance, can have a series of units dealing with environmental concerns, with health and nutrition issues, or with issues of technology; the social studies stream might deal systematically with current events, with upcoming election-year voter decisions, or with a direct treatment of the Constitution and the Bill of Rights; mathematics might lead to a classroom or school store, a treatment of consumer issues, or an economic analysis of the sports industry; language arts might keep its activities aimed at ongoing correspondence with a wide range of pen pals across the country or the world, or at the analysis of language used in advertising, campaigning, or newspaper writing. One can see how common learnings, at least in the elementary school, could replace the more traditional arrangement of subject-area treatment in the curriculum.

Common learnings, of course, do not always call for large group meetings. Some common learnings mandates can be fulfilled with a series of smaller groups that devote themselves to the analysis of various issues. One could easily conceive of a four- to seven-member team making mathematical analyses of how much water is wasted in a typical household in the community (showing through extrapolation cumulative effects), or a team working on an artistic depiction of the cultures represented in the school, or yet another team studying a social problem, such as the care of the aged in the society, that might move them to engage in actions that assist the local senior citizen community.

The community-based facet of common learnings is also quite important. Local problems should, of course, be studied in the classroom through reading, library work, and discussions with peers, but they should also, where possible, be viewed through the lens of a volunteer service organization. Students in high school and middle school might get involved in a study of the quality of life for young children in their community. Based on their studies, the students might state their findings and views to local politicians and

These students are presented with a common learning opportunity, although each one will likely have a different interpretation of the book.

media sources, as well as offer their services to local recreational agencies or to organizations that care for children in need (i.e., battered children or homeless children). Students in elementary schools might find a way to work (with their parents and teachers) on local recycling projects, local food drives, local civic events, and other experiences that aim to assist people in need and that aim to improve the civic life of the community.

One could see that common learnings have a character unlike any other facet of the curriculum. Common learnings are expressly civic in orientation and interdisciplinary in their subject- or content-area makeup. Because of this orientation, many elementary schools are not comfortable with using common learnings to cover the required content areas of the traditional disciplines or subject areas. At the high school, the need to offer students an education in academic areas that is highly specialized and technical would likely make the common curriculum the only place where interdisciplinary studies are conducted. Table 9.4 expresses the instructional possibilities of common learnings in the school.

Academic Growth

Academic growth concerns in the curriculum are most often associated with college entrance demands in middle school and high school and with basic intellectual competencies in elementary schools. Academic priorities are also usually related to the development of thinking skills, which includes skills of inquiry, logic and evaluation, skills of literacy and numeracy, and knowledge in the traditional disciplines. Historically, the academic function of the curriculum has valued specialized knowledge and has been organized along rather strict subject-centered lines. In the high school, this has led to a traditional menu of course work that has covered a discipline-centered knowledge base. In the elementary school, the same type of content has been

TABLE 9.4   SOCIOCIVIC GROWTH AND THE CURRICULUM

Curricular Objective

To provide experiences that deal with sociocivic problems and issues for the purposes of developing social insight and democratic competence

Potential Activities

A. Large classroom initiatives dedicated to examining sociocivic issues. Examples might include classwide letter-writing campaigns to public officials; a classroom store; a monthly preparation of a classroom newsletter; a semester-long preparation of a show dramatizing the problems of the community or society; a collective art mural representing the dynamic dimensions of the community; or a classwide examination and discussion of emerging issues like censorship in the local library or the debate over gun control.

B. Small-group initiatives dedicated to developing an occasional report on an emerging issue. At elementary school levels, topics might include bicycle safety, environmental conservation, the hazards of smoking, or the economy of illicit drug sales. In middle school or high school, topics can deal with sex, the censorship of various materials in the community, the sexist and violent lyrics used in some popular music, the abortion debate, or upcoming election-year decisions.

C. Community-based initiatives that study local problems through the lens of voluntary service organizations. Youth can get involved in service opportunities that aid children (home for battered/homeless children), the aged, and the poor, as well as in projects that aim at civic and cultural enhancement. The idea is not only to participate in the agency but to only become well-versed with the very issues and problems that the agency is committed to improving.

in place, as students jump from mathematics lessons to science lessons to reading lessons and so on. At all levels, academic concerns have been the most dominant concerns in the curriculum.

The Doctrine of Mental Discipline Revisited

Before the turn of the century, the learning doctrine most dominant in the classroom maintained that certain subjects had the intrinsic qualities to strengthen the intellectual potency of the mind. Such a view, known as the doctrine of mental discipline, was wedded to a concept of curriculum that equated learning with knowledge acquisition in an essential body of prescribed subject matter (Kliebard, 1986). The idea was that learning proceeded through an interaction with certain studies believed to be uniquely endowed with the powers to exercise the mind. This view was built on a psychological theory that detailed the landscape of the mind into a series of mental faculties that were waiting to be invigorated by instructional exercises in a select number of disciplines. It was also perpetuated by a conservative philosophical tradition that aimed to use the academic disciplines to transmit the cultural heritage of the society and to keep the school focused on the all-inclusive task of cultivating the rational faculties of the mind.

The biases inherent in the doctrine of mental discipline prejudice certain studies over others, with the effect of giving low priority to the modern social sciences, interdisciplinary subject areas, vocational education, physical education, aesthetics, and other "nonacademic" pursuits. The elevation of certain subjects to the status of being intellective places all other studies in an anti-intellectual position, which itself perpetuates a rather narrow view of what is worthy in the school curriculum.

Over the years, the doctrine of mental discipline has been defrocked in the literature. Studies conducted by Thorndike and others decades ago and verifying studies conducted throughout the century have made it clear that no particular subject has a hold on intellectual development (Tanner & Tanner, 1990). The work conducted by Ralph Tyler in the Eight Year Study also made it clear that traditional academic subjects do not have a superior effect in the development of intelligence. Tyler's evaluation showed that success in college, as measured on academic and social variables, was not dependent on high school achievement in the traditional subject areas but was more powerfully associated with experimental curriculum initiatives marked by an unconventional or antitraditional nature. (Aikin, 1942) There is simply no validity to the belief that certain academic subjects hold intellectual sway over the growth and development of mental faculties like memory, reasoning, and imagination.

Enthroning the Academic Curriculum

In most schools, no facet of the school curriculum is given more attention and more resources than academic studies. State competencies, textbook design, and standard testing each contribute to a climate that gives very high authority to academic curriculum objectives. In the high school, they are often represented as core graduation requirements that simultaneously act as the required course work for admission to an institution of higher education. Throughout the grade levels, academic concerns influence the nature of standardized testing, textbook design, and curriculum development strategies.

Several commentators have reported on the academic nature of the American school curriculum and have characterized it as a highly mechanical and discipline-centered arrangement of studies. Goodlad (1984), for instance, has argued that the instructional treatment of the academic curriculum has been preoccupied with lower intellectual processes. Under these conditions, there is a general failure to see the connection between the subject matter and relevant personal and social concerns. What often occurs in the classroom instead is a highly discipline-centered treatment of the subject matter in which the teacher stakes the lesson to the goal of simple fact accumulation and subject mastery. The subject matter itself, organized often in the most abstract and puristic terms, becomes the curriculum; maneuvering through it with effective instructional procedures becomes the teacher's main concern. The result is not dissimilar to what Friere (1973) called "banking education", where teacher narration gives students a base of academic content, foreign to the needs of the learner and the society, that is uncritically received, memorized, and repeated by them. Under such conditions, students are perceived to be the passive recipients of a narrative curriculum content.

Goodlad's national study of American schooling, which provided a glimpse into the American classroom, lends some support to Friere's description of banking education. Goodlad found, for instance, that in many subject areas, the teaching techniques had a narrative and mechanical character driven by the desire to "deposit" an accumulation of facts and generalizations into the student. In the teaching of social studies, for instance, most classroom activity involved rote and recitation approaches to memorizing the facts; in language arts, the focus was fixed on the mechanics of word recognition, phonics, vocabulary development, and the basics of grammar.

Across all subject areas, Goodlad found that a rather traditional teacher lecture format, pitched to a low level of intellectual challenge, was standard operating procedure in the classroom. When the teacher was not lecturing, Goodlad found that students busied themselves with relatively narrow and unsophisticated levels of individual seatwork.

Part of this failure to abide by a wide curriculum vision in many of today's schools might have something to do with the contemporary restoration of the conservative argument against common and comprehensive public schools. For those supporting the conservative position, the reform of the public schools is believed to be dependent on retracting the school curric   to its most academic and intellectual bases. Such thinking is inspired by an Old World belief that enthrones certain subject areas as intrinsically intellective. Under such conditions, the school curriculum is devoted to the task of immersing youth in the traditions of a discipline-centered, liberal arts curriculum. Any activity that does not meet such a standard is considered anti-intellectual and, hence, is not worthy of treatment in the curriculum. The school experience becomes noteworthy not only for what it includes but also for what it fails to include. The elements typically excluded, or at least relegated in the curriculum, are vocational education, elective study, inter-disciplinary studies, and physical education.

Among contemporary thinkers, Theodore Sizer is well known for his efforts to bring the school back to its academic traditions. Working among high schools, Sizer (1984) has been forthright in acknowledging his bias against the design of the comprehensive school. "High schools cannot be comprehensive and should not try to be comprehensive," he declared, . . . "helping students to use their minds is a large enough assignment" (p. 216). Sizer developed this theme in his widely read work *Horace's Compromise*. Among the teachers portrayed in this book is a high school English teacher named Horace Smith whose life as a professional represents, at least to Sizer, the fundamental problem with schooling today. Although Horace Smith is an

Vocational courses are not generally considered "academic." However, nothing prevents educators from examining the topics of chemistry or physics while engaged in the workings of a car.

PART THREE: THE PRACTICE OF SCHOOLING

educator with considerable talent and enthusiasm for his chosen profession, he cannot simply fulfill his educational charge. He is overcome by excessive time and energy requirements, and he eventually has to resort to a professional life of compromises. Sizer's point is that the problem that Horace faces is systemic to a schooling structure that, by virtue of its comprehensiveness, attempts to do too much and, as a consequence, labors with a highly fragmented and wasteful curriculum scheme. In this manner, Sizer tries to show how the comprehensive high school was an ineffective arrangement for learning, one that ran counter to the central task of developing a student's mind. He captured the logic of this idea by advancing the proposal that "less is more" when applied to the curriculum scope of a school. This essentially meant that more was to be gained by committing the school to the all-inclusive, but less encompassing, task of cultivating the intellect through the academic disciplines.

Disparaging the significance of a wide and extensive educational offering has been the message from several conservative-oriented scholars for many years. Mortimer Adler, a well-known philosopher and longtime critic of progressive education, is a case in point. He denigrates progressive thinkers for trying to bring about a comprehensive school system that attempts to "be all things to all people." To Adler, the school's function should be limited to academic concerns believed to have generalizable effects in the development of one's intellect and character. Such a view, however, places the academic at odds with the nonacademic and reinforces a mind-versus-body dualism. In the case of such a dualism, matters of the mind are separated from matters of the body, with only matters of the mind becoming worthy of the school. Thus, the academic curriculum (i.e., acquisition of discipline-centered knowledge, mastery of basic skills) takes precedent, and other so-called nonacademic phases of the curriculum (i.e., vocational education, interdisciplinary citizenship education, elective study) take on a secondary status in the school.

In 1984, John Goodlad conducted a landmark study of the American school that found, among many other things, that parents wanted more than academic or intellectual objectives stressed in the schooling of their children. In fact, they wanted a balanced and resourceful school experience that strove to meet wide-ranging needs. In other words, when it came to formulating the agenda of schooling, parents wanted and expected a comprehensive curriculum (Goodlad, 1984; Boyer, 1983). This view was reinforced by the fact that most of the parents, teachers, and students questioned in Goodlad's study felt that the day-to-day operations of the school were already heavily weighed in the direction of intellectual goals. Such a view, of course, contradicts Sizer's contention of widespread neglect and compromises in the vital academic cores of the curriculum. If anything, the practice of the American curriculum has had a very high regard for the academic function of schooling, especially as it is reflected on standardized testing measures.

Academic Knowledge and the Curriculum

The goals in the academic sphere of the curriculum are most closely associated with the mastery of mathematical and linguistic skills, as well as with the development of intellectual processes (logical and critical thinking) and the acquisition of subject-centered knowledge. These goals, of course, can be reached through other curriculum outlets, but they generally represent points of academic emphasis.

Much of the debate regarding the academic curriculum revolves around the issue of subject-matter organization. In other words, should the academic sphere of the curriculum necessarily be organized along traditional academic lines? The answer to this question has to account for grade-level differences and for various mandated content requirements, sometimes formed at state organizational levels. In the high school, for instance, there is a clear and pressing need for youth to be given the opportunity to enroll in specialized academic courses, especially as these courses serve the interests of students intent on pursuing a college education. This does not mean that such courses should be offered only to students preparing for college; noncollege bound students should have access to such courses through the individual/exploratory function of the curriculum or as a part of their specialized program in vocational education. If a school, however, chooses to represent academic courses as graduation requirements for all youth (as often happens), there might be some need to fashion the courses along less specialized boundaries and to merge the interests of academics with general education (common learnings). Yet, there is no denying some place for a specialized academic curriculum in the high school.

In elementary school, the academic curriculum need not always take on a specialized tack. There are, of course, state-mandated content directives and, in some states, mandated textbooks that accompany these content directives. The intrusion of the state in the content of the curriculum essentially removes any questions teachers might have about what should be taught in the schools. Over the years, the character of these directives has been typically built along the traditional academic disciplines (science, mathematics, reading, social studies, and language arts). However, teachers can still engage in more interdisciplinary efforts that temper the specialized character of academic instruction. This can be accomplished either in the single classroom or through schoolwide curriculum-planning initiatives involving several classrooms. The idea behind such an initiative would be to lessen the influence of the technical, the procedural, and the abstract in the elementary school and to widen the influence of issues and problems related to the life experience.

It is important to note that the instructional variance in the school curriculum has much to do with retaining a comprehensive concept of schooling. Few people would argue, for instance, with the view that schools should be firmly committed to teaching the fundamental processes of reading, writing, and mathematics. Much of the debate starts when questions are raised over how the basic skills will be taught and the intensity with which they will be embraced in the curriculum. The "back-to-basics" movement of the 1970s, for instance, led to the proliferation of many low-cognitive skill-drill exercises in the curriculum and to a prevailing mentality that equated minimal competencies with maximal achievement. To this day, basic skills instruction is dominated by behavioristic skill-drill strategies and by various self-paced mastery methods, which typically include sequentially developed work sheets and workbooks. In fact, given the school's preoccupation with knowledge acquisition and skill development, most of the instructional strategies embraced in the academic sphere of the curriculum are usually characterized by behavioristic manipulations and expository approaches, such as lecture and recitation methods, and other knowledge-transmission models of instruction.

In other words, when it comes to academic achievement, teachers tend to focus on ways of teaching that convey a base of knowledge or that inculcate an academic competency (i.e., reading, writing). In a highly specialized subject area, like chemistry, physics, or algebra, transmission models make some sense, but in a less specialized arena that features life-experience issues, skill-drill routines and rote and recitation procedures are simply not appropriate. Thus, different facets of the curriculum often call for different instructional strategies.

The premise of elementary education is that it is not specializing. Instructionally speaking, elementary school teachers should aim to construct academic learning activities along less expository and transmissive priorities. The content of the curriculum should be designed to be broad and inclusive of sociopersonal and sociocivic themes. Such themes, moreover, might represent the best context in which to develop mandated skill and knowledge in a subject area.

Most schools convey the official content of the curriculum to teachers by providing scope-and-sequence charts mandated by the state or the district (for each subject area) or by authorizing the use of a textbook that abides by state-directed content. This obviously results in a concrete list of what should be taught. Such a list, however, can be dealt with critically by teachers as they decide what should and should not be stressed in the curriculum, based on their own sense of what is professionally desirable. Such decisions might lead to an extended treatment of a particular topic. A teacher might want to build bridges across certain content areas, which might lead to a specially designed supplemental unit, or the teacher might want to resequence certain materials in the text or offer a set of independent materials as supplemental to a textbook-based course.

At the high school level, the equation changes. The academic tradition has essentially two roles: one that deals expressly with specialized knowledge in the precollege curriculum and another that might have a place in the general education or common learnings function of the curriculum.

Common learnings are openly committed to sociocivic concerns. Many broad disciplines, of course, have insights to offer in such an arrangement. The broad field of social studies is the most obvious, but increasingly one finds educators from various disciplines directing their efforts toward citizenship education. In science education, a movement known as Science-Technology and Society (STS) has burgeoned that stresses the role of thinking in the classroom by using issue-centered themes that touch on critical social topics. Sanctioned by the National Science Teachers Association and sponsored by the National Science Foundation, STS has sought to transcend the discipline-centered lines of traditional science and to deal with points of argument that cut across a broad range of environmental, industrial, technological, social, and political problems (NSTA, 1982; Yager, 1986). Its kinship to common learnings is palpable because it aims to prepare youth for constructive citizenship roles (Hlebowitsh & Hudson, 1991). Similarly, English educators have also mobilized their energies to deal with the relation of their discipline to democratizing practices in the school (Lloyd-Jones & Lindsford, 1989), as have mathematics educators (Mathematical Science Education Board, 1990).

Thus, one way of seeing academic growth in the high school is through the common learnings, which would mingle sociocivic issues with interdisciplinary knowledge. Under such circumstances, the common learnings might seek to deal with social studies through, say, a course on the problems of democracy; science, through a course dedicated to exploring environmental or health problems; mathematics, through a series of courses that deal with understanding sociological phenomena via quantitative means; and English, through the examination of literature that speaks to the social conditions of humankind.

The other side of the academic curriculum in the high school would be centered on providing highly specialized courses, which would be best suited for those who intend to pursue a college education. These courses could also be open to students in other programs. Science, then, might be broached through the standard specializations (biology, chemistry, and physics); mathematics through algebra, geometry, and trigonometry; social studies through civics and history; and English through the standard fare of grammar, composition, and classical literature. The character of these specialized offerings would be very much influenced by college entrance requirements and state-mandated objectives (see Table 9.5).

The academic curriculum is familiar ground to educators. It encompasses most of what they do each day. The specialized tradition of academic knowledge has pervaded the curriculum at virtually all levels and has resulted in the neglect of interdisciplinary schemes in the academic curriculum. At the elementary and middle school, the academic education of students can be tied into a common learnings program without much regard for the specialized academic tradition. In the secondary school, on the other hand, the specialized traditions are central to the precollege curriculum but might also be important in the vocational education program and in the exploratory/enrichment phase of the curriculum.

TABLE 9.5

ACADEMIC GROWTH AND THE CURRICULUM

Curricular Objective

To provide experiences that attend to the mastery of the fundamental processes of reading, writing, and arithmetic, and to offer experiences that lead to the acquisition of knowledge in various academic disciplines.

Potential Activities

A. Interdisciplinary initiatives associated with common learnings that draw out academic skills and knowledge in relation to sociocivic themes. These would predominate in elementary and middle schools but would be reserved within a facet of the common learnings component of the curriculum in high school. The teaching methodology would be less expository and more focused on projects, class discussion, peer teaching, problem-focused inquiry, and other experiential activities.

B. Specialized studies in each of the attendant academic traditions. These courses are designed for students planning to attend college; the style of teaching under these circumstances is aligned with transmittal-expository models, though instructional variance is important in this setting as well. Such courses should not be widely used in elementary or middle school settings because the specialized nature of the offering is foreign to the life experience of learners and to their maturational development. Moreover, specialized academic training, which is the province of higher education, has no compelling justification in the life of an elementary school student.

✦ Vocational Growth

Part of the conventional wisdom about public schooling speaks to its importance in equipping youth with the skills, competencies, and attitudes needed to perform successfully in labor markets. At the university level, "vocational" programs exist for the preparation of accountants, educators, engineers, economists, social workers, musicians, and physicians. In secondary schools, vocational programs exist in relation to employment in the agricultural, health, trade, and industrial sectors. Such programs have long existed in comprehensive school settings, though one can find them in separate technical schools too. Close to 90% of vocational education programs provided in American high schools are in comprehensive schools. (NCES, 1995a) Vocational education also has a role to play in nonoccupational areas like consumer affairs, business theory, the labor movement, and the aesthetics of craftsmanship. In 1992, 97% of all high school graduates completed at least one vocational education course (NCES, 1995a).

Vocational Education and the Curriculum

Vocational education is a phenomenon that applies mostly to middle school and high school settings. Over the years, middle schools have offered courses in the prevocational arts in an attempt to offer youth an opportunity to explore vocational life skills, which usually entail an introduction to the industrial arts. In many secondary schools, however, the bulk of the vocational courses becomes more specialized and more closely associated with the education of youth not destined for higher education. Still, aspects of vocational education can also be weaved into the common learnings facet of the curriculum, perhaps in relation to consumer affairs, to the history of labor-management strife, or to specialized academic programs in the arts and the sciences. Vocational courses, of course, should also be available on an elective basis.

The placement of vocational education in the comprehensive school design has been questioned by a wide ideological range of critics. Conservatives generally argue that vocational programs are anti-intellectual, too costly, and without much value in the actual job market (Adler, 1982; Sizer, 1984; Bestor, 1956). More liberal critics generally argue that vocational education is too specialized and too slow to respond to changes in the technological and occupational conditions of the marketplace. As a result, they criticize vocational education for restricting student career opportunities. Vocational-education students, they claim, may become solely trained as welders and nothing else, which gives them little flexibility in the job market and consequently more restricted options for social and economic advancement (Goodlad, 1984; Broudy, Smith, & Burnett, 1964). In this manner, vocational education, which is largely populated by students from lower socioeconomic sectors of the society, is seen as a mechanism that perpetuates the status quo. It is seen as espousing a decidedly probusiness ideology that gives capitalism the grist that it needs for its oppressive economic mill (Katz, 1975).

The major criticism facing vocational education raises doubt about its worth as a bridge between the school and the workplace. Some researchers have claimed, for instance, that there is no significant relationship between vocational education in high school and future job fate (Mertens & Gardner, 1983). This criticism is often accompanied by the assertion of vocational obsolescence, which is the belief that vocational skills are temporal, especially in today's rapidly changing society (Goodlad, 1984). This is, of course, not a new argument (Hutchins, 1943; Broudy, Smith, & Burnett, 1964), nor is it without some validity. It is actually a criticism that applies to all vocational education, including that which is provided to physicians and engineers, and to those occupations traditionally served in higher education. To deal with this problem, the high school should look toward broad families of occupations. It should also be sure to instill in graduating students the kinds of attitudes that will motivate them to continue to keep up with the changes in their fields (Tanner & Tanner, 1980).

Several commentators have attempted to refocus the curriculum character of vocational education. To avoid a narrowness in training, reformers like Goodlad (1984) and Boyer (1983) have proposed to arrange all vocational studies in general education (common learnings). This approach would ensure wider participation in the instructional programs of vocational education and would help break down the curriculum tracking structure. It would also change the character of vocational education, taking it out of the business of specific job training and into the business of developing more general skills in areas like technological literacy. A vocational program situated in common learnings might stress computer facility and various issues related to understanding economic systems and principles (Goodlad, 1984, p. 344).

Unfortunately, vocational education is in crowded company when placed in the common learnings phase. Goodlad estimates that only 15% of the total school program could be devoted to this objective. For the college bound, this amount may be sufficient. But for those who plan to enter the workforce at the completion of their high school education, such a recommendation might be less than desirable. The placement of vocational education programs in common learnings is appropriate, but it should not be at the expense of comprehensive vocational learning for the noncollege bound.

Even though the evidence bearing on the relation between the school and the workplace is conflicting, there is a general view that vocational education should take less interest in job-specific training and more interest in the development of general skills. In this manner, one might want to look at the vocational-education dimension of the curriculum as semivocational, as having no pretension about training expert technicians or specialists. The idea, then, would be to employ a broad curriculum strategy that promotes communication, problem solving, the social importance of the vocational arts, and the development of vocational skills in a broad range of areas. Under such a reconfiguration, vocational education would equip students with an understanding of the nature of industry and technology; it would also offer some insight into the nature of economic systems and the roles of management and labor unions, while promoting wide categories of vocational skill and competence.

Several commentators have identified several possible vocational categories or clusters (broad areas of study that require a level of competency in language, mathematical, and even applied science skills) that might be used to achieve this reform (Cantor, 1989; Tanner & Tanner, 1980). They might include the following: agriculture; electrical and electronic engineering; marketing, including advertising; health occupations; home economics, including child-care services; office occupations, including computer programming, shorthand, and typing; trade and industrial education, including construction and auto mechanics; and technical education. Each cluster opens to many occupational vistas, not just one or two. However, such programs are expensive in financial cost and school time. It would be difficult to operationalize such programs with anything less than one third of the student school program. Properly designed, the vocational clusters can be combined with academic course work, making each cluster a prevocational preparation for more advanced study in the community college, the technical college, or the four-year university, should students decide to further their education. Table 9.6 outlines the possibilities for vocational education in the curriculum.

 ## *Physical Education, Music, and Art*

Physical education, music, and art have often been perceived as frills in the school curriculum. In truth, they are basic skills. In a comprehensive school arrangement, these three areas can be integrated into the curriculum in any

VOCATIONAL GROWTH AND THE CURRICULUM	TABLE 9.6

Curricular Objective

To provide experiences that develop the skills, attitudes, and habits that will lead to effective participation in economic life

Potential Activities (Middle and Secondary Schools)

Prevocational Courses in Middle School

Several courses might be offered as exploratory initiatives for middle school youth. They could be organized in broad categorical groups through the common curriculum or as elective options. The categories might include home economics education, which would include issues related to food and nutrition, clothing and textiles, child development, family and social relationships, and home management and family economics; or trade and industrial education, which would include an introduction to basic motor mechanics, carpentry skills, drafting, and labor-management relations.

Vocational Education and Common Learnings

The common learnings facet of the curriculum would serve to bridge occupational concerns with sociocivic problems. Courses justified under this category might deal with the problems of capitalism in a free society; the history of unionism in the nation; the role of technology as it relates to the freedoms of a democracy; basic consumer issues; and actual vocational life skills (i.e., motor mechanics, computer literacy, and the skills related to most do-it-yourself home projects). These courses would apply to both middle school and secondary school levels.

Vocational Education and Occupational Clusters

The courses in this category are designed for noncollege bound students. A program of courses would be designed to cover a comprehensive range of occupational skills related to a broad family of vocational competence. The vocational family might include health-services education, which would be preparatory to several occupations. Nurses, medical technicians, physical therapists, dental assistants, orderlies, dietitians, and other health-care related jobs apply. Such a program of courses would be vocational in terms of particular skills, but it would also have a strong academic base, especially as it relates to mathematics and the sciences. Another cluster might be business education, which, besides having a strong skill base in typing, shorthand, and computer facility, would also offer academic course work in mathematics, business principles, and English.

number of ways. Physical education and its associated activities in sport, health, and recreation have an obvious role to play in elements of the common and individualized curriculum. The same may be said of art and music, though art could also have a place in the vocational curriculum and potentially in elements of academic study as well. Still, to underscore the importance of these three areas and to reinforce their place in the school, they should be separated out in the school curriculum. In elementary education, art, music, and physical education-related activities are typical in the daily ebb and flow of experience. However, the comprehensive concept of schooling also assures that these three areas receive a distinct treatment from someone who is expert in the field. Thus, art, music, and physical education classes are usually taught once or twice a week by a specialist. The same idea applies at the middle and secondary school levels, though art and music, as separate and direct studies, are increasingly taught through elective and advanced placement course work.

KEY TERMS

The comprehensive high school
Enrichment education
Exploratory and special interest
   education

General education
Right brain/left brain learning
   styles

Specialized education
Styles of intelligence

KEY QUESTIONS

1. What are the four main curriculum functions in a comprehensive school? Explain their purposes.

2. What would be the main differences between the way that the elementary school and the way that the high school might deal with individual needs in the curriculum?

3. What do you think of the comprehensive needs of youth listed in the chapter? What might you add or delete?

4. What are some classroom possibilities for elementary school teachers wanting to reflect the individual needs and interests of their students?

5. How does knowledge of intelligence styles factor into the curriculum treatment of individual learning?

6. What are the curriculum implications of the right brain/left brain literature?

7. How does general education relate to citizenship education?

8. How might an elementary teacher working in a self-contained classroom operationalize a general education program?

9. How do community issues factor into general education?

10. What role has mental discipline played in the debate over the place of academics in the curriculum?

11. Why have Sizer and Adler argued that "less is more" when it comes to the development of a school curriculum?

12. How might academic instruction factor into general education at the high school level?

13. Why are specialized courses much less necessary in elementary and middle schools than in high schools?

14. What have been the main criticisms against vocational education in a comprehensive high school?

15. Examine the sample schedules provided in the Appendix following Chapter 11 (Figures A.1–A.3). Do you find any problems with the schedules? What might you decide to change?

REFERENCES

Adler, M. J. (1982). *The Paideia proposal.* New York: Macmillan.

Aikin, W. (1942). *The story of the eight year study.* New York: Harper and Row.

Anderson, L & others. (1990) *The civics report card.* Washington, DC: U.S. Department of Education.

Bestor, A. E. (1953). *Educational wastelands.* Urbana, IL: University of Illinois Press.

Bestor, A. E. (1956). *The restoration of learning.* New York: Alfred A. Knopf.

Boyer, E. (1983). *High school.* New York: Harper and Row.

Broudy, H. S., Smith, O. B., & Burnett, J. R. (1964). *Democracy and excellence in American secondary education.* Chicago: Rand McNally.

Butts, R. F. (1989). *The civic mission of educational reform.* Stanford, CA: Hoover Institute Press.

Cantor, L. (1989). *Vocational education and training in the developed world.* New York: Routledge.

Center for Civic Education (1991). *Civitas.* Calabasas, CA: Center for Civic Education.

Cremin, L. A. (1961). *The transformation of the school.* New York: Alfred A. Knopf.

Cremin, L. A. (1965). *The genius of American education.* New York: Vintage Books.

Dewey, J. (1916). *Democracy and education.* New York: Free Press.

Educational Policies Commission. (1944). *Education for ALL American youth.* Washington, DC: National Education Association.

Educational Policies Commission. (1948). *Education for ALL American children.* Washington, DC: National Education Association.

Friere, P. (1973). *Pedagogy of the oppressed.* New York: Seabury Press.

Gardner, H. (1983). *Frames of mind.* New York: Basic Books.

Goodlad, J. I. (1984). *A place called school.* New York: McGraw-Hill.

Hlebowitsh, P. S., & Hudson, S. E. (1991). Science education and the reawakening of the general education ideal. *Science Education, 75*(5), 563–576.

Hutchins, R. M. (1943). *Education for freedom.* Baton Rouge: Louisiana State University Press.

Katz, M. (1975). *Class, bureaucracy and schools.* New York: Praeger.

Kliebard, H. M. (1986). *The struggle for the American curriculum.* New York: Routledge and Kegan Paul.

Lloyd-Jones, R., & Lindsford, A. A. (1989). *The English coalition conference: Democracy through language.* Urbana, IL: National Council of Teachers of English.

Mathematical Science Education Board. (1990). *Reshaping school mathematics.* Washington, DC: National Academy Press.

Mertens, D., & Gardner, J. (1983). The long-term effects of vocational education. *Journal of Vocational Education Research, 8*(2), 1–21.

National Center for Education Statistics (1995). Community service performed by high school seniors *Educational Policy Issues: Statistical Perspectives* Washington, DC: U.S. Department of Education.

National Center for Education Statistics (1995a). *Vocational Education in the United States: The early 1990s.* Washington, DC: U.S. Department of Education.

National Council for the Social Studies (1994). *Curriculum standards for social studies.* Washington, DC: National Council for the Social Studies.

National Science Teachers Association. (1982). *Science-technology and society.* Washington, DC: Government Printing Office.

People for the American Way (1992). *Democracy's next generation: A study of American youth on race.* Washington, DC: People for the American Way.

Report of the Harvard Committee. (1945). *General education in a free society.* Cambridge: Harvard University Press.

Rickover, H. G. (1959). *Education and freedom.* New York: E. P. Dutton and Co.

Sizer, T. R. (1984). *Horace's compromise.* Boston: Houghton-Mifflin Co.

Tanner, D., & Tanner, L. N. (1995). *Curriculum development* (3rd ed.). New York: Macmillan.

Tanner, D., & Tanner, L. N. (1990). *History of the school curriculum.* New York: Macmillan.

Taylor, R. (1982). Vocational education. In *The encyclopedia of educational research* (5th ed.). New York: The Free Press.

Torrence, E. P., & Rockenstein, Z. L. (1988). Styles of thinking and creativity. In R. R. Schmeck (Ed.), *Learning strategies and learning styles.* New York: Plenum Press.

Yager, R. (1986). What's wrong with school science? *The Science Teacher, 53*(1), 145–147.

Ward, L. (1883). *Dynamic sociology.* New York: Appleton.

Wraga, W. G. (1993). *Democracy's high school.* Landam, MD: University Press of America.

10

THE TEACHER AND THE SCHOOL

Here they are, the sixth-grade team at an elementary school in Huntsville, Alabama. Most teachers find that their colleagues are a source of inspiration, assistance, and friendship, yet they also describe teaching as a lonely profession. It is not surprising that the entire sixth-grade team is comprised of women. The great majority of elementary teachers are women. What else is known about teachers? In this chapter, the focus is on the teachers in American schools.

Many questions arise out of this general issue. For instance, what do teachers do in classrooms? How do they design lessons? What decisions do they face when building their day-to-day instructional plans? This chapter explores teachers and their work. Who comprises the teaching force in the United States? How do they view their profession? Are they satisfied in their jobs?

As John Dewey once observed, we are all born to be teachers as we are not born to be engineers or painters. His point was that teaching is preeminently a social act, one that attaches itself to life situations and people. To be human is, in many ways, to be a teacher. The very sustenance of society depends on the capacity of humanity to learn from itself and to encourage social tolerance, social understanding, and the advancement of knowledge. The skills of an educator manifest obviously in the role of parent, spouse, citizen, worker, friend, and colleague. The native capacity for teaching exists, to varying degrees, in all of us.

In this manner, teaching has a nobility about it that few other professions can claim. It is staked in arguably the most important task of a society, the enlightenment of an immature generation of youth for eventual participation in society. Other professions, of course, carry out vital tasks. Doctors, for instance, save lives and lawyers help to preserve justice, but both doctors and lawyers had teachers in their lives who helped to move them toward the development of their professional skills. There is a dignity in the calling of a teacher, a calling of social service that is at the core of helping to maintain and improve society. In this way, the purpose of teaching might be viewed as trying to make life better for those who are yet to be born.

The act of teaching varies according to situational conditions. The teacher of mathematics will likely engage in teaching approaches that will vary considerably from, say, the teacher of reading. Similarly, the kindergarten teacher will engage in actions that will vary from the secondary school teacher. Teachers in different cultural settings and socioeconomic settings might call upon different sets of behavior, but through it all there is a general ground of commonality that constitutes what might be called professional knowledge. Whether one is a "born teacher" or not, all teacher decision making has to be enlivened by what one knows about learners, by how one sees the role of the school in the society, and by the capacity to organize knowledge and experience in a manner that serves the education of youngsters. There is no one way of behaving when it comes to teaching, but there is a principled sense of what it means to be an educator and what it means to make professionally justifiable decisions.

America's Teachers

In preliterate societies, learning took place without the formal institution of schooling. Virtually every action of the society was imbued with life purpose. Food gathering and hunting skills were taught by elders who conveyed their wisdom to the younger generation through life applications. Teaching was not an academic exercise but a life exercise, tied directly into the sustenance of the group. There were no motivation problems and no need to generate learning interest. Learning was *of* interest because it was so vitally associated with the act of living; there was no separation between the needs of living and the act of education.

Today, of course, the role of the educator has been formalized and the educational agenda has a character that is not always tied directly to life. Academic, vocational, social, and individualistic needs are served by formally trained educators who employ formal techniques designed to capture the hearts and minds of youngsters. Lessons are used, objectives are formulated, motivational techniques are considered, and various organization frameworks are weighed. Formal schooling, unlike an informal communal or societal arrangement, has a purpose that is wider than the family or the parochial community. In America, schooling has to bring a multitude of cultures and languages together, and it has to stand for an ideal that transcends all community traditions. The professional educator has to carry out this cosmopolitan purpose in accordance with the highest ideals of the profession.

Who are the people that society has entrusted with the formal education of youngsters? What are teachers' lives like in school, and what are the attitudes and values that they hold toward the institution of schooling and toward children?

One interesting characteristic of the teaching profession is its gender distribution. More than 71% of the nation's 2.5 million public school teachers are women (National Center for Education Statistics, 1994). The percentage of female teachers working in elementary schools is even greater. The dominance of women in the teaching profession probably has something to do with the early development of normal schools, which were teacher training schools that highlighted the teaching of methodology over subject matter. In the 19th century, an education in the omnipotent subject matter, which was embodied in course work in the university or college, was viewed as worthy for only men. A man's intellect, not a woman's, was considered to be equal to the task of learning the subject matter. Long denied access to higher education, women could, by and large, only look to the normal school as a realistic outlet for postsecondary education. The normal school's commitment to the "lightweight" task of teaching methodologies posed no threat to, and generated little interest from, males. The old maxim of "those who can't, teach" had real life application in the minds of many males. Such a prejudice was also buoyed by a cultural perspective that viewed teaching as an extension of mothering. Whereas many teachers recognize that the role they play as teachers often mirrors that of a mother, and most feel this is an important aspect of their job, this very feature has unfortunately devalued their work as teachers. Raising children in Western culture continues to be viewed as unpaid "woman's work," no matter the significance. Interestingly, at the secondary school level, where the children are obviously older, the gender distribution is much more balanced than at the elementary school level.

With respect to ethnicity, the nation's teaching force remains the work of White, middle-class women. Only 13.5% of all public school teachers are members of a minority group (National Center for Education Statistics, 1994). Indeed, even as the public schools' student population is becoming increasingly diverse, teachers are decreasing in ethnic diversity. This situation may grow worse as future demographic patterns in the United States point to an ever-diversifying student population. The ethnic and racial composition of America's schoolteachers, of course, needs to reflect America's population. It currently does not, and the remediation of this problem is viewed by many to be at the very core of any future school reform.

Public school teachers in America are a highly educated group of professionals. More than 47% of all public school teachers have education beyond a bachelor's degree; only about 1% do not hold a bachelor's degree (National Center for Education Statistics, 1994). It should be noted that many school districts have designed structured salary increments that reward teachers who continue to advance their educations. Several states, such as New York, require a master's degree for permanent certification as a teacher. By international standards, American teachers are among the most highly educated in the world (Carson, Huelskamp, & Woodall, 1993).

Contrary to popular opinion, teachers do not work a shortened workweek. Although teachers spend about 35 required hours per week at school, they spend on the average 47 weekly hours performing all their teaching duties (National Center for Education Statistics, 1994).

In terms of salaries, public school teachers across the country report an average salary of about $31,000 (National Center for Education Statistics, 1994). Urban fringe (or suburban) teachers command the highest salaries, while rural teachers make somewhat less. Teachers at the start of their careers can expect to earn an average annual salary of $19,913 and about $33,000 per year after 20 years of experience and a master's degree. Because teachers are typically given about a 10-month contract, they do have an opportunity to augment their annual salary. Teachers' salaries are often determined by negotiated schedules that account for the education levels of the teachers and their years of experience. Interestingly, when asked what proposed changes might best improve the teaching profession, teachers point overwhelmingly to salaries (Carnegie Foundation for the Advancement of Teaching, 1990).

The political and religious character of the teaching profession is balanced, if not slightly tilted to the political right. According to a study conducted by the Carnegie Foundation for the Advancement of Teaching, 29% of public school teachers characterize themselves as liberal or moderately liberal, while 42% characterize themselves as conservative or moderately conservative. The remainder identified themselves as "middle of the road." The overwhelming majority (96%) of public school teachers also claimed to have voted in the last election. One fourth of all teachers see themselves as deeply religious, and another 62% see themselves as moderately religious. Altogether, 88% of the public teaching force considers itself as deeply or moderately religious. This is an important finding because many conservative religious critics of the public school like to describe the school as a cold institution operated by people who have no religious depth. The irony is that the secular nature of schooling is protected and served by highly religious individuals. Only 12% of teachers stated that they were indifferent to religion and only 1% was opposed to it.

What Do Teachers Say About Their Work?

Generally speaking, teachers report high levels of satisfaction with their work. About 86% of a national sample of teachers reported being satisfied with their job in school (Carnegie Foundation, 1990). Despite this overall rating, however, there are some troubling signs in the profession as well. Almost half the teachers reported a decline in morale since 1983, about half also stated that they were not satisfied with the level of control in their professional lives, almost a third reported being less enthusiastic about teaching than when they started, and almost half reported that they subordinated their personal lives to their work as teachers (Carnegie Foundation, 1990). When teachers were asked if they would teach again, if given the opportunity to do things differently, only about 60% answered affirmatively (National Center for Education Statistics, 1993). See Figure 10.1.

Teachers continue to identify drug abuse and inadequate parenting as the fundamental problems facing their schools. From these problems, it seems, others arise. For instance, 30% of all teachers reported that student apathy was a serious problem in their school, 25% identified lack of parental support, and another 19% pointed to absenteeism as a serious problem (Carnegie

FIGURE 10.1

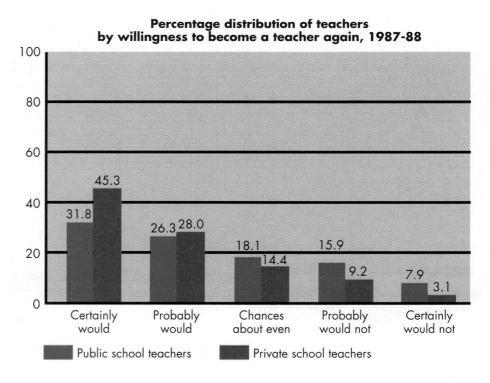

Percentage distribution of teachers by willingness to become a teacher again, 1987-88

Public school teachers   Private school teachers

PART THREE: THE PRACTICE OF SCHOOLING

Foundation, 1990). These reported problems were higher in 1990 than in 1983, when the previous Carnegie survey was taken. It should also be said that teachers did not report theft, vandalism, violence against students, violence against teachers, or ethnic/racial discord as serious problems. Only 5% reported vandalism as a serious problem, and only 1% reported violence against teachers as a serious problem (Carnegie Foundation, 1990). Schools, as it turns out, are among the safest places for children to be, much more so than even the home or family environment (Hyman & others, 1994).

Against this backdrop of problems is a message of academic improvement in the eyes of professional educators. In 1990, more than half the teachers reported that their schools improved in the clarity of their goals and in the academic expectations and requirements for their students, especially in math and science (Carnegie Foundation, 1990). They also reported high levels of improvement in the use of technology for teaching and in the quality of textbooks and other materials. Instruction tailored to student needs and programs for the gifted also drew high self-reported levels of improvement from the teachers (Carnegie Foundation, 1990). At the same time, however, the survey data demonstrated that 51% of public teachers believe that their students are seriously deficient in basic skills (Carnegie Foundation, 1990), and close to half of the public school teachers continue to believe that building literary skills is the most important goal for education (National Center for Education Statistics, 1994). This might explain why at both the elementary and middle school levels teachers spend more instructional time on the language arts than any other subject area. In grades K-4, teachers spend more than twice the amount of instructional time on reading/language arts than on math and almost four times more than on science or on the social studies (NCES, 1993). See Figure 10.2.

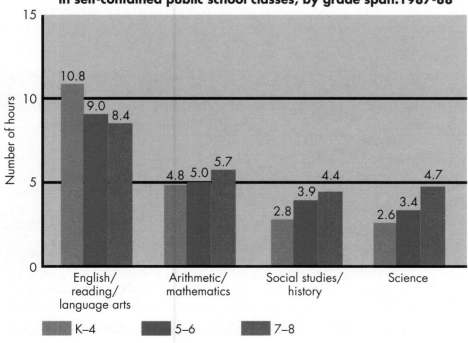

Average number of hours per week spent teaching various subjects in self-contained public school classes, by grade span:1987-88   **FIGURE 10.2**

Number of hours

- English/reading/language arts: K-4 10.8, 5-6 9.0, 7-8 8.4
- Arithmetic/mathematics: K-4 4.8, 5-6 5.0, 7-8 5.7
- Social studies/history: K-4 2.8, 5-6 3.9, 7-8 4.4
- Science: K-4 2.6, 5-6 3.4, 7-8 4.7

Legend: K–4, 5–6, 7–8

The self-reported work conditions of teachers indicate that teachers are still struggling for professional identification. Most teachers reported (56%) less than one hour per day of formal preparation time, and about one third saw their classrooms as too large in size (Carnegie Foundation, 1990), despite the dramatic improvements made with the teacher/student ratio in the schools over the years. (See Table 10.1).Over half also claimed more political interference in education and more state regulation in 1990 than in 1983. About one third of the teachers reported spending between $500 and $1,000 of their own money to support their teaching activities (Carnegie Foundation, 1990). Twenty-two percent claimed that secretarial services were regularly not available to them, a third claimed that word processing reserved for teacher use was regularly not available, and 29% claimed that even typewriters were regularly not available. Amazingly, 9% reported that a telephone for professional use was not regularly available to them (Carnegie Foundation, 1990).

The evaluation of teachers demonstrates some interesting trends. Eighty-four percent believe that teacher evaluations in their schools were either very or somewhat fair, and 94% acknowledged that the major role of evaluating teachers went to the principal. About one third also claimed an improvement in the manner in which evaluation has been handled in their school since 1983 (Carnegie Foundation, 1990). But teacher involvement in the critical curriculum affairs of the school still seems marginal. Only 40% reported to be deeply involved in choosing textbooks and instructional materials, and only 22% reported to be deeply involved in shaping the curriculum and in setting standards for student behavior. Similarly, only 11% reported to be deeply involved in staff development or in-service programs. Most strikingly, 36% of teachers stated that they were not at all involved in setting student promotion and retention policies, and 46% stated that they were not at all involved in deciding how the school budget was spent. An overwhelming majority also claimed not to be at all involved in selecting new teachers, evaluating teacher performance, and selecting new administrators (Carnegie Foundation, 1990). Teachers, however, claimed "a lot of control" in their classrooms with homework assignments and with choice of instructional methods. This turns

TABLE 10.1

PUPIL/TEACHER RATIOS, IN THE PUBLIC SCHOOLS: 1955–91, SELECTED YEARS			
	Public Schools		
	K–12	*Elementary*	*Secondary*
1955	26.9	30.2	20.9
1960	25.8	28.4	21.7
1965	24.7	27.6	20.8
1970	22.3	24.4	19.9
1975	20.4	21.7	18.8
1980	18.7	20.4	16.8
1985	17.9	19.6	15.7
1987	17.6	18.7	16.0
1991	16.9	18.8	14.4

Source: National Center for Education Statistics. *America's Teachers: Profile of a profession.* Washington, D.C. U.S. Department of Education, p. 81.

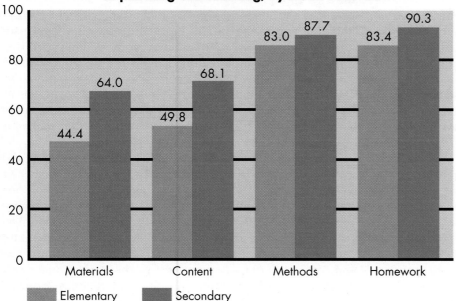

Percentage of public school teachers who reported that they felt they had a lot of control* in their classrooms over selected areas of planning and teaching, by level: 1987-88

FIGURE 10.3

Elementary Secondary

*Teachers were defined as heving felt they had a lot of control if they responded with a 5 or 6 on a 6-point scale of control, with 6 representing *complete control*.

out to be a rather superficial liberty because many teachers failed to claim " a lot of control" in the content and materials of the school curriculum (NCES, 1993). See Figure 10.3. These are not positive signs for the professionalization of teaching.

 ## The Teacher-Technician

For many years, teachers have been viewed as quasi-technicians whose main function in the classroom has been to carry out the instructional directions of prescriptive systems of learning. The popularity of competency-based instruction, mastery learning, teacher-proof materials, performance contracting, low-level accountability testing, and programmed instruction have all testified to this condition. Such instructional ideas tended to reduce the teacher's role in the classroom to its most rudimentary and routine elements. The teacher's action in the classroom became little more than following instructional scripts, handing out premade tests, and cataloging the results.

Teaching, of course, calls for much more than this. It takes creativity and intelligence to plan and implement educative engagements for children. It requires a professional vision that conceptualizes the learning experience in terms that are responsive to the learner, to the values and aims of the society, and to the wider world of knowledge (as it is represented organized subject matter).

Yet, there are data that indicate that teachers continue to respond simplistically to their situation. Goodlad's work in the 1980s showed that teachers were not, generally speaking, engaged in much of a professionally innovative or imaginative approach to teaching. The Old World schemes of rote and recitation continued to prevail in the classroom. In social studies, for instance, most of the classroom activity revolved around acts of memorization, and in language arts, the focus was fixed on the mechanical development of writing, including word recognition, grammar, and phonics. Unsophisticated workbooks and a general climate dedicated to low cognitive exercises seemed standard operating procedure. This is not to say that there was no vitality in the classroom, only that the general tone was traditional in the worst sense of the word. Such an assessment of teaching, however, has to be taken with some caution because there is dynamic variance in the ways that teachers teach within their schools (Pauley, 1991), a fact that makes it difficult to generalize about teachers and teaching in America.

Dewey (1904) once observed that teachers "should be given to understand that they are not only permitted to act on their own initiative, but that they are expected to do so, and that their ability to take on a situation for themselves would be more important in judging them than their following any particular set method or scheme." Needless to say, the freedom to think according to a professional method of action is fundamental to the development of educative environments in the nation's classroom. But there are outside mandates and conditions that often cut against the professional grain and make it more difficult for teachers to actualize their intelligence. Some of these are described here.

Teaching to the Test

Since the early 1980s, standardized testing in public education has gained undiminished popularity and authority in the curriculum. In fact, the penchant for measurement has affected nearly all facets of the school and has been increasingly tied to a host of policy issues on school equity, school effectiveness, teacher evaluation, school accreditation, and student assessment (Ariasian & Madaus, 1983). More specifically, in many schools, tests have served as the primary criterion for school decisions relating to grade promotions, admission to gifted and talented programs, assignment to special education programs, and high school graduation. This has given standardized testing a "high-stakes" status in the curriculum (Madaus, 1988). As a result, educators continue to be persuaded or otherwise compelled into thinking that the best way to improve education (or at least to show improvement) is to raise standardized scores. And this inevitably leads to a form of teaching that tries to conform to the test.

The mandate to teach for the test often emerges from the principal's or superintendent's office. School administrators are quite keen on showing visible signs of growth in their schools, and nothing meets this need better than favorable schoolwide results on norm-referenced standardized examinations. With the public image of the school at stake, administrators will exercise pressures to ensure favorable examination outcomes. Under such conditions, the very worth of a teacher could be, and sometimes is, reduced to student-performance outcomes. In other words, a good teacher is one who can demonstrate high student performance outcomes. Teachers might sometimes rationalize their role in the measurement-driven curriculum by emphasizing the notion that student destinies are dictated by examination results and that educators must do their utmost, like it or not, to boost these all-important scores.

But a serious problem emerges in such a situation. The test, which is conceptually supposed to be part of the curriculum, becomes the curriculum. The curriculum, in other words, gets modified into an apparatus designed around the test. This leads to a phenomenon known as **teaching to the test.** Some commentators have no problem with the act of teaching to the test, stating that whatever works to raise scores should be embraced as a viable strategy. But there are critics who contend that the conformance of the curriculum to the test not only invalidates the test but also creates a training atmosphere that concentrates mostly on the development of low-level skills that are amenable to quantification. It also places great faith in the highly fallible mechanism of standardized testing. Moreover, it also marginalizes the place or priority of anything that is not systematically tested. Thus, a teacher who aims to cultivate certain healthy values and attitudes toward learning or certain higher-order skills might find that such items are not part of the school evaluation and are therefore not very important. Teachers know that what is tested is what is privileged and sanctioned as important.

A study conducted in Texas that compared teachers' self-reported commitment to various instructional strategies against their self-reported commitment to openly teaching to a state-mandated test found that elementary teachers of reading who were committed to teaching to the test also admitted to being overtly reliant on the teacher's manual. Among elementary math teachers, those who reported a high commitment to teaching to the test also reported a high commitment to skill-drill exercises, student memorization tactics, the teacher's manual, independent projects, and peer teaching (Hlebowitsh, 1992). In the instance of the latter two, the teachers did not disclose what kinds of activities they used for independent projects and peer teaching. Still, the correlations in this study pointed to the possibility that teachers who taught directly to the exam were also broadly committed to instructional strategies that were low level and mechanical in orientation.

Some curriculum specialists have also gotten into the act of equating the curriculum to standardized tests. Among the more popular devices emerging from such concerns is a technique known as curriculum mapping and curriculum alignment (Glatthorn, 1987). The central idea behind such an approach to curriculum is to identify specific mastery objectives and align them to the essential activities, experiences, exams, and materials of the curriculum. Because the rhetoric of curriculum alignment describes curriculum development as a process requiring a carefully tailored coordination between objectives, learning experiences, and testing procedures, there is a cosmetic appeal to it. Often, however, curriculum alignment turns out to be little more than a rationalization for teaching to the test because it tends to bring everything into alignment with the all-encompassing priority to raise test scores. In this way, it brings the act of teaching down to its least common denominator.

George Madaus (1988) has been particularly active in his criticism of the manner in which testing has affected the curriculum. His argument is that testing is an important component of a broader curriculum strategy. He also asserts that the elevation of the testings role in the curriculum has allowed it to swamp all other curriculum considerations, resulting in measurement-driven instruction that leads to student cramming, that narrows the scope of the curriculum, that concentrates on the most easily measured items, and that ultimately constrains the creativity and professional judgment of the teacher (Madaus, 1988).

Dividing Instruction From Curriculum

Many problems that serve to limit the role of the teacher in the classroom can be attributed to the way that school professionals treat curriculum knowledge as something that is separate and apart from instructional knowledge. According to Cady (1988), a historical accounting of the professional literature shows that many instructional concerns, especially teaching methodologies, have been typically treated without allowing for basic curriculum principles.

When the domains of curriculum and instruction are treated dualistically, the organic character of the educational situation is undermined and the teacher is left with a stilted knowledge framework with which to make pedagogical judgments. Such a division focuses the priorities of the classroom upon solely instructional manipulations. More often than not, this translates into the development of highly structured lesson plans that articulate the management actions of the lesson. These actions include events dedicated to, say, gaining the class's attention, informing the class of the lesson's objective, or eliciting the so-called desired behavior of the lesson. Preliminary questions about the appropriateness of the objective and/or to the nature of the subject matter are not matters that apparently require teacher thought. The objectives and the content of the curriculum are believed to be preexisting in the textbooks and curriculum materials of the classroom. Thus, the teacher becomes the means by which to deliver fixed objectives, ready-made rules, and prescribed subject matter.

For years, the division between curriculum and instruction in the research literature has kept teachers from exercising a more expansive curriculum vision and intelligence. One of the more recent major insights emerging from this literature, for instance, is the principle of **time on task** (an idea that espouses the need for teachers to keep learners engaged in classroom activities). Obviously, engagement is a prerequisite for learning, but all forms of engagement are not necessarily educative. Because the **time on task** dictum does nothing to highlight or underscore the qualitative character of the task, it is of limited value. Thus, a teacher might achieve high grades in keeping her children on task, but if the task itself is not educationally worthwhile, the level of student engagement is not even an issue. Time on task is clearly an idea rooted in exclusive instructional concerns.

Another manifestation of the separation between curriculum and instruction comes out of the teacher effects research, which is research that has identified certain **effective teaching** practices as measured by standardized test scores. This research has identified generalizations believed to be central to good teaching, including the findings that effective teachers hold to high expectation, convey enthusiasm in their teaching, are vigilant about monitoring student work, and so on. Of course, when the term "effective" is used in this context, one needs to be able to show the criteria by which such a label is being used. The term effective is theoretically neutral. One could be an "effective" thief or an "effective" ax murderer. In the context of the effective teaching literature, the use of the term effective is tied into how well certain practices raise standardized test scores. The problem is that what one might do to raise test scores may not always lead to enlightened pedagogy. For instance, one prominent teacher effectiveness researcher stated that "effective" teachers of basic skills "ask questions at a low cognitive level so that students can produce many correct responses" (Rosenshine, 1979). A preoccupation with asking low-level questions might raise test scores in the basic skills, but it comes at the expense of a vital and dynamic cognitive experience, which should be idea-oriented and directed toward challenging the intelligence and experiences of students.

As Schulman has argued, the empirical research on effective teaching has oversimplified the teaching situation. According to Schulman (1987):

> Critical features of teaching, such as the subject matter being taught, the classroom context, the physical and psychological characteristics of students, or the accomplishment of purpose not readily assessed on standardized tests, are typically ignored in the quest for general principles of effective teaching. (p. 6)

A review of the effective teaching literature substantiates Schulman's point. Of the generalizations that one could derive from the effective teaching literature, there is no substantive mention of the potencies of curriculum knowledge. Indeed, the assumption is that effective teaching is removed from such considerations. Thus, "effective" teachers are expected to, among other things, focus clearly on academic goals, present information clearly, cover subject matter extensively, monitor student progress, and provide quick and well-targeted feedback. But the problem is that it is possible for an educator to abide by these generalizations and still not offer educative experiences in the classroom. It might be important for a teacher to be clear, focused, on task, and organized, but identifying the nature of what a teacher is organizing is equally important. One, after all, can be clear, organized, and vigilant about nonsense. The missing knowledge link in this case centers on curriculum questions related to what knowledge, skills, and values are worth teaching and what organizational, experiential, and pedagogical schemes might best be used to teach them.

Not surprisingly, the findings reported in the educational literature have also been overridden by the popularity of strictly instructional models for school and staff development. The popular Hunter (1980) approach is perhaps best known. Hunter's program, often referred to as the "Seven-Step Lesson" or the "Elements of Effective Instruction," is one of the most enduring features on the educational landscape today. In the early 1980s, it dominated teacher in-service programs throughout American schools, affecting the thinking and behavior of thousands of teachers. Some school districts adopted the Hunter model as their choice for assessing teacher performance and staked it into promotion and salary decisions.

The Hunter approach lists various structural elements of a lesson (anticipatory set, statements of objectives, careful monitoring for understanding, guided and independent practice, and a sense of closure) as the foundation for effective pedagogy. The seven steps to the lesson design are 1) Anticipatory Set: This phase of the lesson is designed primarily to get the students' attention. One of the problems Hunter noticed as she developed her lesson design is that some teachers began to teach before they had the students' attention. The Anticipatory Set helps to focus the learners on what is going to be taught. It is designed to "grab" the students' attention and set the framework for what will proceed; 2) Objective and Purpose: Once the students are attentive, the teacher, in clear and concise language, states what the students will be expected to learn and why; 3) Input: This is the phase in which the teacher provides the information that students need to meet the lesson's objective. A teacher, for instance, might help his students understand how to add fractions by performing examples on the board, asking for strategies that students might have in performing certain manipulations with fractions or providing visual or hands-on demonstrations; 4) Modeling: In this phase, the teacher models or shows students the process, skill, or knowledge that is being taught. The teacher might, for example, anticipate the errors students may make and model how students can correct their own errors. The teacher in this phase may keep in mind that modeling can be enhanced when the teacher "thinks out loud"; 5) Checking for Understanding: During the modeling phase, the teacher attempts to discover how many students understand the lesson's objective and to what degree. Hunter included this phase because she noticed that many teachers would call only on students who knew the answer, or worse, simply ask if there were any questions and move on; 6) Guided Practice: In this phase, the students practice the lesson objective under the guidance of the teacher. For example, the teacher may put a practice problem on the board and help the students solve it together. She may also put a problem on the board and ask a student to work on it independently while she circulates around the room, checking students' work; and 7) Independent Practice: This is the phase of the lesson in which students work on exercises associated with the lesson's objective or objectives independently. In high school classes, independent practice is often used as homework. In elementary school, teachers are more likely to allow students to complete their independent practice in school.

Hunter's lesson cycle has been criticized as overly prescriptive and unsupported by data (Gibboney, 1987). Even Hunter herself has criticized the model, noting that educators were coming to expect too much from her lesson design (Hunter, 1985). One of the main problems is that Hunter focused exclusively on the "how" of teaching and made no effort to try to answer the question of what knowledge and skills were most worthwhile. Hunter's response to this concern was that teachers can make such decisions themselves and that much of "the what" in teaching was inherited by the teacher anyway.

Still, the message received from the Hunter model to teachers is that as long as one follows the seven-step design, good teaching will follow. But good teaching is an incomplete process unless it accounts for the nature of the knowledge and experience that is being used in the Hunter model. The quality of classroom tasks and teacher lessons has as much to do with what is being taught as it does with the methodological issues that concern Hunter. The model can be applied usefully as an instructional component to a larger curriculum vision, but in and of itself it has limited value.

Curriculum Materials

Teachers have often been accused of being held captive by the classroom materials brought to bear in the act of teaching. From textbooks to workbooks and work sheets, to teachers' guides, and to various learning packages, the kinds of materials that teachers employ and the ways in which they employ them are crucial to the educative development of students.

The textbook is among the most potent and durable resources used by teachers in determining the content and the teaching procedures in classroom learning activities. The nature of conventional classrooms continues to be dominated by learnings that are based on or directed by the textbook, although workbooks and work sheets have also emerged as popular resources (Goodlad, 1984). Historically, the teaching of textbook content has been a central responsibility for the teacher. Given the transmissive function of the traditional school curriculum, "teaching the textbook" has often been equated with transmitting what is worth knowing in a particular discipline or area of inquiry. In such a situation, the purpose of the textbook is usually not to expose learners to ideas and unsettling issues but to represent disciplinary knowledge in a linear and puristic format. For all intents and purposes, the textbook becomes the curriculum and the process of curriculum development becomes little more than a matter of textbook adoption. Teaching is believed to be best served by closely and uncritically tracking lessons to the text.

Textbooks and workbooks have been criticized for, among other things, the inordinate concern that their authors place on facts and terms and for stilted and formula-driven writing that often precludes the treatment of ideas and issues in the narrative of the text (Elliott & Woodward, 1990). The body of this criticism shows that teachers may need to work against their own textbooks to bring idea and concept development to the classroom. This is not a trivial problem. During the 1980s, the commercial textbook industry was accused of **"dumbing-down"** its textbooks. At the time, the industry responded to efforts to censor certain materials and topics and to keep the curriculum fixed on unobjectionable facts. In California, State Superintendent Bill Honig criticized publishers for providing science textbooks that were lacking essential material related to evolution, human reproduction, and environmental problems. He later applied the same level of scrutiny to textbooks in other subject areas (Tanner, 1988). Afraid to offend important constituencies in large-enrollment states, the publishers bent over backward to avoid controversy in their books, but in doing so, they created controversy in their industry.

The textbook often includes a series of learning materials that make up what publishers and some school leaders see as a total teaching package for the classroom. Although the nature of these materials will vary, the idea behind many texts and teacher's manuals is to prescribe the knowledge and the instructional procedures of the curriculum. Teachers, of course, might track the text closely or they might use it in a more open-ended fashion, making judgments on emphasis, sequence, and engagement with other facets of the curriculum. In one instance, they might find themselves rejecting entirely the directives provided in a teacher's manual, in another they might follow the directives in a recipe-style manner.

When schools were subjected to increasing demands for minimal-competency testing during the 1970s and 1980s, teachers naturally focused their teaching on facts and skills, resorting to a teaching-to-the-test format that made workbook exercises much more popular. In most cases, the workbook was structured for low-level skill development and low-level fact accumulation. The extent to which educators resorted or even depended on these materials was an indication of the extent to which the "teacher-technician" mentality prevailed. The reliance on rudimentary and routine tasks that comprise workbook activities militates against the development of a professional construct that accounts for the mission of the school in the society and the place of the learner in the teaching-learning process.

Narrowness in the thinking and behavior of today's educators is associated with numerous factors. The exigencies of elevating standardized test scores, the proliferation of "plug-in" instructional models for teachers, the formulations of reductionist materials for teachers (e.g., prescriptive teacher guides, teacher-proof learning materials, and even some forms of computer-assisted instruction), and the exercise of influences working outside the interests of schools all potentially hinder the teacher's ability to use or implement a more orchestral perspective on teaching and learning.

Teachers ought to be taught and encouraged to analyze critically and to reflect on the full dynamics of the educational situation. They should be prepared to make practical decisions on the selection and organization of the subject matter, the promotion of clear-cut learning patterns, and the identification and use of sensitive and responsive assessment mechanisms. They should also be prepared to give critical thought to the educational, social, and moral implications of their pedagogical efforts. It is the teacher's own skill and insight that act as the final judge of what is taught and how it is taught. But the advancement toward a more critically minded teaching profession will be thwarted until teachers are liberated from the bonds of the technician mentality.

 ## Sources for Professional Decision Making

 What are the essential sources for the professional decision making of teachers? The progressive literature provides a clear signal in this area by highlighting the importance of three fundamental factors, or sources, in the educational situation: 1) the nature of the learner; 2) the values and aims of the society; and 3) the world of knowledge represented in organized subject matter (Tanner & Tanner, 1995). These three factors, when taken together, represent a working framework for teacher judgment. Combined, the factors force educators to weigh their decisions in light of the learners' interests and developmental needs, in spirit of the ethical foundations of democratic living, and in regard to some sense of what is worthy knowledge.

The Learner

Accounting for the nature of the learner is a process that involves practical action. It requires teachers to take some stock of their students' lives, interests, and needs.

Teachers, for instance, might take an interest inventory of their students' interests and explore student community life with the aim of identifying prevailing group problems, needs, and traditions. This is not just a matter of reflecting what children like to do but of trying to capture the dimension of a student's life (interests, problems, issues) in the curriculum.

These kinds of judgments not only help the teacher to decide what should be taught, but they also determine how certain skills, knowledge, and values should be taught. A teacher might scan the psychological literature to find insight on the developmental processes involved in teaching schoolchildren. Different-aged learners operate at qualitatively different levels of thinking and are under different social and biological pressures. The psychological literature in these areas might have solid implications for the construction of

The school curriculum, if it is to have much meaning, must link to student experiences outside the shool.

motivation in the classroom and for the development of lesson plans and learning objectives. Where a particular learning problem might arise in an individual, the effort to account for the nature of the learner might reveal a disability or a highly remediable deficiency. The effort to respond to the nature of the learner brings the teacher face-to-face with the literature on developmental processes, the nature of human intelligence, and the character of cognitive and affective process in learning. Howard Gardner's (1983) work on human intelligence, for example, has made it clear that intelligence cannot be reduced, as it has been for years, to purely verbal and quantitative manipulations. Benjamin Bloom's work on cognitive and affective processes (Bloom, 1956; Krathwohl, Bloom, & Masia, 1964) gives teachers working taxonomies that can be used to bring out a wider range of cognitive and affective variation in the classroom. Piaget's (1970) work on developmental processes points the way toward certain teaching strategies as well.

Where group problems might arise, the effort to account for the nature of the learner might call for an investigative strategy. If middle school students, for instance, are experimenting with cigarettes at an alarming rate, the teacher might look to the learner to try to find some insight. She might find that certain advertising gimmicks are preying on preadolescent social pressures, that peer pressures are exerting a strong pull, that the children who are smoking have parents who smoke, and that no fundamental conception exists among the students about the facts of lung cancer. These locally derived insights could then color the pedagogic strategy in the area of teaching about the dangers of smoking or in the more general area of health care. A curriculum plan might include objectives dedicated to learning about the facts of lung cancer and learning about the methods of professional advertising. Pedagogic strategies might stress peer pressure scenarios that provide students with working handles of action and group projects that involve the participation of parents, smokers, and nonsmokers.

In this way, an investigation of the student's school and neighborhood life becomes a fundamental part of being responsive to the nature of the learner.

Any number of tactics can be employed: student interviews, student questionnaires, various testing efforts, social data on the community, newspaper reports, and customized surveys.

Sometimes the investigative effort might be driven by certain professional priorities regarding the teaching of particular skills. Thus, the teacher of reading might want to know what children are reading, if anything, at home, how often they are reading outside of school, and where they are reading. Insight into these questions could very much shape pedagogic tactics that aim to instill in children a love for reading. It might also offer the teacher some insight into what should be read in class.

Accounting for the nature of the learner essentially means holding the teacher responsible for making some effort to respond to the interests and living conditions of students as well as to the fundamental literature of how students learn. It is an essential source for decision making.

The Society

The source of society represents a value and a skills base for the conduct of the classroom. In a democracy, public schooling has to proceed democratically. This means that what one is taught and how one is taught have to be influenced by some judgment of democratic education.

On the question of what is taught, the source of society has much insight. When teachers look to this source, they are required to examine problems and issues that are of relevance to the development of a democracy. Thus, social and personal issues might take center stage in the curriculum, and problem-focused inquiry might arise as an important classroom activity. The study of civic life in the school and the neighborhood emerges as a viable idea under these circumstances. If this source is taken seriously, any educational theory that failed to advance democratic education would have to be found lacking.

The source of society points to the need to teach certain values and certain kinds of skills in the actual life of the classroom. These values and skills transcend subject matter lines. For example, all teachers, regardless of what they are teaching, have to try to embody various democratic processes and values in their teaching. These values might include showing a concern for the well-being and dignity of others. With such a concern in mind, the classroom teacher might try to get children to learn how to consider the consequences of their action in the lives of others, to guard the safety and health of each other, to believe in the worth of each individual, and to offer help to those who are needy. Another value base for democracy might be found in cultivating an awareness of, and a willingness to do something about, the problems that affect the quality of life or in recognizing and finding value in constitutional rights and responsibilities. Accounting for the values of the society might bring the teacher to embrace objectives that teach children to defend the rights and liberties of all people, to think critically about the world, and to believe that each person's participation and opinion are important. It might lead to certain cognitive actions, such as teaching children to seek relevant information and alternative viewpoints, to support open and honest communication, to be able to obtain information from appropriate and various sources, to distinguish fact from opinion/reliable information from unreliable, and to detect logical errors, unstated assumptions, and unsupported statements. These actions are laden with democratic values and aims. They are important for the education of all children in all places and thus represent an important source for teacher decision making.

Subject Matter

There is no escaping the question of subject matter. Students have to be taught something, and the question of what content or what knowledge is most worthwhile has been an enduring one for educators. Thus, using the source of subject matter, one is essentially drawn to the question of what shall be taught and how will the knowledge encapsulated in organized subject matter be used to help with the education of children.

The question of the content of the curriculum is one that is posed in relation to the learner and the society. Thus, the curriculum does not start with some preidentified sense of what is worthwhile but with an honest commitment to offering an education that is allegiant to what is best for learners living in a democracy. Educators go to this source to gather their sense of content and their sense of how to organize the content. An educational theory without a sense of content fails under this framework. The Historical Contexts feature in this section shows how basic reform ideas have failed to honor important sources for professional decision-making.

 Procedures for Professional Decision Making

The essence of teaching and learning is captured in the day-to-day interactions between teachers and students. Many of these interactions are shaped through what is commonly known as a lesson. Indeed, the lesson still reigns as the most popular form of organizing instruction in the classroom (Goodlad, 1984). Nearly all teachers see a good share of their professional duties as associated with planning and teaching lessons (see the Web Points feature for a discussion of on-line lesson ideas).

The character of a teacher's lesson depends on various factors, including the grade level of the students, the overarching objectives of the school, and the nature and organization of the subject matter in the curriculum. A lesson could build on earlier knowledge, be part of a broader teaching unit, and involve several assignments outside of the classroom, or it could be impromptu, on the spot, and conceived according to an emergent question. It could be highly expository in nature, designed to build a particular skill, and be directed at a whole class of students, or it could be marked by questioning tactics designed to create the conditions for a conversation and be directed at a single individual. Whatever its nature, the lesson is always a part of the teacher's landscape; educators, parents, administrators, and even students probably would have trouble conceiving of a school without a teacher who abides by some sense of lesson making.

Why has the lesson become so ubiquitous? Much of it, of course, relates to the need to organize the instructional direction of the classroom by making decisions about time and place in the curriculum and by making judgments about the coverage and mastery of certain skills and knowledge. In most

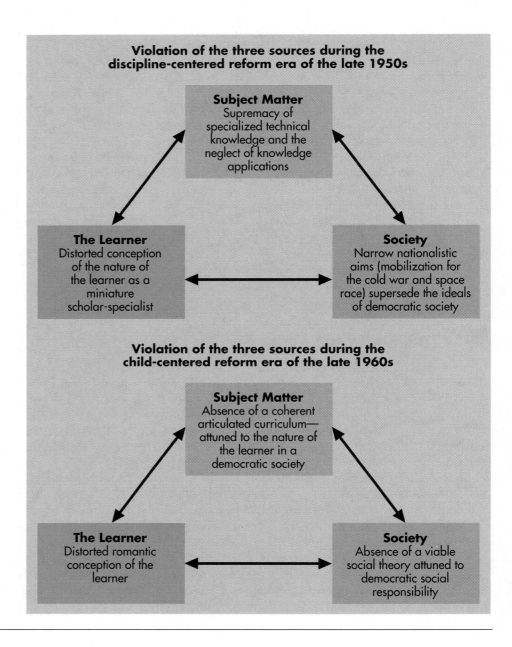

Violation of the three sources during the discipline-centered reform era of the late 1950s

Subject Matter
Supremacy of specialized technical knowledge and the neglect of knowledge applications

The Learner
Distorted conception of the nature of the learner as a miniature scholar-specialist

Society
Narrow nationalistic aims (mobilization for the cold war and space race) supersede the ideals of democratic society

Violation of the three sources during the child-centered reform era of the late 1960s

Subject Matter
Absence of a coherent articulated curriculum—attuned to the nature of the learner in a democratic society

The Learner
Distorted romantic conception of the learner

Society
Absence of a viable social theory attuned to democratic social responsibility

lessons, teachers attempt to communicate a particular idea and see it to closure within a certain period of time. More than anything, the lesson represents an effort to channel the instructional direction of the classroom.

Lessons are always a piece of a greater instructional plan. No thoughtful teacher would think of his instruction as simply a series of unconnected lessons. Yearly goals for student learning usually drive monthly unit plans,

Teacher Talk *and Lesson Plan Ideas*

The web offers those with a little technological initiative the opportunity to "publish" all kinds of materials at little or no cost, especially if they are associated with a university. One good example of such a grassroots publication is *Teacher Talk,* published by the Center for Adolescent Studies at the School of Education, Indiana University, Bloomington, Indiana.

It is located at http://education.indiana.edu/cas/tt/tthmpg.html

Teacher Talk is aimed at the interests of preservice, secondary education teachers and is written largely by students. It is published only as a series of web documents so it is impossible to get a printed copy unless the documents viewed on the web site are printed from the screen. The contents of Volume 1, Issue 2 includes a discussion of different views on classroom management. Students explore their views on management styles such as authoritarian or indifferent. Other Issues in the series include a discussion on the problem of violence in the schools. Any interested reader can respond to the topics by sending an e-mail to ttalk@indiana.edu.

which in turn determine each individual lesson. Various behavioral objectives converge with the content of the curriculum to give the lesson its working material, its sense of what content should be covered and what behavioral objectives should be cultivated.

The traditional image of the schoolteacher is one of a purveyor of knowledge, of someone who values an expository method of telling children about what they need to know. Under such circumstances, the aim of teaching is to transmit knowledge—to cast it forward, more or less uncritically, as something worth knowing. Such a view of teaching is, of course, not wholly bad. Few would deny the need for schools and teachers to fund children with the skills of numeracy and literacy, with knowledge in the sciences, and with the habits and principles that most directly contribute to social democratic understandings. This so-called conservative side of teaching allows educators to build a common culture, to negotiate a common sense of what it means to be knowledgeable in various disciplines of knowledge (science, math, social sciences, and so on), and to develop a reasoned understanding of democratic principles. A problem occurs, however, when such a purpose dominates the thinking and behavior of teachers, when the aim of transmitting knowledge becomes the sole purpose of the school and no alternative or critical sense of knowledge is explored. Thus, teaching must also embrace a purpose that counters the conservative tradition with an open commitment to questioning knowledge and encouraging the development of independent thinking and social criticism. Here the role of the teacher is not to transmit knowledge but to question and problematize it, while also placing it in a context that allows the learner to apply it to life settings.

Teaching entails a vast complex of skills and behaviors that goes well beyond lesson planning and actual teaching. But one way or another, educators have to face several fundamental curriculum questions to teach successfully. These questions were articulated by Ralph Tyler (1949) almost a half century ago: 1) What purposes should the school experience convey and

Tenure, as it is defined by most school agencies, protects teachers from dismissal based on their own political or religious orientation, whether or not that orientation fits the school or community culture. The promotion of any religious viewpoint, of course, is not allowed in publicly funded schools.

support? 2) What experiences will embody these purposes and how will these experiences be organized and developed? 3) How will educators know if these experiences had any effect in relation to their purposes? These questions constitute the heart of teaching and of curriculum development for the classroom teacher. They are basic professional procedures for decision making.

What Purposes Should the School Experience Convey and Support?

The question concerning educational purposes is of course one that involves all types of philosophical judgments about what is worth learning and knowing. For instance, when a teacher decides to plan and implement certain lessons, her judgments will be tied to wider decisions involving the question of what knowledge, skills, and values are most worthwhile. One could work out of a more conservative tradition that places an emphasis on expository or transmissive methods of teaching or a more progressive or even radical tradition that aims to cultivate social criticism and the critical interrogation of all knowledge. In an earlier chapter, the overarching purposes of a comprehensive education were described. They represented an effort to educate youth in a wide range of areas, including education for vocational success, individual needs and talents, intellectual or academic discipline, and socio-civic competency. Each of these areas would obviously implicate a multitude of subgoals or subobjectives that demand a description of what might be seen as educational.

Thus, the sense of educational purpose is reflected in the objectives and the content chosen for classroom study. In thinking about classroom instruction, one should always be directed by a conceptual map of what one wants to accomplish behaviorally with students over the course of a time frame. One decides by weighing the school's mission, by accounting for state-mandated competencies and content requirements that accompany subject and grade levels, by examining critically local school and community traditions and priorities, and by formulating a personal but professionally grounded idea of what all children should accomplish.

Formulating Objectives and Selecting Content

In formulating the behavioral objectives of a unit or particular set of lessons, the teacher, as suggested, should make decisions that are accountable to the nature of the learner and the values of the society. In other words, the objectives set forth in any classroom should be able to pass the test of being appropriate for the learner and appropriate for the schools of democracy. These objectives should be broadly framed with a generalizable tone that captures the spirit of what one wants to accomplish without being too specific and too prescriptive. They should include material related to attitudes, ways of thinking, sensitivities and feelings, and habits or skills to be mastered (Taba, 1962). They might include generic objectives dedicated to thinking skills, inquiry skills, communicative skills, study skills, social attitudes, and social competencies (to name a few). The purpose of these objectives is to act as a compass for action. The objectives are guideposts for conduct, statements that help to animate what one will do in the classroom.

Of course, the objectives must also be accompanied by the basic concepts, ideas, and facts about a unit or some focus of study. Thus, the teacher must also decide what subject matter shall be used in the curriculum, how that subject matter will be organized, and exactly how the content of the curriculum will interact with the behavioral objectives. Often, the subject matter of the curriculum is already provided to the teacher in the form of state or district-mandated decisions on content and skills or in the form of a preidentified body of knowledge covered in a text, a curriculum guide, or even a standardized test. Even if this is the case, however, educators still have many decisions to make about what to emphasize, about how a chosen body of subject matter will be related to certain objectives, about how the subject matter might be organized, and about what teaching strategies should be used to bring the important subject matter to light in the classroom.

These are not steps that can be taken whimsically. The choice of content has to reflect confidence in the learn-ability and appropriateness of the material. It also has to reflect an emerging pattern for the organization of the material, meaning that variously problem-focused, interdisciplinary, or highly discipline-centered approaches might be taken. The layout of the content should be dedicated to an expression of ideas or principles and to a specific description of content.

For explanatory purposes, suppose that a tenth grade high school teacher is planning to develop a unit in the area of civic education. There are, of course, several content possibilities. She has chosen, in consultation with colleagues, to develop a year-long unit dedicated to the following broad content objectives: 1) understanding the nature of constitutional govern-ments and the difference between limited and unlimited powers; 2) under-standing the history of constitutional democracies; 3) knowing the fundamen-tals of the political and legal systems in American democracy; 4) knowing the principles of the market economy 5) understanding current political issues in America, and; 6) understanding the branches of governmental operation in America.

Before further developing the content objectives, the teacher must also identify important behavioral objectives in the curriculum. These are some-times known as *generic behavioral objectives*. They are content-neutral objec-tives that are often tied into areas like thinking skills, communicative skills, study/inquiry skills, social attitudes, and social competencies. The objectives might look something like the following:

Generic objectives

A. Social skills and Social Values

A1. Positive Attitudes Toward Self (the learner)

A1a. Development of self-respect

A1b. Development of honesty, integrity, and healthy self-criticism

A1c. Development of optimistic mind-set
1. Constructive attitude toward school activities

A1d. Development of open-mindedness

A1e. Development of self-interest and self-desire to learn

A2. Social Democratic Skills and Attitudes

A2a. Respect for the dignity and worth of all human beings irrespective of race, ethnicity, gender or economic/social status

A2b. Appreciation of diversity in people, opinions and viewpoints.
1. Sensitivity to others

A2c. Development of tolerance, goodwill, kindliness, and an enlightened sense of justice

A2d. Understanding of democratic purposes and practices
1. Social responsibility and social cooperation
Treats others well
Works to make oneself useful to a social group
Contributes to group discussions
Is open to civil and constructive criticism
Is knowledgeable and tolerant of other viewpoints
Reveals good sense of fair play
Is considerate of the problems facing underprivileged groups
Is politically awareness

A3. Duties and rights of citizenship
Specifics

A4. Intellectual and Aesthetic Values

A4a. Critical respect for scientific truth

A4b. Respect for work well done

A4c. Understanding freedoms of thought, expression, and worship

A4d. Love of beauty in art and in the lives of people

B. Thinking Skills

B1. Engages in the analysis, synthesis, and evaluation of knowledge

B2. Applies scientific method to social thinking

B3. Understands cause and effect relationships

B4. Independent thinking

B5. Ability to analyze arguments and propaganda

B6. Evaluation of authenticity of information

B7. Ability to foresee the consequences of a proposed idea

B8. Ability to understand quantitative reasoning

C. Inquiry and Study Skills

C1. Ability to collect facts and data

C2. Skill in selecting dependable sources of data

C3. Ability to observe and listen attentively

C4. Ability to read critically

C5. Ability to discriminate between important and unimportant facts.

C6. Ability to take notes, and read graphs, charts, tables and maps

C7. Skills in outlining and summarizing

C8. Skills in effective planning and efficient use of time

D. Communicative Skills

D1. Skill in writing clearly and persuasively

D2. Skills in oral presentation

D3. Skills in debate and argumentation

D4. Skills in the preparation of charts, graphs, tables and other nonverbal tools of communication

Source: Adapted from Smith, E. R. & Tyler, R. W. (1948) *Appraising and recording student progress.* New York: Harper and Brothers.

The focus here is strictly on desirable generic behaviors. In some cases, the teacher might want to break down some broad objectives into more specific component parts, as demonstrated with the objective listed under A2. Similarly, an objective such as D1, "the ability to write persuasively," might be further detailed into sub-objectives such as, the ability to write a speech and the ability to express a viewpoint or make a criticism in various literary and nonliterary forms. The level of specificity is negotiable. If broad or general objectives provide enough direction, one may not want to make them more specific.

Once the behavioral objectives are clear, one might proceed to the step of identifying the subject matter. The presumption in articulating content goals is that there is a body of content facts, information ideas, and generalizations that need to be taught and known by students. As mentioned, sometimes the content of what one is expected or required to teach is already drawn out in a school-adopted textbook and in other materials provided by the school. This is more likely in subjects such as math, which are still very much skill-based, than in subjects such as social studies, which have a more wide ranging flavor to their content. The teacher will ask herself what facts, information, principles, and generalizations need to be taught in relation to a year-long 10th grade unit dedicated to the following content objectives: 1) understanding the nature of constitutional governments and the differences between limited and unlimited powers; 2) understanding the history of constitutional democracies; 3) knowing the fundamentals of the political and legal systems in the country; 4) knowing the principles of the market economy; 5) understanding current political issues; and, 6) understanding the branches of government operation. The general idea behind the development of content goals is to describe, with some degree of specificity and clarity, the important facts, information, principles, ideas and generalizations that students should know.

If the behavioral objectives are clear and the content is organized, one can begin to piece the two parts together and set the stage for a series of lessons that will ensure that all identified generic and content objectives will be covered. As expressed in Figure 10.4, the convergence between what one teaches (the content) and the behavior that one wants to develop (the generic objectives), represents a point of birth for the lesson. It allows the teacher to say, "in one set of lessons, I am going to be sure to cover all of the facts and principles related to understanding the nature of constitutional governments and the differences between limited and unlimited powers while also offering children the opportunity to engage in higher level thinking exercises. (See Figure 10.4). Of course, the teacher is also free to combine objectives and content, as well as to skip certain connections that may not be appropriate or applicable. The connections between the generic objectives and content provide the direction for the question of what experiences will embody the school's purposes (see the Objects of Teaching feature in this section).

What Experiences Must Embody the School's Purposes and How Might These Experiences Be Organized and Developed?

The form of pedagogy that one will use in the classroom becomes an issue here. Various instructional approaches might come into play in deciding how a lesson might carry-out various behavioral and content goals. A direct teaching model might be used in one setting and cooperative learning in another; Socratic questioning or a problem-focused solution testing model might also be used. Various teaching models and other methodological techniques find their way into this procedure of developing activities.

The experiences or activities developed in the curriculum must, of course, be organized, meaning that a sense of sequence and emphasis will be constructed. There are two organizational questions to be answered. The first is how will the activities that aim to capture certain combinations of objectives and content be organized in their lesson formats? One way to answer this is to take an organizational approach patterned along three basic concerns: introduction, development, and culmination (Taba, 1962). Introductory activities would essentially be designed to help the teacher and the students to get a flavor for the general spirit of the subsection of objective and content, as well as to arouse interests and develop some involvement. Development activities would get the teacher to think about the full development of the objectives and content. For instance, what readings, projects, committee work, and seatwork lessons will effectively meet the objectives and content? Culminating activities might provide a good segue into the next set of activities and might provide synthesizing activities that capture the requirements entailed in the convergence between objective and content. The second question deals with the overarching organizational framework for the curriculum—the sense of how each of the component blocks of activity will relate to each other. Some curriculum specialists are keen on developing activities that move from easy to difficult, known to unknown, and concrete to abstract. The organizational framework should represent a logical or otherwise reasonable progression of questions, ideas, concepts, and information that will set the pattern for a running sequence of teaching events.

FIGURE 10.4

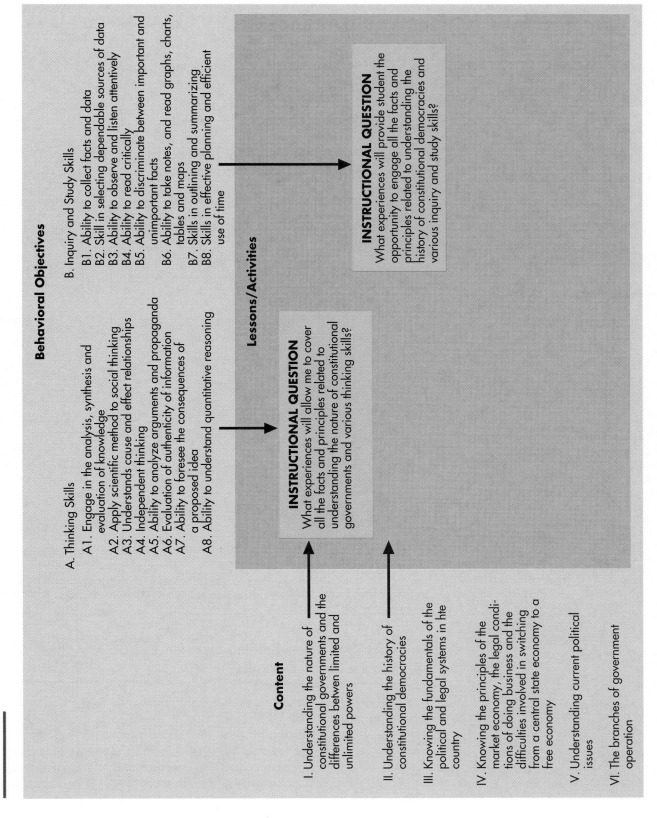

Behavioral Objectives

A. Thinking Skills

A1. Engage in the analysis, synthesis and evaluation of knowledge
A2. Apply scientific method to social thinking
A3. Understands cause and effect relationships
A4. Independent thinking
A5. Ability to analyze arguments and propaganda
A6. Evaluation of authenticity of information
A7. Ability to foresee the consequences of a proposed idea
A8. Ability to understand quantitative reasoning

B. Inquiry and Study Skills

B1. Ability to collect facts and data
B2. Skill in selecting dependable sources of data
B3. Ability to observe and listen attentively
B4. Ability to read critically
B5. Ability to discriminate between important and unimportant facts
B6. Ability to take notes, and read graphs, charts, tables and maps
B7. Skills in outlining and summarizing
B8. Skills in effective planning and efficient use of time

Lessons/Activities

INSTRUCTIONAL QUESTION

What experiences will allow me to cover all the facts and principles related to understanding the nature of constitutional governments and various thinking skills?

INSTRUCTIONAL QUESTION

What experiences will provide student the opportunity to engage all the facts and principles related to understanding the history of constitutional democracies and various inquiry and study skills?

Content

I. Understanding the nature of constitutional governments and the differences bewen limited and unlimited powers

II. Understanding the history of constitutional democracies

III. Knowing the fundamentals of the political and legal systems in hte country

IV. Knowing the principles of the market economy, the legal conditions of doing business and the difficulties involved in switching from a central state economy to a free economy

V. Understanding current political issues

VI. The branches of government operation

Developing Instructional Activities

Content	**BEHAVIORAL ASPECTS OF LEARNING OBJECTIVES**			
	Understanding important facts and principles	Interpreting data and applying principles	Developing skill in making decisions with purpose	Communicating effectively with groups
Science and Humankind				
Functions of Human Organisms Nutrition				
Digestion				
Circulation				
Use of Plant/Animal Resources Energy Relationships				
Heredity/Genetics				
Land Utilization				

Based on this figure, choose a cross-reference between one or two objectives and one or two content areas and design a series of learning experiences. Think about how you might sequence the experiences, organize them, and eventually assess them.

How Do Teachers Know that the Experiences Had Any Effect in Relation to the Stated Purposes?

The last procedure for curriculum decision-making concerns evaluation. The traditional view of evaluation in the curriculum tends to be seen as something that occurs at the conclusion of some area or unit of curriculum study. The curriculum is perceived to be a kind of applied treatment that must be assessed in terms of its predetermined goals and prefashioned outcomes. And although such an aspect of evaluation in the curriculum is certainly important, the idea of evaluation is one that is also continual and that, in certain instances, might be an initiating activity rather than a concluding one in the conduct of curriculum improvement or reform.

Evaluation, as described here, is *of* the curriculum. It is part and parcel of the very essence of the curriculum. Questions related to what to teach, how to teach, and why to teach (all fundamental to the construction of the curriculum) are always accompanied by a desire to know about effects; to know, for instance, whether certain methods of knowledge organization or certain pedagogic strategies met certain expected outcomes, or to know whether the very rationale behind the curriculum was justifiable in terms of its consequences in the lives of learners.

Ideally, of course, the widest range of assessment and testing techniques, including quantitative measures, essays, interviews, portfolios, and various performance and achievement exams, should be used in the curriculum (see The Contemporary Debate feature on the use of student portfolios). This multifaceted strategy toward assessment allows the curriculum to operate without being influenced by the dominance of any particular assessment methodology—it protects, in other words, against the condition of building the curriculum around the assessment approach.

In elementary, middle, and secondary education, there has been an awakening of new forms of assessment in education, many of which have paraded under the category of alternative assessment. The new, or so-called alternative, vision of assessment takes the question of instructional success in the curriculum quite seriously. It is less concerned about standardized forms of assessment that might lead to judgments about certification or student selections and is more concerned about how the curriculum is served by the proposed ends of the schooling experience. Accompanying this new focus is a premium on nonstandardized group assessments, on multidimensional measures (quantitative and qualitative), and on the use of student folders, projects, conversations, and demonstrations.

Alternative assessment, as it is known today, is actually curriculum assessment as it has been known for years. As early as 1949, for instance, Tyler discussed some of the assessment opportunities available to curriculum developers within the framework of his rationale.

This photo of Ralph Tyler was part of the press release to announce the creation of the Center for Advanced Study in the Behavioral Sciences at Stanford University.

> There are a great many kinds of desired behaviors which represent educational objectives that are not easily appraised by paper and pencil devices. For example, such an objective as personal-social adjustment is more easily and validly appraised through observations of children under conditions in which social relations are involved. Observations are also useful devices to get at habits and certain kinds of operational skills. Another method which is useful in evaluation is the interview which may throw light upon changes taking place in attitudes, in interests, in appreciations, and the like. Questionnaires sometimes serve to give evidence about interests, about attitudes, and about other types of behavior. The collection of actual products made by students is sometimes a useful way of getting evidence of behavior. For example, the collection of themes students have written may serve to give some evidence of the writing ability of students, or the paintings students have made in an art class may serve to give evidence of skill and possibly interests in an area. (Tyler, 1949, pp. 107–108)

The point is that the idea of curriculum assessment has long supported an inclusive perspective on assessment, though in the practice of the school curriculum, standardized measures have been dominant. Like alternative assessment, curriculum assessment takes on a role of diagnosing student strengths and weaknesses and of monitoring the general progress of learning in the interests of making subsequent revisions and improvements, not only

Portfolios

How many times have you studied for a multiple-choice test, went on to pass the test, and later forgot everything you supposedly learned? How many times have you felt that the test you took did not reflect what you knew or what you thought was important about the subject? How many times did you receive a grade on a test that seemed unrelated to how much you studied? If this experience sounds all too common, there might not be anything wrong with you. Perhaps it is time to think of a new way of measuring what people have learned.

Many educators have become increasingly disenchanted with the traditional ways of measuring student learning and have proposed substantial modifications. One of the most promising changes is replacing the multiple-choice/true false test with student portfolios. Borrowing the portfolio idea from disciplines such as architecture, many teachers have given students the opportunity to show what they have learned in a portfolio of their work. Portfolios are especially well suited for subjects such as writing, in which students can demonstrate their growth over time. Portfolios also provide students with the opportunity to showcase their best work. For instance, a writing portfolio in any grade can encourage students to think about strategies for improving their writing. Instead of taking a test on punctuation or having a teacher make corrections on students' papers (most of which are ignored anyway), students are asked to self-evaluate their work. Many teachers using portfolios insist that their students not only put a range of their writing (both their good and bad works) into their portfolios but also write a paragraph or two telling why they chose to submit each writing sample.

Educators disagree on whether to grade student portfolios. Some argue that student self-assessment is the primary purpose of the portfolio. Grading the portfolio continues the tradition of a teacher-centered education. Other maintain that schools still require measures of student success. Although grading the portfolio might not be advisable, students must be given a grade. Still others suggest instead of grades that students should be given narrative statements from the teachers about their progress.

Perhaps the most controversial issue regarding student portfolios is whether they should replace the standardized tests that often define the success or failure of a student, a school, or school district. Each year, newspapers across the country print the results of standardized test scores. If a school's average test score is high, then the school is considered a good school. If the scores are low, then the school is bad. Advocates of student portfolios think that scores on standardized tests are a crude and unfair method for assessing student learning. They suggest that samples taken from student portfolios be printed in the paper, then parents and the community could see what students are *doing* in the schools.

in the stated purposes of the schooling experience but also in the general methods used to give life to such purposes. The focus is to move away from student comparisons and to place the role of assessment into the function of program improvement. Thus, assessment under such circumstances is more likely to be criterion based, openly testing for criterion levels of competency or mastery. Such a focus moves away from the kind of assessment that is expressly designed to file students into categories or into a bell curve continuum that necessitates an above- or below-average standing. Curriculum assessment might also look to group standings on systemwide outcomes and to the effect of particular instructional treatments, as well as to overall studentwide performance. But it tries to keep a low-stakes profile.

The distinction between low- and high-stakes testing is an important one. With low-stakes assessment, there is typically no standardization and therefore no basis for comparability. And with such matters out of the way, the concept of objective scoring and traditional concerns over issues of reliability and validity are less urgent, though it should be said that content validity is still very much a factor (Latting, 1992). Assessment, however, that aims at a higher stake (i.e., judging the worthiness of an educator, determining suitability for scholarships or admissions to prestigious programs) immediately brings questions of comparability, impartiality, standardization, reliability, and various forms of validity into the discussion. If teachers and other curriculum leaders, however, are going to take the question of assessment as a curricular and instructional concern, they would be served by thinking about assessment means that are closest to the hands of the student—that embrace student's products, student voices, and student interests. These efforts in the area of curriculum improvement, if exercised over a reasonable period of time, would likely be more valid forms of assessment than anything designed for selection purposes, but they would simultaneously be less reliable, in the sense that the subjective judgment of teachers—what they collect and how they respond to it—will vary (Latting, 1992). Still, the use of internal forms of assessment allows for a sensitivity to local goals and local methods that are not likely to occur with external assessments. It also allows for a more fluid or continual sense of assessment that is symbiotic with the curriculum.

The instructional direction provided by combining working curriculum objectives with a topical sense of content or subject matter is also basic to the question of assessment. In other words, the very nature of instruction and of assessment can be defined by the convergence between what educators teach (the content) and what skills or behaviors educators want to develop (the objectives). In examining objectives number D1—skills in writing clearly and persuasively—and D3—skills in debate and argumentation—in relation to the content topic of civic education, the teacher asks what kind of evidence can be gathered to demonstrate these two skills of communicative competence in the content area of civic education. Writing and debating skills could be assessed using a wide range of approaches to shed light on these concerns. One might require students to write essays from different political standpoints and grade these using holistic scoring techniques. One might in the course of the unit teach specific debating skills and deliberately judge students on their ability to apply such skills in real debate forums. When a summative assessment is considered, the teacher can go through all the objectives and the content areas covered in class and be sure that the test is accountable to every dimension of the planned experience.

The results of the assessments are then used to renegotiate the curriculum and to reconsider its objectives and the means used to achieve them. These results might also lead to a reconsideration of the assessment instruments or to curriculum experimentation that might show a clearer image of an emerging trend. They might also raise flags about certain problems in the curriculum that might require further diagnosis or different sorts of assessment trials. More refined assessment that directly targets phases of the curriculum (instructional strategies or other classroom actions) might also follow. Thus, the assessment of the curriculum is intended to circulate insight about the value of various school experiences and the plans used to energize these experiences.

 ## The Teacher and the Law

One way or another, teachers become inevitably entangled in legal issues related not only to their own rights in the school setting but also to the rights of others, especially the rights of schoolchildren. Being aware of some of the fundamental issues in this area gives educators a working sense of how they might proceed with their own actions and behaviors and how they might react to the actions and behaviors of others. Knowledge of the law allows a teacher to err on the side of caution, to think twice before acting, and to know when to seek professional advice. Teachers, in fact, have been found to have a low level of legally accurate knowledge in the area of education. (Zirkel, 1996).

Due Process

Every U.S. citizen has a constitutional right to due process. Such a right protects the accused from irresponsible and unwarranted punitive actions. Due process essentially means that in certain situations, a set of rules and principles has to be followed when an individual is accused of an act that might lead to his dismissal or that might otherwise affect his livelihood or reputation. In the context of the school, this usually means that a teacher who is subjected to serious charges would have to be informed in a timely manner of any proceedings or accusations taken against him, would have to be given a fair opportunity to answer the charges, would have the right to legal counsel and to mount a defense against the charges, and would have an outlet for appeal. The idea of due process is constitutionally anchored. It is a part of the 14th Amendment to the Constitution: no state may deprive a person "of life, liberty, or property, without due process of law." It is, at its core, an issue of fairness (Fischer, Schimmel, & Kelley, 1991).

With due process to consider, school districts cannot behave whimsically in their actions against teachers. The school has to be sure to abide by due process if the problem involves a liberty, life, or property concern. The courts have, generally speaking, defined a liberty concern broadly, as a concern involving the reputation, honor, or integrity of a person. If one's job is on the line, teachers can claim a property concern, especially teachers with tenure protections. Thus, a teacher accused of sexual discrimination, incompetence, or negligence will likely be facing charges that will affect both liberty and property concerns. As a result, the teacher has to be given a complete and timely description of the charges standing against her. She also has to be given the opportunity to defend herself before an impartial body. Because such charges have to be able to withstand the scrutiny of a hearing and an appeal process, the school has to have a documented and lucidly reasoned argument against a teacher.

Due process protects students also. A student, for instance, facing suspension for a violation of a school rule could claim a liberty interest. As a result, the student has to be given due process before the punishment can be carried out. This means that the student needs to be provided with written notice of the charge and be given an opportunity to present his side of the story. He also should be given a chance to pursue an appeal outlet. It is important to remember that due process applies to charges that implicate a liberty, life, or property concern. Thus, if a teacher punishes a student in class for forgetting his homework without formal due process, there would not likely be a legal issue.

For teachers, due process is a condition followed with great care when it involves a dismissal proceeding. The dismissal of teachers is not always easy to accomplish. Teachers, of course, can be fired for incompetence, neglect of duty, immorality, or unprofessional conduct. But teachers are unique in that some are granted tenure protections against losing their jobs to arbitrary administrative action or to some prejudicial political or religious viewpoint. A principal or a superintendent cannot terminate the contract of a teacher because of the teacher's politics, religion, or lifestyle. However, if the school can demonstrate incompetence in classroom performance or, depending on the state, immoral conduct, such as sexual relations with students or abetting student drinking, even tenure protection will not likely save the teacher from getting fired. The idea of tenure was designed to eliminate the role of political patronage in government hiring processes, to guarantee to teachers the fundamental right of academic freedom, and to recognize the teacher's job as a property concern in the eyes of the law (*Board of Regents v. Roth,* 1972).

Teacher Liability

The dismissal of teachers is one matter, but what legal liability does a teacher carry for his conduct within a school setting? If a child breaks an arm during a physical education routine, can the teacher be held liable? If a student is injured during a mugging on a class trip, can the teacher be found legally accountable?

There is a general rule of thumb followed when liability charges are used against teachers. According to Fischer, Schimmel, and Kelly (1991), several general conditions have to be weighed.

One important question that has to be dealt with is whether the teacher owes a duty of care to the student. In other words, was the teacher expected to look after the student at the time of the incident? Needless to say, the school has a legal responsibility to protect students from injury or harm, so there is no question that there is a duty of care to be fulfilled. But, in the case of individual teachers, the obligation of care may not always be easy to sort out. If an injury occurs to a student under the territorial watch of a teacher (the teacher's classroom or study hall, the appointed monitor of the playground), there is not much debate about the responsibility of the teacher. But if the incident occurred as a student was moving between classrooms or on the way to the bathroom, the issue of "duty of care" is not as easy to determine. A high school, however, that fails to provide any teacher supervision in its girls' locker room because there are no female physical education teachers on staff, would be on shakey ground. If an incident occurred involving a serious injury in the locker room, the school would clearly be in danger of being found liable. The duty of care (of supervision) in the girls' locker room is not being fulfilled in such a school.

Another set of questions has to do with whether the teacher was negligent, whether the negligence was directly related to the injury, and whether the injury itself calls for some compensation. This is where most of the dispute occurs in cases of liability. The basic question here is, To what extent was the teacher's lack of vigilance, lack of action, or lack of foresight related to the occurrence of the injury? Could the teacher have reasonably foreseen the collapse of a bookshelf that broke a student's arm? Were there early signs that the bookshelf might have collapsed? Did the teacher take action to remedy the problem or protect students from potential injury, such as roping off the area until the shelf could be dismantled or repaired? If a student was injured playing baseball, was the injury a function of the normal events associated with playing the game or was it due to a foreseeable problem that the teacher ignored? Was the injury due to a lack of proper supervision? These are the central questions. If a student gets lost on a field trip and is later injured, the questions of liability quickly turn to how the student was supervised and the conditions under which she got lost.

Teachers cannot be at all places at all times. But, generally speaking, they are expected to be able to prevent foreseeable problems, to be on the scene, and to be watchful. If a group of students is left unattended and something happens in the classroom, the teacher is clearly at risk of being found liable. But if a student, for instance, is fooling around with a Bunsen burner during a science experiment and the teacher intervenes by removing him from the group and cautioning him against the dangers of such action, only to find that 2 minutes later he ignored her authority and inadvertently set his shirt ablaze, the teacher would be in a good position to defend herself against an accusation of negligence. The law essentially demands reasonable and prudent action, meaning that there is no expectation of telepathic powers or of superhuman ability, only a reasonable presence of supervision and preventive action.

School districts are familiar with their potential liability. They often provide liability coverage for their teachers. Local teacher unions will also offer teachers inexpensive personal liability coverage. School districts are well known for asking parents to sign consent forms releasing them from liability when students are engaged in activities outside of the school (field trips, sporting events). However, there is still a legal expectation, irrespective of the waiver, that the school will protect and secure the safety and welfare of the children. If negligent, the school and the involved teacher or teachers can still be found liable.

Freedoms of Expression

The concept of academic freedom is an important one. It is a First Amendment right to free speech that allows educators to make decisions about reading materials and to study topics that may not always be popular with local community viewpoints (see The Contemporary Debate feature on academic freedom). However, academic freedom for educators does not translate into allowing teachers to assign any topic or reading material that they desire. There is a standard of professional measure that needs to be met. In other words, teachers are essentially free to choose topics and materials as long as their decisions are professionally defensible. A teacher will not have much of a leg to stand on if he insists on using pornographic readings to teach

Testing Academic Freedom

Springfield, Missouri. When 40 kindergarten children opened copies of Maurice Sendak's *In the Night Kitchen,* they probably didn't notice that an artist had drawn a pair of shorts over the drawing of a nude boy. The work with a felt-tip pen was commissioned by school officials who thought the altered picture "would be in a little better taste for the community standards."

The director of elementary education said: "Obviously we felt there would be a reaction, so we decided that if the book could be changed without altering it severely, we would do it. We didn't want to detract from the story. We felt it was a good story. I think in the public schools we have to be sensitive to the feelings of people. As far as nudity is concerned I guess I'm an old fogey, but I think it should be covered."

If you were a kindergarten teacher who might use Sendak's book, would you consider the school's action an abridgement of your academic freedom? Would this be an issue worth fighting against, or do you find the school's action to be sensible?

Elkader, Iowa. The leader of approximately 30 parents who called themselves Concerned Citizens read a two-hour complaint against books used in the Middle School at Volga. The concerned parent contended that the Ginn 360 Reading Series, the Houghton-Mifflin Action Series, and *A Piece of the Action* by New Dimensions in Education "contained an undercurrent which definitely undermines our American and Christian principles." The protesting parent included these remarks in her complaint. "Among the writers and those given praise in the reading material are: Ogden Nash, Woody Guthrie, Langston Hughes, Joan Baez, Gwendolyn Brooks, Malcolm X, and Dick Gregory. These are all known communists or subversive revolutionaries and sympathizers. Hughes, for example, has authored a variety of subversive 'literature,' including the blasphemous poem 'Goodbye Christ' and a piece he calls 'The Workers Song.' "

If you were a schoolteacher in this district, how might you respond to such a complaint? What actions might you take to deal with such a situation?

Source: Jenkinson, E. B. (1979). *Censors in the Classroom.* Carbondale, IL: Southern Illinois University Press, p. 40–41.

preadolescent children about writing or if he uses blatantly racist materials without having a clear and a high-minded instructional purpose or objective. In the former case, there would be obvious standards of morality that would be violated as well as issues about the appropriateness of the material based on age and maturity factors.

Instructional decisions about curriculum materials and study topics have been challenged in court by local school boards. In ***Hazelwood School District v. Kuhlmeier,*** the courts found that the local school board can act as the final authority regarding what is to be included and excluded in the curriculum as long it has a professionally grounded position. This means that if the school board is going to act against certain controversial materials, its action has to be educationally justifiable. Thus, the board might ask: Are the materials appropriate to the maturity and age level of the students? Do they fulfill sound educational objectives? Are they disruptive to the general educational process of the school? Disputes over what teachers teach and the materials that they use to teach have to be solidly placed in an argument over the educational viability of the topics or materials. They cannot be based on a special interest position taken from a particular religious or political platform.

In a manner of speaking, the courts have tried to define the difference between the idea of censorship and the idea of educational development. School boards that insist on the removal of certain materials because they are offensive to certain political or religious standards in the community are engaging in censorship if their argument does not extend to the educational value of the material. Teachers are held to the same standard. Thus, if a teacher refuses to teach a certain book or deal with certain topics because it conflicts with her personal political, religious, or philosophical belief system, she is engaging in censorship and can be dismissed for such an action. But the decision not to use certain materials can obviously be made if the teacher or some other source of authority in the curriculum asserts that the level of emotional maturity needed to deal with the materials is not yet developed in the students, that the materials themselves advance no palpably significant educational objectives, that the materials might create a condition that undermines the entire educational process of learning in the school, or that the materials violate the most basic standards of morality. Decisions made for educationally legitimate reasons are not considered acts of censorship but acts of educational development. As with nearly all democratic freedoms, the academic freedom afforded to teachers carries clear limitations and constraints. Academic freedom has wide latitude but its boundaries are clearly drawn by the mandate to make a professionally defensible case for the educational legitimacy and value of the educational materials and topics used in class.

Other forms of freedom, of course, involve teachers. Among the more contentious freedoms is the teacher's right to express his personal views in public and in school. Fundamentally, a teacher's First Amendment right is protected in the context of the school. If a teacher is upset about a certain school reform strategy or a particular funding referendum, he has the right to express his views. But even here there are again a few constraints imposed on this freedom.

First, a teacher's right to express herself can be curtailed by the effect that such views have on her performance in the classroom and on the overall educational operation of the school. In the famous *Pickering v. Board of Education* (1968) case, a teacher wrote a highly critical letter to a local newspaper about the manner in which the school board and superintendent were handling some school financing issues. The teacher was fired because the school district maintained that his relationship with his superiors was so damaged by the letter that he could be no longer effectively carry out his teaching responsibilities. The teacher responded by arguing that his First Amendment right to free speech had been violated. Eventually the case made its way to the Supreme Court, and the Court sided with the teacher, stating that the teacher's letter did not hinder the performance of the teacher's classroom duties or otherwise obstruct the educational operation of the school. The Court's test went directly to the question of whether the teacher's expression impeded his ability to teach and whether it had an overall damaging effect on the educational functioning of the school.

There are instances in which a teacher's freedom of expression is not absolutely protected. A teacher, for instance, who verbally abuses her students can be terminated not only because such conduct is unprofessional but also because such conduct harms the ability of the teacher to teach. It is not protected speech. Moreover, a teacher who decides to exercise strong political viewpoints in the classroom may run the risk of being fired if such views disrupt the education process or otherwise make it difficult for the teacher to perform his duties. Such viewpoints, of course, also have to be found to have educational merit. Similarly, teachers who might use unconventional forms of grooming or dress or who engage in unconventional lifestyles are generally protected as long as there is no proof that the educator's professional work is being affected negatively by such things or that any disruption in the educational process is occurring. The teacher's right of expression is subordinate to the educational livelihood of the school.

Interestingly, students have to live with the very same limits on expression. Generally speaking, students' right of expression is also moderated by the question of whether their viewpoints disrupt the educational process of the school. In *Hazelwood School District v. Kuhlmeier*, the Court found that student expression can indeed be regulated if it at all impedes on the educational process and if it is seen as not having educational value or merit. High school journalism students in Hazelwood East High School, in Missouri, contended that their First Amendment freedoms were violated when the principal of their school did not allow two articles to be published in the school's newspaper. The articles dealt with sensitive topics, including a story about some pregnant teenage girls and another about the effect of divorce on teenagers. They involved stories about real students in the high school whose names were changed to protect their identities. The principal's objections to the articles were made on educational grounds. He claimed that the work was poorly researched and poorly written. The Supreme Court agreed with the principal's action, maintaining that school officials can regulate material when it involves a legitimate educational interest. Thus, student speech or student writings viewed to be prejudicial, vulgar, immoral, slanderous, or educationally inappropriate can be regulated.

In another well-known case, **Bethal School District No. 403 v. Fraser** (1986), a high school student presented a student campaign speech to his peers laced with clever sexual connotations, encouraging the student body to vote for him because, to paraphrase one small part of his speech, he was not only firm in character but also firm in his pants. The reaction from the student body was predictably unruly and boisterous. The student who gave the speech was suspended from school but he claimed that his First Amendment right to free speech had been breached. The Supreme Court, however, disagreed, observing that the speech created a disruptive environment and that it sanctioned lewd and indecent conduct, something that the school was well within its right to stymie. It should be made clear, however, that a school cannot restrict a student's speech simply because it does not like what the student is saying. In the famous **Tinker v. Des Moines Independent Community School District** (1969) case, students who wore armbands in protest of the Vietnam War had their right to conduct this silent method of protest upheld and supported by the courts, largely because it was found that it did not disrupt class work or otherwise impede the educational operation of the school.

KEY TERMS

Bethal School District No. 403 v. Fraser
"Dumbing down"
Effective teaching

Hazelwood School District v. Kuhlmeier
Madeline Hunter's lesson cycle
Pickering v. Board of Education

teaching to the test
Time on task
Tinker v. Des Moines Independent Community School District

KEY QUESTIONS

1. Dewey once wrote the following about the role of the teacher in society: "Every teacher should realize the dignity of his calling; that he is a social servant set apart for the maintenance of proper social order and the securing of the right social growth. In this way the teacher is always the prophet of the true God and the usherer in of the true kingdom of God." What do you think he meant by this? How do you feel about such a statement?

2. Why, do you think, is the teaching profession still comprised of mostly women?

3. What are some of the problems with schooling according to professional educators? Do you agree with their assessment?

4. When teachers report absenteeism and lack of student motivation as major school problems, do you think that they should bear any responsibility for these problems?

5. What are some of the issues that might lead one to conclude that teaching still has a long way to go before it is recognized fully as a profession?

6. What is the teacher-technician?

7. What is right or wrong with teaching to the test?

8. Why are some teachers inclined to teach to the test?

9. Do you believe that time on task is an important objective for a teacher?

10. What are some of the theoretical problems associated with the effective teaching literature?

11. What is the process of "dumbing down" textbooks, and why does it occur?

12. Explain the three sources for professional decision making. What do they offer to teachers?

13. Explain the procedure for professional decision making offered in the text.

14. What are some of the important factors to consider when planning assessment?

15. What is due process?

16. What are the basic limits placed on a teacher's freedom of expression?

17. What are the major questions weighed when a teacher-liability issue arises?

18. When it comes to excluding materials from the curriculum, what is the fundamental difference between censorship and educational development?

REFERENCES

Ariasin, P. W., & Madaus, G. F. (1983). Linking testing and instruction: Policy issues. *Journal of Educational Measurement, 20*(2), 103–117.

Bloom, B. S. (1956). *Taxonomy of educational objectives, handbook I: Cognitive domain.* New York: David McKay Company, Inc.

Cady, J. M. (1988). *The curriculum/instruction dualism: Implications for practice.* Unpublished dissertation, Rutgers University, New Brunswick, NJ.

Carnegie Foundation for the Advancement of Teaching. (1990). *The conditions of teaching.* Princeton, NJ: Princeton University Press.

Carson, C. C., Huelskamp, R. M., & Woodall, T. D. (1993). *Perspectives on education in America Journal of Educational Research,* 86(5): 259–310.

Dewey, J. (1904). The relation of theory to practice in education. In the *National Society for the Study of Education, third yearbook,* (Part I, *The relation of theory to practice in the education of teachers*). Bloomington, IL: Public School Publishing Co.

Elliot, D. L., & Woodward, A. (1990). Textbooks, curriculum and school improvement. In D. L. Elliot & A. Woodward, *Textbooks and schooling in the United States. Eighty-ninth yearbook of the National Society for the Study of Education.* Chicago: University of Chicago Press.

Fischer, L., Schimmel, D., & Kelly, C. (1991). *Teachers and the law* (3rd ed.). White Plains, NY: Longman

Gardner, H. (1983). *Frames of mind: The theory of multiple intelligences.* New York: Basic Books.

Gibboney, R. A. (1987) A critique of Madeline Hunter's teaching model from Dewey's perspective *Educational Leadership* 44(5): 46–50

Glatthorn, A. A. (1987). *Curriculum leadership.* Glenview, IL: Scott-Foresman.

Goodlad, J. I. (1984). *A place called school.* New York: McGraw-Hill.

Hlebowitsh, P. S. (1992, Winter). Time on TAAS. *Texas Researcher 3,* 81–89.

Hunter, M. (1980). *Teach more—faster.* El Segundo, CA: TIP Publications.

Hunter, M. (1985) What's wrong with Madeline Hunter? *Educational Leadership,* 42(5):57–60.

Hyman, I. A. & others. (1994). Policy and practice in school discipline: Past, present and future. Paper presented at the Safe Schools, Safe Students Conference. Washington, DC. October 28–29.

Krathwohl, D. R., Bloom, B. S., & Masia, B. B. (1964). *Taxonomy of educational objectives, handbook II: Affective domain.* New York: David McKay Company, Inc.

Latting, J. (1992). *Assessment in education.* Washington, DC: Office of Vocation and Adult Education.

Madaus, G. F. (1988). The influence of testing on the curriculum. In L. N. Tanner (Ed.), *Critical issues in curriculum. Eighty-seventh yearbook of the National Society for the Study of Education.* Chicago: University of Chicago Press.

National Center for Education Statistics (1993). *America's teachers: A profile of a profession.* Washington, DC: U.S. Department of Education.

National Center for Education Statistics. (1994). *Digest of education statistics.* Washington, DC: U.S. Department of Education.

Pauley, E. (1991). *The classroom crucible.* New York: Basic Books.

Piaget, J. (1970). *Science of education and the psychology of the child.* New York: Orion Press.

Rosenshine, B. (1979). Time, content and direct instruction. In P. L. Peterson and Walberg, H. J. (eds.), *Research on Teaching: Concept, findings and implications* Berkeley, CA: McCutchan Publishing.

Schulman, L. S. (1987). Knowledge and teaching: Foundations of the new reform. *Harvard Educational Review,* 57(1), 1–27.

Taba, H. (1962). *Curriculum development: Theory and practice.* New York: Harcourt, Brace and World.

Tanner, D. (1988). The textbook controversies. In L. N. Tanner (Ed.), *Critical issues in curriculum. Eighty-seventh yearbook of the National Society for the Study of Education.* Chicago: University of Chicago Press.

Tanner, D., & Tanner, L. N. (1995). *Curriculum development* (3rd ed.). New York: Macmillan.

Tyler, R. W. (1949). *Basic principles of curriculum and instruction.* Chicago: University of Chicago Press.

Zirchel, P. A. (1996) The law or the lore? *Phi Delta Kappan,* 77(8): 579

LEGAL CASES

Bethal School District No. 403 v. Fraser, 106 S. Ct. 3159 (1986).

Hazelwood School District v. Kuhlmeier, 86–836 S. Ct. (1988).

Pickering v. Board of Education, 391 U.S. 563 (1968).

Tinker v. Des Moines Independent Community School District, 393 U.S. 503 (1969).

11

CLASSROOM CONTROL

Johanna Brown is seated among a few of her students. Her math classes are filled with young adults, some with ideas other than math on their minds. How does a teacher manage up to 200 students per day? How do the general ideas of mathematics penetrate into the minds of restless youth?

In this final chapter, the question of classroom control is discussed. The general theme is that control is not necessarily a negative element in a classroom. Control is a required part of any social behavior. The question to ask is "Who or what is in control?" The general conclusion taken from the theory and research in education is that the curriculum, as it embodies purposeful, engaging activities, is the first step in creating a positive classroom environment. Of course, the teacher's genuine encouragement, accompanied by carefully placed admonishments of unsuitable behavior, is also needed. Teachers cannot rely on the "sugar coating" of boring and dull school activities, nor can they encourage student self-control with unfelt verbal praise. The issue of classroom control is often considered the most challenging aspect of school life.

In *Stuart Little,* E. B. White's well-known book for children, the book's main character inadvertently illustrated an important principle of classroom control and discipline. Stuart Little, a young mouse, is on an adventure looking for his close friend, a bird named Margalo. On his way, he finds a school superintendent sitting by the side of the road who is worried because he is unable to find a substitute teacher for one of his classes. Stuart, with characteristic enthusiasm, eagerly volunteers for the assignment. The superintendent, naturally skeptical that a mouse could manage a class, asks Stuart: "Do you think that you can maintain discipline?" Stuart responds crisply, "I'll make the work interesting and the discipline will take care of itself. Don't worry about me."

In spite of being very much on the right track, Stuart eventually discovers that managing a class is not quite as easy as he had imagined. Managing a group or groups of young people for up to 7 hours a day is challenging and often uncomfortable work, and nearly all beginning teachers find it the most difficult aspect of their job. Even the best laid plans can sometimes falter, and when they do, dealing with classroom chaos can be a most trying and anxiety-provoking experience.

Experienced teachers and principals almost always report that classroom discipline is the beginning teacher's greatest problem, and the research literature seems to bear out their anecdotal reports (Veenman, 1984). What does not seem to get reported, however, is that the lack of control and order in the classroom frequently has very much to do with the lack of quality in the activity of the classroom. The novice teacher's problem with discipline

CHAPTER OUTLINE

often disguises real problems with teaching. Often forgotten is that the answers to pervading questions over control and discipline are tied first and foremost to curricular and instructional considerations.

The purpose of this chapter is to illustrate how classroom management can be accomplished by focusing on the construction of learning engagements and on preventive disciplinary tactics as opposed to reactionary ones. In this regard, classroom management can be viewed as good curriculum development, as an idea operationalized through purposeful learning activities, intrinsically driven motivation, democratic social processes, good organizational techniques, and a general effort to account for the nature of the learner.

The term "classroom control" covers all the factors that go into creating and maintaining an engaging and orderly classroom environment. This not only means all the problems that pertain to keeping a sense of control in the classroom but also all the problems related to providing an educative environment. The ideal is not a smooth and efficient classroom as much as it is a lively and democratically regulated classroom where learners engage in problem-focused inquiry.

The central analytical focus of this chapter is on the idea of control. To most people, the term control has negative connotations. It is often associated with coercion and authoritarianism. The truth, however, is that control elements are essential to every social arrangement and that, one way or another, they will prevail in the context of learning.

Redefining Control

This discussion starts with the proposition that there can be no freedom without control. Imagine driving a car, for instance, without the benefit of traffic signs and traffic signals. One would theoretically be more free because the signs and signals would no longer need to be observed, but in the absence of traffic controls, driving would obviously become more perilous and less liberating. The odds of getting into a serious wreck would be vastly increased and one's own sense of freedom would be undermined by the dangerous vagaries of the traffic flow.

Schooling depends on similar elements of control. The school is a deliberately designed educative environment that aims to fulfill certain goals. It can only have a sense of itself by supporting certain objectives, expectations, and controls. The question, then, is not whether there will be control but what its nature shall be. Most schools will likely operate somewhere between the idea of imposing external controls that are coercive in nature and the idea of cultivating intrinsic controls that are intellectual and emotional in nature. We, of course, are more interested in vesting control in the learning engagement, in opting to place students in control rather than under control. We side with Dewey (1916) in acknowledging that "internal control through identity of interest and understanding is the business of education" (pp. 39–40).

This idea of internal control is rooted in Dewey's belief that education is best conducted by placing it in the language, problems, and spirit of the social group. Thus, things are learned as they are socially circulated and shared with others, in a setting that promotes ideas, problems, controversies, and democratic principles. With respect to teaching, the so-called well-ordered school relies on its activities and its social engagements for control and not on the exercise of threat, coercion, punishment, and other forms of authoritarianism (Dewey, 1938). The teacher does not need to "keep order" as much as find "order" in the learning experience of the school. Such experiences are carried out in the interests of sparking social intercourse and creating situations that "of themselves tend to exercise control over what this, that and the other pupil does and how he does it" (Dewey, 1938, p. 63). Exactly how this is done has to do with responding to the nature of the learner in ways that move the teacher to provide experiences that are satisfying and challenging to learners and in ways that model the values and the aims of democracy. Under these circumstances, "the teacher loses the position of external boss or dictator [and] takes on that of leader of group activities" (Dewey, 1938, p. 66).

 ## Behaviorism and the Psychology of External Control

Behaviorism established itself as a distinct school of human behavior in the early part of the 20th century. Early spokespersons for behaviorism, such as John Watson, believed that they had developed the key to analyzing, interpreting, predicting, and controlling behavior. At the turn of the century, Watson urged psychologists to discard their preoccupation with mentalistic concepts and to focus instead on objective human behaviors and acts. He was convinced that animal behavior held the key to understanding human behavior and stressed the need for experimentation in the area of animal learning.

Given the focus on animal behavior, it was not long before the behaviorists hit upon the idea of the conditioned response. A response, they observed, is conditioned when it is attaches itself or is associated with a stimulus. The Russian psychologist, Pavlov, proved that hungry dogs could be conditioned to salivate at the sound of a bell instead of the sight of food. To early behaviorists, such as Watson, this work with animal learning pointed to the centrality of the stimulus-response bond in human learning. The vast complexity of human behavior could now be studied along its most rudimentary lines, (its stimulus/response bonds), and learning could now be viewed, more powerfully, in relation to the influence of the environment. The behaviorist emphasis on the environment contributed to the popularity of behaviorism to educators because within it was an implicit belief in the educability of virtually all learners. There was, after all, great educational hope in the behaviorist notion that the environment was all-powerful and that through proper stimulus-response arrangements a child can be conditioned into being whatever one wants him to be (Schultz, 1975).

The heart of behaviorism is suggested by its name, which focuses on modifying and ultimately controlling behavior. Other factors in learning, especially those dealing with the learner's ideas, affectations, past experiences, present interests and social interactions, are not ignored but are believed to be of secondary importance. Behaviorism makes no pretensions about understanding and dealing with the learner's purposes and needs. Yet it is not an exaggeration to say that in today's public school classrooms, most instructional and discipline strategies have their origin in behaviorism. Clearly, to understand the functioning of most classrooms today, one must understand behaviorism.

Behaviorism contends that all human or animal behavior can be modified and controlled by structuring the environment in specific ways. The late B. F. Skinner, behaviorism's most celebrated advocate, maintained that teachers must see students as elements to be controlled and manipulated by a series of **reinforcement strategies.** Skinner maintained that "educators are seldom willing to concede that they are engaged in the control of human behavior" (1968, p. 259). At the heart of Skinner's analysis is the belief that motivated students are driven by an environment that has been designed to offer certain rewards and certain punishments for certain types of behavior.

According to Skinner (1968), the act of teaching "is simply the arrangement of contingencies of reinforcement" (p. 33), meaning that virtually every aspect of the classroom, from cognitive learning to behavioral conduct, could be reduced to a grid of operational objectives that is itself realized through conditioned responses. The equation for success is straightforward: behavior that is reinforced will continue to be vital, while behavior that is not reinforced will eventually be vanquished. There is, of course, much truth to such a view, but there is also quite a bit of truth in the view that sees behavior as an autonomous response that is moved by inner forces of industry, pleasure, cooperation, ethics, and interest. Keep in mind that behaviorism does not use the learner's interests and goals as the driving force for motivation but rather resorts to inducements that sometimes try to make intrinsically unattractive endeavors more palatable. Also keep in mind that human beings are complex, and that different individuals will respond to stimuli in varied ways. Thus, what might constitute a reward for one person might be utterly irrelevant to another.

Skinner, like all the early behaviorists, generalized his finding on the prediction and control of behavior from research on lower animals. One of the main principles of behaviorism, a process known as shaping, was actually developed in an early experiment with pigeons. In the experiment, Skinner placed a hungry pigeon in a cage with a colored disk at one end. Each time the pigeon moved a little closer to the disk, he sent a pellet of food into a small cup near the disk. In a very short time the pigeon learned to stand near and even look at the colored disk. Skinner then waited for the pigeon to peck at the disk (pigeons are likely to peck at a good many things given ample time) and then immediately delivered food to the pigeon. Each time the pigeon pecked the disk, Skinner "positively reinforced" the pigeon's behavior with food. Within a short time, the pigeon consistently pecked at the disk to receive food. An association was made between the reinforcement and the behavior.

Skinner also found that after learning to associate pecking the disk with food, the hungry pigeon continued to peck at the disk for some time even in the absence of a food reinforcer. Thousands and thousands of experiments in behaviorism have operated on this general principle of reinforcing behavior, and there is no denying the powerful results. Rewarding behavior is an amazingly effective way to shape actions; it does what behaviorism believes to be most important: it alters or modifies behavior.

The Reinforcement Strategies

The branch of behaviorism most concerned with student misbehavior is known as behavior modification. It is a process that focuses on the consequences of student behavior for the purpose of modifying or correcting poor behavior and maintaining good behavior. There are essentially four conse-quences to any behavior. Generally speaking, all behavior is positively rewarded by providing something enjoyable, negatively rewarded by remov-ing something unpleasant, punished, or ignored.

Punishment is, of course, an oft-used option when a teacher seeks to control behavior. Behaviorism teaches that the introduction of an aversive event will make it less likely that the behavior will reoccur. This is a helpful principle, but teaching is not always responsive to punishment tactics. In fact, to argue for the role of punishment in the classroom immediately raises questions about its form and about the latent messages it conveys to the student. For example, consider that during a science lesson a young boy pulls on a classmate's ponytails, and she screams. After being convinced of the young boy's culpability, which could itself be difficult to discern, the teacher may punish him by making him write an essay on why it is not acceptable to pull a girl's hair.

The rationale for this punishment might be for the boy to think through his behavior, to acknowledge his wrong, and to presumably suffer the strain of writing. Such a punishment, however, carries other messages that are not always very obvious. The fact that the punishment is associated with the act of writing, for instance, could easily be seen as troubling to an educator interested in teaching children to appreciate the communicative powers of good writing. To the student, the punishment might be perceived as a ritual requiring an obligatory confession or admission of guilt, something that may undermine the climate of honesty and openness in the classroom. Do not overanalyze the example, but note that all educators can benefit from looking at the latent or unanticipated effects of punishment. Even if the teacher decided to call the boy's parents, the effects of the punishment would likely

Billy Dean Nave, Jr. teaches at the alternative high school in Turner, Maine. His students, nearly all of whom have already dropped out of "regular" high school, require a special kind of care and attention.

be wide ranging. The parents might treat the phone call from the teacher judiciously, they might ignore it, or they might overreact; the teacher will not likely ever know. Certainly the decision to call a parent will have quite different consequences for different children. But the thing to consider is that punishment often carries with it unwanted side effects, which educators must try to weigh.

From behavioral research, educators know that using punishment will stop or curtail certain behavior, but it could also erupt into escape-avoidance behavior (the student uses virtually any means to escape from the punishment), aggression (the student becomes angry and may act out physically), and in some cases, unhealthy levels of docility and compliance. One should, of course, not dismiss the use of punishment in the classroom, but one should make very careful efforts to try to uncover any of the latent messages that might accompany its use and to make note of any unhealthy signs.

Generally speaking, punishment should be used only after a fair warning and conveyed with a tone that communicates concern and disappointment, perhaps even surprise, but not rage and hostility. The punishment, naturally, should fit "the crime" and should be clearly explained to the student. Even in the context of punishment, there should be an overarching context of fairness. One needs to keep a watchful eye on hostile or aggressive responses and on the tendency of youth to believe that a teacher might hold a grudge against them. Moreover, as others have cautioned, if one resorts to punishment for every discipline problem, one runs the risk of having the punishment associated with the punisher rather than with the undesirable behavior (Borich, 1996).

The controversy surrounding the use of corporal punishment in American schools embodies some of the above-mentioned problems. Although corporal punishments has been banned in most states, there are no federal sanctions against the use of corporal punishment in schools. Thus, some schools in some states still practice corporal punishment quite openly. In most cases, corporal punishment has been defined as a method of punishment involving the striking or hitting of students. Increasingly, however, legal experts are finding such a definition inappropriate because it allows teachers to use physically punitive methods of discipline that do not involve any manner of striking. Thus, a teacher who commands a student to stand erect or run in place for an hour might very well be using physical pain as a punishment, but in manner that might not be viewed as corporal punishment (Hyman, 1993). If corporal punishment is redefined as the infliction of bodily pain, the broadened definition helps to protect students against all forms of physical punsihment, but it also opens the door to an argument that might equate verbal punishment with corporal punsihment, especially if the student's reaction to verbal punishment manifests physically in the form of trembling, nausea, or crying (Hyman, 1993). Thus, the verbal belittling or humiliation of students can potentially be viewed not only as psychological punishment but also physical punishment. Because of the nature of corporal punishment, there is an increased possibility of creating resentment, anger (perhaps even fear) in the student population. There is also the risk of losing the purpose of punishment to a lower-minded desire to seek revenge and the problem associated with teaching children that hitting is an acceptable form of managing conflict. Clearly there are serious latent considerations here. The point is that when using forms of punishments, the educator must try to anticipate negative side-effects.

Another response in the behavior modification repertoire is to simply ignore undesirable behavior or resort to something called omission training. In the hair-pulling example, the behavior obviously cannot be ignored, although if it was a first offense or an otherwise anomalous event, a simple warning might be in order. The teacher, however, could use an ignore response by employing time-out or omission training. The thinking behind this is that the removal of the student from a pleasant or meaningful social environment will negatively reinforce the bad behavior and will likely lead to better behaviors in the future.

This strategy may at first sound like a form of punishment, but time-out differs from punishment. First, it is the removal of the opportunity to be positively rewarded. If the teacher employed time-out for the ponytail-pulling student, she would say very little and calmly tell the student to sit in another part of the room. The boy would not be allowed to participate in the science lesson. The key to this, of course, is for the activity from which the student is being removed to be challenging and rewarding. Time-out is the basic premise of many school discipline techniques (e.g., suspension), but successful time-out hinges on the student being removed from an engaging and meaningful environment. If a student is removed from a dull or aversive situation to correct a behavior, time-out is likely to be ineffective. Again, note that the cornerstone of discipline is the development of attractive and relevant learning experiences. The second important difference between time-out and punishment is that time-out is more likely to circumvent the unwanted side effects associated with punishment. Students will be less likely to try to escape or avoid the situation and will be less likely to become aggressive. This is so because the omission tactic does not have the negativity, authoritarianism, and blaming dimensions that often are part and parcel of direct punishment procedures.

Behavioral modification can also be driven by negative reinforcement strategies designed to increase certain behaviors. Like time-out, negative reinforcement might look and sound a lot like punishment, but again there is a subtle difference. Negative reinforcement is expressly used to increase the likelihood of a desirable behavior by removing something aversive when the desirable behavior occurs. For example, if a student has a history of not doing schoolwork, a teacher might ask the student to stay in at recess until the work is completed. When the student does turn in the work, the teacher removes the aversive situation (staying in at recess), thus making it more likely that the student will do schoolwork in the future. Negative reinforcement, in effect, becomes the removal of a punishment as it is triggered by desirable behavior.

Positive reinforcement, on the other hand, is the introduction of a pleasurable event after a particular behavior, thus making the behavior more likely to occur in the future. The pigeon pecking the disk is a prime example of the power of positive reinforcement, but examples in humans are also compelling.

In the school environment, positive reinforcement can take many forms, though the use of teacher praise and encouragement have been among the strongest. Praise, however, can be overvalued in the classroom. Often teachers will use praise as a contrivance of control and will convey praise in a stilted and less than natural manner ("I like the way that Bobby and Jennifer are working"). Some teachers believe that there is no such thing as too much praise and fix their attention on the frequency of reinforcements as opposed to the careful application of reinforcement as it relates to different student actions (Good & Brophy, 1987).

All children, of course, need to be recognized and praised for their accomplishments, but such praise is usually only effective when it is genuine, not calculated, and when it is delivered with the intention of celebrating students' accomplishments rather than manipulating or controlling their behavior. Praise, in fact, can be overused and can backfire if inappropriately conveyed. The smallest accomplishments should probably not be given effusive praise, even with so-called low-achieving children. Such children can be humiliated by the overreaction of praise, especially if it is an accomplishment that other students have already mastered. It is also generally not a good idea to reward students for behaviors that they are already doing without external reinforcement because, in the end, it might tend to attenuate intrinsic motivational drives (Good & Brophy, 1987). This, in a nutshell, is the fundamental criticism that has been used against the behavioristic tactic of control and management. Behaviorism shows that positive rewards (like praise) and other reinforcement tactics are enough to shape desirable behavior. This might be the case with pigeons, but when applied to the complexities of educating children, praise and other reinforcement strategies may or may not shape behaviors in desirable directions. It all depends on how such reinforcements are conveyed and to whom they are conveyed.

Teachers work in emergent situations, with a classroom of children who each have distinctively different personalities, varied home and family backgrounds, and different levels of ability, interest, and maturity. It is difficult, if not impossible, to find an established model of discipline and management that can be used successfully with entire classrooms or entire schools. There is generally no substitute for teacher intelligence and for the creative application of reinforcement in relation to emergent classroom problems and individual cases, though the logic of behaviorism obviously makes some sense when it is used on an individual basis and when the reinforcement strategies are sensitively constructed to the proclivities of the student.

 ## *Popular Methods of Control*

As mentioned, the conduct of the public school is very much tied into a management logic that makes popular use of external or extrinsic methods of control. Much of this strategy is wrapped up with efforts to boost student motivation and improve behavior with a reward or incentive structure. The following represents a set of control strategies that one is likely to see in American classrooms.

Contracting

The purpose of **contracting** is to hold students responsible to a set of negotiated goals and objectives to which they agree to meet over a specified period of time. The agreement is made in a form of a formal contract that carries with it identifiable incentives. The content of the contract will obviously vary from student to student, but the idea is to connect specific performance desires to specific reinforcements. Thus, a contract for a child might deal directly with goals related to academic achievement (i.e., completing all of one's homework; achieving an average grade of B on the upcoming month's classroom quizzes), or it might deal with a discipline-related issue (i.e., being in class on time each day; receiving no disciplinary referral notices). In either case, each specified goal is associated with an incentive structure, so that meeting, say, the objective regarding the cessation of referral notices might be accompanied with a promise from the teacher for more recess time in the afternoon, extra credit points for a final grade, winning a bag of candy, and so on. Some teachers might have a variety of rewards from which the student might choose, including access to certain games, release time for individual study, and log time on the computer.

Contracting can be used also for a group or whole classroom by setting a level of performance for the group and appending a group reward (a classroom party) to its achievement. One needs to be especially careful with such a procedure largely because of the contribution that one or two persons might make to the failure of the group to meet its goal, a condition that could create deep resentment and alienation toward those who were not able or not willing to assist with the group cause.

One could clearly see the role of behavioristic manipulation in the character of the contracting procedure. The questions already raised regarding reward and punishment structure apply here, as does the concern raised over how external reinforcers turn attention away from making qualitative judgments about the nature of activity in the classroom.

The Authoritarian Climate

Classrooms marked by an authoritarian climate violate the fundamental democratizing principle of schooling. Yet they are popular because they are quite effective at keeping order and control. An authoritarian climate allows the teacher to take on all the characteristics and powers of a dictator. The teacher is not simply an authority; she is an authority who has the last word on everything and whose absolute control can stifle any opportunity for debate, questioning, and spontaneity. Equally distressing, students of such teachers are typically seen as passive listeners whose role is to follow orders and unquestioningly engage in whatever they are told to do. Obviously, these are not the characteristics that educators are attempting to cultivate in democratic schools.

The viability of an authoritarian climate is usually dependent on the exercise of punishment and threat. Where there are rigid rules, however, there will always be students who will fight back and test the limits. In such cases, the authoritarian teacher might resort to quick and severe forms of reprimand, which might include, to name a few probable options, highly emotional outbursts against students, mass punishment tactics designed to show the entire class what happens when one person "falls out of line," an unreasonably ponderous load of homework, and so on. The latent effects of such treatments often further marginalize the student from the teacher and the classroom.

The other characteristic of authoritarian classrooms fatal to the learning process is the notion that the teacher and the curriculum, by virtue of their superordinate status, are beyond reproach. Authoritarian teachers are quick to blame students and their parents whenever there is a lack of success in the

The infamous Joe Clark, displaying the bravado that made both him and his methods the interest of a nation.

classroom. The attitude is that the teacher can do no wrong and that it is the responsibility of students to endure whatever conditions are imposed upon them by teachers. The vital notion of reflective teacher thought and the renegotiation of the classroom in the light of evaluative input and changing conditions are eschewed.

Authoritarianism is imperialistic and at times arrogant but is nevertheless effective at keeping children under control. Inexplicably, it seems to have a supportive following in the media and among a good share of parents. One need only be reminded of the media circus that was built around the school exploits of Joe Clark, the inner-city school principal from New Jersey whose claim to fame was his willingness to impose martial law on his school. Clark's so-called success was not as a curriculum reformer but as a disciplinarian who tolerated little nonsense from the students and little diversity of expression from the teachers. He unabashedly aimed to reform a school through militaristic tactics of control (which was symbolically represented by Clark's need to carry a baseball bat as he monitored the halls of his school). Clark's fame became so prodigious that he found himself on the cover of *Time* magazine and the subject of a major Hollywood motion picture. He was also very much in demand on the television talk-show market and was openly embraced as an exemplary educator by then Secretary of Education William Bennett.

One, of course, has to be sympathetic to the difficulties faced by principals and other educators responsible for the public education of children in low-income, inner city schools. The school condition inherited by Clark was not an easy one. But, his tactics were openly authoritarian, and included, according to some accounts, the arbitrary suspension of children from school, no-appeal disciplinary actions, name-calling of students, and the firing of teachers who were not in agreement with his school vision (Kaplan, 1989).

What is overlooked by those who advocate authoritarian rule in the school is that schools are agencies of democracy and should conduct themselves in a manner that reflects basic democratic values. Clearly, this does not mean that schools should be without rules, but it should mean that teachers frame themselves as authoritative, as opposed to authoritarian, figures in the classroom. As authoritative figures, teachers make their decisions through deliberations on the nature of the learner, the values of the society, and the best available professional knowledge. This is in contradistinction to the authoritarian teacher, whose own unquestioned doctrine is seen as the only way to manage and teach classrooms of youth.

Busywork

If one has ever walked into a classroom and faced rows of children busily and quietly working at their seats, one could probably not help but to be impressed by the sheer silence and engagement of the classroom. But looks can be deceiving, and all engagement is not necessarily good engagement. Increasingly teachers have found that seatwork can indeed be a form of control in the classroom, not because of its educative value or its attraction to the student but rather because of its routine and structured quality. Children do tend to get used to the chains that they wear, and they will begrudgingly accept the structure provided by **busywork,** which is often embodied in workbook assignments. All workbooks, of course, are not of poor quality, but many are, and many fail to even provide youth an opportunity to write a sentence, let alone to actually think deeply about an issue or a problem. In many cases, workbooks call for fill-in-the-blank statements that tend to keep children on task, especially when accompanied by external compulsions. In 1984, Goodlad's reported in his study of schooling that the instructional character of the classroom was heavily influenced by workbooks and work sheets that were used in a way that was not appreciably different from standardized testing.

The use of busywork as a form of control was elevated to new heights when the principle of **time on task** (an idea that espouses the unremarkable conclusion that learners should be engaged in classroom activities) was promulgated during the 1980s as a benchmark for so-called effective teaching. Undeniably, engaging students in learning is important, but all forms of engagement are not educative. Without a broader conceptual sight for their work, educators can fall into the trap of believing that the time on task dictum offers a commonsense criterion for good teaching. Unfortunately, among school professionals, especially teacher supervisors, time on task has come to mean that good teaching is marked by high levels of engagement, irrespective of the nature of the learning engagement. Such an assertion is not driven by educational concerns as much as by controlling concerns largely because the notion of time on task has little worth unless some effort is made to evaluate systematically the quality of the classroom tasks, relative to some overarching curricular purpose. Erickson (1986) described the problem thoughtfully. "If the fundamental [teaching] problem is reduced to keeping people spending time on task," he observed, "then the teacher will learn less and less about how to understand people, activities and tasks" (p. 140).

The history of classroom practice is rife with examples of controlling technologies that are well suited for routine seatwork, including the so-called mastery learning and competency-based instructional packages, programmatic textbooks, teaching machines, and teacher-proof materials. One could tentatively add the microcomputer to the list. Although things are improving, computers in the classroom have too often turned to the very same hollow instructional exercises that were used with teaching machines and programmed texts (Hlebowitsh, 1988). To some commentators, the parallels have been compelling enough to liken the computer to an "electronic workbook." And with ever-developing advances in graphics and programming design, the computer can now offer a titillating and energetic presentation to students that makes them increasingly vulnerable to the controlling powers of technology.

One example of the schools' penchant to use instructional seatwork is the nationally publicized case of how reading was taught in the Chicago Public Schools during the early 1980s. The reading program, known as Chicago Mastery Learning Reading, reduced all instruction to workbook-like materials that led to low-level practice exercises and tests of mastery. Much of the time students were kept busy simply by practicing reading skills on work sheets and by taking tests that demonstrated their mastery of the attendant skills. The result, in the words of a *New York Times* reporter, was "a reading program for elementary school students in Chicago that failed to include an essential ingredient—reading." One could argue that such an overt concern for workbook exercises over the application of reading skills represented a victory of control over learning.

Sugarcoating

Teachers often recognize that what they offer in the classroom does not have much intrinsic appeal to students. To compensate for this, they look for ways to make a lesson more enjoyable. In attempting to do this, they sometimes look past the nature of the activity and instead try to give the activity a superficial layer of attraction. This is a process called **sugarcoating.** The teacher, for instance, who believes that learning the multiplication table can be made enjoyable by constructing a board game that integrates drill-like questions on the multiplication facts is engaging in a form of sugarcoating. In such a case, the very core of the activity is still a rather stale exercise (What is 4 × 3?), but it gets its sugarcoating from the gaming condition, which might include a colorful game board, a competitive winner versus loser logic, and so on.

Similarly, teachers who teach their classes using a highly dramatic and enthusiastic performance in the classroom might be sugarcoating, especially if they fail to offer learning conditions that would still be engaging without the hype. As mentioned, enthusiasm and drama are very important to good teaching, but they cannot save a lesson that fails to strike a respondent intrinsic chord. As Dewey (1902) observed,

> where there is a failure to develop interest and motivation within the range and scope of a child's life, there is a tendency to employ a trick of method to arouse interest, to make it interesting; to cover it with sugarcoating; to conceal its barrenness by intermediate and unrelated material; and finally, as it were, to get the child to swallow and digest the unpalatable morsel while he is enjoying tasting something quite different. (p. 30)

Where there is sugarcoating, the consuming concern is control, and learning is, at best, an incidental effect.

Many educators who supported the behavioral view of learning could be seen dispensing candy as positive reinforcement.

Motivation needs to be constructed in the act of curriculum development, especially as it relates to students' ideas and needs, life experience issues, and democratic processes. Borrowing Dewey's metaphor, one might view motivation as providing palatable and nutritious food to a hungry organism. Once swallowed, the food energizes the body and ultimately provides it with sustenance and growth. For the food to have such effects, however, it has to be of good quality. It has to have nutritional features, be free of contaminants, and satisfy certain taste requirements. It cannot always be cake with piles of icing on it.

Assertive Discipline

Teachers today have also been inclined and sometimes compelled to use various disciplining systems to keep control in their classrooms. Among the most popular modern approach to student discipline is known as **Assertive Discipline,** a program introduced in 1976 by Lee Canter. According to advertising materials prepared by Canter and Associates, over 500,000 teachers have been trained in Assertive Discipline. According to Canter and Associates, 92% of the teachers who have been trained in his program "feel more confident in their ability to handle disruptive behavior effectively" (Canter and Canter, 1976). Canter also maintains that the Assertive Discipline program reduces behavior problems by 80%.

How does this program work? Assertive Discipline begins by assuming that there are three types of teachers: assertive, nonassertive, and hostile. Of course, the assertive teacher is the one believed to be best suited for keeping classroom discipline. She is the teacher who makes it known what she will and will not tolerate in her classroom. She does not get angry or hostile but remains calm while letting children know that she is the one in control. Among the generalizations that the assertive teacher upholds is: "I will not tolerate any student stopping me from teaching or [stopping] another student from learning."

Assertive Discipline is rooted in the reinforcement strategies of behaviorism, which aims, as mentioned, to reward the good and punish the bad. The "assertive" teacher makes his classroom rules and the consequences that result from any infractions to the rules very clear to students. The first infraction of the day in a fifth-grade classroom, for instance, might result in a simple warning. The second might be the loss of morning recess, while the third infraction might result in the loss of both morning and lunch recess. The fourth is typically a phone call to parents, and on the fifth infraction, the student is sent to the office. This is essentially the pattern for all grade levels. The rules and the consequences might vary across grade levels, but the idea of increasing the severity of the punishment with each increasing infraction is consistent.

The student will know when he has broken a rule because the teacher will ask the student to put his name on the board. A checkmark will indicate each subsequent infraction. Some teachers, instead of putting the student's name on the board, will use a bulletin board with a small pocket for each student. Inside each pocket are several different colored cards, each representing ascending infractions. This system is typically used by early elementary teachers whose students may not be able to write their own names on the board. The idea is to provide a public platform for the documentation of each infraction in a manner that does not disrupt the instructional flow of the classroom.

All is well and good so far, but there are some questions that should be entertained. What is the message sent to students when one entire bulletin board of the classroom is devoted to an ongoing public account of who is getting punished? What kind of classroom climate is supported under such conditions? Why is there a need for a teacher's punishment regiment to be visibly conducted? Could it be because, without it, the classroom would have no internal mechanism to stay engaged and fulfilled?

There are also positive-reinforcement aspects to Assertive Discipline, such as the marble-jar-filling tactic used in elementary classrooms. Each time the class behaves appropriately, the teacher puts one or more marbles in a jar. When the jar is filled, the class receives a movie, popcorn, or some other reward. Again, one has to question why there is a need for the teacher to be so preoccupied with a reinforcement strategy, when the real investment in classroom discipline should be made in the learning experience.

Assertive Discipline, as a program, is often recommended to teachers and school districts through testimonial offered by its advocates. As one group of researchers has discovered (Render, Padilla, & Krank, 1989), the data used by Canter to support his program are often wanting. Assertive Discipline is really little more than the application of several common behavioral principals (e.g., swift punishment, group rewards). For his part, Lee Canter has never claimed that Assertive Discipline is anything more than behavioral modification. He has even suggested that many teachers misuse his plan by focusing only on the punishment aspect part of Assertive Discipline (Canter, 1989).

Still, programs such as Assertive Discipline generally ignore the curriculum. As noted, if one asks young people to engage in less-than-meaningful exercises, it stands to reason that they will either misbehave or suffer in silence. Assertive Discipline turns attention away from the character of the learning engagement in the interest of compelling teachers to control youth under any and all pedagogical circumstances.

Assertive Discipline is also limited by its assumption of order and social compliance. Healthy conflict is needed in the school, just as it is needed in a democracy. The school does not always have to be marked by smooth operations and methods of consensual procedure. School is an agency of democracy, though it has some very clear limitations in this respect. It should be a place where life is conducted through conversation, cooperation, and other forms of social mutuality. It should not have the cloud of control and compliance hanging over it, ready to strike a student with its punitive lightning. One can argue that Assertive Discipline teaches children that authoritarian processes are superior to democratic ones, that it puts the teacher in the role of policing rather than facilitating, and that it avoids any discussion regarding the quality of the teaching experience. Under the dictates of Assertive Discipline, students must be engaged in the classroom, not because the learning experience is worthwhile and attractive but because the heavy hand of control is ready to punish anyone who threatens the smooth operations of the classroom.

Punishments and rewards are part of the ebb and flow of life. Teachers will always engage in some form of reinforcement, whether they use programs like Assertive Discipline or not. This is why teachers need to be conscious of rewarding student behaviors naturally and honestly and of punishing offenses in the classroom without undermining important principles of democracy. Commercially available discipline programs should be used judiciously, perhaps with a particularly recalcitrant student. But, in the end, even the most rabid behaviorists will acknowledge the need to teach students to develop self-managing behaviors. They, of course, argue that programs like Assertive Discipline could be the initial means to teaching children to think and act for themselves, according to the rules of the classroom. This could very well be the case, though the evidence does not yet support it. Generally speaking, external contingencies do not easily fade in the classrooms that use them. They remain a major, if not the major, component of many teachers' management plans.

Still, keep one paradoxical principle in mind, one that even the advocates of Assertive Discipline would probably agree with: Good discipline in the classroom is ultimately measured by the ability of the students to be in control of their own actions without resorting to external systems of reinforcement like those represented in Assertive Discipline. Another way of saying this is that good discipline in the classroom means that teachers do not need to be dependent on discipline programs.

 ## *Motivation and Intrinsic Control*

Educators strive to motivate students to be independently-minded, socially conscious thinkers who can regulate their own lives intelligently and derive the lasting benefits of being widely and comprehensively educated. Yet the means used to achieve such an end vary in classrooms and schools.

Some teachers believe that schooling needs to be intrinsically arduous to be educative. They subscribe to the view that students need to learn that "good things do not come easy" and that part of being an educated person

SCHOLARLY VOICES

Dewey on Discipline

The substitute for living motivation in the subject matter is that of contrast-effects; the material of the lesson is rendered interesting, if not in itself, at least in contrast with some alternative experience. To learn the lesson is more interesting than to take a scolding, be held up to general ridicule, stay after school, receive degradingly low marks, or fail to be promoted. And very much of what goes by the name of "discipline," and prides itself upon opposing the doctrines of a soft pedagogy and upon upholding the banner of effort and duty, is nothing more or less than just this appeal to "interest" in its obverse aspect—to fear, to dislike of various kinds of physical, social, and personal pain. The subject-matter does not appeal; it cannot appeal; it lacks origin and bearing in a growing experience. So the appeal is to the thousand and one outside and irrelevant agencies which may serve to throw, by sheer rebuff and rebound, the mind back upon the material from which it is constantly wandering.

Source: Dewey, J. (1902). *The child and the curriculum.* Chicago: University of Chicago Press, p. 29.

means learning to accept the pain of learning. Others might view motivating as a simple inducement strategy designed to make learning as palatable as possible. Such teachers might resort to various reward mechanisms and sugarcoating tactics with more frequency.

Educators should not always look to create or compel interest but should provide experiences that are, in and of themselves, engaging and interesting. The difference is fundamental. In one case, the interest is appended to the experience and is, to paraphrase Dewey (1902, p. 29), held in contrast to an alternate experience, such as receiving a scolding, being held up to ridicule, staying after school, or receiving low marks (see the Scholarly Voices feature in this section). In the other case, interest is umbilically tied, again to paraphrase Dewey (1902) to the consciousness of the child, to her own doings, thinkings, and struggles (Dewey, 1902, p. 29). Motivation is all about making the learning experience responsive to the nature of the learner and the values of society for the purpose of releasing knowledge as working power in the life experience. Hence, interest has to be of the experience, not external to it. In the classroom, student motivation should be driven by curriculum considerations and by efforts to construct learning experiences that are intrinsically appealing to youth. Motivation, in this sense, resides in the quality of the learning experience and is not incidental to instructional concerns, such as questioning procedures, lesson plan orientations, and sincere teacher enthusiasm toward learning.

It is also important to remember that internal motivation is dependent on the fulfillment of the learner's basic internal needs. Maslow (1962) described these needs in hierarchical order, arguing that the most fundamental needs were physiological ones (i.e., sleep and food), followed by a succession of needs that included safety, love and acceptance, self-esteem, and self-actualization. This was Maslow's way of saying that children who come to school tired or hungry will not likely be able to learn. Maslow's work underscored the rationale for the Congressional authorization of the National

School Lunch Act, which provides free or reduced lunches to low income children, and the Child Nutrition Act, which provides free or reduced breakfast to needy children.

Of course, progressive educators, such as Maria Montessori, made early linkages between the need for proper physical nutrition and the cognitive and social development of young children. The implications of Maslow's work, however, go deeper than meeting physiological requirements because of the value that he placed on needs related to safety, love and affection, and self-esteem. Children who attend schools where safety is an issue or who have to deal with some form of dislocation in the home (i.e., an impending divorce or family illness), or who live in homes where love and acceptance might be in short supply, will have their school educations compromised. Similarly, a child who is roundly rejected or ridiculed by his peers, for whatever reasons, will not be poised to succeed in school. Thus, the teacher has a role to play in regulating and managing factors that may often be external to the school.

The Democratic Mandate for Self-Control

The mandate for self-control is, of course, not a purely philosophical argument. When one stakes motivation in the objective of instilling in youth the skills and the responsibilities of self-management within a democratic framework, various classroom procedures rise to the top, including instructional features related to the nature of the learner, group processes related to the values and aims of the society, and a general atmospheric condition that embraces the issues and problems of life.

Questions of motivation should presume that people are active organizers of their own world. Schools should deal with the question of how the socialization of youth enables them to better understand and more effectively regulate their own lives. This does not deny the existence or power of external forces. In fact, it makes it clear that external forces are themselves part of the decision-making process that helps to inform one's choices. Thus, one's actions should not be manipulated by external conditions, as is the case in behavioristic traditions, but should themselves have authority over external conditions. Indeed, how individuals deal with external forces is far more important than are the forces themselves. For example, if a teacher requires a student to complete an assignment and offers points toward a grade as an incentive, the external force (the incentive points toward a grade) is secondary to the question of how the student feels about grades, about the nature of the assignment, and about the teacher. The idea is to compel student behavior from the standpoint of the intrinsic quality of experience.

Unfortunately, it is probably fair to say that there are too few students who are intrinsically motivated toward their school experiences. This lack of motivation can be countered by framing the notion of control in the classroom in terms of giving students the skills and attitudes that they need to control their own educational destinies.

Nothing can be expected from the school curriculum from the standpoint of motivation unless some concession is made to the nature of the learner. This means that the developmental levels of student learning should be considered in formulating a motivational curriculum and that the learner's interests and desires should be considered as well. Although beginning teachers might find it difficult, students need to be given the opportunity to make choices in the curriculum and to set their own goals. This does not mean that the students take over the class, but it does mean that the classroom teacher should show some interest in setting learning goals in accordance with the learner's interests and purposes. This can be accomplished on two levels. First, there should be general responsiveness to what youth raise as being personally relevant, and second, the school should focus on discerning the collective needs of youth, particularly as these needs relate to a wide range of issues, including civic, family, consumer, recreational, and occupational life. Various interviewing methods and other evaluative techniques can be used to discern how students feel about school and various subject areas, what their attitudes and habits are with important practices like, say, recreational reading, and what they see as the fundamental flaws of their own school.

Another important factor tied to the skills of self-determination is related to how well teachers receive and encourage student ideas. Do students initiate discussions and ask questions? Are student views and interests integrated into the learning activities of the classroom? Does the teacher convey respect for students? Does the teacher listen to students and respond to them substantively? Are efforts made to individualize instruction? These questions underscore the importance of conveying to youth the general values of self-exploration and self-dignity.

Motivation is also very much rooted in the active process of testing ideas and sharing insights. In democratic schools, student motivation has much to do with having opportunities to make decisions and with engaging students in cooperative groups that provide an avenue for social expression. In such classrooms, there is a strong sense of individual and group goal settings. Students are self-directed and intrinsically motivated; they are in control. Such a condition cannot prevail unless teachers are themselves inspired by a democratic model of instruction. Teachers become the voices and the models for tolerance, for mutual respect, and for the celebration of each individual's worth and uniquenesses. Having the trust of their teacher, students feel competent in what they are doing and inevitably have higher concepts of self-esteem and self-responsibility.

Of course, the ability of students to control their own lives has much to do with whether or not they learn to think critically. Self-determination is not simply a matter of pursuing one's own whims and fancies but of applying a method of intelligence in the conduct of one's life. Thus, the mandate for self-control must be associated with classroom initiatives that sustain the skills of critical thinking. This means that the classroom needs to supply experiences that go well beyond the traditional skill-drill model of instruction. Learning needs to be idea oriented, which means that it values language and questions of interpretation, as opposed to being fact or information oriented. Learning must also aim to apply the basic skills of literacy and numeracy to the adjudication of various issues and concerns. All content, except perhaps in highly specialized academic studies, should be related to personal-social issues and should be brought out of the abstract and into the concrete and familiar. Lessons should be formatted in ways that inspire curiosity and higher-level cognition.

All in all, the mandate for self-control has to do with being receptive to the nature of the learner, the life experience of the learner, and wider

THE MANDATE FOR SELF-CONTROL IN THE CLASSROOM	TABLE 11.1

Receptivity to the Learner

1. Are student ideas and contributions central to the nature and conduct of the classroom?
2. Are efforts made to deliberately develop the self-esteem of the learner and to cultivate a teacher-student relationship that is built on mutual respect?
3. Do youth have an opportunity to set goals and objectives in the classroom?
4. Is the nature of the learner taken into account, especially in terms of developmental levels and general interests?
5. Are youth given the opportunity to be responsible and think independently?
6. Are youth given the opportunity to explore individual issues and concerns and to further cultivate individual gifts and talents?
7. Is teacher-student interaction built on respect and cooperation?

Receptivity to the Life Experience

1. Are sociopersonal issues and concerns raised in the classroom?
2. Are the characteristics of curiosity and creativity being modeled and otherwise supported in the classroom?
3. Is there an effort to see skill-development in application contexts?

Receptivity to Democratic Processes

1. Are there deliberate efforts in the classroom to cultivate higher level thinking skills?
2. Is the character of the classroom marked by idea orientation as opposed to a skill-based orientation?
3. Does the classroom offer experiences in problem-focused inquiry and in the general testing of speculative thoughts?
4. Does the classroom value conversation and debate and the honest airing of differences?
5. Are communication skills cultivated (i.e., writing, debating, visual arts, critical reading)?

democratic processes. Questions that are central to the development of a classroom marked by the skills self-control are represented in Table 11.1.

The Power of Modeling

The issue of modeling has long been documented as central to the socialization of youth. Teacher behavior will have much to do with the character of climate or atmosphere that is established for learning in the classroom. It will influence, for instance, the degree to which competitive values are stressed over cooperative ones, and vice versa, as well as the degree to which thinking and problem solving are supported in the classroom. It will influence general attitudes toward learning itself and toward the content of various disciplines of knowledge; it will have an impact on students' skills in organization, as well as their levels of responsibility, curiosity, and interest. In terms of the skills of self-determination, the teacher's ability to model independence of thought and problem-focused inquiry is essential. Teachers should verbalize their own thinking to students and, in doing so, encourage creative and speculative thought that can be tested against experience and knowledge. The modeling of these behaviors must convey a passion for ideas and a general commitment to asking questions that have multiple and often incomplete answers.

Teachers should also model the virtues of learning by, among other things, actively using the school library, sharing thoughts over current events and recently read books, engaging youth in honest conversation and debate, and participating in outside educational and cultural events. The climate of the classroom should encourage opinions, conversation, and the testing of problem-solutions and should judge students on the veracity or persuasiveness of their own decisions and views. Students will never become responsible unless they are given opportunities to be responsible. Teachers, moreover, should project sincere enthusiasm for topics and assignments in the classroom, something that students generally will find contagious. This does not mean that each teacher-directed activity become a dramatic production. The goal is not titillation but rather an honest projection of excitement.

The Problem Child

All classrooms will likely have a small handful of students whose behavioral problems will be severe enough to warrant special attention. In fact, youth who are persistent behavioral problems in school will usually, in due time, find their way to the school psychologist. Their problems, if severe enough, might result in special curricular attention, though federal legislation during the past few decades has promoted the mainstreaming of special populations of students in the interests of keeping them in "regular" education. These students, who typically make up approximately 10% of a class, might simply be confused and frustrated in their personal lives; they might be from families whose lives have little consistency and even less love, and they might suffer from any number of emotional or neurological disorders. These students will frequently challenge authority and undermine the educational process of others. They will be ones who will cause some teachers to dread their work. What works for others does not seem to work for them, and one's own anger and frustration with their behavior could result in a spiraling negative relationship that only throws more fuel onto an already burning fire.

Such students will force more teachers to make concessions to external reinforcement strategies because what makes these particular students so frustrating is their inability to develop internal self-control and self-responsibility. But before becoming too behavioristic, there are a few other suggestions that one might want to consider. First, try to keep in mind that some of the problems that a teacher might see in the student could be rooted in any number of familial, medical, or emotional problems. In other words, the behavioral problems witnessed in the classroom could be symptomatic of a broader underlying problem. Asking why the student behaves in the manner in which he behaves is probably a good starting point in attempting to deal with the management of such a child. But be careful. There is a tendency sometimes to explain the student away, to ascribe a pathology to his behavior and to claim that it is beyond the remedial arm of the school. In such a case, the student is typically managed by reaction, which typically means the threat of ever-increasing levels of punishment for misbehavior.

An alternative method would be for the teacher to keep scrupulous observational notes that document the frequency and the character of the misbehavior and that offer an opportunity for analysis. Based on such notes, the school psychologist, for instance, must be able to discern some type of

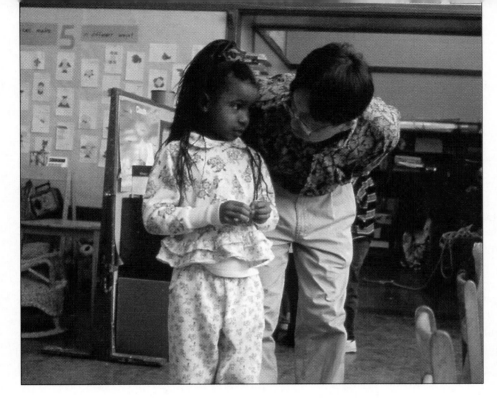

Teachers must be models of virtue and patience. Such a role is not always easy, but children and youth deserve nothing less.

pattern or identify a treatment to be tried. These notes should also be helpful to the teacher as well, in that they would potentially reveal any role that the teacher might have had in triggering or otherwise contributing to the problem at hand. Also keep in mind that for many of these students, the school represents a place of last hope, and for the teacher to admit that the student cannot be taught virtually ensures that she will not be taught.

Second, try to bring as much analytical insight to the problem as is available. This means speaking to former teachers of the student, arranging for conferences with parents, and picking the brains of the school psychologist, learning disabilities specialist, remedial teachers, social workers, principals, physical education teachers, and so on.

Third, there are some therapy tactics that one can apply. Keep in mind, however, that teachers are not trained as counselors, though they often engage in a great deal of counseling, and that any attempt to use psychology and social therapy techniques should usually be done in concert with, and with the approval of, the school psychologist.

Lastly, and perhaps most importantly, try to avoid the creation of a mutually antagonistic relationship. There is a very good chance that with a problem child, the teacher will tend to resort to threats and other conflict-inducing interactions with students. This will essentially doom the student and doom one's ability to make life better for the student and the larger classroom. Continue to stress good behavior, to honestly and calmly voice displeasure with certain behavior, to deal with such misbehaviors firmly and fairly, to consider how to improve upon interactions with the student, and to model the highest ideals of patience and integrity.

KEY TERMS

Assertive Discipline
Behaviorism
Busywork

Contracting
Reinforcement strategies

Sugarcoating
Time on task

KEY QUESTIONS

1. How is control a fundamental attribute of freedom?

2. Why did Dewey make a distinction between external and internal control? What are the pedagogical implications of such a distinction?

3. What are the main problems with reinforcement strategies in the classroom?

4. What precautions should be taken before using punishment strategies in the classroom?

5. Is praise always a good thing? What factors should be considered when using praise in the classroom?

6. What is contracting, and what is its main problem as a method of control?

7. What is the difference between an authoritarian teacher and an authoritative teacher?

8. What makes the notion of time on task problematic in the curriculum?

9. What are the main problems with using Assertive Discipline in a classroom or school?

10. How might a teacher begin to develop the skills of self-control in the students?

11. What steps might be taken to deal with a particularly problematic child in a classroom?

REFERENCES

Borich, G. (1996). *Effective teaching methods.* Englewood Cliffs, N.J.: Merrill.

Canter, L. (1989). Assertive Discipline—more than names on the board and marbles in a jar. *Phi Delta Kappan, 71*(1), 57–61.

Canter, L., & Canter, M. (1976). Assertive discipline: A take-charge approach for today's educators. Santa Monica, CA: Canter and Associates.

Dewey, J. (1902). *The child and the curriculum.* Chicago: University of Chicago Press.

Dewey, J. (1916). *Democracy and education.* New York: Macmillan.

Dewey, J. (1938). *Experience and education.* New York: Macmillan.

Erickson, F. (1986). Tasks in time: Objects of study in a natural history of teaching.

In K. K. Zumwalt (Ed.), *Improving teaching: 1986 ASCD Yearbook.* Alexandria, VA: ASCD, 131–147.

Good, T., & Brophy, J. (1987). *Looking in classrooms.* New York: Harper and Row.

Goodlad, J. I. (1984). *A place called school.* New York: McGraw-Hill.

Hlebowitsh, P. S. (1988). Technology in the classroom: Cautionary notes on a recurring theme. *The ClearingHouse, 62*(10), 53–56.

Hyman, R. T. (1993). Corporal punishment: Just what is it and what should we do about it? Paper presented at the National Organization on Legal Problems of Education (Philadelphia, PA, November, 19–21, 1993) Eric Document 376–563.

Kaplan, G. (1989). *Who Runs Our Schools?* Washington, D.C.: Institute for Educational Leadership.

Maslow, A. H. (1962). *Toward a psychology of being.* New York: Von Nostrand Reinhold.

Render, G. F., Padilla, J. M., & Krank, H. M. (1989). Assertive discipline: A critical review. *Teachers College Record, 90*(4), 607–630.

Schultz, D. (1975). *A history of modern psychology.* New York, NY: Academic Press.

Skinner, B. F. (1968). *The technology of teaching.* New York: Appleton-Century-Crofts.

Veenman, S. (1984, Summer). Perceived problems of beginning teachers. *Review of Educational Research, 54.*

APPENDIX

POINTS OF EMPHASIS IN THE COMPREHENSIVE CONCEPT OF SCHOOLING

	Comprehensive Curriculum Functions			
Comprehensive Needs of Youth	*I*	*SC*	*A*	*V*
1. All youth need to be able to think rationally, to deal with persuasion deftly, to express written and verbal thoughts clearly, to learn how to question truth and common sense, and to understand and live with complexity and ambiguity.	i	SC	A	v
2. All youth need to develop the skills of social tolerance and social cooperation and to grow in their understanding and use of ethical principles and values.	i	SC	a	v
3. All youth need to understand the rights and duties of citizenship and to embrace democratic attitudes and values in their actions.	i	SC	a	v
4. All youth need to develop a realistic sense of self-confidence and self-esteem and to better understand their own inner self.	I	sc	a	v
5. All youth need to understand the communicative power of literature, art, and music and to appreciate the importance of aesthetics in life.	I	sc	a	v
6. All youth need to understand the role of science in relation to contemporary society, to be aware of the limitations of scientific thought, and to understand the basic scientific knowledge related to humankind and its environment.	i	SC	A	v
7. All youth need to develop the skills and understandings needed to become productive and critically minded workers.	i	sc	a	V
8. All youth need to have a critical understanding of a capitalist economy and of the skills needed to be an intelligent consumer of goods and services.	i	SC	a	v
9. All youth need to develop and maintain good health and physical fitness.	i	sc	a	v
10. All youth need to command the fundamental processes of reading, writing, and arithmetic.	i	sc	A	v

I = Individual	SC = Sociocivic	Uppercase letters = major emphasis
A = Academic	V = Vocational	Lowercase letters = minor

SAMPLE SCHEDULE OF A COMPREHENSIVE ELEMENTARY SCHOOL CURRICULUM

	9:00–10:00	10:00–11:00	11:00–12:00	12:00–1:00	1:00–2:00	2:00–3:00
M	IB	A	A	L U N C H A N D R E C E S S	SC	X
T	A	A	IB		X	SC
W	X	SC	IB		A	A
TH	A	A	SC		IB	X
F	SC	A	A		X	IB

Days of the week (vertical, left axis)

Hours of the day

IB = Individualized Block (Enrichment, Remedial, and Exploratory Education)

A = Academic Studies (Reading, Math and Interdisciplinary Studies in Science, Social Studies, and Language Arts)

SC = Socio-civic Learning (Cooperative Groups Working on Socio-civic Issues and Problems)

X = Extra-classroom Experience (Physical Education, Art, and Music)

SAMPLE SCHEDULE OF A COMPREHENSIVE MIDDLE SCHOOL CURRICULUM

	9:00–10:00	10:00–11:00	11:00–12:00	12:00–1:00	1:00–2:00	2:00–3:00
M	IB	A	A		PV	X
T	A	A	IB	L U N C H	X	SC
W	X	SC	PV	A N D	A	A
TH	A	A	SC	R E C E S S	IB	PV
F	SC	PV	A		X	IB

Days of the week

Hours of the day

IB = Individualized Block (Enrichment, Remedial, and Exploratory Education)

A = Academic Studies (Reading, Math and Interdisciplinary Studies in Science, Social Studies, and Language Arts)

SC = Socio-civic Learning (Cooperative Groups Working on Socio-civic Issues and Problems)

X = Extra-classroom Experience (Physical Education, Art, and Music)

PV = Prevocational Courses

SAMPLE SCHEDULE OF A COMPREHENSIVE SECONDARY SCHOOL CURRICULUM

	9:00–10:00	10:00–11:00	11:00–12:00	12:00–1:00	1:00–2:00	2:00–3:00
M	IB	S	S	L U N C H A N D R E C E S S	C	X
T	S	S	IB		X	C
W	X	C	IB		S	S
TH	S	S	C		IB	X
F	C	S	S		X	IB

Days of the week

Hours of the day

IB = Individualized Block (Enrichment, Remedial, and Exploratory Education; Electives and Advances Placement)

S = Specialized Academic Srudied in Math, Science, English and History, or Specialized Vocational Studies in Broad Occupational Clusters

C = Common Learnings in Socio-civic Areas and in Interdisciplinary Academic Studies

X = Physical Education, Art, and Music

NAME INDEX

A

Adams, C.F., 73, 89n.
Adams, J., 19
Addams, J., 72–73, 88, 225–226, 250n.
Adler, M.J., 263, 281n., 309, 313, 317n.
Aikin, W., 307, 317n.
Aleman, S.R., 245, 250n.
Alexander, L., 102
Allen, D.W., 280, 281n.
Anderson, L., 299n., 301n., 317n.
Apple, M., 233, 250n.
Applebee, A.N., 198, 221n., 234n.
Ariasain, P.W., 326, 354n.
Armstrong, L.S., 136, 159n.

B

Bagley, W., 87, 89n.
Baker, C., 247, 251n.
Banks, J., 241, 250n.
Barbanel, J., 109, 124n.
Barber, B., 231, 251n.
Barnard, J., 34n.
Beale, H.K., 12, 34n.
Belenky, M., 152, 159n.
Bennett, W., 231–232, 244, 251n., 263, 273, 281n.
Bereaud, S., 151, 160n.
Bestor, A.E., 254–255, 281n., 287, 302–303, 313, 317n.
Bierlein, L., 264–265, 266n., 267, 268n., 281n.
Binet, A., 86
Biskopic, J., 148, 159n.
Blank, R.K., 266, 281n.
Bloom, B.S., 333, 354n., 355n.
Bobbitt, J.F., 83–86, 88, 89n.
Bode, B.H., 37, 60–61, 62n., 78, 84, 89n.
Boldice, D., 157, 159n.
Bondi, J., 94–95, 124n.
Borich, G., 362, 378n.
Boydston, J.A., 66, 89n.
Bowles, S., 235, 251n.
Boyer, E.L., 209n., 210n., 211n., 262, 281n., 309, 314, 317n.
Bracey, G.W., 163, 221n.
Braddock, J.H., 130–131, 159n.
Brandstad, T., 100
Brinton, R.C., 280, 281n.
Broder, D.S., 244, 251n.
Brophy, J., 364, 378n.
Broudy, H.S., 313–314, 317n.
Bruner, J.S., 255–256, 281n.
Buechler, M., 268n., 282n.
Buell, E.H., 143, 159n.
Burner, D., 34n.

Burnett, J.R., 313–314, 317n.
Bush, G., 100
Butts, R.F., 11, 13, 15, 18–20, 23, 28, 30, 34n., 49, 51, 62n., 76, 89n., 90n., 286

C

Cady, J.M., 328, 354
Caldwell, O.T., 59n.
Calhoun, D., 34n.
Callahan, R., 10–11, 19, 25, 34n., 79–80, 90n., 275, 281n.
Cantor, L., 369–370, 378n.
Cantor, L., 314, 317n.
Cantor, M., 369, 378n.
Carey, N., 131, 136, 159n.
Carson, C.C., 112n., 128, 164, 177, 178n., 179n., 213, 221n., 321n., 354
Carter, J., 27
Catterall, J.S., 270, 279, 281n.
Cazden, C., 243, 251n.
Celis, W., 108, 124n., 148, 271, 281n.
Childs, J., 58, 62n., 66, 78–79, 90n.
Christian, D., 248, 251n.
Chubb, J.E., 272–273, 281n.
Clark, K.B., 239, 251n.
Clark, M.P., 239, 251n.
Clinchy, B., 159n.
Clinton, D.W., 21, 34n.
Clinton, W., 100, 113, 124n., 279
Cohen, D.K., 282n.
Cohen, S.S., 5, 8–9, 12–13, 34n.
Cohen, S., 6n, 9, 12, 13n., 34n.
Coleman, J., 143–145, 159n., 278, 281n.
Coley, R.J., 233, 251n.
Conant, J.B., 256–257, 281n.
Cookson, P.W., 275, 281n.
Coons, J.E., 277–278, 281n.
Cooper, T., 13n.
Cornbleth, C., 241, 251n.
Counts, G.S., 76–79, 88, 90n., 287n.
Cremin, L.A., 3, 7, 12–13, 15, 17, 26, 34n., 55–57, 62n, 66, 72–75, 86–87, 90n., 93, 124n., 127, 159n., 285, 287, 317n.
Cuban, L., 274, 281n.
Cubberley, E.B., 5, 9, 11n., 12, 14, 17, 19–21, 22n., 23, 30, 34n., 48, 62n.
Cummins, J., 236, 248, 251n.
Curcio, J.L., 288n.

D

Daniels, J., 151, 160n.
Darling-Hammond, L., 276, 278–279, 282n.
Davenport, S., 142, 159n.

Delfattore, J., 119–120, 124n.
Dennison, G., 258
Dewey, J., 37, 51, 57, 60–61, 62n., 65–67, 68n., 69–74, 77–79, 87–88, 90n., 227–228, 232, 237, 251n., 286, 317n., 319, 326, 354n., 358–359, 368–369, 372n., 378n.
DeWitt, K., 146, 159n.
Diaz, R.M., 248, 251n.
Dickens, C., 40, 42n.
Douglas, H.R., 8, 30, 34n., 94, 124n.
Dworkin, M., 66, 89n.

E

Edwards, A.C., 69, 90n.
Eisner, E., 280, 281n.
Elam, S., 215–216, 219–200, 221n., 266
Elders, J., 217, 221n.
Eliot, C., 39, 42–45, 61, 62n.
Elkind, D., 174, 221n.
Elliot, D.L., 331, 354n.
Erickson, E., 367, 378n.

F

Farrar, E., 274, 282n.
Fife, B.L., 143, 159n
Finn, C.E., 108–109, 124n., 203n., 273, 281n.
Finney, R.L., 86, 90n.
First, P., 288n.
Fischer, L., 348–349, 354n.
Franklin, B., 15, 32–33
Freidenberg, E.Z., 258
Freire, P., 235–236, 251n., 307, 317n.
French, W.M., 7–8, 14–15, 16n., 34n.
Friedman, M., 269, 281n.
Fromboluti, C.S ., 206, 207n., 216, 222n.
Ford, P.L., 10, 34n.
Fowler, F.C., 273, 281n.
Froebel, F., 47, 51–52, 61, 62n., 66, 73, 88

G

Gallup, A., 215–216, 219–220, 221n.
Gamoran, A., 131, 139, 159n.
Gardner, H., 297, 317n., 333, 354n.
Gardner, J., 314, 317n.
Garms, W.I., 104–105, 106n., 124n.
Geortz, C., 227, 251n.
Gerald, D.E., 155n., 156n.
Gibboney, R., 330, 354n.
Gibson, R., 233, 251n.
Gilligan, C., 150–151, 159n.
Gintis, H., 235, 251n.
Giroux, H., 233, 251n.

SUBJECT INDEX

Elementary school, 94, 96
Ethnic Diversity, 226–227
Experimentalism, 67–68, 79

F

Faculty psychology, 38
Family life, 207–209, 221
   Births to unmarried women, 207
   Divorce rates, 207
   Poverty rates, 206–208
   Prenatal care, 211
   Single-parent homes, 207–208
   Women in the workforce, 209

G

G.I. Bill, 102
Gender bias, 150–158
   Depiction of girls in classroom materials, 151, 153
   Familial roles, 155, 157
   Feminist views, 150, 152
   Gender segregated classrooms, 152–158
   Grades earned in school by girls, 151
   Participation rates in college, 153–155
   Public opinion, 157
   School achievement on standardized tests, 151, 153, 158
   Self-esteem, 153, 157
   Sexual harassment, 152
   Special education placements, 151–152
   The education of girls in Colonial America, 8, 10, 12, 33
General education, 250, 287, 302–303, 311, 316
   Civic education, 301
   Curriculum proposals, 230–233
Goals 2000, 100, 280
Great Books, 38

H

Harvard College, 4, 7, 32
Hazel Wood School District v. Kuhlmeier, 351–351
Head Start, 144
Herbart, 30
Herbartians, 49–51, 56, 85
   Critique of Committee of Fifteen report, 50
   Harris' critique of, 49
   Idea of correlations, 49
   Teaching methodology, 51
   Use of Robinson Crusoe, 49–50
Hidden curriculum, 236–237, 250
Hornbook, 10, 33
Hull House, 72–73
   Dewey's views of the, 73
Hunter lesson cycle, 329–330

I

Idealism, 52

Immigrant rates,
   During the late 1800s, 23
Infant Schools, 21–22, 32–33, 45
Individualized education, 291–298
Intelligence Quotient (IQ), 86–87
   Dewey's criticism of, 87
International Assessment of Educational Progress (IAEP), 165, 167–168, 170–174
   Cross-national outcomes in math, 167, 169
   Cross-national outcomes in reading, 172–174
   Cross-national outcomes in science, 169–173, 174–177
   Percentage of bachelor's degrees in America, 177
   Sampling issues, 174–177
International Educational Achievement (IEA), 165, 170–172, 174–177
International School Achievement, 163–178, 221
   Cross-national characteristics, 164–167

J

Jim Crow Laws, 30
Job analysis (see also Bobbitt, J. Franklin), 83–85
   Criticism of, 84
Job Corps, 144
Junior high school, 94, 96, 130

K

Kalamazoo Case, 29–30, 32–33
Kindergarten, 52
King, Martin Luther, 141
Kiryas, Joel, 121–122, 124

L

Lancaster Method, 21–22, 32–33
Land Ordinance of 1785, 20, 32–33, 93
Latin-Grammar Schools, 6–9, 21, 33, 44
Lau v. Nichols, 245–246, 250
Lesson plans, 335–337
Life situations, 74–75
Lincoln School, 58
Local school board, 100–101

M

Mann, Horace, 27–29, 32, 34
   Disputes with school masters, 28
   Impressions of Prussian education, 28
   Views of church and state, 27–29
   Views on controversy in the curriculum, 28
Massachusetts Bay Colony, 8
Massachusetts Law of 1642, 5, 32–33, 93
Massachusetts Law of 1647, 5–6, 17, 32–33, 93
Massachusetts Law of 1789, 17, 26, 33
Massachusetts Law of 1827, 29

Mental discipline, 38–39, 61, 306–307, 316
   Criticism of, 85
Middle schools, 94, 96–97, 130
Milliken v. Bradley, 147–148
Montessori's diadactic materials, 54
Morrill Act of 1862, 30–32, 101
Motivation, 70, 371–37
   Dewey's notion of, 70
   Intrinsic motivation, 371–373
   Modeling, 375–376
   Self-control, 373–375
Moving school, 16–17, 33
Mozert v. Hawkins County Public Schools, 119–121, 125
Mr. Gradgrind, 40–42
Multicultural education, 237–243, 250
   Additive multiculturalism, 241
   Multiperspective multiculturalism, 241–242
   Particularistic multiculturalism, 238–239
   Reduction of prejudice, 239–240

N

Nation at Risk report, 262–263, 280
National Advisory Committee on Civil Disorders, 144
National Assessment of Educational Progress (NAEP), 101, 180–205, 221
   Math proficiency, 193–198
   Reading proficiency, 180–187
   Science proficiency, 187–193
   Writing proficiency, 198–202
National Center for Education Statistics, View of international school comparisons, 165, 167
National Defense Education Act of 1958 (NDEA), 102, 256
National Merit Scholarship, 102
N.E.A., 42, 75
National standards, 279–280
New England Primer, 10–11, 32–33

O

Object teaching, 48, 61
Office of Educational Research and Improvement, 101
Open education, 259–260
Opportunity-to-Learn (OTL), 168, 170–172, 174, 177, 221

P

Parker, Frances (see also Quincey Methods), 73–74
   Views of, 73–74
Pauper Schools, 12, 20, 33
Pestalozzi, 30, 73
Pickering v. Board of Education, 352
Portfolio assessment, 346
Pragmatism, 66, 67

Project method, 57–60, 62
Prussian Schools, 28, 48
Puritans, 3, 4, 5

Q

Quincey Methods (see also Parker, Frances), 73–74

R

Racial attitudes, 240–241
Reconstruction of Experience, 68–69
Reflective thinking, 68
Reproduction theory, 235–236, 250
Rodriguez v. the San Antonio Independent School District, 105, 124

S

Samplers, 10
Sandia report, 220–221
Scholastic Aptitude Test (SAT), 163, 178–180, 221
  Relation to income, 179
  Sampling issues, 178–180
School building,
  In Colonial America, 9
School choice, 264–279, 281
  And the public interest, 277–279
  Interdistrict choice, 264, 266
  Intradistrict choice, 264
  Parental views of, 265–267
  Views against, 270–271, 273, 277
  Views favoring, 270–271, 272–274, 276
  Vouchers, 269–270
School education,
  Differences between Colonial regions, 3, 12–14, 19–21, 32
  Early critics of state-supported education, 25, 34
  Early state constitutions supporting public education, 19, 29, 32
  In the Colonial south, 12
  Jefferson's proposal for free state-supported education, 19, 32
  Philanthropic movement for free education, 20–21
  Public opinion of American schools, 218–220
  Rice's criticism of, 85–86
School funding, 102–112
  Colonial recognition of property tax, 17
  Differences across local jurisdictions, 103, 105–106
  Early school tax, 25
  Federal expenditures, 102, 107–108
  Flat grant programs, 105–106, 124
  Foundation programs, 105–106, 124
  International comparisons of funding, 109, 111
  Local expenditures, 102–103, 107
  Michigan funding structure, 107–108, 124

Minimal provision philosophy, 103, 107
Overall funding in U.S. schools, 108–112
Relationship to achievement, 108–109
State expenditures, 102–103, 106–108
Tax support for, 102–103, 106
School governance, 93–102
  Colonial roots, 15–17, 33
  Decentralized system, 18, 94
  Dual system, 76
School organization, 18, 22, 30, 93–97
School readiness, 209
School reform, 253–263, 280
  In the Cold War period, 254–257
  In the 1960s, 258–260
  In the 1970s, 260–262
  In the 1980s, 262–263
School segregation, 141–150
  Data on percent of minority students attending segregated schools, 141, 143, 145–149
  De facto segregation, 142
  De jure segregation, 141
  Kansas City case, 148
  Magnet schools, 142
  Majority to minority transfer, 142
  Public opinion on, 149–150, 158
  White flight, 143
Secondary education,
  Comprehensive school design, 75, 97, 124, 286–291, 308
  First high school in Boston, 29, 32
  Magnet schools, 142
  Specialized schools, 97, 124
  Universalization of, 128, 287
Secretary of education, 101
Selectmen, 5
Self-contained classrooms, 94, 96, 123
Serrano v. Priest, 105
Settlement houses, 72
Science education, 45
Scientific management (see also Taylor, Frederick), 80–83
Slave education, 12–13, 33
  Jefferson's views on slavery, 13
Smith-Hughes Act, 101
Sputnik, 255
Social class analysis, 77
Social Darwinism, 56, 61–62, 70–71
Social efficiency, 79–87
Social occupations, 69–70
Social reconstructionism (see also Counts, George), 77–79
  Criticism of, 78
Society for the Propagation of the Gospel in Foreign Parts, 13, 33, 34
Socio-civic learning, 14, 19
  Colonial roots, 14
Southern Christian Leadership Conference, 116

State authority,
  Early authority in Massachusetts, 27
State board of education, 97–98
State governor, 98, 124
State laws,
  Permissive nature of early laws, 26, 19
State superintendent, 97–98
Structure of a discipline, 256
Student violence, 216–217, 221
  Homicide and suicide rates, 216
  Arrest rates, 217
Swann v. Charlotte, 147–148

T

Taylor, Frederick (see also scientific management),
  Standardizing practice, 82
  Work with Bethlehem Steel, 80–81
Teacher liability, 349–350
Teacher-proof materials, 261
Teachers,
  Ethnicity of, 321
  Gender distribution of, 320
  In Colonial America, 9
  Religious and political views of, 321–322
  Salaries of, 321
  Views of the teaching profession, 322–325
Teaching to the test, 326–328, 331
Textbooks, 331
Time on task, 328
Testing,
  Low and high stakes, 347–348
Tinker v. Des Moines, 353
Title IX of the Education Amendment Act, 151, 157
Town schools, 7
Traditional humanism, 38–45, 61

U

Universal manhood suffrage, 20, 24, 33
U.S. Constitution, 4, 18
  1st Amendment to, 112
  10th Amendment to, 18, 33
  13th Amendment to, 30, 32
  14th Amendment to, 30, 113
  15th Amendment to, 30

V

Vocational education, 313–316

W

War on Poverty, 144–145
Ward, Lester,
  Progressive views of, 70–72
Whipping posts, 9
Whittle Corporation, 271–272